ETHICS AS A WORK
OF CHARITY

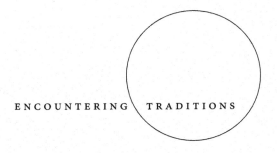

ENCOUNTERING TRADITIONS

ETHICS AS A WORK OF CHARITY

Thomas Aquinas and Pagan Virtue

DAVID DECOSIMO

STANFORD UNIVERSITY PRESS
STANFORD, CALIFORNIA

Stanford University Press
Stanford, California

©2014 by the Board of Trustees of the Leland Stanford Junior University.
All rights reserved.

Printed in the United States of America on acid-free, archival-quality paper

Library of Congress Cataloging-in-Publication Data

Decosimo, Joseph David, 1979- author.
  Ethics as a work of charity : Thomas Aquinas and pagan virtue / David Decosimo.
  pages cm — (Encountering traditions)
  Includes bibliographical references and index.
  ISBN 978-0-8047-9063-5 (cloth : alk. paper)
  ISBN 978-1-5036-0060-7 (pbk. : alk. paper)
  1. Thomas, Aquinas, Saint, 1225?-1274—Ethics. 2. Christianity and other religions. 3. Virtue. 4. Ethics. I. Title. II. Series: Encountering traditions.
  B765.T54D375 2014
  241'.042092—dc23
  ISBN 978-0-8047-9170-0 (electronic)

Typeset by Bruce Lundquist in 10/14 Minion

For Harmony

CONTENTS

ACKNOWLEDGMENTS

Virtue, say Aristotle, Augustine, and Thomas, is exceedingly rare. Anyone who knew my teachers, colleagues, friends, and family would think all three were mistaken. Instead, despite odds and desert, I have been graced to live and learn among the virtuous—pagan and Christian alike.

This book had its beginnings in Princeton University's religion department; it was completed at Loyola University Maryland's theology department. In both places, learnedness, friendship, and joy flourish. I am deeply grateful to my Princeton and Loyola colleagues and friends: John Gager, Eli Sacks, Ryan Harper, Molly Farneth, Amin Venjara, Michael Lamb, Mairaj Syed, Steve Fowl, Jim Buckley, Trent Pomplun, John Kiess, and Rebekah Eklund, to name a few. For encouragement, knowledge, and perspective, I am grateful to Matt Novenson, Joseph and Nora Clair, Caleb and Samantha Cohoe, Adam Eitel, Tuck Bartholomew, Micah Lott, Richard Cowan, Robert Jenson, Calvin Normore, the Aho family, and many other friends and teachers too numerous to name. At Princeton, John Cooper, Qasim Zaman, and Cornel West not only taught me things no one else could but went out of their way to do so. In addition to his friendship, Eric Gregory modeled an inspiring commitment to finding wisdom in diverse voices and asking questions that made new connections.

For generous financial support, I thank Princeton's Center for Human Values, Center for the Study of Religion, and Institute for International and Regional Studies, Loyola's Center for the Humanities and Dean's Fund, and the Institute for Advanced Studies in Culture. I am grateful to the "Encountering Traditions" series editors, especially Jonathan Tran and Randi Rashkover for their support and advice, and to the editorial staff at Stanford University Press, including Emily Jane Cohen and Laura Kenney. I likewise thank Michael Walker for his careful copy editing.

In addition to their friendship, Kevin Hector and Steve Bush gave helpful feedback on the manuscript. I am especially grateful to David Gallagher, Steve Brock, and Fritz Bauerschmidt who read drafts of the complete manuscript and provided exceptionally thoughtful and detailed commentary. The book is better for their generosity and insight.

Without the learnedness, counsel, and wisdom of Jeff Stout and John Bowlin, this book would not be. Each continues to surpass my highest expectations for what it means to be a truly excellent teacher, scholar, and friend. Few have shown me more about true virtue than they.

Scott Davis and Stanley Hauerwas served as the manuscript's reviewers; interacting with them was an unexpected reward. Scott's philosophical acuity, stylistic sense, and capacity to discern the big picture made his pages of commentary a treasure. Stanley championed the project from the outset, offered detailed, perceptive suggestions, and helped me see more clearly what the book should be.

To my family I owe the greatest debt of gratitude. The Honaker and Decosimo families have been supportive in word and in deed: my father, a touchstone in every sense; my mother, by her vivacious joy, recalling me to life's wonder; my brothers, Joseph and Michael, ever faithful friends and encouragers. Nothing I could say here—or say at all—could express my gratitude to my children, Myles, Lucy, and Nora, and, far above all others, to my wife, Harmony. They have brought joy, energy, and love to the entire process, bearing it with patience and reminding me, by their lives, that in writing it, I had better be doing something worthwhile. Aristotle and Thomas agree that many of the most important things we do, we do only by the help of our friends. Harmony, my best friend, has helped and given more than anyone in the writing of this book. I dedicate it to her.

"No effort," Emerson says, "could make my account square." Thomas would cite John's Gospel: "From his fullness, we have all received grace upon grace."

ABBREVIATIONS, TRANSLATION, AND CITATION MATTERS

The following abbreviations are used for frequently cited books or articles. The bibliography provides full details.
All translations of Aquinas are my own. All emphases in his texts are my own.
I have checked my translations against other translations when possible.
Scriptural quotations are from the Douay-Rheims translation.

THOMAS AQUINAS

ADB	*Ad ducissam Brabantiae*
BDT	*Super Boetium De Trinitate*
CC	*Lectura super I ad Corinthios*
CM	*In libros Metaphysicorum*
CNE	*Sententia libri Ethicorum*
DC	*De caritate (De virtutibus quaestio 2)*
DM	*Quaestiones disputatae de malo*
DP	*Quaestiones disputatae de potentia*
DV	*De virtutibus in communi (De virtutibus quaestio 1)*
DVC	*De virtutibus cardinalibus (De virtutibus quaestio 5)*
JC	*Lectura super Ioannem*
PC	*Sententia libri Politicorum*
RC	*Lectura super ad Romanos*
SCG	*Summa contra Gentiles*
ST	*Summa theologiae*

ARISTOTLE

NE	*Nicomachean Ethics*

AUGUSTINE

DCD	*De civitate Dei*

BARTHOLOMEW OF SAN CONCORDIO

Scc   *Summa de casibus conscientiae*

JOHN OF FREIBURG

SC   *Summa confessorum*

MODERN AUTHORS

AA   Thomas Osborne, Jr., "The Augustinianism of Thomas Aquinas's Moral Theory"
APV   Brian Shanley, "Aquinas on Pagan Virtue"
CJ   Solomon Grayzel, *The Church and the Jews*
CK   Jeremy Cohen, *Christ Killers*
FJ   Jeremy Cohen, *The Friars and the Jews*
HA   Joseph Pilsner, *The Specification of Human Action in St. Thomas Aquinas*
LL   Jeremy Cohen, *Living Letters of the Law*
PIV   Thomas Osborne, Jr., "Perfect and Imperfect Virtues in Aquinas"
STA   Jean-Pierre Torrell, *St. Thomas Aquinas*
TA   John Milbank and Catherine Pickstock, *Truth in Aquinas*
TAJ   Stephen Boguslawski, *Thomas Aquinas on the Jews*
TRV   Alasdair MacIntyre, *Three Rival Versions of Moral Enquiry*
TST   John Milbank, *Theology and Social Theory*
TT   Gilles Emery, *The Trinitarian Theology of St. Thomas Aquinas*
WJ   Alasdair MacIntyre, *Whose Justice? Which Rationality?*

For Aquinas's texts, I have relied primarily on the Latin of the Leonine edition or, where there is no Leonine text, the Latin of the Marietti texts listed in the bibliography. For the *Sentences* commentary, however, I have used the Parma text available through *Corpus Thomisticum: Opera Omnia*. In many cases, I have consulted several editions. I have found no textual variations touching on the substance of my translations or claims.

References to Aquinas's and other premodern works are in the common form denoting book or part, question, article, and so on. In the case of Aquinas's commentaries, references are to chapter, lecture, and, for convenience to scholars, the paragraph enumeration supplied by the *Corpus Thomisticum*. Where that numbering is unavailable, I supply the paragraph numbering found in Marietti.

For example:

(I.II 63.2 ad 2) refers to the first part of the second part of the *Summa theologiae*, question 63, article 2, response to objection 2.

(II.II 10.1) refers to the second part of the second part of the *Summa theologiae*, question 10, article 1's "corpus" or body, or, depending on context, to the article in its totality.

(*RC* 10.2.839) refers to *Lectura super ad Romanos* chapter 10, lecture 2, paragraph 839.

ETHICS AS A WORK OF CHARITY

INTRODUCTION:
INTRUSIONS OF GRACE

EVERYTHING THOMAS DOES, he does for love of a God who delights to make strangers, and even enemies, friends. This book is about how Thomas welcomes outsiders and their virtues as an expression of that love. For Thomas, Aristotle is the preeminent outsider. There is, however, no greater insider for Thomas than Augustine of Hippo. As an act of Augustinian love, Thomas unites and transforms Aristotle and Augustine alike to teach charity toward outsiders and their virtues. In each of thousands of interactions with Aristotle, he shows us what charity for a particular outsider looks like. To see how Thomas does this, how he makes ethics itself a work of charity, we must begin where he had to—with Augustine.

Augustine and the Challenge of Pagan Virtue

Writing at the beginning of the end of the Roman Empire, Augustine confronted a problem. It was not hard to critique the declining, decadently bloated empire, but the lives of men like Scipio, Cato, and, especially, Marcus Regulus seemed, to almost anyone, truly praiseworthy. Yet these Romans were obviously not Christians and did not in any straightforward way appear animated by Christ's charity. Their notions of the human end, the ideas that gave their lives an ostensibly virtuous and particularly Roman shape, were not only alien but often contrary to the vision articulated by the church. How then to understand their seemingly virtuous characters? For Augustine, at least as he is commonly read, idolatry and the lust for domination (*libido dominandi*) finally swallowed up any apparent excellence. What mattered most was what these men and their seeming virtues were *not*: ordered to the Triune God. All, therefore, that flowed from lives so misdirected, including the apparent excellences so tempting to praise, was simply one or another variety of sin—the gleaming but poisonous fruit of a wicked heart in pursuit of evil ends.

Perhaps it could not have been otherwise. Augustine was committed, as most Christians are, to the notion that a person's beliefs about the sacred and the holy matter for the life she leads. As well, he held to the essential Christian claim that, more than anything, humans need grace—grace without which it is impossible to please God. And, perhaps most importantly, he lived, as he saw it, in dangerous times. Were he to acknowledge the virtue of Regulus, would that not tempt Christians to paganism? Would that not minimize the reality of sin, the danger of idolatry, and the difference charity makes? Would that not, finally, betray the gospel and, worse, its crucified author?

We live in different times. But we need not share Augustine's history—or his faith—to find ourselves echoing his questions. We confront friends and neighbors whose ideas of what makes for the best sort of human life differ from and sometimes even oppose our own. And, when these people seem morally praiseworthy, we have to figure out how we should understand their ostensible excellence. Do we regard their virtue as somehow independent of their misguided or false beliefs about whether there is a God, what the body is for, which politics are just, or what, if anything, is sacred? Do we, instead, reduce our—and their—deepest convictions to an empty common denominator, downplaying the deep difference or draping it in the suffocating blanket of nonjudgmental niceness, lifestyle liberalism, or the latest ideological kitsch? Or do we swallow our own version of the hard Augustinian pill and regard them with a suspicion ever ready to find its confirmation? Of course, in one sense, all these strategies eventually lead to the same unhappy outcome—if not always hostility and violence, at least distance, closure, and alienation.

That is easy to see when it comes to suspicion—Augustinian or otherwise—for we can hardly be a friend to those we regard as objects for endless unmasking. But it is no less true of the other strategies. What genuine fellowship can come from reducing our fundamental convictions about the most important things to bland sameness? Or, worse, from the outright denial and suppression of such loves and their distinctive shape? Augustine himself—along with countless others—would remind us that what we care about helps make us who we are. Even as we fail to live as we long to, the objects of our love at least ensure that we stumble in a particular direction. Pretending those objects are the same or unimportant buys a semblance of peace at the price of justice, truth, and, most of all, love. Can anything worthy of the name friendship follow from denying the outsider the reality, particularity, or importance of her loves? From performing the same cover-up or amputation on oneself?

In confronting difference, we can seem caught between its denial and the hostile apprehension it tends to generate. The problem of "pagan virtue"— which, whatever our religious commitments or lack thereof, is what we can call this nest of issues—threatens to put us at odds with one another and ourselves, to ensure that we hold either our neighbor or our deepest convictions at a distance. Goods of politics, friendship, and faith hang in the balance. This book turns to Thomas Aquinas to seek a better way.

From Thomas to Us

Thomas Aquinas's neighbors and colleagues were not—like ours—religiously diverse outsiders but members of religious orders, priests, and lay Christians. Jews were the most exotic non-Christians Thomas encountered. In all likelihood, he never so much as met a Muslim. He can just imagine an atheist. Perhaps this very absence of pressure, this lack of impinging, pervasive pluralism, freed him to think through the challenge of pagan virtue with the kind of patient, exhaustive care its complexity and importance demand. Yet, notwithstanding the relative uniformity of the world he inhabited, he held as dear friend and treasured conversation partner a long-dead but, to him, very present Greek pagan, a religious outsider in a very deep sense indeed. He defended the Philosopher, as he affectionately called him, against charges of irrationality brought even by fellow friars, cited him more frequently than any figure save Augustine, and offered more commentary on his work than on any one or any thing but the Bible. And, whatever else it is, his magnum opus represents an extended and embodied effort to welcome that outsider and his virtue in a way that simultaneously honors and imitates the Triune God. In Thomas Aquinas, we have to do with a welcome of pagan virtue that is as generous and deep as it is faithful and true. That, at least, is my claim.

At its core, then, this book attempts to elucidate Thomas Aquinas's complex conception of pagan virtue—to explain just what that vision is and how it relates to both the substance of his ethics and his very way of doing moral theology. Driving this investigation is not only the effort to get Thomas right, but to find in him guidance for our own endeavors—theological or not—to address the

challenge of outsider virtue. To the church first is Thomas's insight most useful
and relevant; however, his way of addressing pagan virtue and doing ethics by
drawing not only on the best of his tradition but the insights of outsiders themselves offers a model for all of us, religious or not. Given my normative interests
and constructive aims, at certain points, I offer rational reconstruction—using
Thomas's texts and concepts to supply answers in his spirit where he has not. It
is a way Thomas himself proceeded in relation to his own interlocutors so the
effort is, in a sense, doubly Thomistic—following after him both in the substance of my answers and the path that leads there.

This book is also an interpretation of Thomas's moral theology—or at least
central aspects of it—in view of pagan virtue. Looking at his ethics in this light
reveals a Triune trajectory we might otherwise miss. As we will see, there are
reasons for this dual focus intrinsic to his thought. Pagan virtue represents a
real but imperfect conformity to the Logos of God whereby men and women
are implicitly caught up in the Father's work of bringing all things to himself
through the Son in the Spirit. Thomas's accounts of goodness, habit, action,
and virtue alike bear the stamp of this Divine movement, calling God's people
to anticipate and welcome it in the lives of those who do not yet know Jesus—
even as they also proclaim the Gospel's necessity and splendor.

Outsiders and Particularity

When the "outsider" gets talked about in philosophy or theology, it is often
in a language of abstraction, far removed from any actual community, place,
or time. In real life, however, the outsider speaks and acts strangely. Her dress
is transgressive. Her worship makes us uneasy and tempts scorn. And she directs this devotion to something alien, even troubling. Any of these differences
can cause us to suspect that behind apparent goodness lurks something sinis-
ter. Few are blind to what can follow when outsiders are thought incapable of
virtue—or the good attainable when they are seen as trustworthy partners in
pursuing justice. Can consideration of an "outsider" whose very otherness remains an abstraction help us grapple with the real challenges religious outsiders
pose? Can it prepare us to respond with justice?

In turning to a particular tradition and an especially deep and apparently
intractable kind of otherness, I hope to refuse an abstraction that, at its worst,
amounts to just another evasion of difference. And while the way one community navigates the challenge will necessarily be its own, this book advances

under the conviction that when it comes to pagans, their virtue, and the task of ethics, Thomas not only has something to teach his church but something to teach us all.

"Hyper-Augustinian" and "Public Reason" Thomism

Given his preeminence both within his tradition and as one of most important interpreters of Augustine, Aristotle, and their legacies, it is unsurprising that Thomas plays a central role in Christian thinking about pagans and their virtues.[1] Within many theological quarters, something like a default interpretation of Thomas's position has emerged—one wherein he regards pagans as incapable of virtue. Alasdair MacIntyre, for instance, declares that for Thomas, "justice cannot flourish, cannot . . . even exist as a natural virtue, unless and insofar as it is informed by . . . caritas" (WJ, 205). Stanley Hauerwas claims that for Thomas, "no true virtue is possible without charity."[2] For John Milbank's Thomas, "there are only two categories of people . . . the fallen wicked and the engraced good" and the "fallen wicked [are] incapable of obeying the natural law [and] cannot do any genuinely 'natural' good," much less attain virtue (TA, 124, 39).[3]

Others protest, declaring Thomas altogether friendly to pagan virtue. Thus, Brian Shanley contends that MacIntyre's "Augustinian leanings skew his interpretation of Aquinas," and Bonnie Kent likewise objects to his "Augustinianism," charging that he transforms Thomas into a "moral provincialist" whose denial of pagan virtue is on intellectual and moral par with sexism.[4]

Both sides frame the contest as one between Thomas's Augustinian and his Aristotelian commitments. Pagan virtue, the story goes, reveals Thomas's deepest loyalties: Augustine or Aristotle, theology or philosophy, faith or reason. It certainly reveals interpretive commitments: not only the ubiquitous either/or paradigm, but the assumption that Thomas either welcomes pagan virtue by betraying Christian commitments and following Aristotle or rejects it thanks to his abandonment of Greek philosophy and fidelity to Augustine, Scripture, and Christ. Such readings, moreover, move beyond interpretation and help fund rival "Augustinian" or, better, "hyper-Augustinian" and "Aristotelian" or, rather, "public reason" proposals for contemporary ethics and politics.[5]

The "hyper-Augustinian" interpreters have been especially influential. On one reading, they regard non-Christians incapable of virtue and seek to sway the church to this view. Faithfulness, they seem to suggest, requires rejecting pagan virtue. Consider a few examples.

Favorably presenting Milbank's and Hauerwas's views, James K. A. Smith raises the question of "whether non-Christians can be good or moral" and, citing Thomas, explains:

> I am inclined toward [the] conclusion [that non-Christians are *not* truly good and moral]: Morality or authentic virtue is possible only for the community of the redeemed. . . . What appear to be instances of mercy or compassion or justice outside the body of Christ are merely semblances of virtue. . . . This is just another way of trying to think through the logic of Aquinas's claim that all the virtues are ordered by charity. . . . Love—and hence true virtue—is possible only within and for the ecclesial community.[6]

Not only the non-Christian's apparent virtue, but even specific acts that appear to be merciful, just, or compassionate, are mere semblances, actually evil. For Milbank, non-Christian thought, practice, and "virtue" are birthed in violence, sustained by conflict, and ultimately directed toward nihilism and death (*TST*, 5).[7] As he has it, "the main gist of [Augustine's] great book [*City of God*] is that [pagan] virtues were hopelessly contaminated by a *celebration* of violence." And, in one sense, the main gist of Milbank's own great book, *Theology and Social Theory*, is that Augustine's claim is a "fundamental truth" (289).[8] Pagan "virtue" is, finally, merely the "worship of violence" in disguise (262). For MacIntyre, contemporary society can produce no moral virtue, only fragmentation and interminable moral conflict.[9] In making charity virtue's presupposition, MacIntyre forsakes Augustinian hope for the good to be sought with Babylon's citizens and abandons his own "tradition of the virtues"—wherein contemporary heirs of Emerson, Hume, and Hegel might, with followers of Abraham's God and others still, find a home (*WJ*, 10–11, 210–25, 401–3). Hauerwas insists that Greek virtue has "no telos other than conflict" and emphasizes that he does "not credit the natural virtues" even to the degree that Thomas is sometimes supposed to have.[10] "It is far from obvious" he says, "that those Christians . . . who have argued so adamantly that pagan virtue is nothing less than sin . . . are so far off track."[11] These criticisms are directed at the virtues of the ancients. What, then, of that which is birthed in the lives of those inhabiting a "world of moral fragments . . . always on the edge of violence . . . [that] lacks the means to [produce] any habits or institutions sufficient to sustain [even] an ethos of honor?"[12]

These and others do not merely cite Thomas as rejecting pagan virtue; they deny the possibility themselves. The declarations even seem to rise from the core of their intellectual agendas: for MacIntyre, late-Western democracies cannot produce people of virtue; for Hauerwas, the church alone can form lives oriented away from violence and consumption toward peace and self-giving love; for Milbank, outside the Christian ontology of peace and metanarrative of love, all is war and death.

Matters, of course, are far more complicated than such slogans suggest. Grant that these readings are distortions, neglecting claims that suggest hospitality, betraying their authors' deepest commitments.[13] Still, the negative remarks remain, often invested with such rhetorical power that they would linger in the imagination even if they did not figure so prominently in the argumentative structure. And these readings are commonplace, forming numerous Christian scholars, pastors, and laypeople who would rather forsake pagan virtue than Scripture's Christ.

If the hyper-Augustinians have a rival when it comes to giving Thomas a voice in contemporary religion, ethics, and politics, it is the "public reason" Thomists.[14] They have had little to no interest in the details of Thomas's account of pagan virtue—perhaps because they regard it simply obvious that outsiders can attain virtue, or perhaps because their vision of ethics has so little to do with virtue to begin with.[15] What Thomas bequeaths us, they say, is a way of safely and justly navigating our pluralistic world and democratic politics by the deliverances of reason alone. Principles sufficiently determinate and clear to guide lives and politics are self-evident to any reflective person, pagan or Christian.[16] And should our eyes be blurry, our minds slow, Thomas adumbrates a list for us in his treatise on law, the meaning of which they will happily explain.

Whatever our theological commitments or lack thereof, we are all governed by natural law, ordered to basic goods. Provided we submit to that governance and choose not against those goods, our lives and communities, Christian or not, will be just and good. Should we disagree, we have, at least, a way to characterize and adjudicate our difference in a neutral, "objective" language that, if not Nature's own, is nearly so. As for matters Christian, "there is," we are told, "no reason to labour the points [Thomas] makes about the evils which ineluctably afflict our present life, and our incapacity to satisfy our desires before the death we naturally abhor."[17] While Thomas himself may, admittedly, stress that friendship with God has preeminence, "fulfillment in some other, say, future, life" goes beyond reason, and so falls in for little or even no attention.[18] How could emphasizing *that* be of help or have a place in our pluralistic context? While these brushstrokes conceal complexity and diversity, this portrait finds real roots in figures like John Finnis, Joseph Boyle, and Robert George, and depicts faithfully their perspective, at least as it converts and shapes scholars, students, and citizens. Against the backdrop of broken politics, a hostile, secularized world, and ongoing battles over the sacred, a solution that bears the imprimatur of Nature, the promise of Neutrality, and the unassailability of Reason—cost what it may in terms of particularly Christian identity or participation—has its allure.

Such, in rough form, are the dominant choices when it comes to Thomas on pagan virtue and in contemporary ethics and politics. Yet which Christians really want to maintain fidelity at the price of hospitality—or welcome pagan virtue by abandoning their identity as a particular people and forsaking the necessity of God's generosity and love for human flourishing?

Our Argument

As Thomas's synthesis is usually understood, he chooses, at each step, between Augustinian and Aristotelian traditions. At best, it's a synthesis of averages, of alternating either/or's reaching a rough balance. Perhaps nowhere is this more evident than when it comes to pagan virtue, where, on nearly every account, honoring Aristotle and reason, he welcomes it, or, keeping faith with Augustine and Christ, he rejects it. What he does not do—or even try to do—is honor insider and outsider, Bishop and Philosopher, alike.

On the dominant paradigms—for Thomas's stance on pagan virtue, his synthesis, and his contemporary significance—he and those who would follow must choose: Augustine or Aristotle, truth or welcome, particularity or public reason. These paradigms of competition, I argue, not only misunderstand Thomas but miss the ethos he would bequeath us. Thomas welcomes pagan virtue *for charity's sake*, not against but because of his Christian convictions, construing pagan virtue itself as the outworking of God's gift—and its recognition as one more instance of giving God the glory he is due. That commitment to charity shapes not just his conclusions but his way of doing moral theology, and more his very life.

Charity's scholarly mode is the multiplication of distinctions in order to preserve truth and honor its inevitably broken seekers—among whom, for Thomas at least, Aristotle ranks near the top. Just where choice between traditions appears inevitable, he finds a way to honor the Philosopher's insights without compromising Christian fidelity. When theological commitments seem to condemn Aristotle, Thomas seeks, in and for charity, redemption. And where Christian or pagan falls short of truth or justice, and charity would be betrayed by his doing otherwise, he offers fraternal correction. Impelled by commitment to Christ, Thomas strives to be Aristotelian by being Augustinian and vice versa, his very engagement with Aristotle performing the capacious stance he commends, his theologizing enacting the welcome he prescribes.[19]

For all of us, Christian and non-Christian alike, Thomas offers a way to grapple with the challenge of difference without betraying our deepest convictions. And for Christians, at least, he models a particular way of doing ethics and being in the world that is at once generous and faithful, hopeful and committed, patterned after God's way with us. Call this stance prophetic Thomism.[20] It sees distinction-drawing, precision, and fidelity as linked arm-in-arm with resistance to domination, critique of empire, and pursuit of the common good. For prophetic Thomism, multiplying distinctions is no rival to the work of justice but a face thereof, enabling the recognition and condemnation of evil and the construction of justice-oriented alliances across lines of difference. Where there is ambiguity in Thomas's work, it opts for a justice in keeping with the best of his thought, and where he falls into error, it corrects, following Thomas's own way with what he found wanting.

If Christian ethics frequently takes tradition and liberation, conceptual analysis and prophetic concern, orthodoxy and inclusion as either/or alternatives—even competing scholarly identities—prophetic Thomism seeks to unite and transform. In both the substance of Thomas's welcome and his way of doing ethics, we glimpse prophetic Thomism at work.

An Ethics for the Church

Suppose there are at least three tasks necessary for articulating an ethics for the church. First, there is the matter of taking sin seriously and giving grace and the grace-giving Christ priority in all things, ethics and spiritual formation included. One has to envision what it means for ethics—as science and practice—to do justice to the ceaseless, prevenient activity of God who, working in, through, and beyond all that humans do, liberates a people, forming them into the image of his Son. A second task focuses on the church's duty to be a primary locus for her people's formation into holiness and virtue. It seeks to articulate a vision and practical regimen of discipleship into God's new humanity, to imagine and enact the practices whereby the regeneration that grace effects will work itself out in active love of neighbor and God. The third task addresses the church's way with what it is not. It asks one to decipher what understanding and conduct most faithfully answer God's call in relation to each of the institutional and cultural orders that are not the church, and, more, who and what even count as "outside." Settling questions about the church's relation to some polity hardly settles questions concerning its duties to the natural world or how it should understand pagan virtue. Arguably, much contemporary political theology has focused almost exclusively on just one or two of the most obviously political dimensions of this task. Certainly it has not usually devoted much energy to the matter of pagan virtue, notwithstanding either its immediate or more indirect political significance. Finally, a complete ethics for the church must not only pursue each of these tasks (and more) but the still more difficult work of coordinating them.

My aim, in contrast, is modest. In forwarding Thomas's vision, I seek to contribute to the third task—primarily that aspect concerned with the church's relation to and assessment of individuals. While this is an inherently political matter, I am not trying to articulate a comprehensive political theology, even as Thomas's way of welcoming pagan virtue and doing ethics models a salutary stance for moral and political theology more broadly, especially ruling out positions rooted in suspicion, competition, or relentless unmasking. In regard to the second task, I believe Thomas contributes profoundly to the church's work of moral formation, and the book's first part especially offers some suggestion of how. In relation to the first matter, the priority of grace, I at least mean to show that Thomas's welcome of pagan virtue does not veer into Pelagianism but honors, expresses, and builds upon the primacy of Jesus Christ and a real grasp of sin's destructive power.

In short, when it comes to an ethics for the church, I seek to address one dimension of one task, the question of pagan virtue, while suggesting the richness and profundity of Thomas's way with the second and the compatibility of both with the priority of grace. Thomas, I argue, gives us an Augustinian welcome of pagan virtue that coheres with, enriches, and depends on Augustinian ways of honoring grace and envisioning the church's pedagogical tasks.

Thomas's Pagans and Ours

Thomas himself never used the term "pagan virtue." And for him *gentilis* or *paganus*, the words we translate as "pagan," refer exclusively to non-Jewish unbelievers, usually ancients like Aristotle but also other less familiar unbelievers.[21] But when we and others treat pagan virtue, we are considering *all* non-Christians—Jews (and Muslims) included. More precisely, we are asking about human capacities for virtue after the fall and apart from redemptive grace—capacities which are common to each of the groups that Thomas's various Latin terms pick out and which do not vary in relation to their referents. In short, the "pagan" in our "pagan virtue" refers to all those without charity.

I use "charity" in two distinct ways in this book. First, as here, to refer to the theological virtue, that God-given habit of grace whereby alone humans are justified, perfectly ordered to, and united in loving friendship with the God revealed in Jesus Christ (II.II 23.2–5). Secondly, and more generally, to name a particular way of being in the world—one marked by generosity, welcome, and love for neighbors near and far; a readiness to find beauty, truth, and goodness even when it is difficult, even in those who would be enemies. This way of being, suggested by the book's title, may or may not be animated by theological virtue, by charity in the other sense. Throughout, context makes clear which sense I intend. In a certain way, that there are these two senses—a recognizably charitable way of life not informed by charity itself—is one of my central claims.

Thanks to his conception of "implicit faith" (*fides implicita*), Thomas may believe that some who do not explicitly follow Christ, who appear to be pagans, are nonetheless, in some way, possessed of charity.[22] The presence of charity would positively affect the sorts of virtue such people could attain and thereby distinguish them from "genuine" pagans. But again, such charity-possessed "pagans" are not the pagans we are considering when it comes to pagan virtue.[23] Our focus, rather, is on pagans considered as those *without* charity—those who appear not to be Christians *and* are not. And this is fitting, for, in the view of Thomas and others, these seem the most distant and so most difficult outsiders. Not those finally like us, but those who do not share our vision of the human good.[24] For, in one sense, implicit faith makes of outsiders insiders: the outsider can be virtuous, one might argue, but only because she is not *really* an outsider. Thus, in considering Thomas's conception of pagan virtue, we attend to what Thomas says non-Christian, fallen humans can attain without charity.[25]

For this reason, the transition from Thomas's pagans to ours is not so difficult, at least for those who share Thomas's faith. Since the question that Thomas poses has to do with human capacities apart from charity, there is at least no *prima facie* reason to think that what he says about pagan virtue is somehow peculiar to ancient Greeks or Romans—to the exclusion of contemporary non-Christians, say. Arguments to follow bear this point out, but an initial remark is important.

For Thomas, all share in both sin's brokenness and a desire for the good. Most basically, a common capacity for virtue is part of what it means to be human at all. Thomas would regard it mistaken or worse to imagine this varied across cultures or epochs. As we will see, individuals experience this capacity differently, and these differences matter for their prospects of cultivating virtue. More importantly, though, it matters what individuals and communities believe and love. It matters how people conduct themselves and what practices cultures inculcate. Certain beliefs and ways of life are obstacles to or even incompatible with virtue's cultivation. Almost everyone, Christian or not, believes that much.

Some might be tempted to think that those formed primarily by contemporary liberal democracies are incapable of virtue. For these, Thomas's affirmation of pagan virtue is without contemporary bearing. Even if Thomas thought ancient pagans could attain virtue—indeed even if he were right—we should not think contemporary Westerners can. The world of difference between ancient and contemporary pagans is simply too great. Pagan virtue is lost in the translation—so the argument runs.

There are at least two paths to this conclusion. The first misunderstands Thomas, mistaking a mere application of his overarching vision—his recognition of ancient pagan virtue—for that vision itself. In stressing that Thomas's concern with pagan virtue is with human capacities without charity, I meant to put that confusion to rest. Thomas sought to elucidate how and why virtue is possible for unredeemed humans, and, in this respect, his vision is no less relevant for our pagans than for his.

Another path recognizes this but assumes societies like ours cannot sustain virtuous pagans. But surely there is as much to recoil from in Athenian or Roman society as in our own. Given the horrendous injustices endemic to ancient life, directed especially at women, slaves, and children, it is hard to see why those skeptical about the capacity of Western societies to sustain virtue should not extend that skepticism to ancient societies too. And, if Thomas found virtue in the ancients—whom he knew exposed their infants, enslaved their foes, and often worshiped idols—why would we think he and those following after him could not find virtue in our own societies, notwithstanding their militarism, greed, and wickedness? For Thomas questions of pagan virtue are not settled by sweeping narratives about liberalism, democracy, or modernity but patient, just, and charitable attention to the concrete neighbor.[26] This work, we will see, is demanding. Thomas's account of pagan virtue gives us good theological reason to believe it is not in vain.

For those who do not share Thomas's theological commitments, their "outsiders" likely have little in common with Thomas's or even the contemporary church's. Indeed, they themselves likely number among those Thomas and his heirs consider outsiders—and vice versa. Yet the salient commonality between the Christian's pagans and the pagan's outsiders is their divergence in conduct, practices, and/or conceptions of the best life. The shared reality and challenge of such differences—whatever the particularities—make Thomas a potential teacher for pagans and Christians alike.[27]

Obviously, the claim awaits testing and vindication by non-Christians. But it also offers the pagan a chance to practice—toward Thomas—the kind of expectant hospitality, anticipation of virtue, and spirit of generosity I believe he himself commends and would have his fellow Christians extend to them. Non-Christian readers are thus invited to conduct themselves in relation to Thomas as Thomas did with Aristotle and his other pagans. The first chapter does some of the ground-clearing work to make that imaginable.

Inviting Intrusions

The challenge of pagan virtue impinges on our lives as we navigate questions of politics and friendship, work and play, love and justice. Can I trust this politician to pursue the common good or will she merely enshrine her religious convictions in law? Will a spouse who does not regard marriage a sacrament persevere in sickness and in health? Will this teacher try to debunk my child's faith or help form her into virtue?

Each of us faces versions of these questions. We must make judgments and draw distinctions to navigate our worlds. Encountering those whose convictions are not ours, we have to make some sense of those commitments and the praiseworthy lives they sometimes sustain. For Christians, these questions get asked in a theological register—in the shadow of Augustine's supposed answer and the ongoing temptation to downplay or even deny the centrality and necessity of the indwelling presence of Jesus Christ for living the best sort of human life. Most Christians, I suspect, would prefer to deny neither their faith nor the outsider's virtue. They want to hold to the supremacy and salience of the incarnate Son and to embrace the goodness in the lives of those who seem to know him not. Thomas, I believe, can help.

It may be that "our age . . . does not have a very sharp eye for the almost imperceptible intrusions of grace," that images of brokenness and banality or our own self-preoccupation blind us to all else.[28] Yet, atheist or theist, call it sacred value or grace, our failure to see it does not mean it is not there. This book is written in the expectation and trust that one locus of that grace and one place that, too often, we do not look, or look and do not see, is the lives of those neighbors whose faith and loves differ from our own. Might not there be some grace for us in that very strange, very distant outsider, Thomas Aquinas? Beginning—but by no means stopping—with him, this book is an invitation to look and see.[29]

I ETHICS AS A WORK OF FAITH

1 THOMAS AND HIS OUTSIDERS

> If what is said about the Jews . . . is true, no punishment would be sufficiently great or sufficiently worthy of their crime. . . . We herewith order . . . that on the first Saturday of the Lent to come, in the morning, while the Jews are gathered in the synagogues, you shall . . . seize all the books of the Jews who live in your districts, and have these books carefully guarded in the possession of the Dominican and Franciscan Friars.[1]

So wrote Gregory IX in June of 1239 in a letter sent throughout Roman territories in concern that Jewish devotion to Talmud was corrupting their loyalty to Torah—and by extension their identity as proto-Christians (*TAJ*, 25).

Understandably, the idea that we could learn something about navigating difference from a medieval theologian is bound to strike some as odd or even pernicious. After all, weren't medieval Christians—especially Dominicans— notoriously intolerant of Jews? And doesn't Thomas bear some responsibility for that?

Consider Jeremy Cohen. In several influential books, he has argued that Thomas's period saw not only a marked rise in the persecution of Jews but the birth of a new brand of anti-Judaism—one aimed at nothing less than the annihilation of Judaism and culminating in the expulsion of Jews from various European realms. During Thomas's era, "ecclesiastical authorities took concerted steps to proselytize among the Jews en masse, persecuting the Talmud . . . , exploiting inquisitorial jurisdiction to harass entire Jewish communities, invading synagogues to preach to Jewish worshipers, and coercing leading rabbis to participate in public, officially sanctioned disputations."[2] In sum, "the very legitimacy of the European Jewish community [was] called into question."[3] Leading this charge, he contends, were the Dominicans and Franciscans who "developed, refined, and sought to implement a new Christian ideology . . . that allotted the Jews no legitimate right to exist in European society" (*FJ*, 14). "By the end of the early

fourteenth century," he continues, "[they] openly advocated that Latin Christendom rid itself of its Jewish population, whether through missionizing, forced
expulsions, or physical harassment that would induce conversion or flight" (14).

In all this, Cohen claims, Thomas Aquinas plays a central role. He does
first through his alleged association with Raymond de Peñafort, whom Cohen
identifies as central to the upsurge in medieval anti-Judaism and its horrors.
Declaring that "Raymond prevailed upon Thomas to compose his *Summa
contra gentiles* as a means of attracting converts to Christianity" (105), he suggests that Thomas shared, shaped, and helped legitimate Raymond's attack
(106, 124). On another level, Thomas is culpable in a far weightier and more
direct sense. "In contrast to . . . theologians from Augustine through the end of
the twelfth century," Cohen contends, "Aquinas taught that [the Jewish] sages
knew that Jesus was the messiah and crucified him in spite of that knowledge.
The disbelief of the Jews derived, therefore not from ignorance but from a deliberate defiance of the truth" (124–25). Until the thirteenth century, Cohen
claims, Jews had been given a right to exist and worship amidst Christians
thanks to Augustine's vision of their ongoing role in salvation history. Thomas,
however, departs radically from Augustine's understanding of the Jews. His
teaching is an invitation—even a goading—to their abuse. In Cohen's story,
then, Thomas may not have been at the forefront of Jewish persecution but,
especially through his treatment of Jewish culpability for the Crucifixion, he
did as much as anyone to foster it.

To be sure, even if Cohen were right, we could still learn from Thomas on
pagan virtue—aware, perhaps, of the irony. Still, for many, willingness to listen
to Thomas on our topic requires considering claims like Cohen's. More importantly, between us and Thomas stand a millennium's distance and interpretive
cacophony. Understanding Thomas thus requires situating him in relation to
the dominant ethos and practices of his day in regard to non-Christians—above
all, his world's most important living unbelievers: Jews and Muslims. While
such contextualization does assuage worries that he's a distasteful teacher, more
to the point, it equips us to read him rightly—as one who, in his era, leaned toward justice and advocated toleration, opposing what he rightly judged as evil,
especially when it came to the treatment of outsiders. Perhaps most suggestive
in this regard is the fact that three centuries later, Dominicans nourished on
and drawing from his thought would number among the only Europeans to
oppose the conquest of the Americas.

Thomas's teachings on the *treatment* of outsiders is vitally distinct from his
vision of their *moral capacities*. Yet, by focusing on the former, this chapter rep-

resents our first step toward grasping the latter. The story it tells is meant to take us to the point where we are not merely willing but able to give Thomas our ear on pagan virtue. Neither fully righteous nor altogether unjust, Thomas is, for us, an outsider—but one from whom, if we imitate his own forbearance and charity, we can learn.

Thomas and His Outsiders

At the time Gregory issued his letter, Thomas would have been about fourteen, a recent arrival at the university in Naples. Only in Paris were the orders followed. And, after notorious public examination and disputations in which the Talmud was put "on trial," in 1242 roughly ten thousand seized manuscripts were burned (*FJ*, 63). Thomas meanwhile was busy studying Aristotelian philosophy, Ibn Rushd's commentaries, and the Jew, Maimonides. Paris, where Jews were persecuted in the street and study of Aristotle's natural philosophy and metaphysics was officially forbidden, was, in more than one sense, a long way away (Torrell, *STA*, 7).

In 1244, shortly after arriving in Naples, Thomas joined the Dominicans—a young, austere, intellectually serious order in which "everything else—organization, studies, rules about poverty and liturgy—was subordinated to [the] one purpose" of preaching the Gospel.[4] The decision was radical enough to cause his family to kidnap him, holding him under "house arrest" in an effort to return him to the respectable, prestigious path they had charted for him when they had first placed their little five-year-old as an oblate at Monte Cassino, the nearby Benedictine monastery. It was a path that would almost certainly terminate in his installment as abbot. Temporarily "imprisoned," surely Thomas had time to reflect on the strange journey that had exposed him, before he was even 20, to two radically different systems of thought and visions of life—first at Monte Cassino as a little boy, to "the age-old tradition of Latin monasticism, richly indebted to Augustine and Christian neo-Platonism," and then in Naples, to "the pagan philosophy of Aristotle, brought to the West by Jewish and especially Muslim scholars."[5] These two traditions—and the relations between them—would be central to Thomas's work for the rest of his life.[6]

The thirteenth century was the height of the medieval era. At Paris and its university, Thomas sat at its pinnacle. There, starting in 1245, he studied theology and Aristotle's ethics under Albert the Great, while continuing his philosophy training with the arts faculty (*STA*, 23–25). After a stint in Cologne, Thomas returned to Paris. Lecturing on Lombard's *Sentences*, he set two trajectories that would mark his entire career.

First, amidst tensions between the arts and theology faculty over Aristotle's philosophy and skepticism even from fellow friars, Thomas included more than two thousand quotations from the Philosopher—more than any other author. Eight hundred of these, the lion's share, were from the *Ethics* alone (41). Secondly, he imposed on the *Sentences'* structure his Dionysian vision of divine *exitus* and *reditus*, exit and return. As Son proceeds from Father, and Spirit from both, and as Son in Spirit "returns," so, Thomas proposes, should all things be seen as coming from and returning to God. Theology therefore treats primarily of the Triune God as Alpha and Omega but also of everything as ordered to him. The very Triune life, both immanent and economic, is distantly mirrored by the movement of all things. Thomas structures his work to trace that reality (43). These two themes, the embrace of Aristotle, especially his ethics, and this profoundly Trinitarian theological vision, characterize Thomas's most mature theological reflection, blooming fully in the *Summa theologiae*. Two minor works also stem from this time, each heavily influenced by the Muslims Ibn Sina and Ibn Rushd (47–50, esp. 49).[7] Like his early appropriation of Aristotle, this engagement with Islamic philosophy would endure.

In 1256, Thomas became *magister in sacra pagina*, Master of Holy Scripture, a full member of the Paris theology faculty called to lecture on Scripture and theology, engage in disputations, and preach. All of this was in addition to his particularly Dominican duties of hearing confession, offering spiritual direction, and forming others to do the same. Thomas returned to Italy, to the Dominican house of study at Orvieto, in 1261. There he began the *Summa contra Gentiles*. While controversy abounds over how to understand the work, it is almost certainly not best understood as a "missionary manual" for disputation with Muslims (104–7). Even the title has little claim to authenticity.

At Orvieto, Thomas trained young Dominicans, almost all of whom would never attend university.[8] In that context, faced with the inadequacy of the materials at his disposal, the unpreparedness of his students, and the weight of what was at stake for them and their future flocks, it is nearly certain that the idea for the *Summa theologiae* was conceived: a work was needed that would prepare students well for lives of service to the Church in hearing confession and preaching. Thomas intended to write it.

Imagining the arid, formulaic, and even chillingly mechanistic approach to caring for souls that would follow from a formation that treated moral theology in isolation from its place in God's overarching work of redemption, Thomas sought a curriculum in which ethics was inextricably integrated with a synoptic theological vision. In Rome, that work began, and by 1268 he had completed the *Prima Pars,* or "first part," of the *Summa*—along with a commentary on Aristotle's *De Anima.* So began his practice of preparing for work in the *Summa* by studying Aristotle's parallel treatments of those topics—the *De Anima* commentary, for instance, coincided with his treatment of the soul in *Summa theologiae* I, and, later, his *Ethics* commentary would coincide with his work on the *Prima Secundae.* In all, Thomas would undertake twelve such commentaries.

In 1268, Thomas returned to Paris—and to controversy. For us, the most important concerned the theology faculty's growing hostility to the study and thought of Aristotle, a stance even many Dominicans shared. Against Aristotle, most held it was rationally demonstrable that the world was not eternal. Defending Aristotle without betraying Scripture, Thomas argued this was not so: Aristotle's position was refutable by revelation alone. On strictly rational grounds, he claimed, it was indeterminate whether the earth had a beginning. It would subject theology—and the faith itself—to ridicule to claim otherwise. Further, it would be an injustice to Aristotle. That, Thomas would not countenance.

Remarkably, amidst the controversies Thomas continued his massive output, in eighteen months completing his *Ethics* commentary, his *De virtutibus,* and the entire second part of the *Summa*—itself nearly thirteen hundred double-columned pages in the standard English translation. Before 1272's end, surely exhausted, he returned to Naples and, following a mystical experience in December 1273, stopped work altogether. In light of his vision, he said, all his work seemed mere "straw." On March 7, 1274, Thomas, still in his forties, died.

Thomas and the Jews

In 1199, only fifty years prior to Gregory's letter, matters for Parisian Jews had been different. It was in that year that Pope Innocent III had issued *Sicut Iudeis,* which would become the most frequently promulgated papal bull concerning the Jews in the medieval era.[9] Addressed to all Christians, under threat of excommunication, it prohibits forced conversion or baptism and declares that "no Christian shall presume to wound [Jewish] person[s], or kill them, or rob them of their money, or change the good customs which they have thus far enjoyed" and that "no one shall disturb them in any way by means of sticks and stones [while they celebrate their festivals]" (*CJ,* 92–93). Steven Boguslawski notes that in issuing this bull, Innocent III was situating himself in a strong tradition of toleration of the Jews that extended back to Gregory the Great's recognition of the impropriety of compulsion and the necessity of gentleness and charity in efforts to sway "even those at odds with the Christian religion to the unity of the faith" (*TAJ*, 21–22). Yet, Boguslawski notes that by the late thirteenth century the repeated reissuance of Innocent's bull, each time with novel proscriptions of still different forms of persecution, testifies to growing hostility toward Jews—animus so great that "by the end of the thirteenth century [they were] . . . beyond any aid from . . . *Sicut Iudeis*."[10] Still, even as late as 1233, the very Gregory who would eventually order the seizure of Jewish texts issued a bull "to end the beatings, tortures, despoiling, and unjust imprisonment of certain Jews" by various French civil authorities (*TAJ*, 24). Throughout, the impetus to protect the Jews was rooted most deeply in the Christian conception of their role as living witnesses to God's fidelity in their own obedience to the Mosaic law, their subservience a just result of their supposed rejection of Jesus as Messiah.

It is in this context that we can, on one level, understand Gregory's letter. For Gregory, Jewish fidelity to Talmud alongside or instead of Torah constituted a betrayal of their own covenantal relationship with God and a displacement from their assigned role in the Christian narrative. Rabbinic teaching could thus seem to threaten the Christian vision of salvation history, to violate the very "Jewishness" of the Jews. To the mind of certain Christians, then, the Talmud was a threat to Jew and Christian alike—and so the Talmud and Jewish adherence to it became the target of Christian attack.[11] Innocent IV continued Gregory's trajectory with a directive in 1244 for the French king to burn Jewish books, citing in particular their crime of "[throwing] away and [despising] the law of Moses and the prophets, and [following] some tradition of their elders" (*CJ*, 251). While the disruption of the Christian narrative of Jewish identity may have been a chief cause of the persecution, Gregory and Innocent both seem to have acted under the impression that the Talmud was largely comprised of attacks on and blasphemies against Christianity and especially the person of Jesus. Thus, responding to the protest of Jewish scholars, in 1247 Innocent IV instructed his representative in France, the archbishop of Rouen, Odo, to return to the Jews those books that were deemed no threat. Odo, however, took the occasion merely to condemn many of the books a second time. Though we do not know what his role might have been, among the forty-four people enlisted in the process of reexamination was the man who would soon become Thomas's teacher, Albert the Great.[12] Such was the atmosphere in Paris one year before Thomas's arrival.

Thomas was not a champion of the Jews. Few if any thirteenth century Christians were. Perhaps the fairest assessment is forwarded by Torrell, Thomas's authoritative biographer. "Thomas," he says, "is sometimes hard on the Jews" (*STA*, 32). Torrell here judges Thomas in relation to our context—and his pronouncement, I think, gets it about right. Thomas is hard on the Jews. He does not hate Jews and would never countenance their persecution. But he does bear the marks of his age.

Thus, it is troubling to hear the Thomas of 1271 agree that Jews should have to wear distinguishing clothing—even as, citing Jewish law, he notes that their own law commands them to do so (*ADB* 8). And it is disturbing that he would favorably cite the dictum that the "Jews are sentenced to perpetual servitude as punishment for their guilt"—even as he insists that they never should be deprived of the goods they need to live and should be allowed to earn their living by honorable work, never forced into usury (*ADB* 1). Yet these remarks, which are culled from *Ad ducissam Brabantiae*, his very brief response to eight legislative and financial questions posed in a letter by Margaret of Constantinople, are actually relatively progressive for their time (*STA*, 218–9). Indeed, Thomas's reply is remarkable only in its departures from standard anti-Jewish practices and its relative friendliness toward and protection of Jews. Further, Thomas indicates that he writes in haste and feels unqualified to render these judgments. Torrell correctly notes that while this letter is often called the *De regimine Iudaeorum*, or *On the Rule of Jews*, "the name is improper because, for more than half of its short length, [it] speaks of the non-Jewish subjects of the recipient" (218).

Moreover, the letter is hardly an adequate or balanced summary of Thomas on Judaism. If anything, it suggests an unjustly negative portrait. Nonetheless, it still shows Thomas pushing against some of the anti-Jewish injustice of his moment. This comes into even clearer light when we consider John Peckham's (1230–92) response to Margaret's questions. As compared to Thomas, Peckham, Thomas's Franciscan contemporary and University of Paris colleague, centrally focuses on the Jews rather than economic matters generally. Specifically, he condemns Jews as usurers, yet forbids them any employment that would bring them into regular interaction with Christians.[13] "The result," Giacomo Todeschini notes, is that "usury is [at once] proscribed but remains the only practicable [business] for Jews."[14] This stands in sharp contrast to Thomas's insistence that Jews be allowed to work for their living and his declaration that a high level of interaction between Christians and Jews is entirely acceptable—even as much as would be involved in their laboring together daily (II. II 10.9).[15] Peckham is not alone in portraying Jews as avaricious, degrading "others" against whom mendicant life must be defended. Todeschini contends that Peckham merely gives explicit formulation to a Franciscan view of Jews as "enemies of Franciscan poverty . . . [and] usurers, [who were] dangerous for the Christian moral and economic order."[16] These commitments, he claims, were shared by Peter John Olivi, Ramon Llull, Roger Bacon, and others—and especially by Bonaventure, who, with Peckham, viewed Jews as "menacing leaders" of avarice and carnality who threatened to destroy Christian society.[17] Whether Todeschini's analysis is fully accurate, at the least it brings Thomas's stance into important relief. Where many deployed the specter of the contemporary "Jew" and Jewish usury in defending Christian life or mendicant poverty, Thomas does no such thing.[18]

As for Cohen's harsh assessment of Thomas, it is problematic on multiple levels. As Boguslawski notes, save one brief citation, Cohen disregards altogether Thomas's most extensive treatment of the Jews: that offered in his *Lectura super ad Romanos*. Boguslawski, in contrast, offers a careful reading of the Romans commentary's treatment of Romans 9–11 and the election of the Jews, arguing that Thomas neither advances the anti-Judaism Cohen blames him for nor simply maintains the "Augustinian" status quo. Instead, Boguslawski contends, Thomas "breaks new ground"—elevating the Jews beyond their place in Augustine's thought and more profoundly guaranteeing their safety and honor (*TAJ*, 4).[19]

Specifically, Boguslawski argues that Thomas deploys conceptions of election and predestination to secure the priority and ongoing place of the Jews in salvation history and "cautions non-Jews against smug self-confidence in the present and promises the future remedy of the Jews in the culmination of salvation history" (7). Noting Thomas's declaration that "'Jew is an honorable [name],'" he contends that "for Aquinas . . . divine election effectively relativizes the status of Jew and Gentile [Christian], *making them equal in their present call, justification, and glorification*" (7, 65, my emphasis). "Thomas," he continues, "preserves the Jews' dignity and their privileged status not only historically, but as essential to the outworking of election in time. . . . There is a necessity and responsibility incumbent upon the Christian church to preserve the role of the Jews in the temporal outworking of salvation history" (65–66).[20] If Boguslawski is correct, then more than simply rejecting his moment's waxing anti-Judaism, in *Lectura super ad Romanos* Thomas transcends Augustinian paradigms, securing a higher, firmer foundation for Jewish flourishing. This is all the more notable given that, while it's uncertain whether Thomas publicly presented the *Summa*, he did lecture on Romans, perhaps even before departing Paris in 1272.[21]

For its part, Cohen's claim that Thomas penned *Summa contra Gentiles* at Raymond's insistence and in order to serve Raymond's efforts with the Jews does not withstand scrutiny.[22] Much less his assertions that the two "shared the same views on how best to convert the infidel" and that this "affinity . . . allowed Raymond to solicit the composition" (*FJ*, 124).[23] Thomas, we'll see, explicitly condemns the abuses Cohen assigns to Raymond's school. Cohen's other charges are equally unfounded. His central evidence that Thomas launched a new brand of anti-Judaism, and thereby abetted in the rise in persecution, is Thomas's purported argument in *Summa theologiae* III 47.5 that the Jews crucified Jesus knowing "exactly who he was" (*LL*, 339–40; *FJ*, 125).[24] But even if Cohen's reading of the passage were correct, this would hardly substantiate his narrative.[25]

Consider first the origin and development of Thomas's teaching on the matter. Cohen repeatedly suggests a connection to a forced disputation in Paris in 1269 or 1270 where the Jewish Dominican Paul Christian, perhaps for his first time, charged the Jews with deicide and nearly sparked a pogrom. "They deserve to be killed," he apparently said, "and woe to those creatures that tolerate them!"[26] "Curiously," Cohen says, implying a link to Paul's attack, Thomas was lecturing in Paris at the time (*CK*, 90).[27]

Actually, as many as twelve years before the disputation and fourteen years prior to writing 47.5, Thomas had considered the role of the Jews in Jesus's death in commenting on 1 Corinthians 2:8, "None of the princes of this world knew; for if they had known it, they would never have crucified the Lord."[28] Grappling with this and Acts 3:17, on the one hand, which suggest the ignorance of those who killed Jesus, and, on the other hand, the parable of the murderous vineyard workers in Matthew 21, which was taken to mean that the Jews acted in full knowledge, Thomas, in typical form, seeks harmonization by mediating between two more rival authorities: a gloss saying the Jewish *principes*, or leaders, knew Jesus to be Messiah but not Son of God and no less a father than Chrysostom insisting that "they knew he was the Son of God" (*CC* 2.2.93). This "new Christian way of imagining the Jew" (*CK*, 89) that Thomas allegedly inaugurates we find in the Gospel of Matthew and a contemporary of Augustine.[29] Even so, rather than simply accept this ancient teaching, Thomas contends that while "the Jewish leaders knew (*scientia*) with certainty that [Jesus] was the Messiah, . . . *the crowds were ignorant (ignorabat) of this*" (*CC* 2.2.93). Against Chrysostom and bending the traditional reading of Matthew, he claims the leaders did not know (*scientia*) Jesus to be God's Son but, due to their sin, had only a vague conjecture (*cognitio*) (93). What's notable and novel in Thomas's remarks is not his qualified submission to what he saw himself bound to accept, but his distinctions and his silence. Dividing knowledge (*scientia*) from a vague sense (*cognitio*), he insists that not even the leaders knew they were killing God's Son. More significantly, unlike his authorities, he not only sharply distinguishes the leaders from the Jewish masses but declares the latter completely ignorant that Jesus was the Messiah, much less God's Son. Finally, he shows no interest in linking any of this to contemporary Jews, about whom he says nothing.

Long before the disputation, driven by Corinthians, and trying to reconcile ancient authorities, Thomas arrived at this teaching about first century Jewish rulers in distinction from unknowing masses and with no eye to contemporary Jews. To my knowledge, Cohen nowhere even mentions this commentary. When Thomas would finally revisit the topic in 1272 or 1273 in the passage Cohen cites and imagines as linked to Paul's attacks, the only real differences in his teaching actually show him *more* friendly toward ancient Jews.[30]

There, Thomas once again finds himself having to say there is some sense in which certain Jews knowingly killed the Messiah and Son only because he is responding to multiple texts that make the claim, including authorities no less ancient or estimable than Jerome, the Council of Ephesus, and the Gospels of Matthew and John.[31] Finding the claim in such texts, he cannot dismiss it. Instead, he mitigates it, confining it to a narrow group of ancient rulers and structuring the article to emphasize the crowd's ignorance as much or more than the leaders' guilt.

Distinguishing *maiores* from *minores*—the leaders from the mass of common Jews—the latter, he says, did not know what they were doing and thought Jesus neither Messiah nor God's Son. Departing from his Corinthians commentary, he even stresses that some of the *minores* believed *in* Jesus (*in eum*) as Messiah and Son of God. These Jews, he means to remind, opposed the Crucifixion. More, Thomas structures the article to make the crowd's ignorance its main point, having the objections claim that Christ's persecutors knew his identity and citing three scriptural texts in the *sed contra* that declare the Jews' ignorance.[32] Finally, as before, he says nothing regarding contemporary Jews.

Indeed, 47.5's only material change relative to *CC* is *more* heavily to stress Jewish ignorance and to add that some trusted *in* Jesus. It's not what we'd expect of someone pleased by Friar Paul's activities, just the opposite. In fact, what Thomas was writing at the time of the disputation was II.II—that portion of the

Summa where he considers the treatment of contemporary Jews and condemns the very abuses Paul was fomenting. And he was likely also preparing and may have begun his lectures on Romans, where he exalts the Jews' vital, ongoing place in God's plan. If we imagine any interaction between Thomas and Paul, surely it should be his rebuking Paul for injustice and scandal or, in outrage, his all the more furiously penning his condemnation of such persecution by which he hoped to turn future generations from Paul's vicious path.

Even putting all this aside, to assign Thomas the role Cohen does requires evidence that 47.5 affected the way people related to or understood Jews, and, in the very way he claims. Cohen offers no such evidence.[33] Nor does he even consider who, if anyone, might have read the article. In truth, if it can be answered at all, the question of *Summa theologiae*'s influence, let alone that of a single article, demands meticulous historical work. What we can say with confidence is this. Likely, the *Summa*'s impact during the period in view was limited.[34] Throughout the era, it circulated almost exclusively piecemeal, in its four parts, and the *Tertia Pars*, where 47.5 is located, was by far the least read of these.[35] By a great deal, the most widely read, in contrast, was II.II, where Thomas considers the treatment of Jews, forbidding their abuse. Despite II.II's relative popularity, until 1500 Thomas's widest readership by far was through John of Freiburg's (d. 1314) *Summa confessorum* (1298), a penitential manual comprised mostly of material from II.II and including other excerpts from Thomas, Peter of Tarentaise, and the like. It became the standard text for training Dominicans in pastoral theology, their main and often only exposure to Thomas, and the primary means by which his thought was disseminated more broadly.[36] The *Summa confessorum* does not include III 47.5.[37] It does, however, recount much of Thomas's teaching on the Jews from II.II, including his prohibition of forced baptism and requirement that Jewish rites and feasts be tolerated.[38]

Without adducing any evidence, Cohen insists that a single article on the knowledge of ancient sages that is entirely silent about contemporary Jews, found in the least circulated part of the *Summa*, and absent from the text by which Thomas's thought was primarily disseminated revolutionized medieval anti-Judaism and abetted persecution. At the same time, he holds that Thomas's detailed, explicit, multi-article rejection of Jewish persecution, located in the most read portion of *Summa theologiae* and included in the *Confessorum*, had no impact at all. Even if we leave aside questions about the quality of such historical reasoning, when it comes to judging Thomas's legacy in relation to

Jews and their treatment, it hardly seems fair to do so not on the basis of how Thomas actually says Jews should be treated but in view of a remark about ancient Jewish leaders. It seems less fair still to do so while neglecting the development of Thomas's teaching, the remark's ancient and Scriptural precedents, its silence on contemporary matters, its focus on the ignorance of the masses, and Thomas's stress there that some ancient Jews placed their faith in Jesus.

In line with the Christian tradition from Scripture to his own day, there is plenty to object to in Thomas's teaching about Jews. But if Thomas is unusual in regard to the Jews, it is only in virtue of being less anti-Jewish than most of his contemporaries and predecessors. If Boguslawski is right, he is a proto-reconciler, sowing seeds that blossomed in twentieth century Catholicism's movement to repent of past wrongs and view Jews in a new light.

Thomas and the Treatment of Outsiders

We turn now to what Thomas says about the treatment of Jews and non-Christians more generally. In II.II, Thomas divides those engaged in *infidelitas* into those who reject the Christian faith *without* or *before* accepting it and those who reject it *after* having accepted it (II.II 10.1).[39] The former includes pagans and Muslims; their sin—because of the lesser character of their resistance—is less. Heretics belong to the category of those who reject Christian faith having accepted it, but so, surprisingly, do Jews. They do, Thomas explains, because in virtue of their Jewish faith, they have accepted the truth *in figura*, in figure (II.II 10.6). To be very clear, this does *not* qualify Jews as heretics in any way for Thomas and certainly does not mean they are to be treated as such. Jewish *infidelitas* is of an entirely different species than that of heretics—just as it is of a different species than that of Muslims. Where heretics "resist" after committing themselves to the "very manifestation of truth" (*in ipsa manifestatione veritatis*), Jews are only committed to Christianity *in figura*—in a way that distinguishes them from other unbelievers but by no means makes them Christians or heretics. Thus, just after his *in figura* claim, Thomas groups Jews with gentile pagans as those "who have *never* received the faith" (*qui nunquam susceperunt fidem, sicut gentiles et Iudaei*) (II.II 10.6).[40] The sinfulness of *infidelitas* is proportionate to the degree of resistance: the sin of heretics is greatest and of one kind, that of Jews less and of another kind, that of Muslims lesser and different still (II.II 10.1 and 6). It's precisely because of Jews having uniquely received truth *in figura*, that, in distinction from all others, their rites are uniquely tolerated

(II.II 10.11). Their protected, enduring place in salvation history for Thomas is inseparable from the character of their *infidelitas*, its relative proximity to yet essential difference from that of heretics.[41] Thomas's taxonomy simultaneously ensures Jews a unique status and protection vis-à-vis pagans, while protecting them from the coercion reserved for heretics.

In this context, Thomas discusses several of the most important practical issues of his day concerning the Christian treatment of non-Christians: disputations, coercion in matters of faith, social interaction, political authority, freedom of worship, and forced baptism.

DISPUTATIONS

Thomas believes disputations permissible only when undertaken by those secure in their faith.[42] Moreover, the audience must be equally steadfast, unless their faith has been shaken because they have been "disturbed or impelled (*sollicitati sive pulsati*) by unbelievers such as Jews, heretics, or pagans who struggle to corrupt their faith," and there is confidence the disputation will restore their faith (II.II 10.7).[43] Importantly, Thomas does not regard all disturbance in the faith of the "simple" as evidence of infidel meddling. He believes innocent social interaction with unbelievers can cause such doubt.[44] Thus, whether someone's faith is shaken and whether an infidel intended this are distinct matters; only if the disturbance is intentional could public disputation become permissible. Even then, the disputant's intention must be to refute some particular error(s), defend the faith from attack, or restore the faith of the "simple." Thomas's concern for the "simple," which demands openness to disputations, is balanced by reticence stemming from his desire not to cause potential converts to scorn Christian faith or otherwise to scandalize them.[45] Such commitments seem incompatible with forcing unbelievers into disputations.[46] His concern to avoid alienating unbelievers comes through clearly in *Ad ducissam Brabantiae*, where he insists that any tax on the Jews not be unreasonable. Citing three scriptural passages, he stresses the importance of not giving Jews unnecessary offense or cause to scorn the church:

> Provisions necessary for life [must] in no way be taken away from them, because it is required that we "walk honestly indeed before those who are outside [the faith]" [1 Thess. 4:11-12], "lest the Lord's name be cursed" [1 Tim. 6:1], and Paul urges the faithful by his example "[to] live without offense among the Jews, the Gentiles, and the Church of God" [1 Cor. 10:32-3] (*ADB* 1).

Scandalizing unbelievers, causing them to curse Christ, is, for Thomas, a betrayal of Jesus, his Gospel, and the task of proclaiming it. It is one of the worst sins a Christian, and especially a *Dominican*, can commit. It is incredible, therefore, to imagine Thomas approving of Paul's disputation, where vulnerable Jews, beholding Paul's "intention to exterminate" them (*CK*, 90), had every reason to curse Christ and his church.

COERCION

Thomas also tackles the question of whether unbelievers ought to be in any way coerced to the faith (II.II 10.8). Heretics and apostates may be coerced, he says, because they made vows for which they may be held accountable.[47] Not so Jews or any others. These have *nunquam susceperunt fidem*, never accepted the faith, and *nullo modo sunt ad fidem compellendi*, are in no way to be compelled to it. Thomas's resistance to compelled conversion runs deep. For Thomas, faith depends on the will—and the will, by its nature, cannot be moved to faith by coercion. Efforts to do so are futile and wrong. Thomas does contend, however, that force should be brought to bear in those cases where unbelievers impede the faith through "blasphemies, malicious sophistries (*persuasionibus*), or even public persecutions" (II.II 10.8). In such cases, it is Christians, he thinks, who are in danger of being coerced to convert. And just as Christians may not compel conversion, so too others must not try to force Christians to abandon their faith. Thus, other things being equal, Thomas believes a duly established non-ecclesial Christian political authority may justly coerce those who attempt to thwart Christian faith. This is the lens through which Thomas understands wars against nonbelievers. However, such wars (and coercive acts) are just only when, among other necessary conditions, the intended end is *not* the conversion or domination of unbelievers but precisely protection of Christian freedom to worship without persecution.[48] As Vitoria would later argue, Thomas's logic entails that not just the persecution of Christians *but of almost any religious group* could become just cause for war and, therefore, that under certain circumstances a non-Christian political authority could justly war against a Christian political authority if that Christian political authority were guilty of unjust religious persecution.[49]

However jarring, Thomas's perspective is not entirely dissimilar to contemporary notions of "responsibility to protect," and his insistence on protecting religious minorities within Christian societies displays a commitment to equity that should keep us from charging him with legitimating imperialism. Importantly, by qualifying his initial statement—those who hinder the faith should be stopped *si facultas adsit*, "if ability or means allow"—Thomas implicitly invokes criteria for the just use of coercion or war that he elaborates elsewhere, especially the criteria of proportionality and chance of success (see, e.g., II.II 43.3 ad 3; 10.11). The persecution of Christians ought to be opposed with force, he suggests, only if there is reasonable chance of permanently stopping the persecution *and* if trying to do so would not cause disproportionate harm to any parties involved, either in the very effort to end the persecution or in its aftermath. Thomas thereby further limits the just use of coercion in matters concerning unbelievers.

Of course, Thomas's language about what constitutes "impeding the faith" is vague. We might especially worry that in mentioning blasphemy as "impeding the faith" he sneaks religious coercion through the back door. While Thomas thinks blasphemy can merit coercion, the question is whether blasphemy is a category so broad it authorizes *de facto* persecution. While we cannot address that concern fully here, the immediate context suggests otherwise. To illustrate just coercion, Thomas takes the case of war against unbelievers who persecute Christians in their midst. It is not in their capacity as *unbelievers* that Christians war against them, Thomas stresses, but in their capacity as *persecutors* of Christians—a *Christian* ruler who persecuted Christians would be no less liable to just attack. Mere adherence to non-Christian faith is neither blasphemy nor grounds for war.[50] Further, only blasphemy that actively impedes or seriously destabilizes the faith could become possible grounds for coercion, not blasphemy *per se.*

AUTHORITY

Thomas additionally takes up the question of whether unbelievers may hold authority or dominion over Christians. In answering, he distinguishes between authority already in place and authority not yet constituted. In the latter case, in Christian societies, Thomas contends that it is unlawful for nonbelievers to hold ultimate authority over believers.[51] Regarding the former case, the Christian/non-Christian distinction is *ex iure divino*, a function of Divine rule, whereas the ruler/ruled distinction is *ex iure humano*, from human law.[52] "Divine law, which is from grace," Thomas explains, "does not destroy human law, which is from natural reason" (II.II 10.10). Thus conversion to Christianity by citizens under non-Christian authority does not *per se* release them from obedience to that authority. While the Church, as bearing God's authority, can so release someone, it only does so when it possesses temporal authority over the non-believing ruler and, even then, only sometimes. Most significantly, other things being equal, the rule of Christians by non-Christians, where that rule is *already in place*, is lawful and just.[53] Thomas's point has major implications, especially concerning the status of non-Christian nations—such as those Muslim nations that Thomas said Christians sometimes war against. Since these nations are already constituted, other things being equal, their rule over Christians is lawful and, as a matter of natural law and grace's status as perfecting rather than destroying nature, *nullo modo* just cause for war. Only if the ruler impedes the faith can war even be considered—and then the full gamut of just war criteria must be met. If R.W. Southern is correct that "the West was never very happy in its justification of the Islamic Crusade," it is clear that to that task Thomas lent little, if any, quarter.[54]

RITES AND FORCED BAPTISM

On two other issues vital for Christian/Jewish relations, Thomas stood against waxing anti-Judaism. First, in a context where Dominicans would occasionally invade Sabbath services to preach, Thomas insists that Jews should be free to worship without interference. Moreover, he cites as an objection a gloss on Galatians characterizing Jewish rites as idolatry. Notwithstanding the preeminent authority he accords Scripture, he implicitly rejects the gloss, claiming that Jewish worship ought to be tolerated precisely "because a certain good flows from it." This good, he says, is "that we have a witness to our faith from the strangers/enemies (*hostibus*) and what we believe is displayed for us *quasi in figura*."[55] Against both traditional and contemporary currents, Thomas defends the Jews' full freedom to worship.[56] Second, Thomas unequivocally rejects forced baptism or the baptism of children against their parents' will. Here we glimpse Thomas in starkest opposition to the anti-Judaism of his day.

Consider two bookends to Thomas's life. In 1201, Innocent III claimed there was a valid distinction between those who are forcibly baptized (picked up and plunged, say) and those coerced to consent to baptism through torture, threat of death, and so on. These latter, he says, "belong to ecclesiastical jurisdiction . . . and might therefore be . . . compelled to observe . . . Christian Faith" (*CJ*, 103). He continues: "One who is drawn to Christianity by violence, through fear and torture, and receives the sacrament of baptism in order to avoid loss . . . does receive the impress of Christianity, and may be forced

to observe the . . . Faith. . . . [They] must be duly constrained to abide." Innocent illustrates the cases he has in mind by referring to seventh-century
Jews coerced into baptism through threat of punishment: these should be
compelled to keep the faith. By implication, his argument includes children
baptized against their parents' will and even legitimates such baptism. In 1277,
after Thomas's death, Nicholas III wrote an inquisitor—a Dominican no less—
explaining that Jews baptized in fear of death who refused to live as Christians
should be subject to the same punishment as recalcitrant heretics, up to and
including execution (*CJ*, 15n.15). And just a generation after Thomas's death,
Scotus would argue for forced baptism of Jewish children—a position Peter
Auriol too would all but endorse.[57]

Thomas's unqualified interdiction against compulsion in matters of faith
forbids *any* sort of forced baptism, any inducement to receive the sacrament
through fear, coercion, torture, or whatever. Thomas is equally categorical in his
prohibition of the baptism of the children of Jews or other unbelievers. What is
particularly noteworthy is less *that* he prohibits this absolutely and more that
he roots this prohibition in natural law. God, Thomas insists, has ordained that
parents have unique responsibility for the spiritual direction of their children
until they reach the age of reason (II.II 10.12 and ad 3). Baptizing a child against
parental objection is as much *contra iustitiam naturalem* as murder—even if,
prior to the age of reason, a child should indicate interest. For Thomas, it is a
matter of natural—and so divine—justice.

Before presenting this argument, Thomas devotes significant space to giving his students a history lesson. Clearly driven by deep pedagogical concerns,
Thomas places this lesson first in his response, even as the *sed contra* summarizes the natural law argument. Recall Thomas's central task of training young
Dominicans. Thomas knew it was extremely likely that many of his students
would one day be asked—or even commanded—to join in coerced baptism,
the disturbance of synagogue worship, forced disputations, and other crimes
against the Jews. Thomas is equipping his students for resistance. It has *never*
been the custom of the Church, he explains, to baptize children against the
will of their parents. He wants the *Summa*'s readers to recognize the acts of
certain friars as the betrayal of tradition and natural justice alike. And so, after
explaining that such action has no precedent, he explains why, focusing on the
fact that the baptism of Jewish children is a gross violation of justice and utterly
inexcusable—and this even if one believes such baptism saves the child from
damnation (II.II 10.12 ad 2).

In sum, when it comes to the Jews, Thomas's shortcomings, however disturbing, are characteristic of his age. His uniqueness lies, rather, in the degree to which he resisted the worst vices of his day.

Thomas and Islam

Aside from Jews, Muslims were the living outsiders with whom Thomas was most familiar. However, since he nearly always groups them in the undifferentiated category of "non-Jewish unbelievers," we have already seen implicitly where he stands on their treatment. Indeed, when it comes to *treatment*, the distinction between Gentile unbelievers and Jews primarily pertains to rites, where his grounding for tolerating Jewish rites is more principled than pragmatic. The rest of his remarks hold as much for Muslims and others as for Jews. Even his claim that the only just cause for war against unbelievers is seeking to end religious persecution is not particular to Muslim but holds for any—even Christian—nations (II.II 10.8). While this tacit sketch answers our needs, we can say a bit more about Thomas in relation to Islam. Doing so returns us to Thomas's youth.

Thomas would have been three or four when his oldest brother, Aimo, departed as part of the sixth crusade. Most simply, the expedition's goal was to reacquire Jerusalem. Through a show of force and negotiations with al-Kāmil, the Ayyubid sultan of Egypt, the city was ceded and conflict largely averted. Aimo, however, was captured on the return home by a vassal of the Christian king of Cyprus and finally ransomed by Gregory IX in 1233. Whether Aimo would have dazzled his eight-year-old little brother with tales of Egypt and Jerusalem, we can only imagine. Surely, though, Thomas would have grown up knowing that his oldest brother had participated in an effort to wrest Jerusalem—and its Christians—from Muslim control. While there is no indication that he had any involvement, by the end of his life, Thomas would have seen three more crusades, including what would be the last in 1272.

Relative to the earliest crusades, popular support was scant for these efforts. The first during Thomas's adult life, undertaken by Louis IX of France, was getting underway just as Thomas arrived in Paris in 1245. Odo, the very archbishop who had enlisted (or conscripted) Albert in his anti-Jewish book-examining campaign, was a close friend of Louis and a constant companion to him following his return from crusade around 1254. We do not know, but, especially given his defense of and devotion to mendicant poverty, it is certainly not hard to imagine Thomas disliking this ostentatious and fractious Franciscan book burner, who lived in luxury, occasionally traveling with a troop of as many as eighty horsemen.[58] Thomas may well have seen in him an image of what he could have become had he followed his family's intentions and become abbot of Monte Cassino. In 1270, in the midst of his second tenure in Paris, Thomas saw Odo leave France as part of Louis's second crusade. When a year or two later Thomas mentions the "faithful of Christ going to war against the unbelievers" in the portion of the *Secunda Secundae* that we examined above, he almost certainly did so with these or earlier crusades in mind (II.II 10.8). Whether out of ignorance, naïveté, or something more troubling, he understood or at least portrayed them as intending the just liberation of persecuted Christians.

The winds of Islam may well have touched Thomas in other ways. David Burrell speculates that Thomas's time in Naples might have nudged him toward greater interest in Muslim philosophy, as compared to northern scholars. Thanks to its proximity to Sicily, a place of Muslim, Jewish, and Christian exchange, Naples may have been more open to such interchange than other parts of Latin Christendom, Spain excepted. Burrell also hints that this ethos might have had something to do with Thomas's choice of Naples for his *studium*, a Dominican house of theological study and formation.[59] All of this is only easier to imagine if we envision a young Thomas sitting, enthralled, listening to some wild tale of Aimo's, frightening and alluring, told in the way that only an older sibling can.

For all this, Thomas knew little about Muslim beliefs and practices, and it seems very unlikely that he would have interacted with any Muslims. Of course, Thomas drew heavily from Muslim philosophers throughout his career, citing Ibn Sina some 450 times and Ibn Rushd (980–1037) on around 500 occasions.[60] He counts these men as authorities. Their being *Muslim* does nothing in his eyes to diminish the degree to which they may be sources of wisdom. From them he gathers insights and distinctions that prove essential, and it is hard to imagine his commentaries on Aristotle without his ongoing textual interaction with the "Commentator," Ibn Rushd. Indeed, it is precisely Ibn Rushd whom Thomas cites when, with profound consequences, he places *voluntas,* or will, near the center of his conception of habit (I.II 49.3 sc). None of this is to suggest he always agreed with such figures. The point, rather, is that he let "a common humanity and intellectual acumen . . . unite [what] alien faith could easily divide," treating Muslims without prejudice as fellow seekers of truth—

men created to know and love Christ even as, in Thomas's judgment, they fell short of that end.[61]

Yet, the gap between medieval Islamic philosophy and *kalām,* or theology, is wide. And the gulf between either and the more "orthodox" faith of scholars of *fiqh,* Qur'an, *hadīth,* and so on—let alone that of average Muslims—was greater still. Thomas knew next to nothing of these distinctions. He was exposed almost exclusively to Islamic philosophy, a genre many Muslims viewed as heretical.[62] What Thomas read had more to do with neo-Platonism and Aristotle than with the Qur'an, the Prophet, or *hadīth.* Further, in engaging Islamic thought, Thomas did not try to probe or reconstruct Islamic religious commitment but to illumine his own questions—some of which were shared with these Muslim philosophers.[63] While Thomas's only encounters with Muslims, through texts by Ibn Rushd, Ibn Sina, and the like, are more engagements with *philosophers* than with *Islam,* in a way that is just the point.

Recent scholarship largely undermines the notion that *Summa contra Gentiles* was directly or indirectly aimed at Muslims. Thomas declares at its outset how scant his knowledge of Islam is (*SCG* I.2). His only text that does talk of Islam in any extended way confirms the admission. *De rationibus fidei ad Cantorem Antiochenum* responds to an unknown figure who seeks guidance in answering Muslim objections to various Christian doctrines: God's Triunity, the Incarnation, and the like. The objections are not even distinctively Muslim; they could have been articulated by any philosophical monotheist. Thomas's short, careful answers display only minimal knowledge of Muslim dogma—little beyond the recognition that Muslims hold God to be one, omnipotent, to forgive without atonement, and so on.[64] What is notable, but by no means distinctive to this text, is Thomas's unswerving commitment to something like what we would call "immanent critique" and to the particularly respectful stance toward one's interlocutor it presupposes and manifests. Thomas holds that one of the best hopes for persuading opponents is appealing to premises they endorse, premises that can vary according to one's religion. Knowing so little of Islam, Thomas nonetheless shows deep respect for Muslims: they are to be addressed as full members of the community of reason-givers, with arguments that do not rest on Scriptures that they reject, and with the primary goal of showing as unfounded their ridicule of Christian dogmas. And this is the approach he seeks to foster in one who will interact with Muslims directly. Along with his readiness to learn from Muslim philosophers, if anything sums up his stance toward Islam—and non-Christians in general—this does.

Thomas and Other Others

Aside from Jews and Muslims, Tatars, Mongols, and other "pagans" on various border regions are the living unbelievers Thomas might have imagined. While some friars found Tatar incursions cause for apocalyptic speculation, there's nothing like this in Thomas. And whatever stir William of Rubruck's *Itinerarium* may have made in 1255, with its tale of his epic journey into the heart of the Khan kingdom and vivid depiction of these peoples, Thomas mentions no *Tartari* in his corpus and—so far as I can tell—offers no specific attention to other living pagans.[65] Still, we can derive a rule of thumb from his approach to *infidelitas*. Recall that rejection of Christianity is the primary factor in the sinfulness of *infidelitas*. In contrast, degree of error, while making *infidelitas* "more grave" (*gravior*) in one sense, is no factor in whether some *infidelitas* is sinful *per se*. Leaving aside the matter of rejection, insofar as Thomas regards religious beliefs as important to moral life, it seems that, other things being equal, his expectations for pagan virtue would decrease the greater the incompatibilities between the outsider's religion and Christianity. Absent refusal of Christianity, though, he would not regard *infidelitas* in itself as sinful. He might, however, expect that religious beliefs that he judges false would make the cultivation of virtue difficult or tend to bear morally unsavory fruit.[66] Conversely, in the case of the doctrinally "nearer" outsider, while any increased resistance to Christianity would entail greater sin, he would expect the greater truth in such beliefs to make moral excellence relatively easier to attain.

Jews Revisited and Our Outsiders

Interpreters differ over whether Thomas held that, ultimately, all Jews would be saved. Certain remarks seem to suggest he does. Concerning Paul's claim in Romans that "all Israel will be saved," for instance, "*non particulariter sicut modo*," explains Thomas, "*sed universaliter omnes*" (*RC* 11.4.916) Translators disagree over whether to read this as saying that all Jews will be saved "not partially as till now, but all universally" or "not in respect to each individually but 'all' universally," *qua* group.[67] Even if one settles the translation, complexities abound regarding Thomas's meaning. His subsequent remarks only muddy the waters.[68]

    In a certain way, the difficulties surrounding such a point express a dynamic at the core of Thomas's conception of the Jews—and our efforts to understand it. It is a conception and task fraught with complexities—complexities that, thankfully, are not those our aims require us further to resolve. Yet, ambiguities not-withstanding, it is a conception that seems to swerve toward charity. Surely it is one that affords us the chance to do the same. For, whoever exactly he meant to include in that *all*, Thomas clearly held that a vast portion of Jews—much more than history or experience seemed to suggest to him—would be saved and that this salvation, "now difficult, [and] almost [marked by] a kind of violence" would, "at the end of the world [be characterized by its] ease," its sweetness, the clarity and excess of its manifestation of the goodness and faithfulness of God (919). Citing Amos 3:12—"As if a shepherd should get out of the lion's mouth two legs, or the tip of the ear: so shall the children of Israel be taken out"—far from endorsing coercion, Thomas depicts Jewish conversion between the times: even as things will one day be different, now, he is saying, in this day, it is against the grain—and even experienced by the community as a kind of violence. The remark suggests a keen sensitivity to Jewish experience. What follows in the text suggests something more.

Speaking of the surety of God's gracious promises to the patriarchs regarding their descendants the Jews, Thomas writes, movingly, of God's covenant and election: "Both are so sure that what God promises is, in a way, already given and whomever he elects is already called" (926). The remark resonates deeply with that of another theologian, one also marked by engagement with and openness to outsiders. Responding to Karl Barth's claim that Jews have the promise but not the fulfillment whereas Christians have both, the self-described Jewish-Barthian Michael Wyschogrod replied: "With human promises, one can have the promise but not the fulfillment. . . . But a promise of God is like money in the bank. If we have his promise we have its fulfillment." Wyschogrod describes what happened next: "There was a period of silence and then [Barth] said, 'You know, I never thought of it that way.'"[69] In the 1270s and without a Wyschogrod to converse with, Thomas had.

Having recounted some of the details of Thomas's way with outsiders, we can move toward his conception of pagan virtue. If his stance against his era's worst suggests that we might, without irony, learn from what he has to say about outsider virtue, the limits of his context also underline the difference between our focus and one on toleration. It's in regard to the former, pagan virtue, that I've commended Thomas. But getting clarity on where he stood on toleration was an essential first step. Our historical work lets us grasp Thomas on his own terms, in his own time, helping us dampen the static that might distort his meaning. We come to Thomas, then, eyes open to his limits and affirming what he so readily confessed of himself—and what, if we have any wisdom, we must admit as well: that, in matters theological and moral, the truth is known only *per longum tempus, et cum admixtione multorum errorum*—after a long time and mixed with much error (I 1.1). Yet, as he did with those whom he saw as mistaken or worse, we come nonetheless, trusting that, amidst error, there is truth and goodness to be found.

2 GOD, GOOD, AND THE DESIRE OF ALL THINGS

AT THE HEART OF THOMAS'S ETHICS is a deceptively simple claim, drawn from Aristotle: "The good is what all desire" (*NE* 1). In *Summa theologiae*, the claim first appears a few questions in when Thomas uses it to help explain the relationship between goodness and *esse*, or existence (I 5.1). Later, in I.II, he says this proposition funds the first principle (*primum principium*) of practical reason, which holds the same place in action as the law of noncontradiction has in any understanding at all (I.II 94.2). This chapter's task is to unravel this simple but cryptic claim and its significance for our topic.

In particular, I will argue that this claim holds the key to understanding Thomas's vision of one vital way in which not only humans but all creatures are deeply and unceasingly related to God: it helps fund his contention that all things—including those who do not believe in God—desire God (I 6.1 ad 2). Perhaps most significantly, because of the way in which it connects all persons to God, this claim forms the basis in his thought for the recognition and appreciation of any virtue wherever it may be found. It specifies with regard to moral capacities and action what is common to humans as humans—whether Christians or not. Put differently, it sets the low threshold for pagan virtue, the minimum excellence present in any human act, no matter the agent.

Thomas's claim that the good is what all desire helps ground a capacious and generous recognition of pagan virtue in a somewhat surprising way: on the basis of an irreducibly theological ethics. In fact, it is not merely a theological but a profoundly Trinitarian and Christocentric vision that founds and propels his recognition of pagan virtue. This richly Scriptural and robustly Augustinian outlook not only enables but actually impels him to welcome and even celebrate the virtue of the outsider. Moreover, this vision itself represents the union of Augustinian and Aristotelian insights—and this where we might least expect: in Thomas's Trinitarianism and his very conception of Christian theology. Striving to be Aristotelian by being Augustinian and vice versa, Thomas, I argue, views creaturely perfection as participation in the Son, good-seeking as Christ-seeking, and, for that reason, he welcomes Aristotle as a genuine seeker, trusted teacher, and wise friend.

These are sketches of what is to come. Their full explication and defense will carry us into later chapters. What we will see here is that insofar as all seek their own perfection, all seek God—and not just any God but the Triune God revealed in Jesus Christ. Exploring how and why Thomas thinks this, what it means, and how it might be plausible is this chapter's goal.

GOD IS WHAT ALL THINGS DESIRE

Secundum rem, Secundum rationem

We begin where Thomas does, with the good in general (in communi): "Are good and being (ens) the same in reality (secundum in rem)," truly identical things (I 5 prooemium)? Thomas claims they are, but this can seem surprising, for it seems one thing for something to be, quite another for it to be good (I 5.1). Many things exist that do not seem good and some good things do not exist. Further, our evaluating something as good seems obviously distinct from our recognizing it as existing—certainly, the latter does not appear to entail the former. Thomas is not blind to this, nor does he fail to see that there are different ways in which things can be good and even different kinds of goodness.[1] Still, he is committed to Augustine's claim, inquantum sumus, boni sumus: inasmuch as we are, we are good (I 5.1 sc). To see what Thomas has in mind in equating goodness and being and claiming the good is what all desire, we move in three steps: grasping a philosophical distinction, elucidating his conception of esse and, finally, examining the details of his argument.[2]

Thomas offers us a way into his notion of goodness when he says that, "goodness and being are one and the same in reality (rem) and are different only conceptually (secundum rationem)" (I 5.1).[3] In distinguishing between res and ratio and declaring being and goodness identical with respect to res but distinct in ratio, Thomas is claiming that the words being and goodness identify the same reality.[4] But his point is not merely linguistic. Goodness and being are the same in res, in that wherever there is being, there is goodness and vice versa. While the terms identify the same reality, they do so under different concepts, and so relate us differently to that same reality. Another philosophical idiom clarifies Thomas's point.

To differ *secundum rationem* means, in part, that applying the concepts *being* and *goodness* involves undertaking different sets of commitments. Take the concepts *writer* and *father*, which differ *secundum rationem,* or in terms of what makes their application appropriate (e.g., authorship and parenthood, respectively) and what follows from such application (e.g., literacy and having had a child). While *writer* and *father* may be identical *secundum rem*—if applied to Charles Dickens, say—they don't *have* to be. *Esse* and *good* also differ conceptually, but unlike *writer* and *father* cannot differ *secundum rem*: they always refer to the same thing, for esse and good are one and the same. *Esse* and *good* are thus like the concepts *Man in Black* and *third husband of June Carter Cash*, naming one and the same reality but authorizing different inferences, relating us distinctly to their objects.

For Thomas, the concept *good* or *esse* implies something about its object that inheres in it apart from our concept use and that makes the concepts appropriate to begin with. Thus, applying *Man in Black* to Johnny Cash highlights aspects of his identity that are present whether I use that concept or not—and which help make the concept appropriate.[5] Likewise, correctly applying the concept *good* calls to our attention something's goodness, which it possesses independently of our so regarding it. For Thomas, things are good in *res* and not merely in *ratio*—indeed, good in *ratio* because good in *res*. We must not imagine Thomas thinking goodness depends for its existence on humans.[6] Given his identification of goodness with esse, this would have him thinking the universe's existence depends on humans.

While Thomas grants that esse enjoys a certain conceptual priority over goodness, he rejects the possibility that one has priority over the other in reality—they cannot, for they are the same reality. Nor in granting esse's conceptual priority does he mean that esse is what there *really* is, yet something to which both concepts can apply (I 5.2). Rather, esse *is* goodness, and goodness *is* esse. One is not actually the "really existent" to which the other is subsidiary. Nor is there some third "behind" or other than goodness/esse to which the concepts are applied. And while it is tempting to imagine *goodness* or *esse* as each referring to different aspects or features of something, for Thomas they do not. They *refer* to one reality—even as they *relate* us differently to it. Most simply, *good* and *esse* identify the same thing: goodness and esse.[7]

How Not to Define "Good"

But what is this? What constitutes goodness in *res* and in *ratio*? Importantly, Thomas does not define the good. Indeed, he *cannot*—at least not properly speaking. For Thomas, following Aristotle, a proper definition articulates a thing's essence by placing it in its genus and detailing its specific difference (I 3.6; 13.1). A human, for example, is properly defined as a "rational animal." *Animal* is the genus term; *rational*, the difference. A proper definition answers the question "*quid est?*" or "what is it?" about a thing's essence. It specifies precisely what makes something the very thing it is and not something else. Goodness, however, is in no genus and so properly defining it is impossible (I 3.5; 5.1).

If Thomas is not offering a proper definition, how should we understand his claims? Some remarks from his commentary on Aristotle's *Metaphysics* offer help. While "only the *ratio* of species, which is constituted by genus and differences, is a definition," Thomas explains, nonetheless, "if a name is set down for other things [than species], there can be a *ratio* disclosing what the name expresses" (*CM* 7.3.23–24). For our purposes, the most important way this can happen is "when some better understood formulation is adduced to elucidate a simple name—so, for instance, to elucidate the name or term 'philosopher' one adduces the formulation 'lover of wisdom.' . . . Nevertheless such a *ratio* will not be a definition, nor will that which is signified by it be that which it is, [its essence]" (*CM* 7.3.24).[8] This describes our case precisely: a "simple name," here, "good," is explained with a "better understood formulation," specifically, "what all things desire." The concept *good* is elucidated in terms of what it signifies—desirability. While we cannot properly define goodness, we can deepen our understanding of goodness and *good* through notions of desirability, even as this neither signifies its essence nor exhausts its meaning.

Some of *Summa theologiae*'s preceding questions along with his commentary on the *Nicomachean Ethics* further illuminate the character and substance of his claim that the good is what all desire. "Goodness," he says,

> is counted among the primary things (*prima*). . . . And it is impossible to make the *prima* known through something prior to them, but only through things posterior to them—in the same way that causes are made known through their effects. Because good properly *is* the mover of the appetite (*motivum appetitus*), it is [here] described *through* the movement of the appetite (*motum appetitus*),

in the same way that the power *to* move is usually revealed (*enuntiaverunt*) by movement [i.e., by its effects].[9] (*CNE* 1.1.9)

Note a few key points. First, in claiming that goodness is among the *prima*—the first and most basic things there are—and in declaring it the *cause* of appetite's movement (indeed *all* movement), Thomas clearly regards goodness as real—more, one of the most fundamental realities. Still, one might wonder whether something is desired because it is good or good because it is desired, whether goodness, however real, nonetheless depends on desire. On that view, goodness is not merely explicable in terms of desire but constituted by it—as fame is not only explicable in terms of being widely known but consists in that. This is not Thomas's view. Desire is the effect not the cause of goodness. Goodness generates and elicits desire, not the other way round.

One of Thomas's most important maxims, variably expressed, conveys this point: "the final end is the first cause"; "the end is the cause of causes"; "the end of a thing corresponds to its beginning" (I 5.2 ad 1; 103.2; 105.5). Later chapters treat such remarks in depth, but the basic point is that goodness causes the first movement of anything at all. So, the good is what all seek, not because what all seek is therefore good, but because goodness elicits the desire that effects everything's movement toward it.

From good's status in *res* follows something about its status in *ratio*, about how we come to know it and what about it we can know.

As among the *prima*, goodness can only be made known in terms of its effects—the desire it causes.[10] While we cannot properly define goodness, we can see its effect—desire—and gain conceptual leverage by characterizing it in those terms, as desire's cause. When something is known through and as the cause of its effects, we can formulate a nominal "definition" of it as: "the cause of these effects." That's what Thomas does: desire is good's effect, and his claim nominally "defines" good in those terms. He says, in essence, "let 'good' be nominally defined as 'that which causes desire.'" This nominal "definition" gives an initial foothold or specification, without which we have no idea what we are inquiring after. It supplies a sufficiently determinate X to begin solving for, even as, apart from its effects, we do not (and cannot) know what goodness is. Eventually, it will enable Thomas to consider goodness explicitly in light of revelation, as related to and most perfectly realized in God. Just here, however, it serves as what Thomas calls a "middle term" in his demonstration that goodness and esse are one and the same in *res*.

Demonstrating Goodness

For Thomas, a demonstration is a syllogism that shows a necessary relationship between a subject and a predicate by giving knowledge of why a conclusion necessarily follows from its premises. Roughly, a middle term is a required term or step within the syllogism that contributes to that movement. In a proper demonstration, the "middle term" is literally in the middle, between the premise's subject term and the conclusion's predicate term. Take the following:

All S are M.

All M are P.

Thus, all S are P.

In this demonstration, S is the subject term, P the predicate term, M the middle term. The middle term is necessary for demonstrating the relationship between subject and predicate. In our case, Thomas wants to show that good and esse are one. That is, he wants to show how and why there is a necessary relationship between the subject term *good* and the predicate term *esse*. While his argument has more than three steps and is not so much a demonstration as a series of demonstrations, he still needs a middle term, a term defining his subject, good. In an ideal demonstration, the middle term is the subject's proper definition. Lacking that, a nominal "definition" can serve as the middle term—as it does here. Actually, Thomas anticipates this earlier when he demonstrates God's existence by using a nominal "definition" for the middle term (I 2.3).[11] In each case, lacking proper definitions, the subject—God and good—is nominally defined as the cause of certain effects. And in each, he seeks both to delineate domains of inquiry in enough detail to prepare for full-fledged, Scripture-informed examinations that will follow *and* to (begin to) establish the identity of the *res* which respectively answer to *God* and *good* in metaphysical theology with those that answer to those terms in Christian theology.

We can now begin to understand what Thomas concretely means in claiming that all things seek good and, more profoundly, God. At the heart of his argument is his notion of perfection, the linchpin connecting his nominal definition of good to esse. I first make that argument's structure explicit and then fill in its details.

"The ratio of good," he begins,

consists in this "that something is desirable," for as Aristotle says, in *Nicomachean Ethics* 1: "the good is what all things desire." It is clear, though, that each thing is desirable to the degree that it is perfect, for every thing desires its own perfection. Insofar as something is perfect, to just that extent is it in act. Thus, we see that insofar as something is good, to just that extent is it esse, for, as was shown earlier, esse is the actuality of all things (*esse . . . est actualitas omnis rei*). And so, from this it is clear that good and being are the same in reality but *good* articulates a *ratio* of desirability that *esse* does not. (I 5.1)

The argument's basic structure is the following:

1. Good is "what all things desire"/"the desirable." (Good is nominally defined in terms of its effects, and that definition will serve as a middle term.)
2. What all things in fact desire is their perfection. (Each thing seeks its perfection.)[12]
3. Perfection is the desirable. (At this stage, we see that the good is perfection. The next step is to show that perfection is esse.)
4. Perfection is "actuality." (To the extent that something is perfect, it is "actual." In other words, degrees of perfection correspond to degrees of "actuality"— the more perfect, the more "actual.")
5. "Actuality" is esse.
6. Esse is the good.

The argument thus moves from showing the identity of goodness and perfection through the middle term of desirability, to showing the identity of perfection and esse on the basis of their identity with "actuality," to the conclusion that goodness and being are one in *res*. Inasmuch as every creature seeks its perfection, every creature seeks to move from what it now is to what it could be, to realize its potential. Thomas describes this as moving from potential to "act": as a creature becomes what it has the capacity to be, it is more "in act," having more of esse. In this way, esse is what all seek: esse *is* the good.

Dividing the argument in half serves to clarify. Thus we begin with the claim that all things seek their perfection and then explore the notion of *esse*, particularly as it relates to perfection and actuality. All this serves our central aim of understanding how and why Thomas thinks "all things seek God" and what that could mean.

Seeking Their Perfection

In Thomas's view, all creatures—angels, humans, horses, oaks, even stones— seek their own perfection (I 6.1). Since our concern is with humans, we put aside angels and nonliving things and grapple with Thomas's claim as it concerns plants and animals. For Thomas, a plant or animal seeks its perfection in that it naturally develops and behaves in ways proper to its kind. Thus, if all goes well, a Corgi naturally grows four legs, teeth, and a lustrous coat, and it eats, mates, barks, and so on. It is impelled to grow and behave in these basic ways, to "seek" these ends (I 18.3; 19.1).[13] And these ends—these "Corgi-ly" features and patterns of life—are its perfection. To the extent it realizes them, it is perfect; to the extent it does not, imperfect. This is what Thomas means when he says that, "something is called *perfect*, when it is lacking nothing according to its mode of perfection (*modum perfectionis*)" (I 4.1). A creature's "mode of perfection" is just that set of features, capacities, and ends that constitute it as the particular kind of creature it is.[14] Thus a three-legged toothless terrier who can't smell and sleeps all day, lacks much according to its mode of perfection—as does a fat vegan bobcat or a diseased maple tree. They are imperfect to the extent that they are deficient according to their modes of perfection. But the fact that the bobcat has no leaves or the maple no eyes does nothing to render either imperfect according to its mode of perfection (I 48.3; 48.5 and ad 1).[15] That, whatever their flaws, they are *living* beings—let us say in my yard right now—does, however, establish them as perfect in one key respect: as substantially existing. Indeed, Thomas delineates three levels of perfection, with *esse substantiale,* or substantial existence (for a creature, existence as a particular thing, I 5.5 ad 3), as most basic, then possession of the features and capacities necessary for its ideal life, and, finally, its living that life, attaining those ends (I 6.3 and ad 2). Creatures seek their perfection at each level, and the degree of perfection they realize with respect to the second and third is limited by their degree of perfection at the more basic level(s). So, the imperfections of our defective creatures concern the second and third levels, but these imperfections would not even be possible, indeed there would *be* no second or third levels for these creatures, if they did not have the first perfection of actually existing.

Thomas acknowledges that some creatures fail to grow or behave in ideal ways but contends that such imperfect creatures are nonetheless seeking their perfection.[16] That we can still recognize something as the creature it is or even a creature at all, he reasons, means that it is seeking its perfection insofar as it can—and actually meeting with considerable success.[17]

In explicating perfection, Thomas's language of "lacking nothing" does not imply a primarily negative conception (I 4.1). Perfection predicates something positive: a creature *lacking nothing* according to its mode of perfection is one that *has everything* according to that mode. "Lack" and "completeness" are two sides of one conceptual coin. Of course, only in reference to a specific, substantive conception of a creature's "mode of perfection" do those concepts have determinate content. Thomas's whole conception thus presupposes rather elaborate ideals against which creatures count as achieving or lacking perfection. Only with some at least implicit notion of an *ideal* Corgi do we judge a *particular* Corgi more or less perfect. But this raises numerous questions: Why does some such ideal rather than another count as authoritative? Why should any ideal have such authority?[18] And, what about his *seeking* claim: In what sense and on what basis can nonrational creatures appropriately be described as "seeking" anything? These questions primarily arise, I think, from our skepticism toward the thoroughly teleological character of Thomas's account. Thomas himself acknowledges this character and supposes not only that every creature has determinate, distinct ends but that all things come from and move toward God (I 103.2; 5.4 ad 1). Moreover, he defends his account against the sorts of challenges these questions pose, even if he could not have anticipated the depth of suspicion with which we raise them or the forms they now take. Examining his responses not only helps us understand his claim that all things seek God but illumines his argument that goodness and esse are one. Thomas himself would find it fitting that these various streams should pour, finally, into consideration of God and God's place in his account, for, as he sees it, God is at once the source and end of all things—and the key unlocking his vision of the good.

God Is What All Things Seek

God, Thomas says, is the highest good, the essence of good, and the cause of all goodness (I 6.1, 2; 100.2, 103.2, 103.6).[19] While we still need to explicate the connection between creaturely and divine goodness, that God is the essence of goodness is key to understanding how it is that all things seek God—for, insofar as all things seek the good, Thomas claims, they are seeking God. God, Thomas also says, is unqualifiedly perfect—perfect not just in some way or according to some type but in every sense and respect (I 4.1 and ad 2). Thomas's notion of a creature's "mode of perfection" actually derives from his conception of God's perfection, which he parses in terms of potentiality and act. Something is imperfect to the degree it is in potential, perfect insofar as it is in act. God, he says, is "pure act with no potentiality whatsoever" (I 3.1, 2; 4.1).

What does this mean? Most simply, potentiality is the property of being *subject to* change—"capable" of *undergoing* change or being *acted upon*. We often think of the "capacity" to undergo change as just that, a *capacity*, and thus something positive. Yet, for Thomas, potentiality is no genuine capacity or potency but incapacity and impotency. To be in potentiality is to lack the sort of completeness and excellence that would make it impossible for any change to be for the better.

Take a painting.[20] It's easy to imagine a good but not timeless (or even great but unfinished) painting that could be changed for the better. For a painting to be like this, is—on a limited scale, in a particular case—what it means to be in potential. If, instead, we take a masterpiece, say Rembrandt's *Return of the Prodigal*, we can perhaps imagine any possible change as being no improvement but a diminution or corruption. Such a painting would be "in act," albeit in the most limited, qualified way, in act *as* the particular painting it was, not as such. Indeed, there are many paintings with excellences it lacks and, more profoundly, different sorts of things—mountains, fish, stars, human beings—that possess excellences no painting, no matter how perfect or "actual" *qua* painting, could possess.[21] To be "pure act," "in act" unqualifiedly, however, is not to be perfect in some particular, limited way or *as* some certain thing or kind of thing, but to be perfect in every way. It is to be such that *any* change would be for the worse. Only God is "pure act" and thus perfect *simpliciter*.[22] To be in act is, moreover, to be an agent, an *actor*. And to be pure act is to be pure agent, agent as such: the subject of no one else's agency, the cause of all movement whatsoever and, insofar as anything exists, the cause of its existing (I 3.1, 2; 4.1).

We must avoid eliding Thomas's conception of perfection and its connection to changelessness with the idea of something's being static, dead, or nonrelational. In characterizing God as pure act, Thomas is insisting that God is *maximally* dynamic, living, and relational. In his vision, God is like a dance so perfectly beautiful that no change could make it more beautiful or better in any respect—and he is so powerful as to be immune to being in any way changed, effaced, or interrupted. There is maximal activity, maximal relationship—indeed, that is the essence of what God is and, we'll see, what occurs in the Triune life—but any change would be for the worse, including the very change that would make God subject to change. That we can hardly imagine such perfection, Thomas would say, speaks to our distance from it, the weakness of our reason, and the degree to which God exceeds our best efforts at comprehension.

In virtue then of being pure act, "not lacking in *any* actuality," God necessarily possesses in himself all perfections (I 4.1 ad 1). "Whatever perfection exists in whatever creature in whatever way," Thomas explains, "wholly preexists in and is possessed by and contained in God in a more excellent mode" (I 14.6; 4.6). This must be the case if God is perfect *simpliciter* and follows too from God's identity as first cause, for as cause of all, God necessarily prepossesses in himself all the effects—all the perfections—that he causes.[23] Just here, we are positioned to grasp the identity between perfection, actuality, and esse—the second main step in Thomas's argument for the identity of goodness and esse.

Esse, Perfection, and Actuality

Connecting the three concepts, Thomas explains that, "<u>esse</u> itself is the most <u>perfect</u> of all things. Indeed, nothing has <u>actuality</u> except insofar as it <u>exists</u>, hence <u>esse</u> itself is the <u>actuality</u> of everything—even of the forms themselves" (I 4.1 ad 3). Esse stands to all things as that by which they exist, that by "addition" of which the sheer potentiality and imperfection of nonexistence moves to actuality, existence. Indeed, esse *is* existence and actuality. That refinement and the scare quotes are necessary because nonexistence *is* nothing: there is nothing prior to and apart from esse for esse to be given to or for it to sustain.[24] Hence Thomas's remark that esse is the actuality "even of forms themselves." Forms reduce matter's potentiality to some particular kind of existence, making matter a particular thing—trout, lion, tulip.[25] As such, forms could seem, aside from God, supremely perfect and actual: while determinate and not subject to change, by them things are made what they are, potentiality reduced to actuality, not just in some matter but in any whatsoever. Yet esse is still more actual, perfect, and complete, for forms are only actual, having whatever existence they have, insofar as they share in esse. If form determines some matter to existence *as* a house, by esse the form and house have *existence*.[26] Thomas further elucidates this link between formality and perfection or actuality with the supreme perfection of esse, when he notes that "esse is the most formal thing of all (*maxime formale omnium*)" (I 7.1).[27] As forms give things the perfection of a particular *kind* of existence, esse gives—or rather is—*existence* itself. And as everything other than God is the creature it is through its form, anything that exists at all, exists because and as some subject of esse. Whatever exists, insofar as it exists, is some subject of esse.

"Just as sound is the first (*primum*) audible," Thomas explains, esse is the first knowable and proper object of intellect (I 5.2).[28] The parallel elucidates esse's priority. His point is not that in knowing some object we first grasp that it exists and then grasp other things about it. That is no more his point here than he means that in hearing something we *first* hear sound and *then* a voice or jazz flute. Rather, just as our hearing a lovely song, rushing wind, or child's call *is* most basically our hearing sound in some form or other, so our intellect's apprehending anything at all is most fundamentally our apprehending esse in some form.[29] As sound is what there is to hear, some or another form of esse is what there is to know and, more profoundly, what, along with God himself, there *is*. Thus, creation and all its perfections at each level are (at least) some form of esse.[30] Esse accounts not just for the bare perfection of something's existing at some time—our first grade of perfection (I 5.1 ad 1)—but strictly *every* perfection is a form of esse: "All perfections pertain to the perfection of existing, for things are perfect in some way because and insofar as they some-how have *esse*" (I 4.2). Grasping esse's identity with perfection and actuality is perhaps easiest when we recognize that as *existence*, nothing can be added to it that does not itself share in esse. Save God, nothing perfects it even as it perfects whatever receives it. And since all that *is* has esse, and every perfection is a kind of existence, God—who authors esse and is his own self-subsistent, divine esse—possesses all perfections in himself (I 4.2).[31]

Of course, the esse of God and creatures are not identical. Creatures have esse not from themselves but from him (I 3.4). And esse stands to their natures as act to potentiality. God, in contrast, is his own esse: his esse is not distinct from but *is* his nature. More, while creatures have *created* esse, and, even so, have it in a qualified, limited way, God is *divine* esse, unqualified, unlimited, uncreated esse (I 3.5; 4.2). Thus, when Thomas says the more a creature attains to God, the more it has of esse (*habet de esse*), he does not mean that creatures and God are "made" of a common stuff called "esse," or that there is a "chain" reaching from created to divine esse (I 3.5 ad 2). Nor does he regard the difference between creaturely and divine esse as a matter merely of degree. The discontinuity between the two is greater than any continuity—so much so that despite our acquaintance with creaturely existence, properly speaking, we do not even know what God's esse is. What we know of God's esse is the limited, partial esse and goodness of creaturely life, a real but distant imitation—what Thomas calls a "participation"—of God's esse. The resemblance is genuine, but like that between an artist and her work—yet more distant still (I 4.3; 44.3 ad 1; 93.6). In this sense does a creature "have more of esse" the nearer it approaches God.

Ideas, Creatures, Perfection, and What God Knows

God, Thomas explains, knows himself perfectly and this self-knowledge is not distinct from his essence, who he is. Unlike me, for example, whose efforts to write are not identical with my identity but particular activities, interrupted by sips of coffee, God's one activity—of understanding, loving, living, and so on—*is* his identity, his essence. Were he to leave it aside (or "could" he), he would not be God; were I to leave aside my writing, I would not cease to exist or be me. Further, God knows himself and all things "through himself" (I 14.2 ad 3). His understanding is not dependent on something outside of himself. In contrast, our grasping this sentence, for example, requires knowledge of English and adequate light—neither of which is identical to any of us. Human knowing involves concepts and, again, we are neither these concepts nor can we learn them without help and the convergence of countless contingencies. God, however, depends on nothing outside himself for his understanding: he is, as it were, his own light and language. God understands himself through himself, and this understanding is his very essence and esse, constituting him as *who* he is (essence), ensuring *that* he is (existence) (I 14.2).

One locus of understanding, Thomas says, can be "in another" instead of "in" the thing we aim to understand. We understand something "in another," when our understanding "X" is coincident with and/or derivative of our understanding "Y." For instance, when we understand a part in virtue of grasping the whole, we understand the part "in" the whole (I 14.5). So, if we understand the position of striker through understanding soccer, our understanding of striker is "in" our understanding of something else, soccer.[32] But God understands himself in himself, and other things not in themselves but in himself, and he does all of this in one essence- and existence-constituting act (I 14.5, 84.2).

Because God knows himself perfectly and is perfect in every way, possessing "whatever perfection had by . . . any other thing and far more," in knowing himself, he necessarily knows every way in which his esse could be manifested by anything else (I 14.6; 15.2). That is, he knows every fragmented, qualified way in which his perfection can be represented or "participated." In so knowing, God knows all that is or might be, since any real or possible existence represents some limited way of being perfect, of being like him. For any thing to exist at all, as what it is, and in the more or less perfect way it does, is for it in some way to participate God's perfection or esse: "The nature of each thing consists in some way of participating the divine perfection" (I 14.6). Thus, in his one act of perfect self-knowledge, God's essence comprehends the ideas of all things, his understanding of every way to participate his perfection (I 14.6 and ad 1).[33]

Recall that as first cause, the effects of whatever God causes necessarily pre-exist in him (I 14.8).[34] They do so as ideas. And these ideas are principles, as it were, of God's creative and providential work. Stressing its deficiency, Thomas often uses the example of an architect: as an architect's idea of the house can serve as plan, so are God's ideas archetypes for his creation (I 14.8; 15.2 ad 2). In this capacity, God's ideas are "exemplars" and belong (as it were) to his practical knowledge (I 14.8 ad 3).[35] And here is Thomas's answer to questions about crea-turely perfection: a creature's exemplar is its determinate, authoritative stan-dard against which its perfection is measured.[36] A creature's perfection vis-à-vis its mode of perfection varies according to its resemblance of its exemplar, God's idea of a particular participation in his perfection.

We must clarify the exemplar/creaturely perfection relation on two fronts. First, "insofar as God knows his essence as admitting of imitation by some crea-ture, he knows it as the proper *ratio* and idea of that creature" (I 15.2). Distinct from a creature's particular relation to her exemplar, her perfection varies abso-lutely according to the degree of participation in God her exemplar represents. Thus, Secretariat might better resemble his exemplar than Socrates, and thus be more perfect vis-à-vis this mode of perfection, but human-exemplar represents a greater participation in God absolutely than horse-exemplar, so Socrates is more perfect absolutely.[37] Secondly, a given creature is more or less perfect, in whatever sense, in virtue of the particular participation in God it actually is. An exemplar is not *itself* a participation, but God's idea *of* a participation. Creatures do not resemble participations of God's esse; they *are* participations. Nor is it through resembling an exemplar—as distinct from simply being—that a crea-ture is constituted as good.[38] As Thomas says, "the proper nature of each thing is some mode of participating the divine" (I 14.6).

Seeking Perfection, Seeking God

Now consider the relation between creaturely and divine goodness and the sense in which creatures seek God. A creature's goodness is both properly its own *and* a fragmentary manifestation of God's. Goodness "inheres" in a crea-ture, but as creator and end, God is that good's ultimate source—in two senses. He *creates* creaturely goodness and *makes* it—*qua* participation in him—good (I 6.4).[39] Yet, a creature's goodness is as much its own as its existence. Because a creature is a participation in God and its perfection the fullest participation in God it can attain, in seeking its perfection it thereby seeks a fuller participation in God. Its good-seeking *is* its God-seeking, for its good is greater Godlikeness, "greater ontological proximity" to God, we might say. "Each and every creature strains to achieve its perfection, which is a similitude of God's perfection and goodness. Therefore the divine good is the end of all things" (I 44.4).

Even if we grant that creatures naturally pursue their perfection and, more, that their perfection participates God's, it is another thing to assign them the agency and intention proper to *seeking*. And Thomas's argument requires that creatures *seek* the good, not merely move purposelessly or accidentally toward it. For Thomas, characterizing physiological development and plant and animal life as "seeking" is nonproblematic because he believes that God directs these processes and creatures to their ends (I 18.3; 21.2 ad 3; 22.1-2). An exemplar, recall, specifies a creature's ends and its mode of pursuit. In creation and providence, God "gives" some creature esse and sustains it in existence, directing it to its end by its distinctive mode. Indeed, God's so specifying and directing makes some creature the particular creature it is. "That '[the good is] what all desire,'" Thomas explains

> must not be understood only of those who have knowledge—who knowingly apprehend (*apprehendunt*) the good—but also of things without knowledge which, by natural appetite, pursue the good. They do not do so as knowing the good, but because they are moved to the good by some intelligence—namely by the ordination of God's intellect: just as an arrow pursues the target through the archer's aim. To so pursue the good is to desire the good. And thus he says they desire good insofar as they pursue it.[40] (*CNE* 1.1.11)

While plants and nonhuman animals do not know the good *as* the good or their perfection *as* their perfection, they still tend toward it—toward the development, behavior, and ends proper to creatures of their kind. Just this Thomas has in mind in claiming that each seeks its perfection. God is the archer "who knows the end not known to the arrow" (I 103.1 ad 1). Yet the analogy, Thomas notes, disintegrates (I 103.1 ad 3), for an arrow suffers a kind of violence as something is added from without in its movement and directedness to the target. Its "seeking" is the impression of an external, alien force that is neither its nature nor in any sense from within. For creatures, however, God's impression—the impression determining and moving them to their ends—*is their very nature*. Neither distinct nor alien, their directedness is precisely what makes them what they are

(I 103.1 ad 3; 105.5; I.II.93.5). The parallel to the creaturely goodness/divine good-ness relation is striking: the creature's movement and directedness is genuinely its own, rising from and constituting its nature; yet its principle is God, superin-tending and directing it and all things to their perfection in himself.

We can now grasp the identity between good and esse, the way in which all things seek the good, and most importantly the way in which, in seeking their perfection, all things seek God. If the good is "what all seek," and all seek their perfection, and if the perfection of each thing is its actuality, and actuality is esse, then good and esse are one. Because creaturely actuality is a participation in God, each creature, in seeking its perfection, seeks God. "By desiring their proper perfections," Thomas explains, "all things desire God himself insofar as the perfection of all things are certain likenesses of the di-vine esse" (I 6.1 ad 2). Elucidating this claim has drawn us into Thomas's rich vision of the God/world relation, where, as in Augustine's cry, "You are closer to me, oh God, than I am to myself," God is intimately present to and at work in all things without in any way minimizing or externalizing their own real-ity or goodness. For Thomas, all goodness is related to God. And goodness is everywhere to be found. His conviction that such goodness is present in everyone, including those who know not Christ, is no betrayal of his theologi-cal commitments, but flows from them. Indeed, the essentially Christological and Trinitarian character of this vision is precisely what enables and impels this celebration of goodness wherever it be found.

Beginning to make good on that last claim—that his welcome of pagans and their virtues stems from his distinctively Christian commitments—is our next task, even as these pages also begin to show something about Thomas's stance and methodology that will govern our engagement throughout: the ex-tent to which his irreducibly theological approach itself enacts the very wel-come he commends.

QUEM ME DICITIS ESSE?
Whose God? Which Thomas?

It is easy to miss the radically Christian character of the vision Thomas has unfolded, to see in all this only *metaphysical* theology. Undertaking so many acts of natural theology, the Thomas whom many readers imagine establishes a purely rational foundation on which to rest the Christian "dimension" of his moral theology.[41] One way to evaluate such interpretations and clarify what

Thomas is about is to ask who this God is whom he says all seek: Is it the God known by reason and adumbrated by metaphysicians or the God who took flesh in Jesus Christ?

Of course, for Thomas, there is only one God, and the identity of philosophy's and Scripture's God is among the very things he means to show. Few interpreters doubt that. Approaching this question rightly then requires putting it differently. We must ask what Thomas is *doing*, what kinds of acts he is undertaking in the *Summa* and, especially, the articles that have concerned us: Acts of metaphysical theologizing or acts of faith seeking understanding? Acts of rational foundation-building or acts that seek no other final ground than Jesus Christ?[42] Answering this question tells us, in the relevant sense, which God it is about whom he is immediately concerned and directly considers in identifying the one whom all seek. To pronounce on this God's identity is thus to take a basic stand on Thomas's project in the *Summa*, and, insofar as it represents the climax of his work, a basic stand on his intellectual identity.[43]

Who then is this God? And how do we—or Thomas—know? With those who see the *Summa*'s Thomas as engaged in *sacra doctrina*, a robustly and inextricably scriptural and theological task, this chapter's remainder contends that the one whom Thomas claims all seek is the God revealed in Jesus Christ, and that he weds an Aristotelian conception of *scientia* with an Augustinian Trinitarian vision to ground this claim in Scripture, and, more profoundly, the person of Jesus himself.[44] Seeing how this is so requires considering the *Summa theologiae*'s first question and overall methodology.

Sacra doctrina and *scientia*

Properly understanding question one is essential to grasping the *Summa theologiae* as a whole, and, especially, the questions that immediately follow.[45] In the *Summa*'s *prooemium*, its programmatic introduction, Thomas declares that his aim (*intentio*) is to present *sacra doctrina*, the holy teachings of the Christian religion. And, immediately following, in question one's *prooemium*, he connects that question to the *Summa*'s overarching goal: to meet the *intentio* the work's *prooemium* just articulated, "it is necessary first of all to explain *sacra doctrina* itself—what it actually is and what it encompasses" (I 1 *prooemium*).[46] Question one, he continues, entirely concerns (*circa*) this. *Summa theologiae*, Thomas says, is *sacra doctrina* and question one explains what that is and what it means for the work.

Specifically, in question one, Thomas uses an Aristotelian vision of *scientia* to elucidate the relation between *sacra doctrina*, revelation, and God himself. Put simply, a *scientia* is a body of knowledge that unfolds some dimension of reality and proceeds in a deductive chain from founding "first principles" (I 1.2). For Thomas, a *scientia* is both held in internal unity and distinguished from other sciences by its "formal object"—the particular dimension of reality it regards in whatever it considers (I 1.3 and 7). Thus, an ecological *scientia* is unified because it regards everything according to its ecological aspects, under that "formality."[47] This formal object also distinguishes it from other sciences. So, a chemical *scientia* might consider the same things as ecology, but it regards them chemically—say, as complexes of elements—according to its distinctive formal object. *Scientia* achieves unity and differentiation like this because aside from being a body of knowledge it is also a power (*potentia*) and habit (*habitus*) of the soul, conforming the intellect to some aspect of reality (I 1.3). Just as a power like *hearing* is unified and distinguished by a formal rather than material object—the "humanly-audible" rather than some particular sound—so it is with *scientia*. Certainly, a *scientia*'s object is not purely formal, rather its primary material object, "what a *scientia* talks about," inherently specifies a formal object (I 1.7 sc). Chemistry, say, studies elements, atoms, and so on, and therefore not only these things but everything in their light. Further, sciences are not merely different ways of seeing but actually disclose reality, truth.

The "first principles" of a science are true, *scientia*-founding propositions that are either self-evident or handed down (*traditia*) as conclusions from a higher (*superior*) science (I 1.2 ad 1). At least for now, it's the latter alternative that concerns Thomas and us (I 1.2 and ad 1). Within the science it founds, a first principle's truth and authority are assumed, given on loan from a higher science where its truth is not believed (*credit*) but known (*novit*). The first principles of generalship, for instance, are handed down from political *scientia*; the first principles of calvaryship, in turn, from generalship. Neither, however, establishes or investigates the validity of its first principles but takes them as true starting points.

In at least two ways does a first principle "contain the whole science virtually within itself" (I 1.7; 1.3 and 4). First, by specifying that *scientia*'s object—what it is about—and thereby the formality or *ratio* under which it proceeds (I 1.7 sc; 1.7 and 1.3). Because this object is concrete *and* formal—*elements* and *things viewed chemically*, say—in specifying its object, a first principle already contains the whole science by stipulating the relation of everything in the science to itself. Like limited-spectrum light, a first principle illumines some aspect of reality, virtually containing what it reveals by dictating both what and how we will see. Or, it contains the science as a recipe contains the meal's taste—virtually, but, in a way, truly.

Secondly, because a science mounts demonstrations from its first principle, in a sense, a science simply unfolds what that first principle already contains. Unfolding a *scientia* renders explicit what is implicit in the first principle. But unlike, say, a seed, which is not a tree but only becomes one, first principles so contain their *scientia* that a perfect mind would comprehend the whole science in comprehending the first principle. Some things are self-evident *per se,* or in themselves, and, thus, to a perfect knower, but are not self-evident *ad nos,* to us (I 2.1). This hints at what it means for a first principle to be self-evident in one *scientia* but not another. A single first principle could be self-evident to God, in his divine *scientia,* but not to us or in our *scientia.* We might say, then, that the whole *scientia* is present in the first principle *per se* but not (or not usually) *ad nos.* While a perfect knower grasps the whole science in grasping the first principle, imperfect knowers unfold the science—to borrow from Thomas—over time, with great effort, and susceptible to much error.

For Thomas, sciences disclose reality. They do so, in part, because in knowing a *scientia* one grasps intelligibilities inhering in the world. And this, in part, thanks to the forms that constitute things as what they are, which stand to living things as inner principles of ordered change and growth, and which one knows in knowing a *scientia.* So, ornithology begins from propositional first principles about birds, which are true because and insofar as by them one knows the bird form, the real principle that makes birds the particular creatures they are. The *scientia* has its order and coherence, because birds are, thanks to their form or nature, the coherent, intelligible things they are. A *scientia's* founding first principles depend for their truth on the real principles that constitute what it investigates. So, propositional first principles are to the sciences they found, as forms or ontological first principles are to the creatures they inform. As propositional first principles contain their whole science virtually, so real first principles contain the whole creature virtually, manifesting themselves as a thing's form. Ontological first principles make *scientia* possible.[48] They are what sciences are *about.*

Consider, then, *sacra doctrina,* the *scientia* that takes as its first principles Scripture or *articuli fidei,* the articles of faith (I 1.6).[49] These first principles are not self-evident to humans, but revealed, handed down from above, believed on God's authority (I 1.6). Like any first principles not self-evident to a *scientia*'s practitioners (*qua* practitioners), they stand in some higher *scientia* as self-evident or conclusions (or both). They have that status, says Thomas, in the *scientia divina*, God's own knowledge (I 1.6 ad 1). Where in *sacra doctrina* they are believed, in "the light of God's *scientia*," by God himself, they are "known" (I 1.5; 1.2). Now, God *is* the Divine *scientia*. His knowledge is not other than his essence; there are no "conclusions" to his act. But *ad nos*, to us, these first principles are regarded and received as if conclusions of a still higher *scientia*, handed down from God's *scientia*. To this we'll return momentarily.

Like any *scientia*, *sacra doctrina* has an object, a reality securing its truth and funding its coherence. Its object, Thomas says, is God himself (I 1.7). Yet God is the object of another *scientia* too—metaphysical theology—from which *sacra doctrina* differs "in kind" (I 1.1 ad 2). Partly, this difference stems from the propositional principles that found these sciences: truths had by revelation and reason, respectively. A difference in propositional principles entails a difference in subjects—or, more precisely, the real-world difference in subject entails the difference in propositional principles. The God known by philosophers is not, for Thomas, some other than the one true God. But metaphysical theology considers this God only insofar as he is known in reason's weak light, itself dimmed by intellect's slowness and hampered by will's propensity to sin. The object of *sacra doctrina*, however, is God "as known to himself alone and disclosed by revelation to others" (I 1.6). These are not two Gods but God known imperfectly, with much error, and largely ineffectually, and God known as he wishes to be and most fully makes himself known, known even as he knows himself.[50] Merely to say that "God" is *sacra doctrina*'s subject, then, is to say too little, to leave *scientia* and object insufficiently articulated. Following Thomas requires saying more. Recognizing that *sacra doctrina* takes its first principles from Scripture helps us do so.

Scripture, for Thomas, is about Jesus. Commenting on John the Evangelist's claim that he writes so that we might believe that Jesus is the Son of God, "all Scripture," Thomas explains, "*Old and New Testament . . . is for this [end]*" (*JC* 20.6.2568). All Scripture, all revelation, is about and meant to direct to Jesus. "They lead unto me, Christ . . . for they 'testify concerning me,'" Thomas has Jesus say. And, more, the Scriptures are only *living* (*vitalia*), only *revelation* "insofar they lead to knowledge of me." (*JC* 5.6.823). Scripture *is* revelation, *is* handed down from God, Thomas insists, to the degree that it is recognized and received as concerning Christ. Christwardness helps constitute Scripture as revelation. At the center of this conception of Scripture is the Word: "Formerly, the only begotten Son revealed knowledge of the Lord through prophets, who proclaimed him insofar as they partook (*fuerunt participes*) of the eternal Word. Thus they said, 'The word of the Lord came to me' and like things. But now the 'only begotten himself', the Son, 'has fully revealed' [him] to the faithful" (*JC* 1.10.221). The one Word, as Thomas has it, is both the content and means of revelation. By the Word, the Word is revealed. By the Word, truth comes from God. And the truth that comes from God *is* the Word—first partially and proleptically, now perfectly in Christ Jesus. Scripture, Thomas says, is not merely about the Word, but about Jesus—or about the Word *because* it is about Jesus. "The word of God leads to Christ, for Christ himself *is* the Word of God by nature. Indeed, every word inspired by God is a certain participated likeness of Christ and thus, since every participated likeness leads to its origin, it is clear that every word inspired by God leads to Christ" (*JC* 5.6.820). For Thomas, Scripture and the *articuli fidei* are about Jesus Christ.

 Sacra doctrina, therefore, is the *scientia* of God as God knows and reveals Godself because it is founded on Scripture. And Scripture is about God in being about Jesus. *Sacra doctrina*'s subject, then, is Jesus Christ. In being *scientia* of Jesus, its object is not other than God. Rather, it is *scientia* of God *because* it is *scientia* of Jesus Christ, God's Word. This is what it *means* for *sacra doctrina* to be our *scientia* of God.[51]

Principles, Processions, Proper Operations

Sacra doctrina is *scientia* of the Incarnate Word, where he is handed down to us as if a conclusion of the Divine *scientia*. Thomas uses an Aristotelian model of *scientia* to relate revelation—God's self-disclosure in Jesus (ontological) and Scripture (propositional)—to *sacra doctrina*, and to relate both to God himself. Like all *scientia*, it depends on real and propositional principles, being and truth: Jesus himself and Scripture.[52] As in chemistry we can distinguish between founding discursive principles and the *scientia* that unfolds from them, just so Scripture is not *itself* the *scientia* of *sacra doctrina* but that *scientia*'s discursive first principles, which themselves answer to the reality of Jesus Christ, somewhat (*only* somewhat) as the periodic table corresponds to actual elements. Jesus himself is a new principle in the world, Scripture the corresponding propositional principles, *sacra doctrina* the corresponding *scientia*.

With that in mind, we can distinguish between (1) Jesus in relation to *sacra doctrina* and (2) Jesus or, more precisely, the Word in relation to *God's* knowledge (*scientia Dei*).[53] Above, we spoke of (1), which, we'll see, depends on (2). We turn now to (2) and the profoundly Trinitarian character of Thomas's theology. More than *Son*, *Word* is Thomas's preferred name for the second person (Emery, *TT*, 177–204). A name for one of the Triune identities must be inherently relational, for the Divine persons are constituted as the persons they are in virtue of their relations to one another.[54] *Word* (*verbum*) satisfies this requirement, for it names "not the activity of knowledge" generally (in which case it would refer to the Divine nature indiscriminately) but that which "really proceeds within the mind," the "*fruit* of an internal . . . conceiving" (182, 184).[55] Linked to *speech* and so a *speaker* (the *Father*), *Word* denotes the *product* of knowledge's act, "the *expression* of the thing known" (182). It thereby denotes the reality of immanent procession that constitutes Son as Son (187; I 34.1 ad 3). And while Thomas might shy from calling the Word a "Conclusion," not least because there's no process in God, nonetheless, within the Triune life, logically but not temporally, the Son does really stand to his Father as Production to Producer, Begotten to Begetter, Conclusion to Principle.

God's act and knowledge are not distinct from Godself and what God knows is himself in himself. The Word is the perfect articulation of God's own self-understanding, which *is* God's very self (I 34.1 ad 3). Because Word is not other than God, he is *also* the *scientia Dei*. Insofar as we take *scientia Dei* as (a) the Divine act of knowing or (b) this knowing's immanent expression, Word is *scientia Dei* either by (a') appropriation or (b') personal property.[56] Either way his status as *scientia Dei* is thanks to who he is *in se*, immanent to the Godhead.

Shift from immanent to economic, Word to Jesus.[57] Jesus is *scientia Dei*— or more familiarly, Word—made flesh. He is perfect manifestation of God's knowledge and God's very self. There is nothing of God missing in him. He is fullness of God in bodily form. These realities underwrite Jesus's status in *sacra doctrina*, his place as the real principle or nature whose being in the world that science would trace. As Word of the Father, he stands as ultimate "Conclusion" to ultimate First Principle. And his movement toward us in incarnation and redemption flows from his personal property, repeats *ad extra* his eternal procession (*TT*, 193). We thus receive him as if "Conclusion" from God's self-knowledge, that status *ad nos* underwritten by Word's identity *in se*. And, in turn, he serves as starting point, real first principle and object, in our own dependent *scientia* of *sacra doctrina*, the discursive principles of which Scripture gives and which we take to be from and of him, "surpassing all other teaching in dignity, authority, and utility because passed down immediately from the only begotten Son, who is First Wisdom" (*JC* 1.11.221). Jesus, then, links our radically subalternate science of God to God's own *scientia*. Because he is *sacra doctrina*'s first principle, its formal object, it views "all things whatsoever" (*omnia quaecumque*) in light of Jesus (I 1.3), as coming from, moving toward, and sustained by him (I 1.7 and ad 2).

Like any *scientia*, *sacra doctrina* does not merely interpret but disclose. It sees all things as Christ-related because they are. All things participate in him.[58] This is the real outworking of Jesus as principle that *sacra doctrina* traces. Indeed, as principle, the incarnate Word inaugurates not just a new *scientia* but stands as a new form, a new presence in the world. This presence is not only the life of Jesus, the Divine person, but that presence and life as in-forming what is not himself. Just as ornithology attends to the bird-form in any and every bird and chemistry not just to elements but to all things insofar as they are chemical—because they really *are* somehow chemical—so *sacra doctrina* attends not just to Jesus himself but to Jesus as he is present in that which is not him.[59]

What is this presence, this form in the world? Jesus is the one through whom all things are *made* and made *new*. The real principle Jesus, as Word of creation, providence, and redemption manifests, most broadly, as the movement toward and participation of "all things whatsoever" in him. *Sacra doctrina* examines this movement of all things Christward, for all things *are* so moved—most perfectly, the church, God's new humanity, but not only the church. Rather, in line with his creational and providential work, strictly all things, including those who know him not, are ordered to and sustained by Christ, imperfectly moving toward him as ultimate-yet-unknown good. Albeit implicitly, this is just what we were seeing in Thomas's account of goodness and God-seeking. "All things are *considered* (*pertractantur*) in *sacra doctrina* in light of God," Thomas says, "because all things are *ordered* to God as the principle and their end" (I 1.7). All things really do seek and participate in Jesus because he really is first principle of creaturely existence, Word through and to whom they were made. The God whom Thomas says all seek is the God revealed in Christ. He is subject of Thomas's *sermo*, of *Summa theologiae*. And the final grounds for this claim is not some metaphysical argument but Scripture and a vision of the immanent Triune life to which creation and providence, God's economy, corresponds. Thomas's acts of "proving" that all seek God are acts of *sacra doctrina*. And the Summa is not merely *theological* and *Biblical* but *Trinitarian* and *Christological*. Christ is its subject—and this corresponds to and reflects Word's identity as proceeding from the Father, revealing God, and being Scripture's heart and life. Thomas vindicates *sacra doctrina* as authentic Aristotelian *scientia* by relying upon an Augustinian vision of God's Triunity, and he joins that Trinitarian vision with the Philosopher's conception of *scientia* to articulate the relation between *sacra doctrina*, revelation, and God himself. In his very construction of the *Summa*, then, Thomas is Aristotelian by being Augustinian and vice versa. His constitution of *sacra doctrina* as *scientia* rests upon his conception of the Trinitarian processions and missions, with the incarnate Word who cannot fully be known apart from his relations to Father and Spirit at the fore.

Gilles Emery rightly warns against letting the *Summa*'s "more Aristotelian terms [of] 'principle and end'"—and we might add *"scientia"*—obscure from us the Trinitarian character of its vision (*TT*, 358). And Gene Rogers notes that while Thomas does not explicitly address Christology until the third part, he

> programmatically announces [his christological prioritization], like a negative sign before parenthesis. . . . The opening parenthesis is the remark that "Christ . . . is the way [*via*] that has been stretched out for us into God" (I.I.2 proem.). . . . The closing parenthesis refers to the same *via*, "the way of truth for us, [which Christ] has demonstrated to us in himself" (III prol.). The great parenthesis opens immediately after . . . Question 1, and closes only at the beginning of christology proper. Everything in the *Summa* is either christology, or marked with a christological sign.[60]

Given the way in which, for Thomas, Trinitarianism frames Christology and Christology the Trinity, we might add: Everything in the *Summa* is either Trinitarian theology or marked with a Trinitarian sign. "The Trinitarian treatise," Emery insists, ought to guide "our reading of the questions on moral theology, . . . Christology, the sacraments, and eschatology" (*TT*, 415). "One could almost say," he continues, "that the rest of the *Summa* is the conclusion to the Trinitarian treatise" (414). I have suggested that this dynamic runs the other direction too, from the treatise back—and, at least in that case, that the relation is reciprocal. This book takes Thomas's moral theology and stance on pagan virtue as unfolding in this context, as *sacra doctrina*.

From *esse* and *bonum* to the I Am and Desire of Israel

"It is not necessary," says Thomas,

> that someone always be *thinking* about the final end whenever one desires or
> does something, but the character of the first intention, which is for the final
> end, abides in every desire [or action] for anything whatsoever, even if one is
> not actually considering the final end. Just as it is not necessary that one who
> walks the road think about the end with each step. (I.II 1.6 ad 3)

For Thomas, as it is in action, so it is with the *Summa*: the Christological and
Trinitarian first principle and last end reign throughout, inflecting and determining the whole, even when they go unmentioned. The end gives each step—and
all together—their fullest meaning. "The end," he says, "is the rule of whatever is
ordained to [it]" (I.II *prooemium*). The "great parenthesis" that explicitly enfolds
the *Summa*'s first and second parts with a Christological sign mark the text as
tracing the missions of the Triune God, especially in Jesus Christ—and, behind
these, the processions and relations of Father, Son, and Spirit.

Viewed outside this context, however, many of *the Summa*'s arguments can
seem just so much metaphysics. Understanding these arguments fully, however, requires seeing them as *sacra doctrina* and in relation to their particular
contexts and purposes. The "Five Ways," for instance, is, *inter alia*, an attempt
to establish the identity of the God of the philosophers with the God of Scripture—he is the real but unintended referent of the Greeks' God-talk. Such
efforts help his students see both that the "God" whom philosophers sought
was, unbeknownst to them, Jesus Christ, and what it means that humans are
"ordered to God as to a certain end that exceeds the comprehension of reason"
(I 1.1). As Paul uses the inscription below an idol, "To the unknown god," to
persuade the Athenians that their longings are met in Christ, so Thomas appro-
priates such philosophical graspings to show his students it is the Triune God
whom Aristotle and others pursued.

Pursued, but could not fully attain. "Because," Thomas explains, "Aristotle
truly saw that . . . humans cannot attain . . . perfect happiness, . . . it is clearly
manifest how much frustration the brilliant character [of philosophers] has endured over time" (*SCG* III.48.16–17). Thus, in a context in which the relationship
between Augustinian theology and Aristotelianism was contested and unclear,
where even the Order's leaders held the Philosopher in suspicion, and a young
Dominican could be confused or insecure about such matters, Thomas seeks

to instill confidence and humility: confidence from seeing how and why *sacra doctrina* is higher, "more universal" than even the best Aristotelian *scientia*; humility from recognizing even the greatest of human minds as ultimately impotent apart from grace to attain the very end to which it is ordered.[61] The arguments, moreover—both in virtue of what they substantively show of the world's structure and insofar as they exemplify philosophy's halting efforts to know God—serve as a concrete examples of God's drawing everything to himself. In Thomas's hands, they become exhibits one through five of the unwitting Christ-directedness of metaphysical speculation. In all this, Thomas commends and displays—in substance and form—charity-driven welcome of the outsider that ultimately enriches and deepens Christian witness.

Still, someone might wonder how all this relates to the chapter's first half: Did it not elucidate Thomas's claims as metaphysical theology rather than *sacra doctrina*, as so many variations on Aristotelian and neo-Platonic themes rather than systematic reflection founded on Scripture?

Yes—and no. First, the objection misleads. Just its competitive, zero-sum framing—*sacra doctrina* versus philosophy, scripture versus reason, Augustine versus Aristotle—the *Summa* seeks to overcome. Striving instead to be Aristotelian by being Augustinian and vice versa, Thomas shows how *sacra doctrina* counts on Aristotelian grounds as a proper—indeed the highest—*scientia*, and he does so by grounding that *scientia* in Scripture, Jesus Christ, and the processions of the Triune life. Even saying that he shows *Aristotle* to represent so many variations of *Christian* themes would betray Thomas. Aristotle is no "Egyptian to be plundered" but a friend to be heard, honored, and loved. Likewise, the "mere variations" language is unhelpful: Aristotelian, neo-Platonic, and other motifs pervade *Summa theologiae*; the point is how Thomas uses them and thus what they mean.

For Thomas, in key ways, Aristotelian theology stands to *sacra doctrina* as acquired virtues, the virtues attainable without grace, stand to the infused or grace-given virtues.[62] *Sacra doctrina* and infused virtue are proper to *redemptive* participation in God's truth and goodness, respectively; metaphysical theology and acquired virtue are proper to *creational* participation in God's truth and goodness. If Aristotelian theology is discursive, theoretical Christ-directedness wherein he remains, to the truth-seeker, reason's unknown God, acquired virtue represents volitional, practical participation in the Son's drawing all things to himself, wherein he is loved as ultimate natural good. Metaphysics is the richest creational answer to God's beckoning as True; the life of acquired virtue the full creational bloom of his enticing hearts to himself as Good.[63] In metaphysics and *sacra doctrina*, then, we have *scientia* under nature and grace, respectively. In acquired virtue and infused virtue, we have *virtue* under nature and grace, respectively. While truly good, metaphysics and acquired virtue alike fall short of the perfection God wills, pursuing one beyond their capacity actually to attain or even perfectly to intend. The *res* sought exceeds the seeking's *ratio*. When possessed with charity, they are not discarded, but, without losing their species, perfected. So, while we only understand Thomas's analysis of good-seeking fully when we see it as *sacra doctrina*, that task involves grasping arguments and claims, many of which are shared between sacred and Aristotelian science. Besides helping explain our way of proceeding, this point suggests something important for those who reject Thomas's theological commitments: whatever one thinks of the *articuli fidei*, there's no reason one can't learn from and engage what Thomas has to say—much of it informed by Aristotle—about human action.

While the chapter's first half did not announce itself as taking Thomas as engaged in *sacra doctrina* or highlight the consequences of so doing, that perspective, now explicit, governed throughout. Considering the Trinitarian shape of Thomas's theology of goodness and Godseeking brings those implicit contours to light. Take Thomas's conception of the Son as *Word*. We've seen how that name answers to the Son's procession, but it speaks to another dimension of his proper role in the immanent Triune Life and, as a result, the economy. Both bear directly on Thomas's account of good and Godseeking.

A word is not merely *spoken*—which answers to the Son's procession—but has a determinate *content*: God eternally speaks himself. The Word is the fullness of the act of self-knowing that is not other than God's essence (I 34.3). As Word, the Son is the one in whom resides the "blossom" of God's self-knowledge. To the Word, then, as function of his immanent identity, belongs the exemplar forms, the plan and shape of creation, of all that is and might be. Indeed, Thomas spends an entire article unfolding the sense in which the name *Word* bespeaks the Son's relation to all creation: "*Word* conveys relation to creatures—for . . . a word . . . refers to everything actually understood. [Thus] because God knows himself and all things in one act, his one Word expresses not only the Father but each creature" (I 34.7). The Word's relation to creation follows from his relation to the Father: precisely because *Word* implies relation to a speaker—his Father—who understands everything in understanding himself, in being related to the Father he is related to all things (I 34.3 ad 4). As

Emery puts it, "in line with the *proper mode* of his procession, the Word bears a special relation to creatures" (*TT*, 197).

It is through the Word that the Father gives the perfection of existence, through the Word that each creature is constituted and sustained as what it is.[64] The existence, intelligibility, and endurance of everything is through the Word; creation and providence a matter of participating, respectively, in the Father's filiation of and self-knowledge in the Son (I 33.3 and ad 1–2). In seeking its perfection, then, each creature seeks the Word—and, thanks to Christ's orientation to the Father, the Father too. Thomas explicitly identifies the "exemplar" or "art" through which the Father creates as the Word. He is Plan and Wisdom of Creation: "God makes [everything] through the concept . . . which is eternally-conceived Wisdom, namely the Word of God, the Son . . . the art full of every living form (*ars plena omnium rationum viventium*)" (*JC* 1.2.77).[65] The "Word of God," he explains, likening the Son to a craftsman's plan (*conceptus*), "is [the Father's] eternal *conceptus* . . . the exemplar likeness of all creatures" (III 3.8). In their very existence and ongoing sustainment all things are thus related to and dependent on the Word, the more so the more perfect, the more fully themselves, they are.

For his part, both within the Triune life as personal property, and in the economy by appropriation, the Father is, for Thomas, *principle*: principle in his identity as unbegotten, and principle of Son and Spirit through begetting and spirating; and, in the missions, principle of creation as pouring forth all things through Son and Spirit (I 33.4).[66] This is why *Father* is his name (I 33.2). The Father is himself the "[end] of the missions of Son and Spirit," the one toward whom, in the Son by the Spirit, all things tend and find their rest (*TT*, 174). As for the Holy Spirit, *Love* is his proper name and personal property, standing to Divine *willing* as *Word* to Divine *knowing* (I 27.3 and ad 3). As Word is the "apex" of Divine self-knowledge, so Love "terminates" the ceaseless act of Divine will. There is a "certain impression" (*quaedam impressio*) of the beloved in the lover "which comes into being in the lover through that which he loves" (I 37.1). This determination of love to its object is a particular impression and impulsion (Holy Spirit) against the backdrop of both love's principles (Father) and the understanding that precedes love (Son). Everything everyone does, Thomas says, is because of love (I.II 28.6 sc). It is love that impels all to seek the Son, and it is the Spirit, Thomas says, in back of this love, generating this impulsion, making all seek the Good. The Spirit's personal property of impulsion toward the Son is manifest *ad extra* in impelling all things Christward (*TT*, 265).

It is the Spirit who causes all to *love* the good, to *seek* the Son. "The movement of created beings, their inclinations" Emery explains, "are all participations in the [Holy Spirit's] personal property" (247).[67] And what Thomas says of the Son and Spirit in redemption is no less true of, if vitally distinct from, their work among all creatures in the order of creation: "Just as the . . . Son's mission is to draw to the Father, so the . . . Holy Spirit's mission is to draw the faithful to the Son" (*JC* 14.6.1958). In creation and providence, Spirit internally impels all toward the Son, who is their perfection and the one conformity to whom points them to the Father. Goodseeking, in short, is an inescapably Trinitarian affair.

While Thomas rejects efforts to deduce God's Triunity from features of the divine nature, he draws connections between that nature and Triunity. Here, God's identity as divine Good is key. To articulate the real relations immanent to the Godhead, Thomas uses action to distinguish the persons: Father *begets*, Son is *begotten*, and so on (I 28.4).[68] Goodness, for Thomas, always has the character of end, and end always implies movement (I 5.4 ad 1). Really and conceptually, action and good are inseparable. The perfectly actual God eternally knows and moves toward himself as absolute Good, peerlessly Desirable, lacking nothing of the perfection of every esse. This very understanding of and movement toward himself just *is* the procession of Son and Spirit, respectively, from and to Father—this *is* the Triune God (I 27.3).[69] The Good that God knows and loves is not other than his very nature, his Triune identity. "The Trinity of the divine persons," says Thomas citing Augustine, "is the *summum bonum*" (I 6.2 sc). The Goodness God knows and eternally moves toward *is* his Triunity, himself in himself. In his one act, he eternally *understands* and *loves* himself as Good, moving ceaselessly in that knowledge and love. Creation and redemption repeat *ad extra* this movement Goodward, drawing what is not God to know and love— and be known and loved by—him. In so knowing and loving himself, God elects that there be creatures to receive the most perfect goodness and joy of loving fellowship with himself. He creates and redeems, says Thomas, "because of love of his own Goodness" (I 32.1 ad 3). While not the processions that constitute his being, creation and redemption are external manifestations of the Trinitarian circle of God's being and love, repeating in time and creation, "the procession of love in him" (I 32.1 ad 3).[70] Indeed, the universe's very diversity-in-unity, says Thomas, is grounded in and distantly mirrors God's own three-in-oneness.[71] "The procession of the eternal persons are cause and ratio of the whole creation" (I *Sent* 14 1.1). "From [them], the procession and multiplicity of every creature is caused" (I *Sent* 26 2.2 ad 2). The multiplicity and diversity of creation are necessary the better to "display the divine Goodness" (I 47.1)—for that Goodness is Triune. No wonder Emery would say that, for Thomas, "we cannot study creation until we have considered God's immanent actions" (42).

Ethics as *sacra doctrina*

Because it chiefly considers God, *sacra doctrina* is a speculative rather than practical science, treating knowledge more than action (I 1.4). And yet, Thomas says, because it *is* concerned with God, *sacra doctrina* transcends *scientia's* normal boundaries, examining everything that relates to God—human action included. It treats "human acts . . . as knowable in divine light" because and "insofar as by them a person is ordered to perfect knowledge of God, wherein lies eternal happiness" (I 1.4). *Sacra doctrina*, thus, concerns itself with ethics, with what people *do*, because it concerns itself with the Triune God, who is and knows himself to be Joy, Rest, Savior, End. And so *sacra doctrina* considers acts, habits, virtues—even pagan virtue—because it cares about a God who cares about the way humans relate to him. Virtues, for Thomas, are means of shepherding oneself and others toward friendship with and likeness to Jesus Christ. Grasping them is part of understanding and, in turn, fostering that movement.

Consider in this light the introduction to the *Summa's* second part: "Having discussed the exemplar, God [in part I] . . . we now examine his image, man, insofar as he is principle . . . , as having free choice and power over his works" (I.II *prooemium*). And the *prooemium* to its first question, which sketches I.II in its entirety: "We must first hasten to consider the final end of human life [Q. 1–5], and then those things through which man can attain that end or stray from it [Q. 6–114], for from the end one must learn the shape (*rationes*) of that which is ordered to the end." Having first considered God himself, Thomas explains, the task now is to treat humans as ordered to him. Concern with *this* God, the one who in three persons eternally knows and loves himself, moving all creatures in their own finite way to enjoy that blessedness, cannot but include consideration of what it means to pursue him as final good. Put differently, Thomas's concern with ethics, with acts, habits, virtues, is a *way* of being concerned with and seeking the Triune God.

Here, Thomas's image of steps on a journey could hardly be more apropos: It is because he is concerned with directing people to Christ that he is so concerned with ethics. His distinction-drawing and analysis map steps on the way to God—a journey he is ushering his students along, not only for their own sake, but so that they might do the same for the people of God. We consider habits and virtues, he says, because, under grace, by them we move toward and become like—better, are moved toward and made like—the Savior, and even before grace, by them we imperfectly imitate the Christ.

In this light, his consideration of the matter of virtue without charity, the virtue we'll see he says was had by many non-Christians, is all the more striking. Given that his whole concern with virtue is driven by the place it finds in the movement of everything Christward, that he considers and remarks on pagan virtue at all suggests that in the broad and full swath of Christian life one issue of importance is the way in which Christians regard unbelievers and their seeming virtues. We need to consider pagan virtue, he suggests, because one aspect of the Christian's path to God concerns her way with those who have not charity. And more, as I have begun to suggest, as part of his pastoral aims, Thomas himself *models* this way in his engagement with Aristotle. "Here," he says to his students and drives home through the *Summa*'s very shape and substance, "is how to relate to the outsider. *Watch me*." To read Thomas's ethics as *sacra doctrina* is, in part and as this book does, to read him in this way.

I began this chapter by claiming that Thomas's distinctively Christian vision, its Christological and Trinitarian shape and substance, not only enables but actually impels him to recognize and even celebrate pagan virtue. We have made some initial headway in explicating and defending that claim. For Thomas, everyone seeks God. And the God whom all seek is the Son, in the Spirit, for the Father. This creational and providential reality comes fully into view only in light of the Triune life. At the same time, Thomas's Trinitarianism goes hand in hand with his devotion to Aristotle. "The doctrine of the Word," Emery notes, "is incontestably the heart of Thomas'[s] Trinitarian theology" (*TT*, 179). And in so prioritizing the Word, Thomas characterizes himself as proceeding "especially according to what Augustine showed" (*DP* 9.5).[72] This *Word*-centric conception of the Son alongside a deeply Aristotelian notion of *scientia* become, in Thomas's hands, a way to constitute *fides quaerens intellectum* as *scientia*, and more, a way to correlate that labor with the work and person of God himself—even in his immanence. Wedding Augustinianism and Aristotelianism, Thomas produces a theory and practice of *sacra doctrina* that is ineliminably scientific and robustly Trinitarian. We have seen too how he unites Aristotle's conception of the good with a vision of the Persons' creational and providential action to produce a vision of good-seeking as Christ-seeking that is Aristotelian in its Augustinianism and vice versa.

Strictly everything, Thomas claims, is related and drawn to Scripture's God. The Son is closer to things than they are to themselves; the Spirit more active in and through them than they are in themselves. And all this is so, for Thomas, without any compromise of creaturely integrity or dignity, without competition between humanity and God. The more a creature is the best version of itself, realizing its unique identity and seeking its singular perfection, the more intimately it participates in God. The more it is good in its own right; the more it shares in God's goodness. In this, we can begin to see how Thomas would be led to recognize the excellence of those outside the faith, for, on his vision, all things, especially humans, are directed and related to the Son. And this, without being less themselves, less the particular individuals they are.

"Of those things that desire God," says Thomas, "some know him as God," some do not (I 6.1 ad 2). Humans, of course, fall into the former group. While with all creatures they necessarily desire their perfection and thereby seek Christ, unlike the rest of creation, they can deliberate and be mistaken about what constitutes that perfection, supposing it to be found not in God, but "riches . . . pleasures or something else" (I 2.1 ad 1). Whereas lesser creatures seek God necessarily and in such a way that success or failure is largely out of their hands, it is in a vital sense up to humans whether or not they make God their end. It is due to this distinctive feature, this freedom, that Thomas says that, "what has a will is said to be good insofar as it has a good will" (I 5.4 ad 3). The next two chapters trace the implications of these particularly human capacities for Thomas's conception of pagan virtue and do so in light of the way in which the Augustinian character of his theology, its shape and substance as *sacra doctrina*, impels him to commend and enact the welcome of outsiders.

3 THE PERFECTION OF HABIT

TO GRASP THOMAS'S CONCEPTION OF VIRTUE so that we can understand his claims about pagan virtue, it is tempting to begin with his explication of Augustine's definition of virtue. That definition is succinct and elegant. He endorses it in the two texts that constitute his most extended treatment of virtue—*Summa theologiae* and the more specialized *De virtutibus*.[1] And he refers to it throughout those treatments. That is not, however, where Thomas himself begins.[2] Instead, in both cases, he begins by asking whether virtues are habits.

Whatever else Thomas wants us to know about virtues, first and foremost he wants us to know they are habits. We must grasp this, he insists, if we would understand virtue at all. To that end, he devotes five lengthy questions to examining habit before even beginning the *Summa*'s treatment of virtue (I.II 49). While the habits treatise, along with that on the soul's powers, is necessary to explain "the intrinsic principles of human acts" and thereby explicate human agency, more than anything, the habits treatise—placed *not* adjacent to the powers treatise in the *Summa*'s first volume but immediately prior to the treatise on virtue—paves the way for his analysis of virtue (I.II 49 *prooemium*). Even if we tried to begin with Augustine's definition or elsewhere in the treatise on virtue, we would eventually find ourselves backtracking to grasp the complex conception of habit at the heart of Thomas's account.[3] Thomas, in fact, allows himself a single modification to Augustine's definition: where Augustine says that "virtue is a good *quality* of the soul," Thomas insists that "quality" should be replaced with habit (I.II 55.4). That he would so amend his chief churchly *auctoritas* suggests something of the place habit holds in his conception of virtue.

Getting clear on habits also helps us avoid some mistakes we might make in parsing Thomas on pagan virtue. In understanding that a virtue is a sort of habit and what that means, we can recognize that some inclinations, tendencies, or patterns of behavior that we might be tempted to call virtue—or that Thomas might, loosely, label as such—are not in fact virtues. They are not because they fail to meet one or another of the criteria necessary to constitute something as habit. Whatever qualifies as genuine virtue must at least attain habit's essential features. As distinctions pile up, Thomas's language can confuse: he refers, for instance, to "natural virtue" (*virtus natura*) and elsewhere to virtue that is "wholly imperfect" (*omnino imperfectae*) (I.II 60.3; *DVC* 2). Failing to grasp what a habit is makes it easy for us to be misled, to miss, for example, that "wholly imperfect virtues" and "natural virtues" are not, in the salient sense, really virtues at all.

This chapter, then, explicates Thomas's conception of habit in a way that answers to our basic aim of understanding his welcome of pagan virtue. Along with the next chapter, it also finishes the story the preceding chapter began about the distinctively human way of pursuing and desiring the good, what it means that a human's goodness is, by and large, up to her.

An Initial Sketch of Thomistic Habit

Consider the following cases. You spend most of the winter catching cold after cold—tissues and chicken soup ever at the ready—while your roommate stays healthy. Curt Schilling throws pitch after flawless pitch—even as his foot bleeds, the temperature drops, and the pressure mounts. A grumpy economist in a slow-moving checkout line quickly teaches her daughter why the grocery store is always so crowded on Sunday afternoons. The businessman, texting his broker, fails to notice the child next to him fall off the platform.

Few will read these and think: "Habits, of course." For Thomas, however, habit is what each exemplifies: bodily habits of bad and good health; a habit of excellent pitching; an intellectual habit of economic *scientia* (and perhaps a habit of impatience); and an "operative" or action-focused habit of self-absorption. Thomas's conception is not ours and the risk of confusion is significant enough that, despite Thomas's identification of virtue as a kind of habit, Servais Pinckaers would entitle an article "Virtue Is Not a Habit."[4] The chances of misunderstanding Thomas by reading our notions of habit into his thought is so great, Pinckaers recommends abandoning the term altogether. Best then to put standard ideas of habit out of mind.

Another error tempts. The past century saw several influential social theorists formulate a concept they labeled "*habitus*" and give it a central place in their theories.[5] Using the Latin they sought to distance their concept from notions of habit proper to their native languages. They also meant to evoke and, in some cases, connect to premodern conceptions of human identity, agency, and embodiment, especially as present in medieval concepts of *habitus* and ancient Greek notions of *hexis*. The extent to which their *habitus* relates to premodern notions is up for debate. And reading contemporary conceptions into Thomas's conception would only muddy that conversation. More importantly, doing so would risk our fundamentally misunderstanding Thomas. Given that danger, I refer throughout to Thomas's understanding of *habit* rather than *habitus*.

Four features of that conception concern us.[6] Habit is a perfection of a capacity. It is necessarily either good or bad *in se*. It is difficult to change. And it enables action at will.

Take the habit of bike riding. Some may be better disposed than others, but anyone of sound mind and body has the capacity to acquire that habit. Humans naturally possess bodily and intellectual capacities that, through training, can become disposed so that a person has the habit. Yet nobody can ride a bike simply by having been born human. We are not biologically determined to have the habit—as we are to grow limbs, see, or digest.

The capacities for movement and thinking that a bike-riding habit disposes are not determined to bike riding alone but are capable of many different dispositions.[7] Thus the same (or nearly the same) capacities that bear a bike riding habit can also bear habits of unicycle, motorcycle, and scooter riding and much else. Habits are dispositions that give a more determinate direction and shape to capacities that are not disposed in sufficiently narrow ways, that might be variously developed. Some capacities—like those that constitute the ability to breathe or grow scabs—terminate in a singular function or shape appropriate to the creature whose capacities they are and do so from nature.[8] Such capacities do not bear habits.[9] They lack the potentiality and indeterminateness that make habits necessary and possible. So, while there can be habits of bike riding, economics, and self-absorption, there cannot be habits of circulating or bile production. Habits determine powers by disposing them so that they are oriented to a more determinate end.

According to Thomas, this orientation is always either for good or ill. Considered *per se*, apart from the end to which it is ordered in some action, every habit is either good or bad. Which it is depends on its relation to the capacity it disposes. Capacities have certain natures defined in terms of function, and dispositions count as more or less fitting in relation to them. (Thomas describes this in terms of a habit involving the relation of a thing with itself.) For example, the intellect's nature is to know the true: a habit of economic *scientia* is good *per se* because it disposes the intellect to know the true (relates it well to itself); a habit of anti-Semitic thinking is bad *per se* because it disposes the intellect to falsehood (relates it poorly to itself). The habit of bike riding is good *per se* because bike riding is among the myriad activities well suited to the nature of those capacities. Of course, a habit that is good *per se* like bike riding could be put to evil use—say, running over stray cats. And a habit that is bad *per se* can be put to good use—disabusing someone of his anti-Semitism. Habits, then, are creatures of potentiality that perfect for good or ill a capacity that is capable of being disposed in various ways. In Thomas's words: "A habit is a disposition whereby that in which the habit resides is well- or ill-disposed to the nature of that very capacity or to the operation to which the nature is ordained" (I.II 49.3). Virtue, we can note in passing, is a good habit of using oneself and one's habits well, a habit disposing one to use itself and all other habits and capacities for exclusively good ends.

According to Thomas, habit is difficult to change, *difficile mobile*. A disposition is not a habit unless it is firmly settled, endures over the long haul and in the face of difficulty. While it can eventually be weakened or overcome, it is such that, even after interruption to its use, dormancy, or acts that oppose it, it endures. Someone with a habit of bike riding could refrain from riding for years, hop on, and ride just fine.

Suppose, however, that the rider is Lance Armstrong and the time off has been two decades during which he has become obese. Returning to the saddle, he will certainly not immediately ride as well as he used to, maybe never. Even if he has remained fit, it is unlikely that he would ride as he used to. Yet, if the habit has faded at all, it is not in the sense we might initially think. Surely, in either case Lance cannot ride as well. But, for Thomas, this is due to his obese or aging body, not habit's diminution. Properly, this habit resides not in the body, but in his soul—in the powers of his soul whereby he moves the body. It resides in the body only secondarily, insofar as in the body there is a "certain disposition to promptly serve (*prompte deserviendum*) the soul" (I.II 50.1). For Lance to lose the habit would require that he forget how to cycle, lose his bike-riding know-how. This has not happened, even if thanks to his body he can no longer ride or ride very well.[10]

Those who love to ski but rarely get to know what Thomas has in mind. On the slopes after a long absence, it takes time to return to our prior level of skiing. It is not that we have forgotten how and are having to reacquire the habit we attained when we first learned. Rather we *know* what we need to do and how to do it, but we find our bodies slow to comply, strangely disobedient. What has faded is not the habit, but the body's prompt disposition to comply. After a few days we do not say, "So *that's* how to ski," but "I'm getting my ski-legs back." And similar stories can be told about habits of tennis, knitting, typing, and so on. These habits, along with economic thinking, self-absorption, temperance, and many more, are all what Thomas calls operative habits. They concern humans as agents, as sources of action—whether that movement is intellectual, like mentally running through a mathematical proof, or, like dancing, involves the body more centrally. Operative habits reside essentially in the soul and only secondarily, or by participation, in the body. For this reason they are difficult to change.

Some habits, Thomas says, are "bodily," they reside in the body essentially and concern the body in relation to its form—whether the body is well- or ill-disposed in relation to its biological function by being healthy or ill and whether it is well- or ill-disposed in terms of its shape and features by being beautiful or ugly. Coming pages explain further, but bodily habits include things like your roommate's good health, your bad health, and Hepburn's (take your pick) beauty. Operative habits answer perfectly to the *ratio* of habit. Bodily habits do not. Lance's case suggests why.

Bike riding is an operative habit and thus *qua* habit difficult to change, but because it involves the body so centrally it is easy to render it ineffective, to prevent its full realization in the riding of a bike. If this is so for an *operative* habit that merely *involves* the body, we can imagine what holds for those habits that are *essentially* in the body. Bodily habits—as essentially bodily—are essentially easy to change. Health disappears as quickly as we catch the flu; ugliness fades with the slice of a surgeon's knife. So, in Lance's battle with cancer, his habit of health was destroyed, but his habit of riding endured and would have only been destroyed had cancer ended his life or his capacity to think. Operative habits, genuine habits, are difficult to change.[11]

Further, habits enable one to act at will. Assuming bodily integrity, a bicycling habit requires that one *consistently* be able to ride, not merely that one be able to pedal a few times before crashing. Being able to do "acts of reading"—recognize certain words, decipher occasional short sentences—does not amount to a habit of reading. Habit brings a consistency and ease like that proper to strictly natural action—like seeing or breathing. If Herb struggles to ride a bike (not because he is out of shape, wounded, on tough terrain, but just to *ride*), he lacks the habit. Other things being equal, someone with a bicycling habit can ride at will. Take the painter of public television fame, Bob Ross. However we judge his work, the man has a habit of painting: he can paint at will. Most of us know how to paint—sort of—but we fall short of the habit in that we cannot paint at will. Our trying to paint does not coincide very well with our succeeding. We struggle to depict the tree. Ross's "happy mistakes"— the errant falls of his brush that he effortlessly transforms into some feature of his cheesy dreamscapes—are, on our canvases, just mistakes.

"A habit," Thomas explains, "is a disposition whereby that in which the habit resides, its subject, is well- or ill-disposed to the nature of that very subject or to the operation to which the nature is ordained" (I.II 49.3).[12] Thomas calls that which possesses a habit most immediately a habit's *subject* and speaks of a habit as being *subjected* in a place. When considering habits, "subject" is shorthand for whatever it is some habit most immediately disposes, wherever it is that a habit resides: the subject of *scientia* is the intellect; of moderation, sensible appetite; of health, the body. The qualifier "most immediately" distinguishes the subject from the creature who possesses the subject, for in many cases the subject is not identical with the creature. While our economist possesses and is disposed by an economic habit, since she is not identical to her intellect, she is not technically that habit's subject—her intellect is, for it most immediately possesses and is disposed by the habit. Your roommate may have a habit of health, but her *body* is that habit's subject. In many ways, habit stands to its subject as form to matter, giving determinate shape and orientation where they are naturally lacking and, given the subject's nature, needed. It is in relation to its subject's nature that a habit is either well- or ill-suited, good or bad. It is in relating a subject to its nature that a habit puts a subject "in relation to itself."

Every subject has a particular fitting determination (or range thereof) appropriate to its nature, is open to being differently determined by various habits, but requires habit to be sufficiently determined at all. A good habit gives its subject an appropriate determination; a bad habit some other. But every habit gives its subject *some* determination. That every habit does so is why Thomas says every habit is a *perfection*. All habits are perfections, because all habits bring the perfection of completion. They move some subject from potentiality to actuality. These formulations have been intentionally skeletal and removed from exegetical detail, paving our way for the work ahead.

Natures, Bodies, and Habits

Recall Thomas's remark that "habit principally and in itself (*primo et per se*) causes relation (*habitudinem*) to the *nature* of a thing (*naturam rei*) . . . [that] its essence or *ratio* is to be related to nature" (I.II 49.3). Yet he also says that "according to the *ratio* of habit, it is proper in some way to *every* habit to be ordained to *act*," and further claims that "habit implies not only relation to the *nature of a thing* itself, but also, consequently, *to operation* [or some sort of movement]—insofar as operation is the end of nature or leads to that end" (I.II 49.3 and ad 2). Thomas says all this in a single article and reiterates these points throughout the treatise on habits. Habit, he seems to insist, is related essentially to *both* nature and operation. This is puzzling. It is challenging enough to grasp what he means in claiming that habit is related to nature. In what sense is habit essentially related to both nature and operation?

This question generates others still. Take Thomas's claim that habit is related to a nature. I said we should take that to mean that a habit is related to its *subject's* nature, but we might wonder whether Thomas instead means that habit is related to the nature of the creature whose habit it is. And even if we're sure he holds the former, we can still be unclear about what exactly that means or what a subject's "nature" even is. It turns out that we have some challenging questions to answer just to grasp the basic details of Thomas's account. Happily, answering them does more than resolve thorny conceptual and textual issues. It leads us, in due course, to Thomas's account of operative habit, the sort that most centrally concerns him and us, the sort that, when good in the right way, is virtue.

In I.II 49.3, Thomas first outlines his conception of operative habit and claims that while not every sort of habit is related to operation in the same way, every habit is related to operation. Those related to it more immediately and directly than others are operative habits. Since every habit is essentially related to its subject's nature, if some habit is related to a nature "that *itself* consists in a relation to an act" then that habit "principally implies relation to an act" (I.II 49.3). Some natures, Thomas is saying, are essentially about operation—operation is what they are in the sense that they are a capacity for operation, an ability to move or be moved. Because habits are essentially related to a nature, if a given nature is "capacity-for-operation," "readiness-to-act" then, *because habit is related to that nature*, that habit is principally and essentially related to operation: "If the nature of the thing in which the habit resides itself consists in readiness-to-act (*ordinem ad actum*), it follows that the habit principally implies readiness-to-act." The habit, in other words, is principally related to operation.

This remains abstract. What sort of thing, of its very nature, is readiness-to-act, capacity-for-operation? Consider sensitive appetite, our desire for sensible pleasure, for things like food, sex, comfortable temperature, and so on. For Thomas, sensitive appetite is, of its very nature, a capacity to be moved. We smell the hot brownies and are stirred to hunger for them. This hunger, our internal inclination toward them, is the very movement or operation of sensitive appetite. Sensitive appetite is the capacity to be inclined toward sensible pleasure (and away from sensible pain). It is one of what Thomas calls the powers (*potentiae*) of the soul.[13] Each power of the soul is an internal principle for a certain sort of generically or formally defined movement or operation. So, vision, for example, is a power of the soul. As a power, vision is not just a capacity to see this or that thing, say, puppies or shapes, but a capacity for *seeing* as such. Its object is the *seeable*. This is what it means to say that a power of the soul is a capacity for a *formally* defined operation. The seeable is vision's formal object.[14] And *sight* or *seeing* is the operation that vision is a power or principle for. Likewise, the power of hearing is the internal principle that effects the operation of *hearing*, the formal object of which is the *audible*.[15] Sensitive appetite, then, is the power whose formal object is *sensible pleasure and pain*; its operation *sensible desiring or averting* or *resting in the sensibly pleasurable*. We can note quickly that will (*voluntas*) is a power whose formal object is *good* and whose operation is *rational appetite*—inclination toward what intellect grasps as good. Not unlike sensitive appetite, will's operation is a certain sort of inclining or desiring, albeit an essentially reason-laden one.[16]

Anticipating our initial question about what sort of things are of their very nature capacity-for-operation, Thomas explains that the soul's powers (*potentia*) are. The very "nature and notion" (*natura et ratio*) of a power is capacity-for-operation (*ordinem ad actum*). In relating to a nature that is itself readiness-to-act, habits residing in powers are related immediately, principally, and essentially to operation: "Every habit that resides in some power as its subject principally implies relatedness-to-operation" (I.II 49.3). Some habit of the sensitive appetite is itself essentially and primarily involved in disposing sensible desire, causing it to incline to certain things and not others and to do so with more or less intensity. It relates essentially to operation because operation is power's very nature. Operative habits are habits of powers and, insofar as every creaturely power is a power of the soul, habits of the soul.[17] The path to operative habit, habit immediately related to and disposing act, runs right through the essential character of habit as disposing a nature.

But there is another way in which habit is related to operation, a way in which *every* habit is so related. For that matter, there is another sense in which habits are related to natures—or, more precisely, another sense of "nature." And in that different sense, only some habits are related to natures. Before addressing these two complexities, we can say definitively now which nature every habit is essentially related to and what it means for a habit to be related to a subject's nature.

Recall that operative habit is related immediately to action because it is related to a power's nature. A power is not a creature but a dimension of a creature's soul. I.II 49.3's explication of operative habit depends on the fact that a habit is related to the nature of that habit's subject—*not* the nature of whatever creature possesses that subject.[18] Otherwise, Thomas's argument would disintegrate. Take our economist, Jane. Her *scientia* is subjected in her intellect, and thus the nature that habit relates to is the intellect's, that of habit's subject. Jane's nature is not her intellect's. Her economic habit does not dispose her intellect well or ill in relation to *Jane's* nature—at least not immediately. Rather, her economic habit disposes her intellect well or ill in relation to *itself*, to its *subject's* nature. Intellect's nature is *to know truth* whereas Jane's nature is to be a rational animal, and the operation that is her end is not simply to know truth, but to know and love God and neighbor. Thus, an economic habit might dispose Jane's intellect well because it answers to her intellect's nature of knowing truth. But Jane *herself* is not ill- or well-disposed by it, ill- or well-disposed in relation to *her* nature: she may use that knowledge to oppress the poor by establishing optimally profitable usury rates or to construct markets that maximally benefit the poor. In considering whether a habit of Jane's intellect is, in itself, good or bad, we must look immediately not to Jane's nature but intellect's.[19]

The next chapter returns to these matters, but in identifying which nature habit relates to, Thomas is not being frivolous—nor, in troubling over it, are we. Conceiving habits in this way allows him and those he is training to identify what is involved in helping someone acquire or overcome some habit: for example, if a student's difficulties with the *Categories* are due to his intellect's limits, this suggests a different response than if they stem from a habit of illness or laziness. Recognizing such possibilities—and that and how they are distinct—is no small thing. Take Heidegger. On Thomas's account of habit (not metaphysics!), we can appreciate and learn from Heidegger's intellectual habits without thinking that doing so need imply any endorsement of his vicious moral habits.

While a habit immediately disposes and relates to its subject's nature, that subject is itself always some creature's. So too the subject's habit. Indeed, the creature's nature is itself essential to understanding fully the subject's nature. As memory, intellect, or eyes exist *for* a human, so every subject exists for the creature, to serve and complete its nature. Thus, a creature's nature helps us see what a subject's nature is properly for, how it should function, the completion that a habit good *in se* brings. In serving their subjects, habits serve and are had by the creatures whose subjects they are.

We can now grasp the sense in which strictly every habit is related to operation. Not every habit is operative because not every habit belongs to a power. Thomas notes this in drawing 49.3's key distinction, one between those habits that *are* "primarily and *per se*" related to operation and those that are not. Yet, the article's main thrust is that all habits are nonetheless related to operation in some way, and that this is essential to habit's very *ratio* (see too, e.g., I.II 54.2). Here again, habit's essential relation to its subject's nature does the explanatory work: every habit is somehow related to operation because every habit is essentially related to its subject's nature, and every nature is somehow ordained to action, to an end (I.II 55.2 ad 1). "Habit," Thomas explains, "implies not only relation to the nature of a thing itself, but also, consequently, to operation [or some sort of movement]—*insofar as operation is the end of nature or leads to that end*" (I.II 49.3). All creatures, Thomas reminds, are ordered, finally, to operation. And all that is within a creature is ordered to the creature's good and, just so, ordered mediately to the operation that is that creature's end.

We are recalled here to the fundamentally theological character of Thomas's vision. In being ordered to natures, all habits are ordered to operation for all things seek the Triune God. Being so impelled by the Spirit, so ordered, is not other than what a creature is. As participations in the Word, creatures are what they are by participating in the One who is himself complete operation. All of the subjects of habits within a creature, including those not immediately ordered to operation, are nonetheless ordered to the creature—which is itself ordered to operation (I.II 55.2 ad 1). Thus every habit *as such* is essentially—if not immediately—ordered to action. And habits, as perfections of creatures' natures, completing for good or ill various dimensions of those natures, establish a creature as participating in God more or less fully.

Bodily Habits

There are then two distinct senses in which habit relates to operation: one immediate and particular, distinctive to operative habit; the other mediate and common to habit as such. Fully grasping operative habit, however, requires distinguishing it from bodily habit—beyond the mere fact that, unlike bodily habit, it relates directly to operation. Two key interpretive challenges, both related to I.II 50.2, remain: an ostensible denial of I.II 49.3's claim that all habits are related to *both* operation and nature and an apparent claim that non-operative habits are related *not* to the *subject's* but the *creature's* nature. Addressing these textual difficulties further illumines operative habit and its distinction from bodily habit.

"Habit," Thomas says, "implies a certain disposition related to *either* nature (*naturam*) or operation (*operationem*)" (I.II 50.2). This is surprising. Above, we saw Thomas establish all habits as essentially related to *both* nature *and* operation: some to operation "primarily and principally" because they relate to natures essentially about operation; non-operative habits to operation insofar as all natures (and subjects) are ordained to operation in seeking God as end. This article, however, seems to pose an exclusive alternative: habits relate *either* to operation *or* nature. Thomas even says that "a habit whose subject is a power does *not imply ordination to nature* (*natura*) *but to operation*" (I.II 50.2 ad 3). Moreover, beginning in the prior article and stretching into this one, Thomas indifferently alternates between speaking of nature and form (*forma*), as though the nature to which some (or is it *all*?) habits are related are *forms*—as though "nature" just *means* "form." He even talks of habit "dispos[ing] its subject to *form*," where, ostensibly contradicting what we have seen, that form or nature to which habit relates appears to be the creature's rather than the subject's (I.II 50.1).

Consider, in fuller context, Thomas's remark: "If we speak about the disposition of the subject to *form*, then it is possible for a habitual disposition to be in the body, which stands to the soul as subject does to form. And in this manner health, beauty, and like things are said to be habitual dispositions" (I.II 50.1). Here, habit seems related to the creature's nature, the soul, rather than the subject's. But recall what a body and its nature are for Thomas.[20] Take the habit of health: in disposing the body well in relation to the soul, health actually *is* disposing its subject well in relation to its subject's nature. Yes, the subject's nature here is also the creature's—but only because *body* is the subject. For health or other bodily habits, habit's subject *is* the body, and body's nature *is* the soul: the soul precisely in its capacity as body's form. "In the constitution of the human," Thomas says, "body is had as matter, soul as form" (I.II 55.2 and 1).

Body is constituted *as body*, by soul; it is matter-informed-by-soul. This is why Thomas holds that at death the "body" is, properly speaking, no longer a body but a corpse.[21] Body's nature is the soul—in soul's capacity as form. And, for this reason, body shares its nature with the creature. As subject of health, illness, and so on, body is well- or ill-disposed to *itself*, its own nature, precisely in being well- or ill-disposed to soul, its form. Because habit relates subject to subject's nature, bodily habit disposes to soul, body's nature—even as soul is *quodammodo*, in a certain way, creature's nature too. Thomas speaks alternately of nature and soul because, for bodily habits, the two are identical.

Bodily habit disposes the body fully in relation to the soul—perfecting it, as habit does, in relation to its form. Yet soul makes a body the very body it is— human, marmot, antelope. What room does that leave for bodily habit, for a fur- ther determination of body in relation to form? For Thomas, there is some bodily completion that form does not itself effect. Indeed, form dictates that aspects of body remain indeterminate, *effecting* that matter's incompleteness, as an artist might design an installation to be complete only after weathering sun and rain. Soul leaves body in potency to different completions—some more fitting to the soul, others less. The body, then, needs various habits—such as health or illness, beauty or ugliness—to achieve its completion. Such habits are called "bodily" thanks to their subject and their effecting perfection in relation to form primar- ily and operation only derivatively. Because their subject is never immediately ordained to action and the nature to which they relate is always a form (a nature in that sense), Thomas occasionally describes bodily habits as related to "nature" or form *instead* of operation.

This he does in I.II 50.1 and 2, distinguishing bodily and operative habits as related to nature and operation, respectively. Certainly, in disposing bodies (which are ultimately ordained to operation) bodily habits relate to operation in some way but not immediately. Their subject's nature is not essentially op- erative, for bodily habits relate body to soul not in soul's capacity as "principle of action" but *qua form* of that body. In contrast, consider Thomas's claim that *operative* habit, as "a habit whose subject is a power, does *not* entail ordination to nature (*natura*) but to operation" (I.II 50.2 ad 3). "Nature" here refers not to the nature of habit's subject, which strictly every habit relates to, but instead to form, body's nature. And operative habits are not related to "nature" so understood but essentially and uniquely related to a power's nature, operation. Hence Thomas's depiction of bodily and operative habit as related to nature and operation, respectively, and hence the consistency between that claim and his insistence on habit's essential relation to nature and operation alike.

These points suggest that whether subjected in a power or a body, every habit is somehow related to the soul. Only soul has the qualities to make habits possible. In treating whether soul itself is habit's subject, Thomas distinguishes between soul in its capacity as: (a) body's form and (b) rational power and principle of action. In respect of (a), the soul itself does not admit of habit. As form, it is already fully determined in regard to itself, not in potential. Otherwise, by having a habit a terrier, say, could become a Labrador, Bengal tiger, or mushroom. As body's form, soul cannot be related to itself for it is, in the relevant sense, *already* determinate—the form of *this* species. It lacks the requisite potentiality to be habit's subject. While soul itself does not bear bodily habits, the body's capacity for habits depends on its relation to soul. At his most precise, Thomas stresses that bodily habits are not found in body *simply* but in body-by-reason-of-its-relation-to-the-soul (I.II 50.2). Such habits are neither in the soul *qua* form nor the body *qua* piece of matter but in the particular complex of form *and* body.[22] The body is essentially subject of such habits, for it brings the potentiality that makes habit necessary and possible. As form, soul brings a nature sufficiently determinate for habit to relate to, while not itself so determining body that no room remains for habit. Only in this relational complex can such a non-operative habit exist.

In its identity as rational power, the soul itself admits of habit, for a rational power is a principle of action not determined to a single action but capable of a whole range. As rational power, soul needs further formation to achieve an orientation and disposition that perfects it, one more or less fitting its own nature. Habits are thus proper to the soul as they are not to the body, and, just so, operative—unlike bodily—habits answer perfectly to habit's *ratio*.

Creatures of Potentiality, Perfections of Powers

Habits are creatures of potentiality. They dwell only in subjects that are not, by their nature, determined to one thing but stand in potency to different ends. Subjects' natures are such that certain of these orientations are fitting, others not. Good habits bring a subject to a disposition befitting its nature. Bad habits dispose subjects in ways unsuited to their nature. But every habit is a perfection, determining its subject, completing what a creature's nature naturally leaves unfinished.

Some things, however, nature completes of its own accord. A creature's nature just causes such-and-such to be the case: the brook trout's having gills, the human's having a thumb, the falcon's having keen eyes. Thus, many aspects of creatures and many creatures themselves have no need or capacity for habit. Provided all goes well, the rose seed or deer embryo terminates in a fully developed rose and deer, respectively, which live in characteristic ways. With respect to what they will be, how they will behave, and so on, they are on the whole not indeterminate, not open to a whole host of different ends. Here, what nature begins, nature completes. In humans too, capacities related to what Thomas calls the vegetative powers—powers that humans share with all living, earthly creatures and that direct biological function and development—are determined and, if all goes well, perfected by nature (I.II 49.4 ad 3). The development and function of lungs for breathing, a digestive system for digesting, a circulatory system for circulating—these are all functions of the vegetative power and do not require habits for their various perfections (I.II 50.3 and ad 1 and 3). None of this suggests that nothing can go wrong with roses, deer, or human vegetative capacities. Rather, if something like this does go wrong, this represents a failure of nature or an instance of misfortune. It is not due to bad habit that a rose fails to bloom, a deer fails to mate, or a man is born blind. In contrast, that humans only learn a language if taught, represents no failure of individual or human nature but a natural feature of that nature, something nature requires habit to perfect.

A human can will and pursue as good what is not in fact perfective of her nature, thereby ruining her digestive system and coming to have a bodily habit of ill health. Subsisting on chips, donuts, and soda and never exercising, she will almost certainly acquire a retinue of health problems that will, together, constitute a habit of illness. The development of such a habit in a manner for which an individual bears responsibility is a function of the facts that humans possess operative capacities that require habits to achieve perfection and that humans require a variety of habits to ensure that they flourish. All the capacities of a human are ordered to the perfection of the creature. The highest part, the rational power, is, in its capacity as appetite for what is perceived as good, essentially a subject of habit. In habituating that highest capacity—which includes a capacity for commanding the operation and movement of the creature itself—the effects echo through the whole person. Even capacities that in themselves are not immediately subject to reason or in no way obey reason's command, are not insulated from consequences of will's willing and directing the creature. The course reason charts as effected by will carries consequences for all of those human capacities.

So, by choosing to smoke, I can eventually ruin my respiratory system although it is not itself immediately subject to habit or my command—I can hold my breath but cannot will my lungs to stop absorbing oxygen. By exercising and eating well, in contrast, I can strengthen my circulatory system—but I cannot just will my arteries to unclog themselves. Thomas is guilty of no pernicious dualism here. Precisely because the vegetative powers are not subject completely, immediately, or even directly to reason, things can go for good or ill with various capacities irrespective of the character of someone's habituation. So, the fit runner suffers a heart attack at twenty while the high-stress smoker reaches his nineties. Or, a Stephen Hawking or Stevie Wonder makes a good life in a way that an animal similarly challenged could not. The relation between the capacities that need habits and those that do not is dynamic and reciprocal, with each shaping the other in various ways, to various degrees. It is in this sense that humans are creatures of habit—creatures who by nature need habits to become the creatures that they are meant to be.

That habits complete their subject implies that prior to their advent the subject already has a trajectory, an initial directedness somehow expressing the subject's nature. Habits work from this particular character. Say we stumble on a half-written novel. It could be finished in many ways, but as far as it goes it is coherent, with an interesting plot, complex characters, and beautiful writing. With care, we can sense how the author might have proceeded and finish it in a way that suits the story thus far—giving it a fitting, even excellent, conclusion. Or we can finish it in a way inconsistent with its trajectory, making it a poor work indeed. Subjects, at least, have a relatively narrow range of completions truly befitting their nature. They have a seed, an initial-directedness, and "habit is to [that nature or] power as complete to incomplete" (I.II 50.2 ad 3). As *perfecting* its subject, habit works with given ingredients and finishes what its subject starts (49.4 sc).

Without habit, hunger, for instance, is for whatever is humanly edible. Appetitive habits give determinate orientation to this general appetite so that certain things and not others are consistently and readily desired. Thus, through habit a former burger-lover turned vegetarian might eventually find meat unappetizing and hunger instead only for kale, soy protein, and the like. Note well, though, habit does not *cause* appetitive power to desire food—that desire, instead, is what habit works upon, shapes and perfects. The subject habit perfects always has an initial but insufficiently determined direction or inclination, the inchoate, underdetermined beginning of a disposition, a quasi-disposition—and "quasi" precisely in virtue of being insufficiently determinate. The habit itself is not this beginning but what habit presupposes (I.II 50.5 ad 1 and ad 3). This point is essential for understanding what Thomas is referring to when he talks later, in 63.1, about "natural virtues" (*virtus inchoata* and *natura*).

Difficile mobile, virtus inchoata, and Pagan Virtue

Habits, Thomas says, must be difficult to change: if a disposition is easy to change, it is for that reason not a habit (I.II 49.1 ad 3; 49.2 and ad 3). The point is rooted in habit's function: habit could hardly *perfect* its subject if the disposition it brought was not long-lasting. Completion that is easily changed, that does not last, is, in this case, *incompletion*. The perfection of completion demands habit's endurance. A disposition not settled and long-lasting makes for a subject—and a creature—that lacks the essential perfection of stable identity, the good of operating in particular, consistent ways. Where determination is needed, instability and change entail imperfection. As perfecting, habit must be difficult to change.

But what exactly does that mean? Consider bodily habits. For Thomas, they are by their nature easy to change and for that reason an imperfect sort of habit. As material, the body is easy to change, subject to decay, brokenness, and death. So it is with any habit of that subject. Even if bodily habits are taken as more enduring than particular bodily features—so that health could survive loss of a limb, say—the difficulty in changing them is still only relative (I.II 50.1 ad 2). That is, only in *relation* to other aspects of the body or other dispositions are they *difficile mobile*: your beauty more stable than your health or mine, say. Perhaps, some bodily habit is only changed or destroyed if the body itself is. Still, it is not *simply* difficult to change, for no bodily habit is more difficult to change than its subject, body—which is essentially easy to change (I.II 50.1 and 49.2). The soul, in contrast, is "simply difficult to change," *difficile mobile* by its very nature as spiritual. So too are soul's habits.[23]

This point bears directly on our consideration of pagan virtue. The feature of being *difficile mobile* that essentially characterizes genuine habit necessarily characterizes authentic virtue too. As a complete habit, one answering perfectly to habit's *ratio*, there is no full-fledged virtue, nothing attaining its *ratio*, that is not difficult to change. Early in the habits treatise, Thomas explicitly distinguishes between habit and disposition precisely along the axis of changeability—where disposition is characterized by failing to be *difficile mobile* (I.II 49.2 ad 3). After noting that in another sense *disposition* denotes a genus in which habit stands as a particular species, he notes that, alternatively, *disposition* can be taken as distinct from or opposed to habit in two different ways:

(1) (a) *Disposition* can denote bodily habit—habit that, thanks to its subject's nature, is essentially easy to change. (b) *Habit*, in contrast, here denotes that which is over against disposition so understood. It is operative or nonbodily habit—habit whose subject, soul, is essentially difficult to change.

(2) (c) *Disposition* can denote a stage of growth along the way to habit, so that it describes some state in which the degree of unchangeability proper to habit has not yet been achieved. (d) *Habit*, in contrast, names that orientation of soul that is truly *difficile mobile*, firmly held, and so attains habit's *ratio*. On this usage, he says, a disposition becomes a habit as a boy becomes a man; disposition and habit stand as imperfect and perfect *within one species* (namely (1b)).[24] Yet the imperfect specimen, Thomas says, is more properly called "disposition," not "habit."[25]

Given its importance and complexity, we need to consider this passage in some detail. For clarity, I use *determination* to refer generically to the various orientations of body and soul Thomas has in view.

(1) is the more basic distinction. We have (a) determinations that as subjected in body are by nature essentially easy to change, bodily habits, and (b) determinations that as subjected in soul are by nature essentially difficult to change, operative habits. We can, Thomas says, call (a) *disposition* and (b) *habit*. In one sense, the *difficile mobile* criterion divides (a) from (b), marking distinct species within a broader genus. Yet, it does so entirely in view of the *in principle* difference in changeability proper to subjection in body as opposed to soul— dividing according to the changeability of *subjects* not their particular determinations. It is a distinction that obtains irrespective of what *actually holds for some determination's changeability*. Put differently, (1)'s division simply traces the body/soul distinction vis-à-vis changeability, irrespective of what actually holds in regard to changeability for a given determination of body or of soul. Thus, some determination of soul could in fact *fail* to be difficult to change—or even be easier to change than some bodily determination. Yet on this usage of

habit and *disposition*, the determination of soul could still be called *habit*, the bodily determination, *disposition*, for *habit* here means "any determination of soul irrespective of its actual stability"; *disposition*, "any determination of body irrespective of its actual stability."[26] Knowing that some determination is *habit* or *disposition* in this sense allows us to infer (next to) nothing about its actual changeability and so its status as habit properly speaking. What it authorizes is knowledge of where a determination is subject, whether in soul or body. More precisely, knowing something is a disposition in this sense rules out its being habit properly speaking, but knowing something is habit in this sense is necessary but not sufficient for knowing whether it is a habit properly speaking, for its actual stability remains in question.

(1)'s habit/disposition distinction is like that between man and dog. While rationality is proper to human nature, it is a different question whether someone belongs to the human species and whether he is in fact rational. Likewise, it is a different question whether some determination is a determination of soul—and in that *species*-sense a habit—and whether that determination is *in fact difficile mobile*.[27] To remind ourselves what Thomas has in view with this distinction and these terms, call these *S-habit* and *S-disposition*.

(2) above, traces a distinction within (1b), a distinction within *S-habit*. Specifically, it is a distinction generated not by a merely "in principle," abstract, or as-to-subject's-nature application of the *difficile mobile* criterion but by its actual, concrete application, its application to given determinations. There are, Thomas explains, (d) soul-determinations that are in fact *difficile mobile* or *habits* and (c) those that are not, *dispositions*. In this (but not the other) sense, dispositions become habits as boys become men, standing as imperfect and perfect, respectively, within the common species *S-habit*. And this common species, recall, gets its identity fundamentally from its subject, its over-againstness in relation to body with respect to changeability, not from whether its various members are in fact *difficile mobile*. The upshot: something can belong to *S-habit*—be *operative* as opposed to *bodily*—without actually being *difficile mobile* and so without actually being a habit most properly. Being *difficile mobile* is essential to some determination attaining habit's *ratio*. Disposition lacks this. It is "habit" only in the sense of being subject in soul rather than body. In fact, it falls so far short of habit's *ratio* that Thomas insists on calling it *disposition* rather than *habit*. That is, even its species membership, its being *S-habit*, does not make it most properly called *habit*—and this precisely because it lacks a feature essential to full-fledged habit, the very feature which helps generate the

S-habit/S-disposition distinction to begin with: it is not *difficile mobile*. This disposition can be called "imperfect habit," but only insofar as we understand that to mean "imperfect *S-habit*" more or rather than imperfect habit. It is no more an imperfect habit than a child is an imperfect adult—a child is an imperfect *human being*. Whereas in that case we have differing terms for the species and the perfect member thereof, *human being* and *adult*, who (ideally) realizes the species-constituting difference, in our case we have one term for both—*habit*. And hence my labeling Thomas's distinction—*S-habit/habit*.[28] Now, as a child can have some use of reason prior to adulthood, the most developed disposition may attain some share of *difficile mobile*—the least, none at all. The analogy falters, however, and instructively so: while infants, say, have no use of reason, no animal (for Thomas) could have any use of reason, much less surpass some human's share. Yet, even a progressing member of *S-habit*, a disposition *in via*, could well be surpassed in *difficile mobile* by a bodily habit, an *S-disposition*. What secures disposition's membership in *S-habit* is simply its being a determination of *soul* rather than body. What distinguishes it from habit is its failure actually to be *difficile mobile*.

We can note in passing that Thomas's boy/man analogy captures a difficulty inherent in his reliance on *difficile mobile* to distinguish true habit from disposition, a difficulty in his division between true habit or virtue and those determinations that thanks to the *difficile mobile* criterion fall short, by a little or a lot. In so falling short, they fail to attain habit's *ratio*, fail to be virtue— even if, in view of their species membership, they are called "imperfect habit," "imperfect virtue." The difficulty concerns vagueness, a version of what we can call the problem of the heap. At the extremes, it is easy enough to distinguish six or ten leaves from a heap—as it is a toddler from an adult. Other cases are closer calls, the difficulty increasing as leaves are added or the child ages. For Thomas, a bright line divides habit (and virtue) from disposition. Yet, like the "age of reason," his criterion for separating childhood from adulthood, the *difficile mobile* criterion raises a vagueness problem: while obviously determinate across numerous cases, it appears difficult to apply nonarbitrarily when it comes to close calls. Nonetheless, Thomas is clearly and steadfastly committed to a sharp distinction between authentic habit or virtue and its near neighbors—let alone its distant antecedents. Chapter 6 treats this vagueness problem in detail—how, when it comes to close calls, Thomas keeps the line between virtue and its closest antecedents bright without making it arbitrary.[29] Happily, however, the cases that most concern us—the "true but imperfect (because disconnected)" or "loosely held" virtue that interpreters propose as being "pagan virtue"—fall so obviously short of stably generating good acts done well there is no doubt about their failure to be *difficile mobile*, their status as mere dispositions, their falling essentially short of being habit or virtue in any more than the specific sense.[30] Most simply, when it comes to the dominant "negative" interpretation of Thomas on pagan virtue, vagueness issues just don't arise. This passage reminds us that in being sometimes called "imperfect virtue," these dispositions are simply being identified as determinations of soul that are, at least, not usually bad and thus specifically distinct from false or counterfeit virtue, those habits that *seem* good but are in fact bad.

In *both* (1) and (2), Thomas identifies changeability as essential to dividing dispositions and habits in either senses. In different ways, it lies near the heart of both distinctions between habit and what falls essentially short of habit's *ratio*, disposition. Habit alone denotes a deep degree of unchangeability, a "certain long-lastingness" (*diuturnitatem quondam*). Disposition does not. This characteristic is so important to habit's *ratio*, that even when a determination's subject is *difficile mobile*, if the determination itself is not, then it is more properly called *mere disposition* than *habit*. True habit entails *difficile mobile*—not merely as to its subject's nature but as to its own.

"If someone should have a *scientia* imperfectly (*habere imperfecte*), so that he be subject to losing it easily," Thomas explains, "he is more said to be *disposed* to that *scientia* rather than said to *have* (*habere*) it" (I.II 49.2 ad 3). Saying such a person *has* the science incorrectly ascribes to him the *habit*. But this person has no such habit, for "*habit* implies a certain long-lastingness; *disposition* does not" (I.II 49.2 ad 3). She who "has" *scientia*, but in a way that is not long-lasting, *difficile mobile*, and so on does not actually *have scientia* but merely a disposition *for* it. She is, again, "more said to be *disposed to* the science rather than to *have it*" (*magis dicitur disponi ad scientiam quam scientiam habere*) (I.II 49.2 ad 3). To be sure, this is *scientia* under discussion, not health—an *S-habit*, not an *S-disposition*—but it is another matter still whether she actually *has* the habit, has *scientia*. To have *scientia* is to have a habit, something essentially marked by *actually*, not merely potentially, being *difficile mobile*. To have what is easily lost, not firmly held, is necessarily not to have *habit* or *virtue* but something somehow preparatory to it, a propensity or disposition to *acquire* it.

This echoes a point Thomas makes in the first—and immediately preceding—article about habits (I.II 49.1 ad 3). Using "disposition" as a general category, he distinguishes between determinations within that broader group that "are in preparation and propensity not yet perfect, such as *scientia* and virtue *inchoata* [or incomplete]" and those that are "perfect dispositions, which are said to be habits, things like *complete (complete) scientia* and virtue."[31] Here, unlike I.II 49.2, he does not explicitly cite changeability as the reason this *inchoata scientia et virtus* count as incomplete.[32] Nonetheless, he essentially draws the same sharp, basic distinction in the same way—basically, that within *S-habit*, between (c) and (d), preparatory disposition and habit. In both passages, there is, on the one hand, a beginning, a certain propensity that is incomplete, imperfect, *not* attaining to habit but remaining mere disposition. And, on the other, there is completion, "perfection," true habit. The contrast—imperfect/perfect, easily lost/firmly held, disposition/habit, *inchoata scientia et virtus/scientia et virtus complete*—runs across both passages. Habit, they concur, denotes completion, perfection, unchangeability. It excludes disposition's provisionality, changeability, and on-the-way-ness. What is loosely held, easily lost is not—cannot be—habit or virtue but a disposition *for* habit, *for* virtue.[33]

Thomas's diction, especially his use of *scientia* across the texts, the details of his claims, and the close proximity of the passages invite us to read them together: I.II 49.1 ad 3's *scientia inchoata*, antecedent of *complete scientia*, parallels I.II 49.2 ad 3's "easily-lost *scientia*," which Thomas says is, properly, not *scientia* at all, but a mere disposition to it. Both *scientia inchoata* and "easily lost *scientia*" are described as imperfect, "in formation," dispositions rather than habits. Indeed, even if 49.2's easily lost *scientia* should represent a development beyond 49.1's *scientia inchoata*, since the former fails to be authentic habit, much more does the latter. Properly speaking, they are not virtue at all. We might still wonder whether or in what sense 49.1's *virtus inchoata*—while not *complete* or *perfect* virtue—might be true virtue. Reading the passage synoptically clarifies: easily lost virtue and *virtus inchoata* belong to *S-habit* or, as we might say given the focus here, *S-virtue*.[34] They are determinations of soul, and in that sense, imperfect "habits" or "virtues"—but, lacking something essential to habit's very *ratio*, unchangeability, they fall short of habit or virtue proper. To be sure and to anticipate coming discussions, they are importantly, even specifically distinct from false virtues or vice—indeed as much distinct from either as *S-disposition* from *S-virtue*—but, in the sense Thomas and we care about most, they are not, and are not appropriately called, virtue. They fail to be virtue as disposition fails to be habit.

Habits, Thomas insists, are essentially marked by unchangeability, which distinguishes authentic habit from disposition (in either sense). Any determination *not* truly *difficile mobile* is not true virtue for Thomas. It may be virtue in the sense of being virtue's precursor, determination of soul rather than body, belonging to *S-virtue* rather than *S-disposition*, and it may be true in the sense of not being counterfeit, vice in disguise. But changeability is incompatible with its being habit or virtue in any sense beyond these. Any half-decent orientation of will is "virtue" in this sense—no matter how easily lost, how infrequently generative of good action.[35] Affirming this as all pagans can attain hardly amounts to affirming pagan virtue, at least by Thomas's lights. For him, if we want to talk about authentic virtue, we must recognize that virtue is a habit and that habits are, essentially, *difficile mobile*. Being *difficile mobile* is not some optional extra when it comes to virtue in more than the mere *S-virtue* sense, but proper to virtue *per se,* absolutely essential to its *ratio*. Consider in this light a very common interpretive strategy.

Take Thomas Osborne, for instance, who represents many in claiming that Aquinas denies that outsiders can attain connected moral virtue—virtue that extends beyond any but the narrowest spheres of activity.[36] At the same time, such interpreters want to avoid claiming that Thomas disallows the possibility of pagan virtue altogether, since he clearly does not. Osborne thus points to these passages as supporting his claim that pagans are capable only of what he calls "true but unconnected" virtue. While noting that I.II 49.1 ad 3, 49.2 ad 3, and the texts that have occupied us throughout this chapter, represent "Thomas's [primary] discussion of how virtues develop and persist," he pays them scant attention (*PIV*, 49). Citing 49.2 ad 3, he claims "an agent could have true virtue and yet only as an imperfect disposition that can easily be lost" (49). He is claiming, in other words, that Thomas here declares that such a disposition is a virtue, that by having something "easily lost" one nonetheless has virtue.[37]

For Thomas, however, virtue is a kind of habit—and whatever else habit is, it is not easily lost. That's precisely what divides it from disposition. Further, 49.2 ad 3 claims that one with an easily lost disposition does not *have* virtue but merely a *disposition for it.* This easily lost disposition is just that member of *S-habit* or *S-virtue* that is mere disposition rather than virtue. It is at best a non-evil determination of soul. And it is "true but imperfect virtue," only if that means "imperfect *S-virtue*," and only if we drop "true" as redundant. It is "true" only in being not *counterfeit* virtue—which is to say only in belonging to *S-virtue*. It is not "true," however, in attaining virtue's *ratio*, in being habit rather than disposition.[38] Indeed, perhaps that's why Thomas himself never describes such a disposition as *vera sed imperfecta*, true but imperfect, virtue.[39] As used by interpreters like Osborne, in contrast, that label can obscure how radically far from a habit of virtue this is. What they are actually claiming Thomas regards pagans capable of fails even to be habit for Thomas, much less true virtue.

Acting "at Will" and the Distinctively Human

Part of Thomas's insistence on the *difficile mobile* criterion has to do with the way an instable completion is not really a completion. It is hard to imagine Jane's economic science perfecting her intellect if, turning to her daughter to hold forth, she found she could not remember why the line was so long after all. The example illustrates the connection between a habit's being *difficile mobile* and that whereby "we act at will" (I.II 49.3 sc). Habits, for Thomas, have an essential connection to will. And in one sense, saying that habits enable us to act "at will" merely expresses that relation, the priority of operative habit—from whose article the phrase comes. By giving a power a determinate, settled disposition, habit enables that power to act "when we will" (*cum voluerit*): enabling it both to complete its particular operation and do so with ease. Possessed of *scientia*, Jane's mind is economically primed. She does not have to try to recall various economic principles and theories or struggle to apply them. Literally, without thinking twice, she begins her analysis. Habit transforms subject into a hair-trigger, fully formed capacity for determinate operation, making operation "at will" not only by giving it a hair trigger but by determining and setting its whole course. It renders operation easy to complete, not just to begin: Jane doesn't merely spring into analysis but carries it through—not getting stuck at the harder parts or struggling to figure out what comes next. Or take Michael Phelps's swimming habit: he does not dive into the water at will only, halfway through, to slow down and have to think, "Okay, so it's stroke, stroke, stroke, *then* breathe."[40] Habit enables one to *operate* at will, not just to *begin* to do so.

"The soul," Thomas says, "is principle of operation through its powers . . . [and] habits are in the soul according to its powers" (I.II 50.2). All of a creature's operations, from walking to willing, are traceable to the soul as principle. For operations "not determined to one," those requiring habit's perfection, soul is readied for action by habits of those powers (I.II 50.1). Such habits enable soul to function more perfectly as principle of all the creature's operations. Thomas is not suggesting that the will is the subject of every operative habit: intellectual habit is subjected in intellect, for instance; the bad habit of gluttony in sensitive appetite. Jane's intellect is ready-at-hand for economics and the glutton's appetite is at the ready to crave too much food and to help propel him to decide to eat it.[41] Absent habits, action is stunted: it may get under way and even reach completion, but not with habit's ease.

Habits are not just that by which *subject* is readied to operate, but that by which *agents* are. Bringing the distinctively human more fully into view, we turn then to the "at will" character of habit relative to the use of oneself that will and its habits effect. Above we described habits as hair triggers, here we liken them to trigger fingers. Will is one power of the soul among many, but it plays a special role in regard to habit: "From the very *ratio* of habit insofar as habit is that which one uses at will—it is evident that it is principally related to will" (I.II 50.5). As a rational power, not fully determined to some particular good among all that intellect can grasp as good, will needs habit to orient it to some sort of fixed good (I.II 50.5 and ad 3; 51.3). But this does not explain will and habit's special relation, for in needing a habit due to its indeterminateness will stands with all subjects. Will's special relation to habit stems, rather, from will's special relation, among the powers, to operation. Will alone is the efficient cause of the exercise of any of those habit-bearing powers, insofar as they can obey reason's command.[42] *Usus* is Thomas's term for will's special operation whereby it causes other powers to execute their operations. In use, Stephen Brock explains, "one applies his power *over* that power to an operation, namely the operation of using that power. His power *over* that power is a power of his will; it is precisely his power to use the other power. If he did not have this, his use of the other power would not constitute a genuine control of it."[43] While will's use executes (and is thus subject to) reason's command about what to do, that reason even operates to issue a command is itself thanks to will's using it.[44] As efficient cause of any habit-bearing subject's operation (*qua* piece of human action), will has a special relation to operation. Will is that whereby the soul uses itself and any of its powers that can be subject to reason's command. And will alone, among the powers, is able to *use* itself—having its own use in its power.[45]

Given habit's essential relation to operation, one can see why Thomas would say that habit by its very nature is principally related to will—that whereby reason-grounded operation is efficiently caused in the soul.[46] It seems clearest that this is what Thomas has in mind when he considers how some—especially tamed—animals seem to possess habits, dispositions hard to change and not strictly natural: the horse bears a rider; the lion lets Bozo put his head in her mouth. Granting that these dispositions are habit-like, Thomas's insistence that they are not genuine habits is instructive: "[animals] do not have that dominion over *using* or *not using*, which seems to pertain to the *ratio* of habit; and therefore properly speaking they can have no habit" (I.II 50.3 ad 2). It is *use* that Thomas says is missing in these quasi-habits, that keeps them from being true habits.

Usus is an act of the will whereby a person orders something to some end, puts something to use for the sake of some end. So, Lance uses a bike by riding it to win a race or visit his aunt. Yet it might still seem that tamed animals have use of their apparent habits: Tucker the terrier knows various tricks, and, sometimes, does a trick for a treat. Has not Tucker the power to *use* this trick? Has not Tucker habit?[47] He does not because *usus* demands a capacity for reflectivity that Thomas believes dogs and other animals lack, one that involves knowing some end *as end*, some means *as means*, and the relation between the two. Tucker lacks not only this but the capacity for the most basic use of all—use of himself. Tucker cannot ordain *himself* to any ends; his ends are just given by his nature. That and how he seeks a treat is not a matter of his *conducting* himself, choosing among means, but of circumstance and appetite. For Tucker to use himself, he would have to have some hand in determining his ends. Instead, he is ordained to them apart from *any* self-determination; they are given by nature and instinct. Putting something else to use requires that one first be able to put oneself to use—to put oneself to use in using it. But putting oneself to use is not just a matter of *moving* oneself, responding to stimuli, or even pursuing something desired, but of actually *ordering* oneself to an end.

Certainly, Tucker moves himself: runs to get food, pees to mark territory. His doing tricks for treats is not (relevantly) different. In doing such things, he does not *use* himself. That he moves is not explained by any self-ordering on his part, but by instincts, training, and circumstance. When it comes to his ends and how he gets them, he is *moved* rather than *mover*, *used* rather than *user*.[48] As Thomas puts it, "through desiring the end by natural instinct, [animals] are *moved* to the end—*moved* as if by another" (I.II 12.5 ad 3). As principle, end helps determine action's course. Lacking any mastery of their ends, animals are used and determined *by those ends*—whatever movement they may elicit. In having a role in determining their ends, some power to ordain themselves to one or another end, humans have the capacity to be, to some extent, masters of their actions, selves, and habits, the capacity to use themselves and any habits they might have. This is what Thomas has in mind in declaring habits essentially rational and saying they enable action at will.

Whatever we think of his account, in claiming that habit is principally related to will, Thomas stresses genuine habit's reason-laden character. Where there is habit, there is will. And where there is will, there is reason. Genuine habit, therefore, necessarily involves reason or participation in reason (I.II 55.4 ad 3). A power that does not participate in reason cannot bear operative habit. Thanks to the indeterminateness and openness to use it has due to its share in reason, appetite can be so habituated that it tracks someone's considered food-related judgments. Her hunger, sealed with reason's stamp, embodies reason's verdict about what is good to eat. It is essential, then, to habit's *ratio* that it be subject to reason's command and will's use.

Bodily habits, in contrast, are not so subject. Will uses the body and is responsible for many of its movements, but it does not directly use or move body in respect to its relation to form. It can impact bodily habits, but only mediately—by using the body *operationally*. Will's relation to bodily habit always depends on its using the power of movement. It cannot immediately operate or use the subject within which health resides, for that subject is the body—not *qua* instrument of movement but *qua* matter to soul's form. By willing (the body) to exercise, it indirectly helps instill health; by willing (the body) to visit a surgeon, beauty. But it cannot simply will health or beauty—only the operations that help bring those things about, for those habits are subject to will only indirectly, insofar as will *moves* the body, uses it as instrument of movement.[49] Use is not identical to the capacity to have an effect on something or bring something about. One can cut off an arm and thereby destroy health—quite an effect. But in cutting off the arm, one is not *using* a habit of health or any other bodily habit. One is using one's power of movement to destroy a subject and habit inherently beyond will's use. If one could destroy health by using the body *qua* subject of bodily habit, why go to the trouble of cutting off the arm? If health were within will's power of use, no one would need to go to the gym—it would be enough to will health as we move an arm, answer a call, or finish a section.

Habit's Evidence

Because habit enables us to act at will, our habits become visible in what we do (or try to do) and how we do it. Action from habit is marked by a certain ease or pleasure. Sometimes, this is only relative: the courageous protester may not *enjoy* the life-endangering march, but she finds it less difficult than the rest of us. In less extreme contexts, however, one of habit's key markers is its facilitating not only ease *of*—but ease *in*—action. It conduces to a certain pleasure and ease in the performance of habit-related actions. As a kind of second nature, habit brings to actions that are not strictly natural at least the comfort and often the pleasure associated with well-functioning natural actions, like sleeping or even relieving oneself.

Thus, the measure of gluttony as a habit is gauged not just by how much or how unhealthy the food but the ease with which the glutton eats and the pleasure he finds in doing so. Or a geometrician finds a certain pleasure in running through the proofs—not the satisfaction of seeing it all work out, which even the habit-less person can get—but a certain ease in the naturalness with which the work is done. Likewise, while the glutton takes pleasure in the food itself, the key pleasure in gauging the habit is in the *ease* of the over-consumption, the way it "feels so right." There was once a time, we can imagine, when the glutton *struggled* to finish the cobbler—he enjoyed every last bite, but the eating was work. To the extent that those days are but a memory, he has the habit. This "feel" of habit is perhaps more readily recognized in its absence. Think of the care-laden attention of the not-quite-but-nearly-fluent speaker: she knows the language and can express what she wants, even quickly, but not with the utterly unselfconscious effortlessness of fluency, of habit.[50]

The Significance—and Danger—of "Natural Virtue"

We have spoken about the way in which habit presupposes an initial, incomplete orientation that it perfects. "Habit," Thomas reminds, "is to power as complete to incomplete" (I.II 50.2 ad 3). In the case of the habit of virtue, this initial inclination is natural virtue or *virtus inchoata* (I.II 63.1).[51] Natural virtue is just that initial incomplete orientation of a power that virtue completes, what it presupposes and works upon (I.II 50.5 ad 1 and ad 3). At I.II 51.1, Thomas asks whether any habits are in us *a natura*, from nature. The notion seems contrary to habit's very *ratio*, let alone virtue's. As expected, Thomas says there are no habits in human beings *a natura*. But he also goes on to draw quite a few distinctions.

No habits are in us, Thomas says, *entirely* (*totaliter*) *a natura*, but we must clarify what is meant by "from nature," or "*a natura*," and "habit." Proceeding, he distinguishes first between something being *a natura*: (1) *specifically* (*secundum naturam speciei*), that is *a natura* with respect to the nature of the *species*; and (2) *individually*, that is with respect to the nature of the *individual* member of that species. Thomas illustrates: human risibility is *a natura specifically*—it flows from the very nature of the species; it is *a natura individually* that one person is more prone to health or illness (or laughter) than another. The former is a function of the human soul as possessed by any human; the latter a function of the particular body-soul union that constitutes some person as the particular person she is. Thomas further distinguishes between the possibility of something being: (A) *entirely a natura*; and (B) *partly a natura*. For example, someone who is healed of sickness entirely by himself has a habit of health *entirely a natura* because his nature has disposed him well. Another who is healed only with the help of medicine has his health partly *a natura* and partly from an external principle, the medicine—thus his habit of health is *partly a natura*. Or, we might imagine two movie stars: one has his beauty just naturally; the other with help of syringe and knife. This distinction between (A) and (B) can be made with respect to both (1) and (2), so that, for example, someone could be risible thanks to his nature as a human (*a natura specifically*) but, especially risible, thanks to his habit of spending most days tripped up on nitrous oxide. Risibility is not, in itself, a habit, but this guy's risibility is (B) partly from his (1) natural species.

The sort of habits that centrally concern us, *moral* virtues, are all either subjected in will, the rational *appetitive* power, or possessed by their subjects in virtue of the relationship their subjects have to the will.[52] None of these habits, Thomas insists, no habits of the *appetitive* powers, are *a natura specifically*, even in part or "according to their beginning" (*secundum inchoationem naturalis*). No moral virtue is present in a person from her specific nature, and, properly speaking, from specific nature there is not even a *beginning* of the virtue. That is not to say that there are no *inclinations* due to specific nature—there must be lest the human form not specify a *human*. However, whatever inclination specific nature effects is no part of any habit's or virtue's substance. In the case of moral virtues, what specific nature contributes is only the initial underdetermined inclination that habit perfects. And this, he says, is no part of habit itself.

Thomas actually notes that we might be tempted to think that there *would* be a beginning of virtue thanks to specific nature—and immediately rejects that possibility. There are in the soul naturally known principles, the principles of the common or natural law, whereby we are naturally *inclined*, albeit in the most general way, to goods genuinely perfective of our nature—things like life, bodily integrity, knowledge, friendship, and so on. Such principles, he notes, "are said to be seeds of virtue" (*dicuntur esse seminalia virtutum*) (I.II 51.1). And insofar as these principles incline their subjects to ends and operations proper (*propria*) to them, it could *seem* (*videtur*) that they are beginnings and thus parts of habits. Yet this, he says, must be rejected: these inclinations do not properly belong to habits. They belong, rather, to the powers, the appetites, that are subjects of these habits. In fact, these inclinations pertain to the very *ratio* of the powers (*pertinet ad ipsam rationem potentiarum*). They are precisely those profoundly underdetermined, insufficiently narrow inclinations that habits work to perfect. And they are called seeds of virtue not because they are themselves part of virtue, so that in possessing them one has some share in virtue. (In possessing them one has a share in *humanity*.) Rather, they are so called because they are those indeterminately disposed inclinations that habits perfect and determinately orient and that virtues perfect well.[53]

In this sense, Thomas rejects the possibility of appetitive habit or moral virtue present *specifically a natura*, even in part. These inclinations help constitute humans *as* humans; that they are not themselves habits or virtues helps explain how and why humans differ from other animals: humans have the capacity and obligation to orient their appetites so that they use themselves *well, virtuously*. A human must give herself a habit to make herself good. Specific nature and its inclinations are the field that make us human and virtue possible. And this possibility of using oneself well, becoming virtuous, belongs to *every* human just in virtue—and precisely because—of her nature.

When Thomas considers the possibility of an appetitive habit being in humans *a natura individually*, he reaches an importantly different conclusion. In the soul/matter union that is a given individual, due to variations in that body's relation to soul, a person *can* have a habit's beginning insofar as, by natural temperament, some dimension of her appetitive power is naturally more or less submissive to reason. Appetitive habits have to do with the ways in which various appetitive powers are disposed in relation to reason's judgment mediated by will. The appetitive powers are by nature somewhat obedient to reason, but precisely *how* obedient they are prior to training has to do with their particular strength or weaknesses—and this, Thomas says, is a matter of a person's individual nature. Thus a person might have a beginning of the virtue of chastity because his sexual appetite is relatively weak and thus more easily guided by and submissive to reason and therefore more readily trained to a habit of moderation that is a good disposition or virtue for that appetite. Conversely, a person might have the beginning of the corresponding vice, licentiousness, because his sexual appetite is especially strong and harder to submit to reason's rule. In such cases, these beginnings are actually part of the substance of the habits. Why? Because they are not merely insufficiently determinate inclinations that are of the very essence of the subject in which the habit abides, like those that arise from the principles of common law. Instead, they are themselves the beginnings of more determinate dispositions. Further, with the exception of the virtue of legal justice, which involves giving each person her due and thus attains what Thomas calls the "real mean," the moral virtues, habits of the appetitive parts, must attain a "relative mean"—a moderation of appetite appropriate to some person given that person's appetite. So, when Phelps and I buy dinner, legal justice dictates that we pay the amount due: our acts of legal justice will in this respect look identical. Not necessarily so our acts flowing from appetitive moral virtues. At the buffet, the acts produced by Phelps's temperance would be, for me, acts of gluttony; my acts of temperance, insensibility for him. Thus, because the appetitive virtues involve the relative mean, the balance between too little and too much that is appropriate for the perfection of the person whose appetites they are, *and* because some have appetites more easily or difficultly moderated by reason than others, a person can have a real beginning of a virtue from their individual nature—or a real beginning of vice.[54]

Natural virtue, then, is both the vague inclination to true goods common to every soul *and* the particular shape those inclinations take thanks to an individual's body/soul matrix. Call the former "shared natural virtue"; the latter "individual natural virtue." (In I.II 49.2's language, individual natural virtue would stand at (or near) the far end of S-*habit*'s disposition; shared natural virtue would not be on the scale but helps make the scale possible.) While individual natural virtue can be a beginning of habit or virtue, it is still so far from true virtue that Thomas regards it a very dangerous thing. Sam's individual natural virtue involves his having a weak appetite for food, say, and so he could easily cultivate moderation. But thanks to that same individual natural virtue, he may fail to appreciate the joys of a delicious feast with friends. Insensible to these delights, he may come to despise such affairs so that he becomes disdainful of pleasure in general—a prude. Thomas imagines more troubling possibilities: "The natural inclination to the true good is a sort of inclination to virtue but it is not virtue. For the stronger the inclination, the more deadly it can be, unless yoked by right reason, which enables the right choice concerning what is suited to the due end" (I.II 58.4 ad 3). Some are inclined by individual natural virtue to pursue the same truly good ends the virtuous might pursue. But they are not inclined to pursue them in the same *way*, for, among other things, the truly virtuous ensure the justice of their means. Not so the person possessed only of individual natural virtue. And the stronger an individual natural virtue, the more dangerous it may be, for the more intense the pursuit of the end, the more dangerous the neglect of means. Grave injustice looms, for in light of a truly good end a person may choose whatever means ensure its achievement without regard to justice. Thomas compares this person to a galloping, blind horse—a terror to itself and any who falls in its path, "the faster it runs the harder it will crash, the graver it will be wounded" (I.II 58.4 ad 3). So far is natural virtue from virtue.

In his account of natural virtue, Thomas sketches key features of his substantial but broad conception of human nature, what he believes all humans share. We share a capacity and need to make ourselves what and who we will be. There are certain very general inclinations for food, friendship, knowledge, and so on. They are not determined to a single fulfillment, but open, capable of diverse satisfaction. This openness is chiefly manifest in one of the most important things we share: a capacity to consider and pursue things as *good*. A capacity to *will*. We cannot avoid a certain commonality of freedom: pursuing much of what we do because we believe it worth pursuing. These commonalities predict, and indeed, demand the presence of habits across time and culture representing efforts to make our pursuit of what we believe choiceworthy more efficient, more successful. Humans, he believes, cannot get by without habit. His account of natural virtue requires that he expect to find habits and at least some virtues wherever there are people. For, wherever there are people, they are individually and communally pursuing what they believe to be good and using the "tools" of habits to do so. Corresponding to the various capacities humans have for relating to and desiring good and the characteristic difficulties that attend human life and the pursuit of diverse notions of flourishing, he expects to find habits belonging to each of those capacities—habits for coping with the difficulties each capacity faces. Even if such virtues remain unnamed, implicit, or undistinguished, there will be a virtue like justice governing a person's life in community and coordinating her own desire for the good with that of others; a virtue like courage dealing with a person's capacities for anger and fear, the passions she has when pursuit of the good is difficult; a virtue like moderation concerning desire for sensible pleasures—food, sex, and so on; and a virtue like prudence concerned with choosing well with respect to what she does and how she does it, how she conducts herself.

Yet, the selfsame account that leads Thomas to anticipate very broad commonalities in the habits human cultivate in pursuit of the good and in virtues, those habits that are excellent, leads him also to expect a great diversity of habits and virtues within and across cultures. For the very openness that makes virtues necessary entails the possibility of diversity. The natural virtues are so open-ended that they admit of an incredibly wide array of good and bad completions. Different cultures, places, and times will produce different virtues, different ways of perfecting the natural virtues in the face of different challenges and priorities. His expectation of difference prepares him to welcome the unfamiliar habit, to consider whether it might represent a more excellent perfection than he had previously imagined. One can even read Thomas's distinction between natural and human law as a variation on this theme (I.II 91.2 and 3).

In Thomas's account of natural virtue, we can also see an outworking of his vision unfolded in chapter 2: natural virtues represent one way in which God is drawing humans to himself. Through the natural virtues, Thomas believes, a human is *in via* to God. That which makes humans *human* is also that by which they are on their way Godward. In Trinitarian terms, Word's pattern and Spirit's impulsion are two faces of a single dynamic leading humans to the Father. The way in which humans are on their way helps constitute them *as* humans. That way is one in which a person's further or lesser participation in God is, in many respects, up to her. The natural virtues facilitate a choice: participate more or less fully in God by habituating oneself more or less well. Humanity and God are not in competition so that more participation in God comes at freedom's expense. Rather, in perfecting oneself through virtue, one participates more fully in God. As one becomes more oneself, the best version of oneself, one becomes, Thomas contends, more deeply God's.

Augustinian Infused Virtue as Aristotelian Habit

Thomas's conception of natural virtue helps ground a distinction between human and infused virtue, virtue attainable by outsiders and virtue dependent on an infusion of grace. The human virtues are, in principle, attainable without charity by everyone because they perfect and are founded on the natural virtues. For Thomas, it is entirely possible that some or even many outsiders are, with respect to this kind of virtue, more virtuous than many Christians, many who have grace. In contrast, the virtues exclusive to Christians, infused virtues, are caused solely by God's grace and are not rooted in natural virtue. They are an entirely different species of virtue from those virtues Christian and non-Christian can share (I.II 63.4).[55] Due entirely to grace, the virtue that distinguishes Christian from pagans is one for which the Christian deserves—and should see herself as deserving—no praise. It leaves no room for pride.

In closing, we can note that it is Thomas's account of habit and natural virtue that explains how something not acquired by habituation could nonetheless be a habit, how an *infused* virtue is no less a virtue, no less a habit. This account enables Thomas to vindicate Augustinian infused virtue as Aristotelian habit. It shows him, once again, being Augustinian by being Aristotelian and vice versa. An operative habit's subject must be the sort of power that Thomas, following Aristotle, calls a "moved mover": "mover" in respect of its being a power, having some proper operation; "moved" in respect of its depending on some principle more active than itself in order for it to commence its operation (I.II 51.2 and ad 1 and 3; 51.3). The active moving principle need not be the will, for while these powers require will for their *use* (which is distinct from their *operating*), that is not the sense in which they are *moved* movers. As patient or object of will's use they are like those powers that are not *moved* movers but simply *movers*. The intellect, for example, is a moved mover: it is a power and can be the subject of a habit, *scientia*, but intellect's operation of reasoning about conclusions, working out demonstrations, and so on requires "an active principle in a self-evidently true proposition" (I.II 51.2). Intellect's proper work depends on an active principle—a self-evident proposition—neither its own nor self-generated. That active principle, by which it is *moved*, enables its operation—its *movement*. As demanding an "external" principle for its proper operation, it is moved; as power, as having such an operation, mover. Will can "try" all it wants to use intellect to enact some operation, but absent the self-evident proposition, intellect is powerless to execute it.

Consider habit's cause—since habit is necessarily subjected in a moved mover. The features of an operative habit's *subject* are inextricably tied to the way in which that subject's habit is caused: a subject must be passive in order to *receive* a habit; but must be a power, a mover, for the habit received to be *operative*. Habit perfects or fully *actualizes* its subject, bringing it from potentiality to greater actuality. Habit acquisition, then, is a process in which subject is passive with respect to some shaping it undergoes (even if this shaping occurs as it moves, since this moving itself depends on the subject's first being moved). Subject is somehow *shaped* or *disposed*: moved from potentially to actually *shaped*, indeterminately to determinately *disposed*. And, because habit gives some power actuality, perfection that, by definition, it does not have of its own nature, there must be some principle other than the power—something more perfect and actual than it—from whence shaping (and the greater actuality) comes. There must be a shaper. From *whence* this shaping comes is inessential;

only it must be an external, active principle—something which can shape the power, overcome its "actuality deficit."

The aspect of the power that is *already* in act, that by which it is a *mover*, passes on, as it were, the external principle's higher degree of actuality: passes it on to that which power is and has as *moved*. Thus in the exercise of the power enabled by the more perfect principle, the power becomes more and more actual than it is just in itself. An excess of actuality, so to speak, flows through that part of the power that is already in act, already a principle, to actual*ize* that aspect of the power that is still wanting in actuality, capable of being shaped. The power cannot be perfected in respect of that part of it which is *mover*, in which it is *already* perfected by its nature as a power. Nonetheless, in respect of that part of it which *remains* in potential it can be transformed. Habit is that transformed reality.

Hence Thomas's explanation: "insofar as the power moves by being moved by another, it receives something from the moving, [from what moves it]: and thus is a habit caused" (I.II 51.2 ad 1). The "something received" is that whereby the power's imperfection, its incapacity to shape itself, is overcome. "A habit," Thomas sums up, "is generated by act inasmuch as a passive power is moved by some active principle" (I.II 51.3). All of these types then are essential in any habit's story: the in-some-way-rational-and-submissive-to-will subject that is both moved and mover in need of shaping it cannot give itself; the stronger more active type able to give such shaping; and the sooner-or-later product of their union, habit. The essential point in all this is that on Thomas's formulation of this Aristotelian account, the active, habit-causing principle need not be a "natural" active principle: it may be will or a self-evident proposition, but it may be God himself. Only it must be more actual than the passive power it habituates, more in movement than the moved mover it moves. This is why infused virtues, those effected by God, are not strange creatures for Thomas. They are not, for him, missing *any* of what is essential for habit but achieve the *ratio* of habit perfectly well from the start. The virtues that God gives are, for Thomas, paradigmatic with respect to the essential *ratio* of habit and the essential *ratio* of virtue. But fully to grasp that last point requires us to see just what virtue's essential *ratio* is. And before we talk of virtues given by God, we must speak of virtues acquired by women and men.

4 PAGAN VIRTUE:
Perfect, Unified, and True

QUESTION I.II 55 begins Thomas's explicit treatment of virtue in the *Summa*; this chapter begins ours. From 55 through 61's penultimate article, Thomas treats "human virtue," virtue as "proportioned to human nature" (*secundum conditionem suae naturae*) (I.II 61.5).[1] All these articles—and their generic talk of virtue—concern it, whatever else they additionally encompass. Building on the preceding chapter's account of habit, our initial task is to grasp Thomas's conception of human virtue, which, for now, following Thomas, we can simply call "virtue" (I.II 61.1). More fundamentally, though, this chapter begins to make the case for understanding Thomas as welcoming pagan virtue as true, unified, and—in a vital sense—perfect. A number of his readers have claimed that Thomas regards pagan virtue as true but disconnected. For these interpreters, pagan virtues are unstable, easily thwarted propensities to do good in relatively, even extremely, narrow domains. This chapter shows such "virtue" to be a mere shadow of what Thomas envisions and their reading to be conceptually and exegetically unsustainable. Unity, it turns out, is essential to Thomas's very conception of virtue.

Early in the virtue treatise, Thomas distinguishes between moral and intellectual virtue. Though both are types of virtue, with Thomas, our primary interest is in moral virtue—and this for three reasons (I.II 58.1–3). First, as a function of our topic, which has to do not with the uncontroversial capacity of pagans to possess intellectual virtues, like logic or astronomy, but to attain moral virtues, like justice and courage. We want to know whether pagans can be good; not whether they can be fine mathematicians or excellent cooks. Secondly, for Thomas, moral virtues answer more perfectly to the very idea or *ratio* of virtue than do intellectual virtues. As we will see, moral virtues are virtues *simpliciter*; intellectual virtues, save those specially related to will, are not (I.II 56.3). Finally, Thomas himself devotes far more attention to moral than intellectual virtues.

Still, grasping Thomas's conception of moral virtue requires distinguishing it from intellectual virtue and understanding how and why it attains the *ratio* of virtue more perfectly. Indeed, prudence itself, reckoned chief among moral virtues, is properly an intellectual virtue (I.II 58.3 ad 1; II.II 56.1 ad 1).[2] So, what is a moral virtue?

Virtues: Good Operative Habits

In one sense, we already know, for virtues are, first and foremost, habits. Recall how Thomas places this at the fore: it not only occupies him in the virtue treatise's *prooemium*, but the treatise's first three articles elucidate virtue in terms of habit (I.II 55.1–3). Even in 55's final article—his treatment of Augustine's definition of virtue and the only article not centrally focused on habit—habit manifests itself. Where Augustine says virtue is a good *quality* of the soul, Thomas insists, "it would have been better if he had said *habit*" (I.II 55.4). So, a virtue is a habit, namely a good operative habit (I.II 55.2 and 3). That it must be an operative habit is unsurprising: in view of their resistance to change and their connection to will's *usus*—their enabling action at will—only operative habits perfectly attain habit's *ratio*. Were it otherwise, virtue would fail to be a habit most completely. Virtue is an operative habit because it is concerned with humans as agents, creatures who have their own use in their power.

Pointing to the etymology of the Latin *virtus*, Thomas reminds us of its roots in notions of manhood, strength, and might (I.II 55.2). While he notes that bodily habits of health and beauty answer in their own ways to such notions of strength, his interest, he reminds us, is in *human* virtue and thus the distinctively human. Humans are unique among animals in that they can possess operative habits due to the human soul's rational powers (I.II 55.2 and ad 2). Thus, a concern with human virtue—with human power for action and, especially, human self-use—cannot but be a concern with operative habits. Virtue, then, facilitates and is a principle of human operations or actions (I.II 55.2 and ad 1–3). As a habit, it is an ordered disposition related to its subject's nature—in this case, a nature fulfilled in operation (I.II 55.2 ad 2).

"Virtue," Thomas explains citing Aristotle, "is that which makes the person who possesses it good and renders his activity good too" (I.II 56.3; 55.2). In other words, virtue is a *good* operative habit (I.II 55.3). It is the sort of operative habit that disposes its subject *well*, fittingly in relation to its nature's particular operation. Specifically, it is a perfection or completion of an insufficiently determinate human power—both in the sense that strictly every habit is a perfection and in the narrower sense in which only a good habit is, by *well* perfecting its subject.[3] As a good *operative* habit, its goodness has to do with its being well suited to its immediate subject's nature and, since that nature is a power of the soul, its being well suited to the operation particular to that power. Ultimately, what counts as well suited to some power's operation is a matter of the creature's nature and the relation between the power and the creature's end. Thus, from the operation that constitutes a human's end we know what counts as a *good* habit of some power: for example, since the this-worldly human end involves eating, a good operative habit of the sensitive appetite disposes that appetite so that its hunger tracks the agent's right judgment about what is good to eat. This habit relates the power well to its (and its creature's) nature: to desire food perfective of humans. An operative habit is good insofar as it disposes its power well vis-à-vis that power's own nature, and a power is well disposed to its nature insofar as it is well disposed to the creature whose power it is. This remains abstract; a comparative glance at intellectual virtue offers clarity.

Moral Virtue, or What Intellectual Virtue Is Not

The intellectual virtue of *scientia* perfects a power, the intellect. Moreover, it is a good habit for it disposes the mind to know certain nonpractical truths and knowing such truths is part of what intellect is for, something that suits it well in relation to the human (I.II 56.3 ad 2; *DV* 7). Indeed, the sort of knowing the virtue of *scientia* enables is central to humanity's end. Art, for its part, is a non-speculative intellectual virtue distinguished by its concern with *making*—from the production of artifacts and athletic and artistic performances to activities like typing, farming, or doctoring (I.II 57.3 and 4).[4] It renders such "makings" good (I.II 57.3). If we left off here, we might think *scientia* or other intellectual virtues answer fully to the *ratio* of virtue, that they "make both a person and his activity good." But consider two essential points.

MORAL VIRTUE MAKES A PERSON *ACT* . . .

First, the intellect depends on will's *usus* for its contribution to human action.[5] Having a geometric *scientia*, for instance, means that one is disposed to operate well intellectually in the sense that one knows geometric first principles and can correctly and quickly run through various proofs. Yet it is perfectly compatible with having this or any other *scientia* that one not use it: instead, one ponders where to eat, not thinking geometrically or speculatively at all. Or one could think speculatively but non-geometrically by considering Boolean algebra, say, or Arabic verbal forms. It is also compatible with having (and even using) this *scientia* that one think about geometry in intentionally incorrect or amusing ways—perhaps writing deliberately fallacious proofs for kicks.[6] Nothing proper to geometric *scientia* or any intellectual virtue rules out such possibilities or makes them less (or more) likely.

Indeed, in itself, nothing intrinsic to intellectual virtue makes it any more or less likely that one will use it or use it well.[7] Rather, this depends on one's will: whether and how one *wills* to use it. Thus, even as they enable production of things like proofs and paintings that, considered in themselves, are good, intellectual virtues (aside from faith and prudence, which each have different sorts of relations to the will) are not entirely *good* habits. They are not because they lack an orientation to their own use. Simply having them does nothing to incline one to use them well (as opposed to comically, sloppily, intentionally badly, etc.) or to use them at all.[8] They fail to make one's work anything more than *potentially* good: good, provided one chooses to use them and use them well. That is a not a matter of ability alone but of desire, will, and love. And intellectual virtues do not bear on love.

Consider the student who easily scores perfectly on every geometry test. She has the science. But her having it does not in itself, in its capacity as *habit* and so principle of intellect's movement, involve or entail her wanting to exercise it.[9] If it did, she would necessarily find herself more inclined to use it the more she had it, the better she knew geometry. Instead, as class progresses, the better she knows it the more she *hates* it, the *less* she wants to use it.[10] We can even imagine her beginning the class with enthusiasm but coming to despise geometry, her desire to do it decreasing in proportion to her mastery. Getting her A+, she burns the textbook and swears off geometry for life. But, for all this, purely in virtue of her hatred she does not have the *scientia* any less—any less than if she loved geometry.[11] Inclination to its use varies independently from its possession.[12] While teachers might wish it otherwise, having an intellectual habit does not incline one to the *love* of truth that would make one want to engage in *scientia*. *Scientia* and other intellectual virtues involve an aptness to act well *provided one chooses to so act*.[13] This is not the same as an aptness actually to act (or act well)—an aptness not only to act in some way *provided* one chooses to act but an aptness *to choose to act in that way*.

Admittedly, this seems counterintuitive. Many of us have tried something new, not liked it at first, and then found ourselves liking it more the better we got at it, the more we had the habit. This happens often enough that it could seem that our acquisition and mastery of the habit are directly and essentially connected to our love for its use, that in itself the habit does involve our desire to use it. But note several points. First, we must disentangle the improvement or habit acquisition from our love or desire to put the habit to use. The possession of a habit does bring a pleasure of performance to the act that is lacking prior to habit's presence. So, there is a pleasure to dancing or doing algebra habitually that is absent prior to the habit, but that pleasure itself may or may not be something we love or that inclines us to put the habit to use. Imagine someone who, solely in order to qualify herself for an elite MI6 position, after years of training becomes an excellent skier. Thanks to her habituation, she now finds a pleasure in the act of skiing that she did not before. Where once it was laborious, even painful, it now comes with the pleasant, unselfconscious ease of natural activity. But for all that, whether she loves or even likes to *ski* (or the attendant feeling of naturalness) is a separate matter. Perhaps she hates it, despising its distinctive feel, its rhythm and sound, everything about it. Conversely, the worst skier may well be the one who loves and finds the most pleasure in *skiing*—even as he lacks the pleasure associated with skiing even half-decently, much less habit's natural ease. That ease of action which habit enables is not the same pleasure as finding *joy* in the action itself, as *loving* it. It is not even the same thing as finding joy in the ease of action peculiar to habit—much less being motivated to perform the action by it.

If we think otherwise, we are probably confusing the background pleasure that just doing the action habitually enables (or the experience of that pleasure) with loving the *activity* habit enables (or, a different matter still, loving the pleasurable ease enabled by the action's status as habitual).[14] Most simply, the distinction is one between the act itself and the ease with which it is done. Experiencing the pleasure habit in particular enables is not identical to taking pleasure in or liking the *action* or *operation* itself, for the pleasure peculiar to habit is (at least) the pleasure of the *ease* with which the action is performed. That ease which habit brings in distinction from less expert performance may or may not factor into whether a person loves the *action*. Presumably many people who work an assembly line develop habits that enable them to do with ease actions that were at first difficult or even painful—willy-nilly, they experience this ease and so, a kind of pleasure, when they do the action. Knowing that this is

the case tells us nothing about whether such a person loves to do those activities, whether they like doing the action—or for that matter whether they even
like the ease with which they do it. Perhaps a janitor cleans toilets with ease
thanks to his toilet-cleaning habit—and, regarding the work as degrading, he
feels anger and shame at the ease with which he does it. He takes no pleasure in
the pleasure; he despises it.

In sum, when it comes to intellectual virtues, being good, even excellent at
something has no *intrinsic* connection to liking or wanting to do that thing.
The best flutist, tennis champion, or logician may despise playing the flute, hit-
ting volleys, or doing proofs—even though, thanks to their habits, they find a
pleasurable ease in those activities that eludes the rest of us. While that pleasure
can become a reason for them to perform the activity, its doing so depends,
among other things, on their taking pleasure in that pleasure, their regarding
it as desirable.[15] Many are the children trained to be expert violinists, soccer
players, or competitive spellers who eventually hate the activities in which they
so excel. The phenomenon of the "burnout" testifies to Thomas's point. While
some "burnouts" become so because of extrinsic factors—think of the cliché
sports movie where the protagonist needs to escape from the spotlight and return to the game's "pure" form—surely many "burnouts" have actually come
to hate even the "purest" form of the activity. The thought of one more swing
makes them feel sick. Conversely, many love such activities, but never attain the
excellence or attendant pleasure that habit brings—loving and taking pleasure
in actions that they do poorly or painfully. Intellectual virtues do nothing in
themselves to incline a person to put them to use or use them well. While intellectual virtues may supply us with new *objects* or *candidates* of love, they do not
effect desire for those objects or for their own use. Insofar as they are principles
at all, they are principles of the act that they enable *when will commands them.*[16]

In contrast, consider a moral virtue, justice. While the just person has a capacity or faculty (*facultatem*) to act justly as the scientific or artistic person has
a faculty to think scientifically or act artistically, unlike either, the just person,
precisely by her habit of justice, is inclined to act according to justice, to *use* the
capacity. This wedding of capacity with inclination distinguishes moral from
intellectual virtue. Justice or any other moral virtue is not merely a disposition
to act justly or virtuously *provided one choose to do so*, but, as well, a disposition
to *choose to do so* (I.II 56.3). It seeks to make itself principle. Both moral and
intellectual virtues give a person the faculty to act in a certain way, but only
moral virtues incline one to use that faculty—and use it well.

. . . AND ACT *WELL*

Secondly, moral virtues not only incline to their own use, they incline to their own *good* use—they cause a person to choose *and* "choose aright," to *do* good and do *good* (I.II 58.1 ad 2). Drawing from part of Augustine's definition of virtue—"no on can use [virtue] for evil (*nullus male utitur*)"—Thomas explains that only habits that can be used exclusively for good count as virtues (I.II 55.4). While one can make bad use of virtue "insofar as it is taken as an object," say, if one is proud of one's virtue, in such cases, the virtue is not a *principle* of action (I.II 55.4 ad 5). What Thomas means is that "virtue cannot be a principle of bad *usus* so that an act of virtue be evil." It can only and always be put to good use, never to evil use.

We'll elucidate the point further, but for now, contrast this with an intellectual virtue.[17] Say Jane is engaged in an economic science, using her habit as a principle of operation. Is she doing good or evil? It depends. If she is using the habit to intimidate her insecure graduate student with her mastery of the discipline or when she should be nursing her dying friend, she is using it evilly. In contrast, as principles of action, moral virtues cannot be used evilly. They produce exclusively good action.

On the one hand, the point is stipulative. Virtue just is a habit inclining one exclusively to good and incapable of evil use. On the other hand, it is diagnostic. Where someone might appear to exercise a virtue—say, because of her ease in facing dangers of death—she does not have (or is not using) the virtue if that action is ordered to evil or in any way fails to be good.[18] Courage, for instance, is not in use when one risks death to commit adultery or fraud; nor when one pursues a good end in a gratuitously or unnecessarily dangerous way. Whatever habit impels me to run through the fire to rescue a child when I can save him just as well by going around the back where the flames are absent is not courage. In contrast, an intellectual virtue is no less in use by Jane when she uses her economic expertise to oppress the poor than when she uses it to advise an NGO. And, likewise, an intellectual virtue of painting is equally in use when one employs it to make fascist propaganda or to create art for the resistance.[19] Intellectual virtues are *good*—but not *exclusively* good—habits. They can as readily be put to evil as to good use. In contrast, "Virtue makes one act well, not just merely have the capacity (*facultate*) to act well" (I.II 56.3). Justice, for instance, is an inclination to *will* and will *justly*.

Thomas's distinction between the different formal and material objects of intellectual and moral virtues clarifies further. Intellectual virtues are directed to some good materially: they have truly good things—like truth or knowl-edge—as their proper matter. That is why they count, in a limited way, as good habits, virtues. Formally, however, intellectual virtues do not regard their mate-rially good objects as *desirable* or *good* but as *true*. They do not relate or order one to their object in terms of *desire* but *knowledge*. They cannot: intellectual virtue is ordered intellect not ordered desire, capacity to know the truth, not inclination to seek it. A relation to truth or anything else as good, as desirable, is the work of will.

Intellect and will and their respective habits can even have the same *material* object, for example, truth. But they relate to it under different "formalities": rational appetite or will relates to its material objects under the formality of *goodness*; speculative intellect under the formality of *truth* or *knowability*. Stephen Brock makes the point well when, echoing Hegel, he notes that the more we know a thing, the more we know its opposite, what it excludes.[20] In knowing X, intellect relates equally to or knows equally well that which the thing known *excludes*, $\sim X$. The better I know 3; the better I know ~ 3—that 3 is not *red*, *i*, *edible*, and so on. The more intellect knows the one, the more it knows the other. So, the knowing intellect is more intimately related to the known object the more it is related to that which the known object excludes. Indeed, our very effort to elucidate moral virtue has enacted a variation on this theme: distin-guishing moral from intellectual virtue, we come to know it better. Conversely, the more appetite *desires* something—appetite's proper mode of relation—the more it abhors, averts, or disinclines from that thing's negation. More deeply to desire my son's flourishing is necessarily to abhor more deeply his corruption. Yet I more precisely *know* his flourishing the better I understand his corruption, the negation of his flourishing.

Rational appetite relates to the true as something it loves or hates; specula-tive intellect relates to the true as something it knows or does not. Moral and intellectual virtues alike have materially good objects, but moral virtues alone have the good as *formal* object, relating to the materially good object *as* good: desiring *good* (material); and *desiring* good (formal).

"Good according to the *ratio* of good," Thomas explains, "is the object of the *appetitive part* (*appetitivae partis*) alone, for good is that which all things *desire* (*appetunt*)" (DV 7). The linguistic parallel between the adjectival *appe-titivae* (appetitive) and the verb *appetunt* (desire) underlines the connection between appetite and good's *ratio*: appetite (*appetitus*) desires (*appetere*). The very *ratio* of good, recall, is *desirability*; not to know *that* something is desirable, but to relate to it *as* desirable—which one does just by desiring it.[21] Moral virtue alone involves a person in *loving* good, for only appetite, where moral virtue resides, includes "to desire" (*appetere*) among its operations. In *inclining* to the good, moral virtues elicit action; in inclining to the *truly good*, they make one act well.

MORAL VIRTUES MAKE A *PERSON* GOOD

In doing so, they "make a person good and her work good likewise." Intellectual virtues fail to make a *person* good, and, more, their possession is compatible with a person being evil (I.II 56.3; 57.1). The scientist is as likely to be an abuser as a loving parent; the artist as likely to be greedy as generous. Which she will be is a matter not of *intellectual* but *moral* virtue. One is not a good *person*, Thomas says, by being a good artist or scientist—one is just a good *artist* or *scientist*: "Through scientific knowing or artistic expertise, a man is not said to be good *simpliciter* but only good in some respect, according to some qualification (*secundum quid*)—a good grammarian, say, or a good carpenter" (I.II 56.3). In contrast, one is a good *person* by the moral virtues, for they incline to their own necessarily good use. And that good use, in turn, governs the use of any other virtues or habits an agent has. Governing what one does, they thus make a person and her work good. Intellectual virtues and voluntary capacities generally serve at the beck and call of the will and its virtues. The intellectual virtues, Thomas explains, "are not called virtues *simpliciter*, because they do not make activity good—except for granting a certain ability [to do good should one happen to choose to]—nor do they make the person good" (I.II 56.3).

For the virtuous person who acts virtuously, her virtues are in use whenever she uses intellectual virtue or does anything. And even when moral virtue is not in use or possessed, still, behind (or, better, governing) intellectual virtue's act, effecting any human action at all, is an act of will—a sought good, an intended end, a chosen means. Since an act of will effects every human action, we can see why Thomas insists that all human action is moral action, ethically significant.[22] All human action expresses an act of will; it involves a person relating herself to some good. All human action is rooted in *love* (I.II 62.2 ad 3). And in matters of love, it is always fair to ask whether what is loved is worthy of being loved or being loved in that way, to that degree, at that time, for that reason. While intellectual virtues lack a disposition to their use, much less their good use, all desire-related habits are *moral*. Habits of powers other than the will become morally significant thanks to the relation in which they stand to the will and its habits. They find their place and meaning in relation to the moral fabric of someone's life. It is love, as Thomas has it, that makes a person who she is.

These points emerge with special clarity in considering prudence, which our talk of intellectual virtue has mostly excluded. While subjected in reason, prudence's special relation to will makes it different from all other intellectual virtue (I.II 56.3; 58.5). Specifically, prudence, by which one judges about means, as much presupposes will's inclination to a right end for its existence, as *scientia* does first principles (I.II 57.4; 58.5).[23] It thus depends on will uniquely among intellectual virtues, for not just its beginning but its whole operation (I.II 58.5 and ad 3; 58.3; 61.1). And moral virtues equally need prudence: to effect good action and be *good* (I.II 58.2, esp. ad 1 and 4; 58.3; 58.4 and ad 1). Thus, notwithstanding its incapacity to incline to its own good use, prudence both presupposes and, through its relation to will, effects that good use. As perfecting *practical* reason, it makes its possessor and her work good and thus, while properly an intellectual virtue, "count[s] among (*connumeratur*) the moral virtues" (I.II 58.3 ad 1) and "in a certain way is [one]" (I.II 61.1). For simplicity and following Thomas's lead, my references to *moral virtue* below include prudence.

Human Moral Virtue Is Virtue Simply

In all this, we have begun to see both that and why moral virtues—*human* moral virtues—are virtues simply (*virtutes simpliciter*).[24] "Since virtue is that 'which makes the person who possesses it good and renders his activity good too,' these sort of [virtues] are called virtues *simpliciter*" (I.II 56.3).[25] Making possessors and their work good are what moral virtues do.[26] They are virtues *simpliciter*, answering perfectly to virtue's *ratio* (I.II 56. 3 and ad 1 and 3). They do so because they attain Aristotle's definition on which Thomas's first few articles on virtue depend (I.II 55.2 and 3). In relation to Augustine's views too, Thomas affirms human moral virtues as virtues simply: we should understand Augustine's claim that "all virtue is love," he says, as referring to virtue *simply* (I.II 56.3 ad 1). Augustine's remark is true just because it speaks of virtues of the appetitive part and those specially related thereto. Further, contrasting nonmoral to moral virtues, Thomas variously characterizes the former as: "not called virtues simply," "divided against virtue (*contra virtutem dividitur*)" "virtues according to some qualification (*secundum quid*)," "imperfect," and "virtues in a relative sense" (I.II 56.3). Moral virtues, then, are virtues *simply*, virtues in a *nonrelative sense*, virtues *without qualification*. Making one act not just as right reason would dictate but actually *with* right reason's participation, they are, Thomas says, "perfect virtue[s]" (I.II 58.4 ad 3).

This characterization of human moral virtue extends to *De virtutibus quaestio 1*, which aside from his *Ethics* commentary, represents Thomas's most extended treatment of virtue outside the *Summa*. *De virtutibus* describes moral virtues, prudence included, in similar terms: they "have the form of virtue chiefly or above all (*potissime habent rationem virtutis*)" (*DV 7*). "They are," as McInerny translates it, "virtues in the strongest sense."[27] In contrast, nonmoral virtues, "can in *some way* (*aliquo modo*) be called virtues, but not . . . properly as [moral virtues can]." Moral virtues, Thomas continues, "more *perfectly* and *properly* (*perfectius et magis proprie*) have the form of virtue" (*DV 7*). Thomas applies these terms—perfect, proper, simple, unqualified—to moral virtue in characterizing its relation to virtue's very essence.

To be sure, there is a comparative note in some of these remarks, situating moral in relation to intellectual virtue. But that hardly exhausts Thomas's point. Except in God's case, perfection is always relative, Thomas's usage always variable.[28] Ascriptions of perfection always imply completion or actuality, and thus some incompletion or potentiality in respect to which the perfection stands as complete, actual. It is, then, no strike against Thomas's characterization of moral virtue as perfect that it sometimes comes as he compares it to intellectual virtue. That no virtue could be more perfect, true, and unqualified than God's exemplar virtue hardly counts against other types (I.II 61.5). In any case, it is not only in comparison to intellectual virtues but in relation to virtue's *ratio* that Thomas characterizes moral virtues as virtues *simpliciter*. Indeed, just after noting the superiority of "heroic" to human virtue, Thomas declares human virtue to be "virtue *simpliciter*" (*CNE 7.1.10*).[29] Such depictions of human moral virtue are, we'll see, essential to grasping Thomas's understanding of pagan virtue.

By now, we have seen why, for Thomas and us, a focus on virtue leads to a focus on moral virtue. And we have seen Thomas's characterization of human moral virtue as perfect *qua virtue*, virtue "in the strongest sense." Often, Thomas foregrounds this terminology: these virtues are *said to be* (*dicuntur*) or *called* (*dicit*) virtues simply (I.II 56.3 ad 1 and 3). His diction demands attention. Thomas uses this language to make explicit his awareness of the usage governing these terms, that he believes these terms matter, and, most importantly, that, here at least, he is deliberately adopting such usage. Far from speaking carelessly, he self-consciously embraces a vocabulary in which human moral virtues are virtues *simpliciter*, in which talk about *virtues* can, other things equal, be taken as talk about *human moral virtues*. "When we speak simply of *virtue*," Thomas explains, making this linguistic point, "it is understood that we speak of *human* virtues" (I.II 61.1). From *virtue* we can infer human moral virtue; calling it *virtue* is the norm.

The linguistic point, recall, follows from how things actually are with human virtue. The language goes this way because of what I.II 56.3 and other articles show.[30] Human virtue is rightly called *virtue* because human virtue *is* unqualified virtue, virtue *simpliciter*. Terminology aside, that's what Thomas labors to show. In one standard, well-attested context, then, Thomas regards human moral virtues as true, perfect, and simple. This is no small thing, for as we will see, human moral virtues are precisely the virtues he believes outsiders can attain. When it comes to naming and grasping pagan virtue, all this has major implications for those who would be Thomas's heirs.

Complexity and Context: Augustine's Definition

Grasping Thomas's conception of pagan virtue requires attending to multiple texts and their complexities—and showing sensitivity to context and its import for labels like *simple* and *perfect*. For instance, even as Thomas here declares human moral virtue to be virtue simply, elsewhere he says otherwise (I.II 65.2). Many efforts to address our topic have not reckoned sufficiently with these dynamics.[31] When Thomas's thought is so complex that recognizing five sets of distinctions still proves insufficient to give the full picture, such shortcomings are understandable (*PIV*, 51). But understanding his conception of pagan virtue requires parsing his numerous distinctions and tracking his variable terms. At stake is nothing less than whether he believes religious outsiders can attain virtue truly worth the name. Part of our task then is coping with and working through the complexity, recognizing that a virtue perfect or simple in one sense may not be so in another, and, more significantly, that even when it is not, it can still be every bit the virtue that we—and Thomas—think worth caring about.

Such complexity, along with the importance of context in negotiating it, is on display when in I.II 55.4 Thomas cites Augustine's definition of virtue, the final phrase of which—that virtues are "worked in us, without us by God"— can seem contrary to the immediately prior articles. Only what God infuses, it seems to say, are virtues. Thomas "dispenses" with the difficulty by saying that with the phrase included the definition "applies to infused virtue." "If this little bit is removed, the remainder . . . will hold for all virtues generally, both acquired and infused" (I.II 55.4). Yet this remains unclear.[32]

One might think only infused virtues count as virtues simply, for only they live up entirely to the "altogether excellent definition." But that is incompatible with the immediate context and what we've seen Thomas says in following articles. Perhaps then the "excellence" of the unredacted definition has to do with its excellence as a definition of *infused* virtue, its final phrase implying nothing about what counts as virtue as such. That, with minimal modification, it defines virtue generally only enhances its excellence. Or perhaps he praises it in view of its excellence as a definition of virtue broadly understood but disregards the last phrase in doing so—he "dispenses" with it, counting it inessential to the definition and virtue as such.[33] There is, however, another explanation for why Thomas might have created this trouble for himself—and one with which the preceding possibilities are also compatible.

After elucidating distinct aspects of Aristotle's conception of virtue in 55's first three articles and even citing Aristotle in each *sed contra*, Thomas adduces Augustine's definition in 55.4.[34] And he devotes the corpus to systematically showing how that definition fits each of the Aristotelian criteria. Thus, corresponding to 55.1, which establishes that virtue pertains to a rational power, Thomas notes that Augustine's definition stipulates that virtue is a habit *of the mind*. In relation to 55.2 and 3, which concern virtue's status as *operative* and *good* habit, respectively, Thomas explains, in turn, that Augustine's definition concerns operation and exclusively good operation. Thomas thus structures the corpus to show that Augustine's definition clearly fits the Aristotelian conception of virtue that the preceding articles and habits treatise articulate. As our final chapter will show, he eventually aims to demonstrate how even the infusion clause realizes Aristotelian commitments. So, while positing God as virtue's cause could seem impossible to reconcile with Aristotle, if we recall his own insistence that virtue is a power's limit, conducing to the best end, we can begin to see that given Scripture's teaching about human ends and nature, Augustine's definition alone can fully satisfy Aristotelian criteria. Ultimately, Thomas means to show how infused virtue is, by Aristotelian lights, the limit of *our* power. And already his construction of a notion of habit that satisfies Aristotle and Augustine alike and on which God-given habits meet Aristotelian criteria represent a major step in this direction—so that even now infused habit can seem plausible by Aristotelian lights.[35]

Thomas's use of Augustine's definition, then, infusion clause included, makes sense when we recognize him as striving for a genuinely transformative synthesis—all the more when we realize that this particular definition was the definition of choice among those of Thomas's contemporaries who rejected pagan virtue and regarded Aristotle with suspicion or even hostility.[36] Thomas thus highlights the Aristotelian and Augustinian reconciliation he is effecting—even though the work is not yet complete, as the dangling infusion clause suggests. But, even now, his one modification, replacing "quality" with "habit," underlines what he has already accomplished, both displaying the definition's Aristotelian character and making it, in his view, better. That revision itself leaves no doubt that being Augustinian by being Aristotelian and vice versa, not mixing water with wine but making a new vintage, is what he's up to. The cost, for now, is some temporary ambiguity as to just how the infused clause relates. Still, he is very clear in I.II 55.4 and in what precedes and follows, that human virtue is authentic virtue.

Whatever complexities and further distinctions later passages introduce, in the texts we have treated, Thomas declares human moral virtue—precisely what concerns us—to be virtue, *vera* and *simpliciter*. We want to know whether Thomas thinks pagans capable of this and, if so, in what sense, for this answers to Aristotle's conception of virtue, to many of ours and, at least here, to Thomas's.

The Unity of Virtue

To that end, we turn to what could seem an unlikely topic: the unity of the virtues. This is necessary for two related reasons—first, to further clarify just what Thomas thinks pagans attain in attaining virtue; secondly, to dispel the common claim that he believes non-Christians capable only of virtue that is true but imperfect in lacking unity.[37] The unity of the virtues, we will see, is an essential feature of Thomas's notion of human virtue, inherent in its conception. For one habit to be good in the way it must be to count as virtue requires the other virtues.[38] Possession and connection rise and fall together. Unconnected "virtue," for Thomas, is mere disposition to virtue.

That Thomas affirms the unity of the virtues is clear (I.II 65.1). The doctrine stipulates that to have any virtue, one must have them all. Take prudence, "right reason of things to be done," the virtue whereby practical intellect reasons and judges well regarding what ought to be done and how and issues its conclusions as commands for action that will effects (I.II 56.3).[39] Prudence, however, presupposes justice, rectitude of will: the will's desiring the right determinate good (I.II 56.2 ad 3).[40] It does, because the end to which will is inclined, what a person loves, serve as a principle or starting point for prudence's work. As Thomas often reminds, "the end is the rule of whatever is ordained to the end" and "in action, the last end is the first principle." Justice supplies practical reason with *good* first principles, so that the ends loved and sought are genuinely good. As *scientia* is a habit of speculative intellect that reasons well from first principles to conclusions; so prudence is the habit of practical intellect that reasons well from will's end to a course of action for its attainment. Will's orientation posits the goal prudence works to achieve. If Bob wills that his heirs be financially secure, prudence charts the course—deliberating about the integrity of various attorneys, the merits of different trusts, and so on. Subjected in intellect, prudence does not and cannot generate this desire to provide for his heirs; rather, it presupposes that end and determines how best to achieve it.[41]

Yet prudence, in its relation to the ends toward which will disposes, is importantly different from *scientia* in its relation to first principles. Whereas speculative intellect's first principles contain the whole *scientia* virtually and concern only noncontingent things, and whereas *scientia* traces one correct demonstration to its necessary conclusion, prudence concerns itself with accidents and contingencies. It does, because human life involves accidents and contingencies. The lines of geometry contend with neither potholes nor traffic, but even the simplest human act is subject to the vagaries of fortune.[42] And prudence's ends are often such that there are numerous efficient and just ways to achieve them. Human actions, Thomas reminds us, "concern particulars that can be other than they are" (I.II 57.4 ob 2). If Joe wills a "green" lifestyle, he is faced with innumerable variables, many in flux, so that slow deliberation can render what is wise in one moment foolish in the next. Without justice, there can be no prudence, for the principles from which practical intellect would reason about what to do would fail to possess the goodness of justice, of rightly ordered loves. Just as an erroneous starting point corrupts a mathematical proof, no matter the subsequent steps, if will's end is unjust, practical reason's deliberation about the means will itself be vitiated by the end's wickedness. There is no truly prudent way to plot a murder, embezzle a trust, or orchestrate a genocide.

Prudence presupposes not only a will perfected by justice but a sensitive appetite perfected by moderation and courage. The passions of sensual desire— for food, sex, and other pleasures—and the irascible appetite—anger, fear, and so on—can mislead practical reason unless they have, respectively, habits of moderation and courage (I.II 58.5 and ad 3; 58.2). These nonrational appetites can obey reason in two ways (I 81.3). First, in their own operations, so that, in response to reason's thinking about something—say, a delicious burger or a coworker's slight—one feels hunger or anger.[43] In this sense, reason can exercise a kind of control: provoking or quelling. Secondly, they can become submissive to reason by an act of will. For example, if a person repeatedly refuses to will the act that would fulfill their operation—eating the burger, retaliating against the coworker—they become more obedient to will in such matters. With enough training, they can come reliably to track one's judgment in such cases about what really is sensually desirable or worth fearing or being angry about. Thus, by repeatedly laughing off the coworker's derisive comments that once enraged, one no longer feels the angry urge to retaliate. Reason's rule, in either of these modes, is never so complete that the passions cannot resist in some respect—for, by their nature, they are not fully obedient to reason but "have something of their own." Even after years of ignoring the colleague's insults, he could say something so offensive that one's anger was stirred—despite one's judgment that it was not worth getting angry toward him even for this. Unlike the body's movement, to which (other things being equal) reason stands as absolute tyrant, the passions can rebel.[44]

"The work of prudence," Thomas explains, "cannot proceed unless the impediment of the passions corrupting [its] judgment and command be removed . . . by moral virtue" (I.II 58.5 ad 3). Passions do not quickly and easily follow right reason's judgment unless a habit cause them to do so. They can cause someone to ignore or neglect the general principles of right and wrong that bear on the situation at hand as well as the relevant particulars—the things it is right reason's job to consider. Thus, lacking moderation and beholding a delicious slab of carrot cake, my desire could be so strong that I ignore or neglect the fact that it belongs to my friend who has stepped away from the table and the general principle, "do not steal." Instead, gripped and prodded by hunger, I attend to the fact that it is good to eat and, say, the general principle, "nothing good to eat is forbidden," and decide to eat it (I.II 58.5).[45] In itself, the practical syllogism is valid—the carrot cake is good to eat and nothing good to eat is forbidden—but it is not the right one to govern my action just now. My judgment accords with *reason*, but not *right* reason; it fails to register the salient principles or particulars. Or, I might realize that I should not eat it since doing so would be theft—and decide not to. But as my friend lingers, it might "go over and over in my heart" (*versatur in corde*) that it is permitted to eat what is tasty, and, failing to execute my earlier decision, I give in and eat (*DM* 3.9 ad 7).[46] Here, "passion trumps or comes before (*praeveniens*) the judgment of reason," preventing it from issuing the right command effectively and so short-circuiting right reason's work (I.II 59.2 ad 3).[47]

As well, the moral virtues presuppose one another: temperance and courage presuppose justice and vice versa and so on, throughout the combinations. An example or two suffice. "When because of anger someone hits another person," Thomas remarks, "in the very undeserved blow, justice is corrupted" (I.II 60.2).[48] Here, irascible passion leads a person to do and—provided she is not utterly blinded by rage—to *will* to do what is unjust.[49] Justice concerns those of our actions that affect others. But, really, nearly all our actions are of that sort. "It is clear," explains Thomas,

> that all who belong to some community stand to it as a part to the whole . . .
> so that whatever is the good of the part is ordainable to the good of the whole
> community. . . . Thus the good of *anyone's* virtue—*whether ordering some person
> in relation to himself [as temperance does, for example] or to . . . others*—can be
> ordained to the common good. (II.II 58.5)

Justice, for Thomas, is implicated even in someone's governance of and relation to herself. In our contemporary, interconnected world, the point is especially easy to see: my solitary consumption of or unruly appetite for non-fair-trade coffee or shoes produced by child labor, not only implicates me in the failure of right internal order that is gluttony or vanity; it entangles me in a global web of injustice. Unless a person lives entirely in solitude with complete self-sufficiency, nearly *everything* a person does affects others in some way. Anger, especially, easily leads to injustice—snapping at a colleague because of a professional disappointment or pursuing revenge against an obnoxious driver, unjustly endangering everyone on the road.

Or, consider courage. Whether we envision battlefields or protest lines, it is easy to see that lack of courage—say, too much fear for one's safety—can lead to the betrayal of justice that is desertion. And undisciplined attraction to the pleasures of home, poorly ordered concupiscible appetite, can contribute to the lack of courage and act of injustice that desertion involves. The spouse whose lust leads to adultery is drawn by his undisciplined appetite to betray justice, loving and choosing what he should not. Lack of virtue in the sensitive appetites is thus incompatible with a habit of justice in the will. Justice cannot reside in the will of one whose other appetitive powers are unruly, for those appetites make it difficult for her to will genuine goods, order the will's loves rightly, or, in relation to others, give each her due. Conversely, absent justice, a person does not love the right things or love them appropriately, and so courage, which requires fear for the right things, and temperance, which involves the right appetite for the right things, are not really possible.

Finally, just as prudence cannot exist without the virtues of the appetitive part, there can be no virtue of justice—or any appetitive virtue—without prudence (I.II 58.4). A will cannot be just—cannot love and use according to right reason's judgment—if reason is not right, for practical intellect's command, which will effects, will be out of accord with what it is actually right to do.[50] Thus will's use, *while in accord with reason's command*, will fail to be just. For example, beholding my friend's cake, suppose I do will to give my friend her due (will's act) by not eating her cake (practical reason's command). It is hers, I reason, eating it would be theft. But it is delicious, I think. She returns—to find a mound of salt, one edge of the cake protruding. "I value our friendship," I say, "so I didn't eat your cake!" Prudence has failed spectacularly, but note the failure of justice that attends. The salt-dumping that will effects at reason's command is unjust. When practical reason does not command a just act, what will effects lacks the good of justice.

Cum ratione recta, or Virtue Loveth Adverbs

Were this all we could say about the unity of the virtues, there might still be room to object that their unity is not really intrinsic to Thomas's conception of virtue *per se*, that the preceding account only shows that in certain circumstances some virtues require others. Such an objection is misguided. Thomas holds that virtue and its act are not merely *according* to right reason (*secundum rationem rectam*) but *with* right reason (*cum ratione recta*) (I.II 58.4 ad 3). Put differently, an inclination that merely led to the right thing being done, that merely inclines one to do *what* right reason would dictate, would not be virtue.[51] Virtue, rather, requires that what is done actually be done *with* right reason's activity. Right reason, its counsel and command, needs to be involved in the doing of the act. Virtue, then, bears not only on *what* a person does but *how* she does it; this is one key sense in which that is so.

For Thomas, virtue has an essentially adverbial aspect: it makes the good thing be done *well*, with the active involvement of right reasoning about what ought to be done (I.II 57.5). The good life for a human is a matter of not only *what* a person does (*quid faciat*), but *how* a person does it (*quo modo*); the human end is not only a doing-what but a doing-how (I.II 57.5 and ad 1 and 2).

To do the good thing *well*, it is not enough that the right thing be done, but that it be done in the right way. And that means, first, that the agent must do it *knowing* it is the right thing and with truly good reasons. The human good involves discerning and living a specifically rational life, one that manifests the goodness of right reason through right choice (*rectam electionem*), through *choosing* to live with right reason (I.II 55.4 ad 4; 19.4).

If a knife's end is cutting and being sharp, it is no defect that it not make *itself* sharp or make *itself* cut, no defect that it not make *itself* well-suited for its end.[52] But it is a defect for a human not to make herself well-suited to her end, for *making oneself well-suited* to that end is, for Thomas, partly constitutive of that end. Part of the human end is not just being, but having a hand in making oneself, rationally sharp.[53] Prudence is that whereby we so sharpen ourselves. Thomas, at one point, imagines someone who in all his acts obeys the counsel of the most virtuous, prudent person imaginable. While such a person does exclusively good deeds, he nonetheless fails to do them well, in the way it is good for humans to do them. His activity is not *with* right reason even as it is perfectly *according to* right reason.

Central to his defect is his failure to make himself do well in the way he is able, his failure to cultivate—or try to cultivate—prudence. "If he do a good action," Thomas explains, "nevertheless he does not do well simply (*bene simpliciter*)—and *that* is to live well" (I.II 57.5 ad 2). Humans are such that their perfection involves the perfection of their practically-oriented rational power, the perfection of themselves as principles of rational action.[54] Simply to take even the best orders from a person of flawless counsel is not to live the humanly good life but to abdicate it, to live a purely—we might say—"knifely" existence. To use oneself in this way is not properly to *use* oneself—it is to lend use of one's self (and indeed one's use of self) to another. In contrast, the human good depends on a person using herself well insofar as it is up to her—and that requires perfecting the rational dimension of herself insofar as it is a principle of action.

Every human action is for the good, and every human action involves practical reason. But only in certain human acts is the good desired truly perfective here and now, and only in certain acts does practical reason identify that good and a just and prudent path to it. For someone to do the good act well requires that she act for it because of the goodness it has thanks to its being truly perfective—its being in accord with right reason—and that her practical reason be active in discerning that goodness.[55] Pursuit of the good *so understood* is essential for virtue. Discussing what he calls the "honest good" (*bonum honestum*), Thomas explains: "Something is called [an] honest [good] . . . insofar as it has a certain beauty from the regulation of reason. That which is according to reason's regulation is naturally fitting (*conveniens*) to man, and each one naturally delights in [what is] fitting to him. And thus the honest good is naturally delightful to man" (II.II 145.3). The truly good act sets things right in the world: immediately through speaking truth in love or turning away from temptation, say, and/or mediately, through giving someone a living wage, writing a just law, and so on (II.II 57). The virtuous person regards this act and state of affairs as good—and desires to realize it in her life and the world because of its goodness, which it has because it is truly right.[56] Doing good acts *well* requires that one act for that goodness, something inherently desirable, beautiful, and fitting to humans. It requires too that one's own practical reason correctly discern that goodness—both as partly constitutive of fully virtuous action and because, otherwise, one could hardly experience that good's pull, hardly act *for* it. And, in the case of virtue, all of this has to happen consistently, promptly, and with ease.

"When someone does a good action," Thomas explains, "not in accord with the deliverance of his own reason but moved to it by the counsel of another, his act is still not entirely perfect—this thanks to [deficiency in] reason's directing and appetite's movement. Therefore if he do a good action, nevertheless he does not do well simply—and *that* is to live well" (I.II 57.5 ad 2). Merely to do good deeds or even consistently to do and incline to them does not a virtue make. Virtue requires that they be done well; it is as much a habit of *choosing* good action as of doing it. And that requires the presence and activity of right reason—both as habit in intellect and as that in which the appetites habitually participate. It requires that one's sensitive appetite not interfere with but incline toward and obey reason's judgment.

Further, virtue's adverbial character is not confined to the contribution of prudence; the right participation of will and the appetitive powers are equally necessary. This is so because effecting the goodness proper to virtue requires active cooperation between well-ordered appetitive powers and right reason. Without will and passions alike the good act cannot be done well and thus virtue is absent. Thomas explains: "The good of anything is determined by the condition of its nature . . . [and] the good operation of a human being is *with passion*" (I.II 59.5 ad 3).[57] The sensitive appetite, for instance, contributes a certain, fitting pleasure and joy to action, for "virtue *produces* appropriate passion" (I.II 59.5 ad 1). The just person, then, takes pleasure in just action, doing it with ease and delight—this helps mark the difference between her and the not-quite virtuous person. For, "it does not belong to virtue that it *deprive* those [powers] subject to reason of their proper acts, but [cause them to] *follow* reason's command, performing their proper acts" (I.II 59.5). Other things being equal, the more perfected a person in virtue, the more pleasure found in virtuous action (I.II 59.5). Not merely prophylactic, the appetitive virtues contribute positively to the act prudence commands. "For a man to do well (*agit bene*)," Thomas says, "it is necessary not only that reason be well disposed by [prudence], but, *moreover, that the appetitive power[s] be well disposed through a habit of moral virtue*" (I.II 58.2). The good act done well—and thus *virtue*—requires that one do the rational good *feelingly*. By their virtue, the appetitive powers participate and move with their own distinctive operation in action's performance: the truly virtuous woman *feels* compassion for the beggar she helps, anger at the injustice that put him on the streets, delight to bring him comfort. The very notion of virtue, then, requires possession of the appetitive virtues, for many good acts cannot be done well without passion's contribution. In fact, in the absence of the appetitive virtues, prudence itself would fall short of virtue's definition by failing to make a person be good or act well; its goodness would be lost, as it were, in translation.

This insistence that practical reason and the appetitive powers alike must be well perfected for a person to act well entails the unity of the virtues. "Reason," Thomas says, "is the good of the soul." It is by inclining a person to act *with* right reason that virtue makes a person and his act *good* (I.II 58.2; 59.4). And if virtue would make a person be and do good, it must stretch as far in him as can right reason, reaching all that admits of habit ordered to it. Of course, this includes practical reason and the will or rational appetite, but the sensitive appetites have a share in reason too and so can share in right reason's goodness. It is incompatible with possessing virtue that someone should lack the appetitive virtues, right reason's good in those powers. Otherwise, that goodness—and so virtue—would not be in a person or her act.

There is one more way to see the connection between Thomas's conception of virtue and their unity. "Human virtue," he says, "is a habit perfecting man for operating well (*bene operandum*). In man there are only two principles of human action: intellect or reason and appetite" (I.II 58.3). Reason alone is the first principle of human action; appetite a principle insofar as it participates in reason (I.II 58.2). Moral virtue is—and makes a person good as—a principle of action, inclining one to act with right reason. In one sense, human action originates in a unity: practical reason, in itself and as participated by will and sensitive appetite. Virtue requires the perfection of that principle, for any deficiency in the principle corrupts the resultant action. Virtue therefore demands perfection not just of practical reason, sensitive appetite, or will (as if any could be perfected independently of one another), but the perfection of the *unified principle of human action*—the perfection of a person *qua principle of action*, participant in reason. In fact, virtue *makes* a person a unified principle of action, bringing order and harmony where division and disorder could reign. Absent virtue, an agent can be divided against herself so that sensitive appetite rebels against practical reason or will inclines to what a person might think it should not. Virtue excludes such division.[58]

Yet, whether unity obtains or not, practical reason, will, and sensitive appetite are all, for better or worse, involved in any human action. And imperfection in any one entails imperfection in the act produced, for action comes from all together, whether they do act harmoniously or not.[59] "An operation," Thomas explains, "which proceeds from two powers [namely, reason and sensitive appetite] cannot be perfect unless *each power* be perfected by its due habit, [the habit proper to that power and its operation]" (I.II 58.3 ad 2). Truly virtuous action requires *all* of action's principles to be perfect. Any corruption in action means that no habits implicated in their production—however good they seem—are virtues, for virtues conduce to good acts done well. Since together they generate action, action is only as good as the least good habit—and, just so, if any be less than good, all are less than virtuous. The worker's product, Thomas notes, is only as excellent as her tools allow: imperfect tools; imperfect work. So it is with human operation.[60] Both agent and instrument, practical reason and appetite, must be fully good for action to be virtuous. Yet, unlike carpentry, where the worker may be good, hampered only by shoddy tools, in the case of action, if it is not virtuous, *none of its principles are.*

"Prudence," Thomas says, "stands to human acts—to *usus* of powers and habits—as art does to external productions because each is perfect reason with respect to the things about which it is concerned" (I.II 57.4). As art is the right know-how for making and instills its goodness in its product, prudence is the right know-how for self-use, for living well, and it instills its goodness in given actions (I.II 57.5 ad 1). Just here another instructive disanalogy intervenes: where art's tools and objects just (and merely) are receptive or passive, prudence's instruments, the other powers, require *habits* of receptivity—*habits* inclining them to obey. Whether they share in and effectively "pass on" right reason's goodness depends on their inclining to the good of operation with right reason. Thus, later, when Thomas says that "virtue is the art of good conduct," he explains that this applies to practical reason essentially as it possesses prudence but that it holds for other powers by participation, "insofar as they are inclined to obey and be directed by prudence" (I.II 58.2 ad 1). Right reason "is in *all* the moral virtues through participation, in so far as prudence directs them all" (I.II 58.2 ad 4).

Right reason's goodness, though, cannot simply be "put" into other powers as an artist's goodness into her art. Even if prudence could exist without the other virtues it could make neither action nor the other powers fully good. It discerns the order of right reason conformity to which renders appetitive powers virtuous. But those powers only have right reason's goodness insofar as they incline by habit to obey (I.II 56.4). The artist's tools are mere vessels mediating her skill to her work. Not so the appetitive powers in relation to prudence. In being *themselves* inclined to obey right reason, they manifest right reason in their inclination and operation. And only when they do so—by *actively* cooperating with prudence—can the agent produce acts that have right reason's goodness. They positively contribute to action's goodness in a way unlike the sculptor's chisel or painter's brush, adding something, in a sense, beyond "mere" prudence.

The qualification matters, for it is right reason's good, the good proper to prudence, that they "add." But, they are no mere vessels or containers. The case is like that of a police officer and her K-9. The relevant goodness of the dog is wholly thanks to the training—and so the goodness—of the master, a goodness proper to and instilled by her. Yet the dog does not merely mediate that goodness, he participates it, giving it a particular and uniquely canine flavor. And this canine-ly participation, precisely in virtue of its canine-ness, adds to the unified crime-fighting activity of master and dog so that there is something more in the activity than there would be were the master working without the dog or with a less excellently trained one.

The good order prudence bestows on practical reason is necessary for the possibility of courage and moderation. Only insofar as the sensitive appetite obeys prudence can it be subject of virtue—fearing, being angry at, and desiring the right things in the right way (I.II 56.4; 59.4). Importantly, however, those virtues perfect their subjects not merely by bringing them in accord with the judgment of reason—a *vice* does that much—but with the judgment of *right* reason.[61] Following reason's lead is a far cry from following right reason's lead. Appetitive habit's obedience to reason is conditional: an appetite is not trained to obey reason's command *as such*, but a particular *variety of reason's command*. This is a vital point.

Say a virtuous person decides to do something unjust, to embezzle a trust. Having decided, it does not follow that she will not deeply fear—even be terrified of—getting caught. And this even though she has the virtue of courage and would fearlessly (or with appropriate fear) risk her life to save a friend. Through its habit of courage, her irascible appetite is trained to obey, follow, and participate in *right* reason's judgment.[62] When reason's command goes astray, her passions do not obey. This is part of why doing wrong is harder for the virtuous person than for someone else—her virtues make their presence known, if not through active resistance then at least through the resistance that is the absence of their cooperation.[63] (Like driving with the emergency brake on.) As well, this is what it means for it to be true that a virtue cannot be put to bad use. If courage strengthened the irascible appetite as our friend pursued her embezzlement, then her courage would be used for ill. The habit would assist in the doing of evil. If it could be so used, it would not have been a habit of *courage* to begin with. Indeed to what ethical or spiritual advantage would a habit be that made wrongdoing easier? Moral virtue obeys and moves the appetite according to *right reason's* judgment. If the good habits of the appetitive part are lacking, no matter how correctly prudence may seem to proceed, such a person has not virtue: her operation will not be good, for the principle of that operation will be imperfect. Perfectly disposed reason could not produce perfect action unless sensitive appetite, which it moves and which itself contributes to the action, were also perfect.

Later chapters revisit this account, unfolding its significance more fully. For now, note that this connection between Thomas's conception of virtue and their unity has primarily to do with virtue's *breadth* rather than its *ends*. Certainly, virtue's end, that to which it conduces, bears on its breadth, the degree to which virtue fully inhabits each power that bears it. Here, however, our emphasis is on the necessary unity of human moral virtue, the way it inheres in Thomas's very conception. We can also speak of the *ends* of virtue, considering the extent to which some virtue's end is the best to which humans can be ordered. That is, apart from the matter of unity—a necessary feature of virtue as such—we can consider virtue in terms of whether it orders to the end that is truly final and perfective for humans *simply* or whether its end is the best attainable without charity. Virtue, we will see, can be perfect as to breadth—in the sense of unity, disposing all in an agent that needs disposing. And it can be perfect in another sense, disposing someone to the best end attainable.[64] The former perfection does not presuppose the latter. Virtue's unity does not presuppose its perfection in terms of end.

In I.II 65.1, Thomas explicitly endorses virtue's unity, but that passage comes after he has ceased talking so primarily of human moral virtue. There, he declares these unified virtues perfect. While he says this to distinguish these virtues from natural virtues—which we have seen are not really virtues—his characterization of human virtues as "perfect" has led some to insist that such virtues are unattainable by non-Christians. Since Thomas elsewhere declares that perfect virtue requires charity, such interpreters seem to imagine that unified virtues, since they are perfect, cannot be attained by outsiders. But this is both to lose track of the different senses in which virtues can be perfect and to misunderstand the relation between virtues and their unity—the way their connection inheres in Thomas's very conception. I have meant to lay these confusions to rest: by noting some of the variability of his perfection language; by showing how his very conception of human virtue entails their unity; and by deriving my account from portions of the virtue treatise where human virtue is primarily in focus and where none of the perfection/imperfection distinctions concern the quite different perfection distinction(s) proper to the difference between the virtues of pagans and Christians. In short, I've tried to show the conceptual incoherence of a disconnected Thomistic virtue and to do so on the basis of texts where human moral virtue is in view and where perfection language implicates no Christian/pagan distinctions.

Chapter 6 analyzes I.II 65.1, showing its perfection is in fact proper to human virtue as such, a sort attainable without charity. That text neither stipulates an additional criterion for habit to count as virtue nor a criterion distinguishing perfect from true but imperfect virtue. Dismissal of virtue's unity amounts to dismissal of Thomas's conception of virtue. For Thomas, ascribing "true but disconnected" virtue to pagans is, if not simply incoherent, not really to ascribe them virtue at all.

Cardinal Virtue and Virtue's Perfect Ratio

We have seen so far what it means for virtues to be good operative habits, why moral virtues are virtues *simpliciter*, and that the unity of the virtues is intrinsic to Thomas's definition of virtue. Thomas calls human moral virtues "perfect" and says they are virtues "simply," "unqualifiedly," and so on, even highlighting the propriety so describing them. That he does underlines the wrongness of imagining that all perfect/imperfect distinctions mark a single boundary—that between Christian and non-Christian virtue.

Considering whether the moral virtues should be called cardinal virtues, Thomas notes that to count as cardinal, a virtue must somehow be principal (I.II 61.1). The cardinals are principal in standing as the source of special, narrower virtues that subdivide what the cardinals address (e.g., justice [cardinal] to piety [special]) (I.II 60.3). And they are principal in attaining preeminently to virtue's *ratio* (I.II 61.1). In declaring human virtues cardinal, Thomas forecloses any attempt to view them as somehow deficient, second-rate. Making his case, Thomas explains that those human virtues that make their possessor and her work good, human moral virtues (prudence included), "answer to the perfect definition of virtue (*perfectam rationem virtutits*)" (I.II 61.1). Intellectual virtues, in contrast, are "called virtues only according to an incomplete definition of virtue (*secundum imperfectam rationem virtutis*)" (I.II 61.1). By claiming they attain virtue's *perfect ratio* (*perfectam rationem*) and explicitly linking cardinality to perfection, Thomas implies what he later makes explicit, that human moral virtues themselves are perfect. For, only insofar as moral virtue *itself* is perfect and does not merely attain a perfect *ratio*, is it (not just its *definition*) *prinicipalius*, "more principal."[65] Thomas not only declares human moral virtues to be virtues *simpliciter*, he recognizes them as perfect, attaining virtue's perfect *ratio*.

Later, in 61.5, Thomas distinguishes four sets of cardinal virtues, that is, the human cardinal virtues and three other species: social or human (*politicas*), purifying (*purgatorias*), purified-of-spirit (*purgati animi*), and exemplar or cardinal virtues as possessed by God.[66] While social virtues rank "lowest" here, he says nothing to diminish them. "Social" (*politicas*) virtues are "human" (*humanae*) virtues, those by which one "carries on well (*recte*) in human affairs." And he declares that these are the virtues he has been considering since Question 55:

> Because according to his nature man is a political animal, these kind of virtues—just as they exist in man according to the condition of his nature—are called 'political [or social] virtues,' just as, to be sure, man's carrying on well in human affairs (*recte in rebus humanis gerendis*) depends on his having these virtues. Up to this point, it is *this* kind of virtue [i.e., *human* virtue] that we have been talking about. (I.II 61.5)[67]

Virtutes politicae refer to the virtues concerned with the whole life of humans as social animals.[68] With the Latin *rebus humanis*, Thomas characterizes these as virtues that bear on "all the human stuff"—politics, vocation, recreation, family life, friendship, and everything else. "It must be carefully noted," he stresses, "that it belongs to the social virtues—as they are denominated here—not only to [cause man] to act well toward the community [as a whole] but also to its parts, whether a household or . . . some single person" (I.II 61.5 ad 4). Social virtues thus bear on one's relation to individuals—including the individual that is oneself—as well as the common good and everything in between. Throughout the treatise on virtue, then, Thomas interchangeably uses the terms "human (*humana*) virtue," "moral (*moralis*) virtue," "social (*politicae*) virtue," and "virtue." These and what I have called "human moral virtue" all refer to one thing— which satisfies the perfect *ratio* of virtue and which Thomas declares perfect (I.II 58.4 ad 3; 59.5).

I.II 63.2: Pagan Virtue as Human Virtue

Perhaps as well as any passage, I.II 63.2 shows that Thomas believes human moral virtue is attainable by outsiders, without charity. Question 63 centers on virtue's causes, and 63.2 concerns whether "virtues can be caused in us through habituation (*ex assuetudine operum*)." It explicitly addresses the question of whether virtues can be attained by human acts *apart from grace*.[69] The two articles that follow investigate whether moral virtue can be caused by grace (I.II 63.3) and the distinction between grace-generated virtues and those caused by habituation (I.II 63.4). If 63.2 concerned virtues acquired by grace, 63.3 would be unnecessary. Additionally, 63.4 treats habituation and grace as distinct, mutually exclusive causes of virtue. This context thus underlines that in 63.2 Thomas is concerned with habituation *instead* of grace as a cause of virtue.

63.2 primarily focuses on the possibility of acquiring virtue without grace by habituation (*assuetudine operum*), and its argument distinguishes between virtues that require and those that do not require grace for their attainment. The article centrally depends on sharply distinguishing between habituation and grace as causes of virtue. Specifically, Thomas deploys that distinction to address the article's primary objection. Responding to authorities like Augustine who seem to deny that *any* virtues are attainable without grace, Thomas insists that human virtues can be acquired by habituation apart from grace. Such authorities, he says, refer not to human virtues or virtues as such, but to infused virtues. Infused virtues, those virtues that lead to the beatific end are unattainable without grace; not so human virtues, those ordered to the political end.

Understanding Thomas's affirmation and its significance requires grasping two points. First, we need to see that habituation here means habituation *without grace*, habituation-as-cause excludes grace-as-cause. Secondly, we need to recognize that Thomas is asking about virtue, nothing less. Easily he could have said that habituation caused something virtue-ish but less than genuine virtue—perhaps a disposition to virtue. Given Augustine's apparent rejection of virtue's attainability without grace, surely Thomas considered both that denial and a "virtue-lite" strategy for coping with it. Indeed, the immediately preceding article, 63.1, offers a kind of precedent: it concerns *virtus inchoata* and the "seeds of virtues," which, recall, are not virtues but their precondition or, at most, their beginnings. There is both reason and precedent for Thomas to make a similar distinction here in 63.2. He could simply claim that whatever humans can attain without grace falls short of virtue, thus honoring his Christian authorities while at least nodding toward Aristotle. Instead, in 63.2, Thomas speaks of nothing less than full-fledged virtue, whether human or infused, and he claims the former but not the latter can be attained by habituation apart from grace.

Human virtue, Thomas reminds us in 63.2, perfects a person in relation to the natural or political good, the good in accord with reason. Delineating between that good and the absolutely final good that is determined by Divine law, exceeds human capacities, and requires grace, Thomas explains that human virtues, the virtues that lead to and in their operation help constitute the political good, are attainable by human acts without grace. These virtues, he says, the "virtues of men that are ordered to the good which is determined according to the rule of human reason, *can be caused by human acts (potest ex actibus humanis causari)*, insofar as such acts proceed from reason, whose power and rule establish that good" (I.II 63.2). The implicit comparison is vital: these acts proceed from and accord with reason *as opposed to* and *in distinction from* proceeding from grace and in accord with Divine law. Most simply, human virtues are attainable by humans apart from grace. Thomas regards this claim, preceded by *igitur*, "therefore," as his argument's *conclusion*. In addressing the primary objection that virtue is not attainable without grace, his response is *not* to distinguish between (a) grace alone as virtue's cause and (b) the cooperation of grace and human action as its cause, and then to suggest that human virtue is attainable through such cooperation. Nor is it to distinguish between the capacities of (c) sinful and (d) integral or pre-Fall human nature and then to suggest that human virtue is only attainable without grace for integral human nature. On the contrary, he proceeds by distinguishing between different types of virtue and their corresponding causes. Both in the article and its context, virtues *either* require grace *or* can be attained by human action—attainability by human action is necessarily attainability without grace. Thomas's insistence that human virtue is attainable by human acts is thus a claim that they can be had without grace. By acting in accord with reason's rule, he says, one can acquire virtue apart from grace—specifically, *human* virtue or the "virtue of men . . . ordered to the good determined by reason." And the virtues of 63.2 that Thomas explicitly says can be so acquired apart from grace are precisely the human virtues of I.II 61.5 and of the treatise on virtue's first six questions, virtues *simpliciter*—virtues he declares true and perfect and which, by their very nature, are unified.[70]

In a sense, 63.2's first objection, citing Augustine and Romans 14:23 and claiming that no virtue can be had without grace, is the objection of all who contend that Thomas believes that no virtue or only a shadow thereof is attainable apart from grace. Such interpreters regard themselves—and Thomas too—as Augustinian in rejecting the possibility of true virtue without charity or at least denying its connectedness. While Thomas sees himself as following Augustine, he explicitly rejects a position that denies either that virtue can be attained by habituation or that such virtue is less than genuine human virtue. Instead, distinguishing infused from human virtue, he claims the former leads to beatitude, and insists that Augustine's and Scripture's claims refer to infused virtue alone. Human virtue eludes Augustine's objection by conducing to the social good, *not beatitude*. Both species of virtue are true, but human virtue is attainable apart from grace, *potest ex actibus humanis causari*.

The following two articles, 63.3 and 4, further substantiate all this. 63.3 argues that some moral virtues can *only* be had by infusion: the *infused* moral virtues, which work directly with theological virtues and have their proximate end set by beatitude.[71] What that article regards as puzzling is not the acquisition of moral virtues without grace, but the notion of moral virtues acquired any other way. Following 63.2, 63.3 simply presumes human moral virtues are "caused in us by our acts" (*possunt causari in nobis ex nostris actibus*) without grace (I.II 63.3 ad 1 and ob 1, not denied). These virtues, it says, are cultivated from the *virtus inchoata*, the natural principles of virtues (*principia naturalia virtutum*); they do not exceed but are proportioned to human nature. "What can be done by a secondary cause [for example, by humans]," Thomas explains, "is not done by God immediately, unless perhaps sometimes miraculously" (I.II 63.3 ob 1, not denied). That is why infused moral virtues are *infused*: they instill a moral virtue no human could otherwise acquire (I.II 63.3 ad 3). For God to give *human* virtues by infusion is possible, but a kind of redundancy—the kind we are accustomed to call a miracle (I.II 63.4 ad 3).

Pagan Virtue and This Age

Someone might still object that in affirming human virtue's attainability without grace Thomas has in view prelapsarian human capacities, not such capacities as exist here and now, stained and limited by sin. These passages, the objection runs, thus say nothing about what *fallen* humanity can achieve without grace and so nothing concerning pagan virtue.

In 63.2's first objection, Thomas cites Augustine's claims concerning Romans 14:23 that without grace "the whole life of the unbeliever is sin" and thus that any apparent virtue in those lacking grace is merely *apparent*. "Virtue," Augustine says, "is false even in those [unbelievers] with the best character." Both the Romans passage and Augustine's comments obviously concern the postlapsarian eon, human nature and capacities *after the Fall*, and they declare such humanity incapable of virtue without grace. There is no question here of an untouched, integral human nature. Moreover, the second objection centers on the presence and opposition of sin to virtue: only when considering the postlapsarian epoch are worries about sin's effects on human capacities for virtue coherent. The article's question is whether and how *sinful* humans can achieve virtue; the challenge it faces that fallen humans seem incapable of achieving virtue without charity. It would be no *response* to say that fallen humans cannot achieve virtue, that only prelapsarian humans can. That would reverse the article's structure and give its objections the day.

Thomas might have proceeded differently—framing his claims about virtue's attainability without charity as concerning integral nature and fully embracing Augustine's famous critique of pagan virtue as vainglory, which he well knew.[72] But he does not.[73] Instead, he welcomes outsider virtue as faithful to Augustine's spirit and explicitly declares that the argument's corpus itself constitutes a response to the first objection. That objection is answered not because only unfallen humans can attain virtue without grace but because its claims, Thomas says, concern infused virtue. And it counts as an *objection* because, in regarding fallen humanity, it represents an initial challenge to Thomas's own claim that fallen humans can attain human virtue without grace.[74] Clearly, then, Thomas here claims that postlapsarian humans can attain human virtue without charity. Here and now, *human* virtue—simple, perfect, true, and inherently unified *potest ex actibus humanis causari*—can be caused by human acts, attained by pagans without charity.

Coming chapters treat other passages that bear on our topic. But we already have strong evidence that Thomas affirms pagan virtue and a good sense of what his affirmation amounts to. Thomas allows for pagan virtue, virtue attainable without the grace necessary for beatitude. And this virtue, which he regards pagans as capable of attaining, answers precisely to our interests. More, it is a sort Thomas himself regards as perfect, simple, inherently unified, and true. Indeed, he esteems it so highly that he begins and, in a real sense, founds his entire treatment of virtue on it. Whatever comes later, this much is clear.

Still, as we have seen, he does not think human virtue is the best virtue humans can possess even if it is the best they can attain without charity. At certain points he even says things that suggest that human virtue is in some sense imperfect or not virtue simply. Many have seized on and prioritized such remarks to the neglect of I.II 63.2 and other texts. How are we supposed to understand such passages in which it might seem that what Thomas gives with one hand he takes with the other? Just what is the imperfection in human virtue and, given our interests, what difference does it make? These apparently disparate questions are closely connected. It is the work of the book's next part to answer them—and in so doing show how.

II ETHICS AND THE THINGS OF THIS WORLD

5 "THE VIRTUE OF MANY GENTILES"

PERHAPS THE SINGLE MOST IMPORTANT PASSAGE for our topic is I.II 65.2 where Thomas declares that a certain sort of moral virtue was present *in multis gentilibus*—in many Gentiles or pagans. Many believe Thomas there claims it is precisely acquired or political virtue that these non-Christians possessed; others say the passage shows that outsiders *cannot* attain virtue at all or only a disconnected, highly imperfect sort.[1] Such contrary readings suggest not only divergent interpretive commitments and competing understandings of the article's context, but the complexity of the passage itself. While ostensibly affirming pagan virtue, it can appear to suggest that such virtue is disconnected, for it can seem to claim that the prudence necessary for acquired virtue's unity is unattainable without charity.[2] Like the other texts that this book's second part addresses, this one has not received the attention it requires.

In what follows, I try to untangle the knots, showing that this passage affirms that outsiders can possess acquired virtues—which are, of course, necessarily "connected." It's no mistake that we approach 65.2 only now; the preceding chapters offered essential background and preparation. The next three chapters elucidate related, equally important texts and themes. Like pieces of a complex mosaic, each passage raises points and questions vital to our topic without itself giving the whole picture. It's not immediately clear how or whether they even fit together. Facing the exegetical and conceptual difficulties particular to each passage and their relations, the coming chapters show how together they comprise a rich, unified theological vision in which, not against but because of Thomas's Augustinian commitments, the outsider is welcomed as capable of a virtue fully worth the name.

A First Look at I.II 65.2

I.II 65.2 finds Thomas asking whether the moral virtues (*virtutes morales*) can be had without charity. Initially, it's ambiguous just what he means by "moral virtues." Given that 65.1 spoke of *virtutes morales* but seemed to focus exclusively on *acquired* virtues, we might expect the same here.[3] Instead, Thomas distinguishes between two species of *virtutes morales*, acquired and *infused*: acquired virtue, he explains, can be possessed without charity (*acquisitae sine caritate esse possunt*); infused virtue cannot. Infused moral virtues are perfect, he says, because they conduce to beatitude, the final end. Acquired virtues do not and, in this respect, are imperfect.[4]

"Virtues that generate good works proportionate to the supernatural final end," Thomas says, "have the *ratio* of virtue perfectly and truly and cannot be acquired by human acts but only infused by God. And such virtues as these cannot be had without charity" (I.II 65.2). Dependent on charity, infused virtues lead to beatitude and alone "have the character of virtue truly and perfectly." Earlier in 65.2, Thomas declared the political virtues attainable without charity. "Just as I said above," he begins the article, "moral virtues—insofar as they lead to good works ordained to an end which does not surpass the natural capacities of men—are able to be acquired by human works. They [i.e., acquired virtues] are able to be acquired *without charity*, just as they were in many pagans" (I.II 65.2). Note his backward glance: *sicut supra dictum est*, "just as it was said above." At the *respondeo*'s outset and as support for his claim that political virtues are attainable without charity, Thomas reaffirms and explicitly directs us to I.II 63.2's contention that precisely the political virtues, virtues unified of their very nature and directed to the end proportionate to human nature, are attainable by fallen humans without charity.

As the preceding chapter showed, Thomas repeatedly characterizes acquired virtues as virtues perfect, simple, and true. Here, however, they are imperfect. Given the relative, contextual character of Thomas's perfection language, this is unsurprising. Acquired virtues are and are not perfect and unqualified: perfect insofar as they attain virtue's perfect *ratio*, the *ratio* of the species he elsewhere declares perfect, simple, true; imperfect insofar as their species falls short of another. Here, they fall short precisely by failing to conduce to beatitude.

Thus far, the interpretation is straightforward. Some might challenge my identification of acquired virtue here as political virtue or my claim that this is the virtue he says many pagans obtained, but few would dispute the basic point:

that Thomas distinguishes acquired and infused moral virtues, that infused but not acquired require charity, and that infused but not acquired perfectly attain virtue's fullest definition and are thus perfect where the others are imperfect.

Continuing, Thomas deploys claims about the unity of the virtues to build his case for infused moral virtue's dependence on charity. Invoking earlier arguments, he notes that prudence and the other acquired moral virtues are interdependent: "It was remarked earlier that the other moral virtues cannot be without prudence; prudence also cannot be without the moral virtues inasmuch as the moral virtues make one well disposed to certain ends from whence prudence's work proceeds" (I.II 65.2). Prudence presupposes a just will's principles and requires that passions not disrupt its operation. Likewise, those virtues require prudence's right command in order to manifest virtue's goodness. This is familiar enough, but the argument's next step can generate serious misunderstanding.

Which Prudence? What Dependence?

"It was remarked earlier," Thomas explains,

> that the other moral virtues cannot be without prudence; prudence also cannot be without the moral virtues inasmuch as the moral virtues make one well disposed to certain ends from whence prudence's work proceeds. Now for the right reasoning of prudence it is much more necessary that a man be well disposed to the final end, which happens through charity, than that he be well disposed to other ends, which happens through the moral virtues—just as in speculative reasoning right reason needs most of all the indemonstrable first principle, that 'contradictories cannot simultaneously be true.' Hence, it is clear that neither is infused prudence (*prudentia infusa*) able to exist without charity, nor, consequently, the other moral virtues (*aliae virtutes morales*), which, without prudence, are not possible. It is evident, therefore, from these words, that the infused virtues alone are perfect and said to be virtues simply, because they order man well to the final end simply (*finem ultimum simpliciter*). Other virtues—certainly the acquired virtues—are virtues *secundum quid*, in a qualified way, not virtues simply: they ordain a man well with respect to the final end in some genus (*genere*), not with respect to the final end simply (*finem ultimum simpliciter*). (I.II 65.2)

Perhaps the most significant interpretive issue concerns the underscored sentence. Taken with the sentence that precedes it, it can seem to say that acquired virtues are *not* possible without charity or, perhaps, that acquired virtues "in their connected form" are not.[5] Either way, the sentence is taken to concern *acquired* virtues and their dependence on charity. When Aquinas refers to "other moral virtues"—"neither is infused prudence (*prudentia infusa*) able to exist without charity, *nor, consequently, the other moral virtues (aliae virtutes morales)*"—some imagine he refers to *all* the moral virtues, infused *and* acquired (or at least acquired). Likewise, the sentence that precedes it can seem to claim that without charity there can be no prudence, for prudence is more dependent on charity's principles and orientation than it is on justice's or on the good disposition of the nonrational appetites. Such interpretations underwrite denials of one or another sort that virtue or "connected virtue" can be had without charity.

For instance, 65.2 and this passage in particular figure significantly in Thomas Osborne's claim that Aquinas thinks pagans cannot attain "connected" virtue, that disconnectedness is part of pagan virtue's imperfection. Conceding that "acquired moral virtues are connected through prudence," Osborne insists that "the real issue is whether the virtue of prudence can exist in someone who lacks charity" (*AA*, 298). Referring here to *acquired* prudence, he says the real issue is whether it can be had without charity.[6] And, citing 65.2, he says it cannot:

> For [the] interpretation [that pagans can possess connected acquired virtue] to be correct, Thomas would have to be arguing not only that the acquired virtues are connected through prudence, *but also that someone who does not have charity can have prudence*. There are no hints . . . that Thomas so argues. Moreover, as we have seen, Thomas's discussion in [I.II] 65, article 2, would *contradict that conclusion*. (298, my emphasis)

Osborne explains that if Thomas thought "connected" acquired virtue were attainable without charity, he would have to believe that *acquired prudence* could be so attained.[7] But Thomas does not hold this, he claims. 65.2, he says, *contradicts* "that conclusion," the conclusion "that someone who does not have charity can have prudence" (298). Osborne thus reads 65.2 as showing that acquired prudence requires charity and cites the sentence I underscored above as evidence, footnoting the Latin without translation or explanation (*AA*, n.53).[8] His denial that "connected" acquired virtue is attainable without charity commits him to denying that acquired prudence is. His "true but imperfect virtue," it turns out, is without prudence, right reason, and so merely an inclination to good acts, a "virtue" so imperfect as to fall essentially short of virtue's *ratio*.

Return, then, to our passage. While Thomas here says that acquired virtues, including acquired prudence, are imperfect, he is not saying their possession requires charity. When Thomas says, "it is clear that neither is infused prudence (*prudentia infusa*) able to exist without charity, nor, consequently, the other moral virtues (*aliae virtutes morales*), which, without prudence are not possible," this sentence's *aliae virtutes morales* refers not to *acquired* but only to *infused* moral virtues—the infused virtues that are *other, alia,* than *infused* prudence. Difficulties arise because 65.2 tends to refer to moral virtues or prudence without always labeling them as either infused or acquired, leaving us to examine the context at each point to determine which sort are under discussion. The complexities multiply because his argument rests on a structural parallel between *acquired* prudence's dependence on *acquired* moral virtue and *infused* prudence's dependence on *charity*. As he shifts between different sorts of virtues without always announcing which are in view, we must decipher what Thomas has in mind.

After establishing the distinction between (a) acquired prudence and acquired moral virtues and (b) infused prudence and infused moral virtues in the article's first sentences, Thomas sets about his central task: showing why infused virtues require charity. First, just before the underlined portion, he reminds us of prudence's character. Prudence—of whatever sort—is concerned with means and thus presupposes an end that something other than prudence itself must supply. He makes the point by reminding readers of "what has been remarked above": various points about the interconnectedness of prudence and moral virtues and especially prudence's dependence on the moral virtues for its principle. Specifically, he has in view texts on the interdependence of prudence and moral virtues, such as I.II 58.4 and 5, which the previous chapter considered, and, especially the immediately preceding article, I.II 65.1, which we treat below.[9] All these texts are concerned exclusively with *acquired* moral virtues: "what has been remarked above" about virtue's unity has concerned *acquired* prudence and *acquired* moral virtues. 65.2 represents the first consideration of the unity of any virtues *other* than the acquired, but at first, Thomas refers to *acquired* prudence and, when he speaks this time of "*aliae morales virtutes,*" the other *acquired* virtues, that is, acquired virtues *other* than acquired prudence.[10] Invoking what he has shown about acquired prudence, he means to make a point about prudence of every sort, highlighting the *ratio* of prudence as such: as concerned with means, something else must supply it with an end.[11]

Next, he sets up a parallel between that (acquired) prudence/(acquired) moral virtue relation, and the structurally identical relation between prudence and charity.[12] Specifically, prudence as such depends on other virtue(s) for its principles: in the case of acquired prudence, acquired moral virtue supplies principles; in the case of infused prudence, charity. Like acquired moral virtue, charity belongs to appetite and supplies (in charity's case, *infused*) prudence with principles. These principles derive from charity's distinctive end, beatitude. Notwithstanding the missing labels, the passage's second sentence refers to *infused* prudence, for it is infused prudence that *requires* charity to supply its principles. In contrast, earlier articles and even the prior sentence speak exclusively of moral virtues as filling that role for acquired prudence; they say nothing of a requirement of charity.

"Now," Thomas explains, "for the right reasoning of prudence it is much more necessary that a man be well disposed to the final end, which happens through charity, than that he be well disposed to other ends, which happens through the moral virtues—just as in speculative reasoning right reason needs most of all the indemonstrable first principle, that 'contradictories cannot simultaneously be true.'" If acquired prudence needs acquired virtue's principles to consider means in regard to the limited domain of political life, much more, he says, does prudence need charity's principles to reason well about the much more universal, supernatural end. There are two points here, at least. The first we have noted: given prudence's *ratio* there can be no practical reasoning about how to act in light of beatitude if one be not inclined toward it through charity. The second concerns this parallel between (c) the charity/prudence relation and (d) the moral virtue/prudence relation. We'll qualify this intentionally vague formulation shortly, but the point is something like this: If prudence needs the moral virtues to reason well about means to those "other" subordinate ends to which moral virtues dispose, much more does prudence require charity to reason well about means to the ultimate, much more difficult and comprehensive, beatific end. Yet, it is not immediately clear how the parallel works, what precisely it's between, or what sort(s) of moral virtue and prudence are in play at each point. Our understanding of whether and/or which prudence depends on charity hangs in the balance. In speaking of the dependence of prudence on charity, is Thomas intending to make a claim about *acquired* prudence, *infused* prudence, or both?

While we saw that 65.2's first reference to the interdependence of prudence and the moral virtues concerns acquired virtues and acquired prudence, here in his claim that "much more" does prudence require charity, Thomas again leaves *prudentia* unlabeled. More, in the sentence cited above, he explicitly refers to this *prudentia* only once but nonetheless he speaks of *two* different dependencies of prudence. Prudence does double duty in the argument even as it appears only once graphically: first, as related to charity ("charity is more necessary . . .") and, second, as related to the moral virtues (the moral virtues are necessary for its function since charity is more necessary). There are, then, two issues before us: (1) which *prudentia* depends on charity and (2) whether it is that charity-dependent *prudentia* or some other *prudentia* that depends on the moral virtues. We also need to grasp the relation between the answers to these questions. We begin with (1), the question of which prudence depends on charity.

Infused Prudence, Infused Moral Virtues

We can rule out first the idea that the claim that prudence depends on charity concerns acquired prudence *alone*. If that were his claim, he would fail to have shown anything about *infused* prudence and its relation to charity, failed to accomplish the article's central task. Further, this would make nonsense of his argument's conclusion—*therefore it is clear* (*unde manifestum fit*), he says following the parallel, that *infused* prudence (*prudentia infusa*) cannot exist without charity. Without numerous steps that simply are not there, claiming that acquired prudence required charity could hardly generate the conclusion that *infused* prudence does.

Could he be referring to both? Saying that prudence of *whatever sort* requires charity? The reference to two dependencies, on moral virtue and charity, might tempt us to think he's claiming that both sorts of prudence require charity. But that cannot be, for the article begins with and centrally depends on the claim that *acquired* virtues do *not* require charity—and, as he explains elsewhere and even within this article, acquired moral virtues require and count among their number acquired prudence.[13] Moreover, the article ends by reiterating that claim and each response to an objection depends on it. Declaring here that *both* acquired and infused prudence required charity would render the article incoherent, collapsing a distinction essential to its case.

Thus, it is necessarily *infused* prudence alone that Thomas here says depends on charity.[14] Recognizing this helps resolve the second puzzle, (2), what to make of the two dependencies. And, really, this asks us to decide on the argument's structure. This much is clear: it is infused prudence that depends on charity and this dependence is analogous to, yet more profound than, the dependence of prudence-of-some-sort on moral-virtues-of-some-sort. The argument's form is:

> *just as (sicut)* ____ requires ____, *even more (multo magis)* ____ requires ____.

And more precisely:

> *just as* ____ requires <u>moral-virtue-of-some-sort</u>, *even more* <u>infused prudence</u> requires <u>charity</u>.

Since Thomas explicitly mentions prudence only once, and we know he is at least claiming that infused prudence requires charity, we might be *tempted* to imagine the argument is:

> *just as* **infused prudence** requires <u>moral-virtue-of-some-sort</u>, *even more* <u>infused prudence</u> requires <u>charity</u>.

If that were the case, the moral-virtue-of-some-sort could only be *infused* moral virtue.[15] Possibly, he has this in mind (a few lines later he speaks of infused moral virtue's dependence on infused prudence), but it seems unlikely because, until now, he has said nothing about relations among the infused moral virtues *and* in the immediately preceding sentence he has spoken instead of the dependence of *acquired* prudence on *acquired* moral virtue. Much more likely then are two alternatives: that he is referring to the dependence of *prudence in general* on *moral virtues in general* or the dependence of *acquired prudence* on *acquired moral virtues*. Either way, the argument has this structure:

> *just as* A requires B, *even more* A* (infused prudence) requires B* (charity).

In both options, the parallel involves some prudence *other* than infused prudence. Either charity is even more necessary to infused prudence than: (1) acquired moral virtue is to acquired prudence *or* (2) moral virtue is to prudence. Just as *acquired* prudence or prudence as such requires *acquired moral virtue* or moral virtue as such, even more does *infused* prudence require *charity*. One of these possibilities seems most likely.[16] In any case, and even on the unlikely infused prudence/infused moral virtue pairing, none of these suggests that *acquired* prudence requires charity. The key point is clear: it is *infused* prudence that is even more dependent on charity than prudence (of whatever sort) on moral virtue (of whatever same sort). Only reading Thomas as *not* claiming here that acquired prudence requires charity can cohere with the article as a whole or his explicit reference to *infused* prudence in this portion's conclusion.

Charity, the Principle of Noncontradiction, and the More Necessary

Following his "even more" argument, Thomas parallels infused prudence's dependence on charity to speculative reason's dependence on the principle of noncontradiction ("PNC"), comparing prudence's need of charity to speculative reasoning's need of the PNC: there is no right speculative reasoning without the PNC as there is no infused prudence without charity. But what about acquired prudence? If charity stands to it *exactly* as PNC stands to speculative reasoning, acquired prudence would be impossible. That, however, would not only contradict my interpretation of this article, but Thomas's explicit affirmations, here and elsewhere, of acquired virtue without charity. More, it would contradict those instances where nearly everyone concedes he countenances at least *some* true if imperfect acquired virtue and prudence as attainable without charity—if only in Eden. This hyperliteral take on the analogy is untenable.

Further, the profound differences between PNC, charity, and their roles, show that charity cannot stand even to infused—much less acquired—prudence exactly as PNC stands to speculative reasoning. First, PNC's role in speculative reasoning is primarily formal, structuring thought but lacking substantive content.[17] While charity informs prudence, Thomas here stresses charity's substantive role in relation to infused prudence: it disposes to beatitude's determinate finality, it supplies prudence with that principle. While PNC cannot itself give rise to any particular knowledge, charity generates particular, substantive acts. Secondly, PNC is self-evident and naturally available to all; not so, charity. While speculative reasoning without PNC is impossible, there can be right (if imperfect) reasoning about non-ultimate ends and means without charity, for grace perfects nature. Infused prudence is as dependent on charity as reasoning on PNC; not so acquired virtue and prudence, which can be had without charity. 65.2 declares acquired virtue imperfect for failing to conduce to beatitude—and charity does not change that.[18] PNC does not so relate to speculative reason.

There is, we will see later, one sense in which charity is necessary for the fullest flowering of even acquired prudence. For now, however, treating another aspect of 65.2 brings two points to light: charity is as necessary to *infused* prudence as PNC to speculative reasoning, and charity can be, like PNC in its domain, implicit in each act of prudence, infused and acquired.

We know why charity is *necessary* for infused prudence, but need to see why Thomas declares it *"more* necessary"—*"much more necessary* that a man be well disposed to the final end . . . through charity, than . . . well disposed to other ends . . . through the moral virtues." Two reasons stand out. One concerns prudence's *ratio*. As a virtue, prudence just is more concerned with the more comprehensive, inclusive, and final end than proximate, even penultimate, ends. Its special matter is rightness of means in pursuit of its chief object, the highest, most comprehensive good.[19] Attending to what Thomas says about other virtues clarifies and vindicates the point.

Take courage. Where the good sought is regarded as difficult or dangerous to obtain, passions of fear and daring come into play, and courage so disposes those passions that, despite the danger, one pursues the good and does so with the right feelings of fear and daring. Thus, courage can be exercised whenever the good pursued is difficult to obtain: winning a race, speaking truth before a hostile audience, and so on. Nonetheless, like all virtues, courage has a "special matter" (*materia specialis*): fear and daring in the face of the gravest dangers of all, dangers of death (II.II 141.3). Courage's chief act, then, is to confront such dangers. So, while courage regards any difficult good, it is tested to its utmost when its task is most difficult: governing passions of fear and daring where the situation is most trying, most likely to elicit foolish, rash, or cowardly action due to irascible appetite's unruliness. And this is in the face of death. Virtue, as "the utmost strength of a power," is vindicated *in extremis* (I.II 56.1). As fitness is gauged against the most strenuous activity, so virtue is measured against that challenge most powerful to sway its subject from right reason. To have courage, irascible appetite must habitually hold to reason's measure even before death. And the person courageous when her life is on the line will (other things being equal) be courageous where lesser dangers are concerned.[20] As the limit of a power, virtue must hold firm in limit cases.

Now, consider prudence. Its formal object is reasoning well about things to be done. Amidst countless, ever-changing singulars, it must discern how rightly to pursue some end. If prudence were to have a special matter what would it be? What would count as its operation *in extremis*? Prudence's task is greatest when it concerns the most singulars and the most complex relations in judging what to do and how to do it: it does this most of all when its end is most comprehensive, inclusive, ultimate. Thus, given the end of eating a healthy lunch the singulars and principles prudence faces are relatively delimited as compared to the end of being a loving spouse, which, in turn, is relatively delimited as compared to the end of pursuing the common good.[21] As the good pursued is more comprehensive, so the relevant singulars, principles, and occasions for error multiply exponentially. In a certain way, the more comprehensive good includes in its aegis an ordering of various less universal goods to it, and thus its pursuit implicates some of the complexity proper to pursuit of those less universal goods.[22] Moreover, the more comprehensive good requires one to deal not just with numerically more considerations but with more complicated questions of how to order and honor various subsidiary goods in relation to one another and the final end. Thus acquired prudence in ordering means to the political end, the highest end proper to it, operates *in extremis* even as it does not concern the ultimate, beatific end.

Just as it is of courage's essence to confront death's dangers, it is of the essence of acquired prudence to reason about the attainment of the comprehensive political end and, in the case of infused prudence, the final, supernatural good. And, thus, it is *more necessary* to prudence that someone be disposed to the ultimate end by charity—for, it is more central and essential to prudence's task to face the challenges posed by pursuit of *that* end than those posed by any lesser ones. It is more necessary that prudence reason about means to not just any but the *final* end as it is more necessary that courage confront not just any dangers but those that threaten life.

Charity is also more necessary to prudence thanks to its role in actually disposing a person *well*. Moral virtues supply prudence with principles but also ensure that the appetites happily comply and do not interfere with prudence's work. If prudence requires that in the less comprehensive realm of the political end, then where beatitude is concerned it is even more necessary that will not only offer no resistance but wholeheartedly, consistently, and single-mindedly impel the agent forward. These are among charity's effects.

When charity is effective, one can (in principle at least) explain how each good act—at least mediately—conduces to beatitude and how its doing so contributed to the act's choiceworthiness. Charity requires that *each act* finally be ordered to beatitude, and that at each step along the way that end not be acted against (*DC* 11 ad 3). Prudence needs charity for this work. Further, since proximate goods really are good, in pursuing such a good and reasoning about how to do so, one can choose in some way that while appropriate in relation to and in pursuit of that good, is not or not maximally so in relation to the final good. Insofar as prudence successfully walks this line, it bears charity's stamp. In part, this is what it means with respect to prudence for charity to be the form of the

virtues. Each act of prudence is informed by charity. Charity is "more necessary" for the operation of infused prudence because for prudence to reason
well about means to the final end, charity must safeguard each of prudence's
decisions along the way.

The Unity of the Infused Virtues

The remainder of 65.2 is relatively straightforward. Having shown that infused
prudence requires charity, Thomas shows that the other infused virtues do too:
they can no more function without infused prudence than acquired virtues
without acquired prudence. "It is clear," he explains, "that neither is infused
prudence (*prudentia infusa*) able to exist without charity, nor, consequently,
the other moral virtues (*aliae virtutes morales*), which, without prudence
(*prudentia*) are not possible" (I.II 65.2). That sentence can seem to claim that
acquired prudence and *acquired* moral virtues *all* depend on charity, because
or as infused prudence does. The misreading tempts because *infusa* disappears
when Thomas refers to prudence in the sentence's second half, because earlier
aliae virtutes morales did refer to *acquired* moral virtues, and because of the
article's overall complexity. By now, we know better. The article aims to show
that *infused* virtues depend on charity and how they do so. This sentence represents the culmination of that case. It would hardly count as success if he only
showed that infused *prudence* depends on charity without showing that the *infused* moral virtues do too. Here he does just that: *infused* moral virtues depend
on charity because they depend on something that depends on charity, *infused*
prudence. If this claim concerned *acquired* virtues, he would undercut 65.2's
first and chief distinction and fail to make the article's main point.

Part of the reason for so carefully examining 65.2 was to guard against the
misreading that takes Thomas to claim here that acquired prudence requires
infused prudence or charity. At no point in 65.2 does Thomas make or imply
that claim. To the contrary, he contends that the acquired virtues, including
acquired prudence can be and actually have been had without charity.

Thomas's conclusion to the corpus, as well as his objections and responses,
further confirm this interpretation: "It is evident, therefore, from these words,
that the infused virtues alone are perfect and said to be virtues simply, because they order man well to the final end simply (*finem ultimum simpliciter*).
Other virtues—certainly the acquired virtues—are virtues in a qualified way
(*secundum quid*), not virtues *simpliciter*: they order a man well with respect to

the final end (*finis ultimi*) in some genus (*genere*), not with respect to the final end simply (*finem ultimum simpliciter*)." Thomas reiterates the supremacy of infused virtue, which alone conduces to beatitude, but notes that the acquired virtues are nonetheless virtues—the sort that he has repeatedly declared true, simple, and perfect, even as here, in view of beatitude, because the political end to which they lead is not final *simply*, he calls them virtues *secundum quid*.

65.2's objections, responses, and broader context further corroborate the reading I've given. In objection two, for instance, Thomas refers simply to "moral virtues," with no further specification and claims that these virtues can be had without charity. The response clarifies the ambiguity of the phrase "moral virtues," explaining that the objection holds only for *acquired* moral virtues. Without explicitly saying what species of prudence and moral virtues are in view, objection three claims that charity surpasses (so as to be unrelated to) prudence and that prudence and the moral virtues are therefore not connected to it. The response makes the very point we saw in the corpus and with nearly identical language: prudence depends on charity and, thus, all the *infused* moral virtues (*omnes virtutes morales infusae*) do. Where the objection and the body's parallel remark spoke simply of *virtutes morales*, the response refers explicitly to *infusae virtutes morales*: the *infused* moral virtues are those requiring charity. The prudence that links *infused* moral virtues cannot be other than *infused*—that is the prudence in view here and at the corpus's parallel point, where it remains unlabeled. *Infused* prudence and *infused* moral virtues alone are under discussion at these points; they alone require charity.[23]

In sum, nothing in I.II 65.2 suggests that charity is necessary for *acquired* virtue to be "connected." Thinking otherwise flows from confusing its claims about *infused* virtues for claims about *acquired* virtues, especially: confusing its insistence that *infused* prudence and the *infused* moral virtues it connects require charity with claims that acquired prudence and moral virtues so depend; and/or eliding the infused/acquired prudence distinction or thinking acquired depends on infused. I have meant to put such misreadings to rest, addressing especially the two passages most likely to generate these misunderstandings.

The (Limited) Deficiency of Acquired Virtue

I.II 65.2, we have seen, stresses that as compared to infused virtues, acquired virtues are essentially imperfect. They immediately concern the final good *secundum quid* rather than the final good *simpliciter*. For this reason they are imperfect—

even when had by Christians. Whatever difference charity makes to their possession, they cannot relate to beatitude as infused virtues do.[24] Yet their classification
as imperfect is not pejorative. It does not devalue them or imply that Thomas
holds them in less than high esteem. We've seen, rather, that he views them as
essential for a vitally important sort of human flourishing, necessary for living
well and for such happiness as can be had in this life.[25] Without acquired virtues,
even those possessed of infused virtue will miss some of the joy and goodness
God intends for humans; their contribution to the common good will not be as
rich, as full, as it could be.

It is with respect to the political good, life and conduct in this world, that
we are centrally concerned. To be sure, charity and the infused virtues matter
now, allowing and enabling deeds of love and sacrifice that testify to the coming kingdom, the brokenness of this world, and God's patient generosity—that
extends to loving even the enemy (II.II 27.7). Yet these, for Thomas, are transcendent, supernatural perfections; their absence, whatever defects it entails,
does not in itself negate or vitiate the real and profound, if finally partial, goodness of the life of acquired, pagan virtue.[26] That life, in regard to the common
good, is truly praiseworthy. That this virtue is deficient as compared to that
directed to beatitude is no reason not to recognize and celebrate it as true, as
good. In pursuing the limited but real good of life together in this world, Christians have every reason to welcome, befriend, partner with, and learn from
those virtuous neighbors who know not their Lord. Insofar as such pagans act
according to their virtue, they are, for Thomas, to be admired and trusted in
matters concerning the common good.

"That Many Gentiles Attained"

The point of supreme interest to us in I.II 65.2, we have held for last. Doing
so has allowed us to answer most of the objections that would detract from
Thomas's affirmation of pagan virtue here. This affirmation is twofold: (1) initially distinguishing acquired from infused virtue, he refers to I.II 63.2 and
declares that acquired virtues are attainable without charity; (2) he says that
precisely these virtues, *acquired* virtues, were actually attained by many non-
Christians. Having already considered (1), we turn to (2): "Just as I said above,
the moral virtues—insofar as they lead to good works ordained to an end
which does not surpass the natural capacities of men—[that is, the *acquired*
virtues] are able to be acquired by human works. They are able to be acquired

without charity, just as they were in many pagans (*multis gentilibus*)" (I.II 65.2). Pagans, Thomas explicitly affirms, are capable of acquired virtue (or, as some problematically call it, "connected acquired virtue").

Acquired virtues just are the political virtues: the political good is the end "not surpassing the natural power of man," the end proportioned to human nature.[27] As the corpus later says, they conduce to the "last end in some particular genus of action"—which is just what the political good is. The acquired virtues possessed by "many of the pagans" are political virtues, the virtues we care about, those that have occupied us throughout. The affirmation of acquired virtue's attainability without charity is *sicut supra dictum est*, just as said above, in I.II 63.2. There we saw how, even after the fall, the virtues proportioned to humanity are attainable without charity. 65.2's acquired virtues possessed by many "Gentiles," are 63.2's acquired or political virtues: all that is true of them as to perfection, inherent unity, and authenticity is true of these.

That "many Gentiles" attained these virtues substantiates and clarifies that the humans capable of attaining these virtues without charity are humans as actually living in our postlapsarian, sin-ridden world. This forecloses any suggestion that here, in 63.2, or elsewhere Thomas is referring to integral human nature in affirming pagan virtue. Whatever original sin's consequences, it does not entail that humans cannot attain the political virtues, which of their nature are inherently "connected."

Consider too 65.2's second objection and response, where Thomas affirms that acquired virtue can be had without charity, citing *Nicomachean Ethics* II.1–2 as showing that "moral virtues can be acquired by means of human acts." The virtues Thomas has in mind as attainable without charity are, in his view, not other than those *Nicomachean Ethics* II.1–2 considers. In the relevant sense, he regards himself and Aristotle as treating specifically identical virtue. Indeed, his commentary explicitly identifies Aristotle here as discussing virtues as excellences of character in accord with *recta ratione* (*CNE* I.10.12, II.2.3 and 9). Nothing less than habits of will and appetite participating right reason is the sort of virtue Thomas here declares attainable without charity. These are full-fledged "connected" virtues imbued with *recta ratione* by prudence. Certainly, nothing here, in the *Ethics*, or in his reading of Aristotle suggests he has in mind "unconnected" or loosely held quasi-virtues in saying pagans attained acquired virtues. It is nothing less than full-fledged acquired virtues—imperfect though they be relative to infused—that Thomas explicitly declares attainable without charity.

In 65.1, Thomas distinguishes between perfect and imperfect moral virtues, where perfect moral virtues are true virtues, political virtues—virtues "connected," stable, and participating right reason. 65.1's imperfect virtues, in contrast, include individual natural virtue and inconsistent dispositions to narrowly good ends.[28] This imperfect virtue—so imperfect that Thomas says it lacks virtue's essential *ratio* by lacking right reason—is what some claim Thomas says can be attained by pagans in 65.2. Given the complexity, the confusion is understandable.

I.II 65.2 may constitute Thomas's most explicit affirmation of pagan virtue, however easy it may be to misunderstand. By now, we've seen that the article offers a strong, definitive affirmation of pagan virtue, that its acquired virtues can be attained without charity, and that they are the political or human virtues, those that concern Aristotle, us, and, through much of the virtue treatise, Thomas himself. They were attained by pagans and are attainable by postlapsarian humanity. In being human virtues, they are necessarily "connected"—Thomas envisions no other possibility for authentic acquired virtues, not in 65.2 or anywhere else. We turn now to two texts that have been in the background throughout this chapter, especially in matters to do with virtue's unity: I.II 65.1 and *De virtutibus cardinalibus* 2.

6   BOUNDARIES AND ENDS

FOR THOMAS, unity, stability, and the robust participation of right reason are essential to constituting virtues as virtues. There are no authentic virtues, no genuine habits of doing good well, that are not *difficile mobile*, interconnected, imbued with right reason. These things, we've seen, flow from virtue's very *ratio*. And Thomas insists on a firm division between that which attains this *ratio*—good habit or virtue—and even its nearest dispositional predecessors, let alone its most distant antecedents. Yet, as chapter 3 noted, criteria like stability, connection, and right reason confront us with vagueness problems. There's no doubt that a loosely held disposition to do good in some limited domain is no real virtue but, granted the incremental character of habituation into virtue, what of those states where unity, stability, and right reason have in some real measure begun to obtain? Those conditions immediately prior to full-fledged virtue? How can we even declare some such state *prior*? That Thomas sometimes couches this distinction in the language of perfection and imperfection does not resolve such questions; it simply changes the vocabulary. We're left wondering how to divide imperfect from perfect, disposition from virtue. This chapter confronts these and other challenges by considering two texts vital to our topic: I.II 65.1 and *De virtutibus cardinalibus (DVC)* 2.

As the preceding chapter indicates, 65.1 is essential to the question of pagan virtue: it explicitly confirms that the acquired virtues are, of their essence, connected and thus that in attaining acquired virtues outsiders necessarily possess connected virtues; it further refines our conception of what acquired virtue is; and it explicates one of Thomas's key imperfection/perfection distinctions, that between what truly is a virtue and what in some essential way fails to be. *DVC* 2 closely parallels 65.1 and while both are essential, *DVC* is the more complex of the two, incorporating and expanding on nearly everything in 65.1 while also covering material that appears in I.II 65.2 and in II.II 23.7. Accordingly, while beginning with 65.1, we take *DVC* 2 as our primary focus.

I.II 65.1 and the Breadth of Imperfect Virtue

65.1 distinguishes perfect from imperfect moral virtue. Perfect moral virtue is connected; imperfect moral virtue, not properly virtue at all, is not. Synthesizing much that came before, the article illustrates the variability of Thomas's perfection language and contends that moral virtues are necessarily connected. Defending the *sed contra*, which, atypically, cites four authorities—Ambrose, Augustine, Gregory, *and* Cicero—Thomas even declares the unity of the moral virtues a doctrine "nearly all hold."

As we will see, fully grasping this text requires recalling chapter 4's lessons. In one sense, we can read 65.1 as elucidating and applying I.II 49.2 ad 3's distinction within *S-habit*. While here the distinction is within *S-virtue*, it is structurally and—as regards the *difficile mobile* criterion—materially identical, dividing authentic virtue from mere disposition, that which is inherently connected from that which is not properly virtue. To be sure, 65.1's perfect and imperfect virtue both stand within the broader species *S-virtue*. But that merely means they are neither bad nor bodily habits but dispositions of soul with at least minimal proclivity to good action in limited domains. Species membership is insufficient to constitute a disposition as an authentic habit of virtue. A world of difference stands between virtue and disposition thereto, a habit of doing the good well and something less, I.II 65.1's perfect and imperfect virtue.

65.1's imperfect virtue falls *essentially* short of virtue's *ratio* (I.II 65.1 ad 1). 65.1's perfection, connection, belongs to moral virtue *as such*, along with stability and other features that constitute it as virtue, as distinct from mere disposition. Stability and unity mutually implicate one another and are inextricably related, inhering in virtue's *ratio*. Pertaining to the virtue side of the division within *S-virtue*, they help constitute that line. "Connected moral virtue," then, is no perfected subset within the habit of virtue, any more than "person having attained the age of reason" is of "morally responsible human." Nor is unity an independent addition that turns imperfect virtue perfect. Unity, *difficile mobilie, recte ratione*, true virtue—these rise and fall together. When unity is absent it is never absent alone. Rather, a whole host of features constitutive of virtue's essence are necessarily missing too, especially, right reason's habitual participation. For Thomas, a bright line divides 65.1's imperfect and perfect virtues and disconnection is merely one facet of imperfect virtue's essential deficiency, of a piece with the rest. This line is so bright and significant, I.II 49.2 ad 3 and earlier chapters show, that what falls on the imperfect side is not strictly speaking virtue at all but a disposition to virtue. It's no *habit* of doing good well. Calling it *imperfect virtue* conveys correctly that, unlike false virtue, it can be virtue's precursor, a step *in via,* even as it falls essentially short. And the terms *perfect virtue* or *connected virtue* avoid redundancy only when *virtue* means *S-virtue,* when the broader species is in view. When we have in focus virtue proper, excellent habits of character, speaking of *connected* or *perfect virtue* is a confusing redundancy. Connection inheres in virtue's *being* virtue; disconnected dispositions are not properly virtues at all. This chapter further substantiates these claims and sketches an account of Thomas's sharp division that honors his insistence on the dividing line's brightness while keeping the vagueness problem—as much a function of unity as of stability—at bay.

Imperfection, *ex assuetudine*, and Perfection

"An imperfect moral virtue," Thomas explains, "such as [imperfect] temperance or [imperfect] courage, is nothing other than a certain inclination (*aliqua inclinatio*) in us for doing some good deed. And such an inclination may be in us from nature (*a natura*) or from habituation (*ex assuetudine*)" (I.II 65.1). Thomas does not exclusively identify imperfect virtue with inclinations *a natura,* individual natural virtue, but refers as well to inclinations that are *ex assuetudine,* from habituation or custom. Imperfect virtues are inclinations to good deeds in us due either to our particular nature or habituation.[1] This habituation may involve efforts at self-cultivation or may stem, more narrowly, from culture's socializing power.

What counts as *ex assuetudine* are not just inclinations unwittingly adopted through upbringing or enculturation or even those that additionally require some consent or participation on the agent's part. Also included are those acquired thanks to intention and deliberate self-exercise, even those acquired in pursuit of virtue. Responding to the first objection, Thomas contrasts one who acquires perfect virtue with one who acquires only imperfect virtue. In each case the same verb describes what the person does: *exercitetur.* She "is exercised" or "trained" or "exercises" or "trains herself." Since not just imperfect virtue but virtue proper is characterized as acquired *ex assuetudine,* what counts as acquired *ex assuetudine* is not merely that which is acquired through acculturation or other relatively un-self-reflective avenues but that which is, like virtue proper, acquired precisely through deliberate pursuit. She who acquires true virtue has sufficiently exercised herself in *all* the activities of the virtues; she who acquires imperfect virtue exercises herself inadequately or only in some or one of the activities.[2] At least one variety of imperfect virtue shares perfect virtue's basic etiology. Any differences in their pathways are due not to the absence of intention or self-cultivation but its character, longevity, or the like.

In two senses can imperfect virtues be had *ex assuetudine*. They can be present thanks to a *process* of habituation, even if the inclination is not itself rooted in a full-fledged habit. Thus, thanks to habituation, Joe could have an inclination to do good deeds in matters of courage even as this inclination fell short of being (or being rooted in) habit.[3] Alternatively, he could actually have a habit thanks to his habituation—that is, his inclination could itself qualify as or be rooted in a habit.[4]

Insofar as it produces *good* deeds, this habit will have a very narrow scope, a limited range of success, and a kind of stable inconsistency.[5] This is so because it will produce good actions only in those extremely straightforward, exceedingly rare cases where, say, matters of courage *alone* impinge, where the agent's lack of the virtues, including courage, does not result in his courage-related action being bad. Understood precisely, the habit will not be one of *doing good acts* in matters of courage but, as Thomas puts it, of "restraining anger" (*refrenandum iras*), of not letting anger regularly corrupt one's judgments in matters directly concerned with anger (I.II 65.1 ad 1). It is not a habit of doing good but a habit bearing on irascible matters, occasionally producing good acts in that sphere. This variety of habit would belong to some soldiers, say, who lack true courage but, due to good courage-related battlefield acts, appear courageous (II.II 123.1 ad 2). It will have a stable inconsistency: leading as often to *wrong* as to right action. Its instability, we will see, goes deeper still: it is unstable even as a *determinate* inclination.

For now, note the very wide scope of states Thomas here characterizes as imperfect virtue. In speaking of it as inclination either *a natura* or *ex assuetudine*, he includes everything from individual natural virtues to dispositions for courageous acts to habits of "restraining anger." None is virtue proper, for none is a habit of acting fully *with* right reason, with prudence judging as to means and right reason forming the appetitive subject that bears the habit (I.II 57.5 and ad 2; 58.2; 58.4 ad 3). At best, they incline, inconsistently, to good actions within some limited sphere or circumstances, such as actions involving restraining anger or resisting lust *when nothing else is implicated*. Still, there is great and important difference between the opposing poles that demark imperfect virtue's terrain. On one end are individual natural virtues, which lack even virtue's roots in habituation. On the other are inclinations present through habit, deliberate self-cultivation, that nonetheless lack virtue's participation in right reason. In grouping such traits together, Thomas does not deny these differences. On the contrary, only their falling short of true virtue constitutes them as a common class. The point is key. Missing it can let one imagine that imperfect virtues just *are* individual natural virtues or similarly impoverished inclinations.

And thinking that can generate interpretive errors as one tries to make room for the wide range of character states between individual natural virtue and true virtue. One can, for instance, imagine that true virtues, thanks to unity alone, are a perfected variety within a common set "virtue" that includes an otherwise identical disconnected, imperfect type, and that these together are essentially distinct from individual natural virtue. Recognizing that Thomas constitutes the category of imperfect virtue as broadly as he does helps quell such misreadings. Mere inclusion in that category does not imply that Thomas regards everything included therein as equally praiseworthy—only that he regards them all as essentially distinct from perfect virtue, true virtue.

"A perfect moral virtue," Thomas explains, "is a habit inclining [one] to do a good act *well*. And taking 'moral virtues' in *this* way, it must be said that they are connected" (I.II 65.1). Perfect moral virtues are *habits of doing good acts well*. While some imperfect virtues may be habits, they are not habits of doing good acts, much less good acts well.[6] They are not because, *qua* habits, they do not stably conduce to good acts, but at best to acts that, in certain narrow, favorable circumstances, are good. The distinguishing feature of these acts is not goodness but, say, restraining anger or lust. Such a habit may generate the right act, but in many instances—and with no failure relative to its identity or function *as* habit—it will not.

In contrast, 65.1's "perfect virtue" is a habit of doing the good act well: acquired, political, or human virtue, which is necessarily connected.[7] Thomas here stresses that prudence connects the virtues, particularly emphasizing its role in discerning right means to will's end. Absent prudence, inclination to truly good ends will not necessarily lead to good actions. Recall, Thomas's portrait of the person with individual natural virtue as a blind, stampeding horse. Say through habituation I acquire an imperfect virtue of liberality, inclining me to earn and generously give money. Say, too, I have even acquired an imperfect liberality focused prudence. As *imperfect*, it exclusively concerns reasoning about means *in relation to attaining money and giving it away* and thus does not involve right reasoning in relation to other goods implicated in these choices or choices more generally.[8] I decide the best way to earn money to give away is through investing, including investing in a brothel. With no flaw in their very exercise, this imperfect liberality and its prudence result in generous giving but lead as well to unjust action.[9] Prudence guarantees against undertaking evil means in pursuit of the good end to which some moral virtue disposes. Without it, one will do evil as frequently as good.

Each moral virtue is thus connected to and dependent on prudence. "Without prudence," Thomas says, "no moral virtue can be had for it is proper to moral virtue to conduce to a right choice since it is a choosing habit (*habitus electivus*)" (I.II 65.1).[10] That is, moral virtue conduces exclusively to *right* action—but for this to obtain requires that moral virtue be possessed *with* prudence so that an inclination to a good end yields not brothel-funding or like evils: "Right choice (*rectam electionem*) requires not only inclination to the due end, which is directly by a habit of moral virtue, but also that one choose (*eligat*) [well] concerning that which is ordered to the end, which is directly through prudence" (I.II 65.1).

But prudence itself, Thomas reminds us, depends on *all* the moral virtues. As *scientia* needs first principles, prudence's right reasoning requires that moral virtues supply it with good ends. Further, prudence's operation must not be undercut by problematic desires—bad ends, unruly appetite. Perhaps undisciplined sensible appetite and the thought of certain benefits contribute to the brothel investor choosing this particular unjust means. Absent temperance shaping sensual desire or justice informing will, imperfect prudence stands little chance of success, little chance of generating good actions.

Aside from his labeling inclinations to good acts as "imperfect virtue," all this is familiar. Thomas even refers explicitly to I.II 58.4 and 5's earlier arguments concerning unity. The perfection under consideration is proper to virtue as such, the connection/disconnection distinction derivative of that within *S-virtue* between virtue and what fails to attain virtue's *ratio*, disposition. While virtue generates good deeds done well and cannot be used badly, imperfect "virtue" falls short on both counts.

Clearly, 65.1's perfection is not I.II 65.2's. 65.2's perfection concerned virtue conducing to beatitude—something *infused* virtue alone can do.[11] Certainly, infused moral virtues are connected—to one another and the theological virtues—and so are "perfect" in 65.1's sense (or something analogous to it). But this is only to say they *are* virtues. 65.2's imperfect virtue, the virtue of *multis Gentilibus*, is 65.1's perfect virtue, human virtue. As *human virtue*, 65.2's imperfect virtue is necessarily connected, but 65.1 underlines that point and clarifies the sense in which outsiders can possess perfect acquired virtue: perfect according to its *ratio*, perfect in being true, unified virtue; imperfect in not conducing to beatitude. It's the disposition of the perfect to the second best.

DVC 2, Instability, and the Limits of Imperfect Virtue

While covering similar ground, *DVC* 2 is importantly different from I.II 65.1 and 2. Viewing it as synthesizing those passages neglects the ways its distinctions are not necessarily theirs. Specifically, in *DVC* 2, Thomas asks "whether the virtues be connected so that he who has one has all" (*DVC* 2). He answers by distinguishing between imperfect and perfect virtues and then between two varieties of perfect virtues: acquired and infused virtue. Both perfect varieties are necessarily intraconnected; imperfect virtue is not. Three "grades" of virtue correspond to these three distinctions: wholly imperfect virtues (*omnino imperfectae*), acquired virtues or virtues perfect in the sense of attaining right reason's rule but not simply perfect, and infused virtues or virtues conducing to beatitude and simply perfect.

Wholly imperfect virtues "exist without prudence, not reaching the [rule of] right reason." They incline to some good action, but not to it *as* good action, *as* right. Using *sicut*, or "such as," Thomas adduces individual natural virtue as an example: "inclinations that some have to the works of some virtue even from birth." "Such inclinations," he continues, "do not have the *ratio* of virtue because virtue may not be put to evil use . . . but someone can use these inclinations evilly and injuriously." Unsurprisingly, his example of the stampeding, blind horse follows. That wholly imperfect virtues result in good acts is more a matter of circumstance and fortune than deliberation: the very inclination that yields a courageous act today yields gross injustice tomorrow.[12] Concluding, Thomas cites prudence's absence and wholly imperfect virtue's capacity to be used evilly to distinguish wholly imperfect virtue from *DVC*'s true but imperfect virtue. Wholly imperfect virtues, thus, seem to be any dispositions to good acts that lack true prudence, prudence that attains right reason's rule. They seem coincident with 65.1's imperfect virtues—the whole spectrum of inclinations, however acquired, sometimes conducing to good acts but lacking right reason's full participation.

An objection here in *DVC* 2 and in 65.1 imagines someone who deliberately tries to cultivate a single virtue. Say, Jane exercises herself exclusively in courage-related matters. The objection claims that a virtue can be attained in this way, all by itself, and thus that acquired virtues are not connected after all. Thomas responds that, ultimately, whatever is acquired in this way is just another variety of imperfect virtue. Still, this case of someone who *tries* to cultivate a single virtue or to train herself to do good acts in one virtue's matter surely represents one of imperfect virtue's far reaches.[13] Significantly, even this falls short of genuine virtue, acquired virtue. Some suggest that just this is what Thomas believes outsiders can attain—and that this is not included within *DVC* 2's and I.II 65.1's wholly imperfect or imperfect virtue. But in claiming pagans can attain acquired virtue, Thomas is *not* claiming that this, just another variety of imperfect virtue, is what they can attain. We need to see why this inclination falls short of virtue and how far it is from acquired virtue in its inherent instability.

In both *DVC* 2 ad 9 and I.II 65.1 ad 1, Thomas begins by noting that some activities and challenges are common to every human life. The matters of the cardinal virtues are such that nobody can go through life without facing them even daily. We all must do something about our appetites for food, sex, and so on, and our anger and fear. Everyone has to live with and relate to others. And everyone has to consider what ends to pursue and how to go about pursuing them. These are, respectively, the matters of moderation, courage, justice, and prudence. For Thomas, these dimensions of human life are common to all. In both passages, Thomas claims that unless one exercise oneself well in all of these matters, one will, in the end, exercise oneself well in none. To acquire the virtues, one must (try to) do good deeds consistently and for the right reasons, in the right way, and so on, in all these dimensions of life (*DVC* 2 ad 9 and 10).

If one does good deeds in just one of these dimensions of life, he claims, one will not acquire even the single virtue whose works one tries to do.[14] Take Thomas's illustration in 65.1, "We see [someone who] from some natural tendency (*complexione*) or habituation is prompt to works of liberality even as he is not prompt to works of chastity."[15] Thomas roots the example in observation; it's something he thinks we can see.[16] We encounter people, he says, who are quick to give away money but slow to avert a lustful gaze—or prone not to avert it at all. And most of us do know people who seem admirable in some respect—courageous on the protest line, temperate in relation to drink—but less than admirable in other moral dimensions—quick to anger, say, or greedy. Or perhaps, they are just "average" in most areas and appear to excel in one dimension of moral life.

Thomas claims that one who deliberately does good works where anger is concerned but not in all matters common to life can acquire some habit (*habitum aliquem*) of restraining anger.[17] In calling this "habit," he characterizes it *not* as a habit of *doing good or courageous acts* but of "restraining anger." This because in many cases it *fails* to produce good or even courageous deeds— it is *not* stable *qua* inclination to *good deeds*. In the case Thomas envisions, someone has failed to exercise herself in good deeds pertaining to sensitive appetite. She easily and readily governs herself in matters concerning anger (alone) but fails to have her sexual desire informed by temperance. This anger-related habit, Thomas explains, "will not have the *ratio* of virtue because of the lack of prudence—which is spoiled in matters of lust" (I.II 65.1 ad 1). Recall that for prudence to reason aright in *any* matter it needs to reason aright in *all*—and for that it needs *each* appetite rightly disposed.[18]

The point is easier to grasp with another example. Suppose someone has exercised himself well in food-related matters so that he is good at restraining his appetite, not overindulging, and his appetite usually tends not to desire too much food. Yet he has neglected to practice good deeds in matters of justice or anger. He typically desires and eats moderate amounts of healthy food *when other things are equal*, when decisions about food do not implicate principles or passions other than those related to food. This is a disposition to do good deeds when the only difficulty is that posed by food and desire for it *per se*. However, if his lover has just left him or he's feeling depressed, angry, aroused, or distracted, or if there's not enough food to go around, he does not conduct himself well *even* in regard to food—his food-related deeds are not good. They are not because his practical reasoning about how much food to eat, when, where, and so on, is corrupted by the ends his will and appetites wrongly dispose him toward or the principles they call, or fail to call, to mind. Practical reason is polluted with improper principles, blinded to the right ones, and handicapped in its deliberation concerning the matter of erstwhile strength. So, in his emotional or distracted states he overeats or desires too much or the wrong sort of food, or, in the situation of scarcity, he takes a moderate amount given his own needs but an unjust share given someone else's.

Imperfect virtues of the sort discussed here in 65.1 ad 1 and *DVC* 2 ad 9 conduce to good actions when other things are equal. But in life other things are usually *not* equal. Rarely does one face a decision that implicates the matter of one virtue alone. There will very frequently and perhaps almost always be matters other than those strictly related to food that impinge when it comes time to eat. Justice is required to behave well in matters to do with others. To have the last piece of pie may not be immoderate, but if my child is hungry and there is nothing else to eat it will be unjust. Practical reason must attend not only to whether, relative to health, this piece of pie is good to eat but to the needs of others and my parental duties.[19] Thanks to a lack of justice, however, practical reason is corrupted. Prudence is absent. I eat the pie. My child borders on starvation.[20] In short, the scenarios in which it is *only* the good of food and the desire for it that are in play are at least equaled and likely far outnumbered by situations in which matters are more complicated, goods more varied, desires more diverse. Easily, then, my disposition could produce bad action as often as good. The same holds for any disposition to do good limited to any one matter—or any less than all matters—of the virtues.

This is just what Thomas has in mind in *DVC* 2 ad 9 when he says that

> It is *necessary* that a person, while exercising himself in the act of one virtue, either simultaneously exercise himself in the acts of the other virtues, and thus acquire all the habits of the virtues together or else that he act well in the one and badly in the others and, in so doing, acquire a habit *contrary* to one of the other virtues and, consequently, the corruption of prudence—without which the disposition acquired by any virtuous act does not have the proper *ratio* of virtue.

Thomas says that this is *necessarily* the case. If one performs the acts of just one or some of the virtues then whatever habit or disposition one thereby acquires will fail to be virtue. It will because it will not produce action with right reason since practical reason will be corrupted in those matters where one has not exercised oneself. And thus, that habit will not participate right reason—because there will be no right reason *for* it to participate—nor, for the same reason, will it produce action that is *with* right reason.

What is more, as I illustrated and Thomas notes, the corruption of practical reason thanks to unruly habits or inconsistent (or incontinent) desires will necessarily spill over into matters where one has exercised oneself in good works. Eventually, if one lives long enough, practical reason becomes corrupted concerning the very matters where one inclined to good works.[21] As a result one will not do good works in that matter so that, eventually, the initial inclination will not merely fail, as it always has to produce good *with* right reason, but even to produce good *according* to right reason. Where an individual natural virtue might endure on account of its origin in one's particular human nature, this sort of self-made imperfect virtue will have no such endurance. It will finally disintegrate thanks to one's negligence in other matters or one's other bad habits. This sort of imperfect virtue actually contains the seeds of its own destruction from and in its very inception. Earlier I noted the deep, fundamental instability of imperfect virtues even as determinate inclinations. This is what I had in mind.

Speaking about natural virtue and why one cannot be naturally inclined to *all* the virtues, Thomas remarks that

> The natural disposition which inclines to one virtue inclines to the contrary of a different virtue—so, someone who is naturally disposed to courage, which is pursuit of the difficult, is thus less disposed to meekness or gentleness (*mansuetudo*) which consists in bridling the irascible passions. Hence we see that animals which are naturally inclined to the act of one virtue are inclined to the vice that is that virtue's contrary—just as the lion which is naturally bold is also naturally cruel. (*DV* 8 ad 10)

The point holds for self-made imperfect virtue as well. Inclination to a limited good, a good particular to one virtue, is necessarily inclination away from the good of another, and so inclination to some vice opposed to that virtue. Over time that inclination develops into vice and so spells destruction for *any* and *all* dispositions to virtue, including that which initially appeared so virtuous.

In sum, without prudence, this inclination is not really virtue but lacks the "proper *ratio* of virtue" (*DVC* 2 ad 9). Without prudence, it is inherently unstable, always decaying, and, finally, impotent to consistently produce even *merely* good actions (*DV* 8). It is easy to see why these habits are grouped in the category of "imperfect virtues." And it is easy to see why Thomas would declare them just like individual natural virtues. If the virtues are to be acquired at all, they must be acquired together. While inclinations acquired by one sort of good act may for a time, under some description, be habits, they are essentially imperfect virtues. As acquired through self-exercise, they participate reason, following its lead in a particular matter, under certain circumstances. But following *reason*'s lead is a far cry from following *right* reason's lead. Imperfect virtue enables not obedience to *right reason*. Whatever end in relation to which someone exercises herself, to that end is her passion ordered and obedient

to reason. At one point, Thomas explains that intellectual virtues are disconnected because they are each "ordained to some particular goods," some *bona
particularia* (*DVC* 2 ad 8).[22] And he goes on to say that in being so ordered,
they are disconnected for the same reason as imperfect virtues. Imperfect virtues, his remark reminds, are always ordered to some *particular* good, not the
good-according-to-right-reason. An appetitive habit is conditionally obedient to
reason, not obedient to reason's command *as such*, but to a particular *variety
thereof*. Its prompt obedience to reason is nontransferable. That is why courage
does not help the embezzler with her fear. That is why the one-trick virtue is
not really virtue at all.

DVC 2's remarks concerning acquired and infused virtues are similar to
what Thomas says in the other texts we've examined. Grade 2 virtues are acquired virtues and, unlike wholly imperfect virtues, "attain to right reason but
do not attain to God himself through charity" (*DVC* 2). Echoing 65.2 and reso-
nating with II.II 23.7, Thomas explains that such virtues "*are* perfect, in a way,
in relation to the human good, but they are not perfect *simpliciter* because they
do not attain to the first rule, which is the final end" (*DVC* 2). While perfect in
respect to the human good, because this good is not ultimate, acquired virtues
are perfect *aliqualiter*, "in a way."

In I.II 65.2, II.II 23.7, and *DVC* 2, these virtues are perfect or true in view of
the political end, but *secundum quid* in view of beatitude. Here Thomas notes
that they "fall short of the true *ratio* of virtue much as (*sicut*) moral inclinations without prudence" (*DVC* 2). The comparison can mislead. Thomas's point
is merely that acquired virtues are like wholly imperfect virtues in that *both*
fail to attain the ultimate end. Neither does the work of simply perfect virtue.
But the similarity ends there, for Thomas counts acquired virtue *as virtue* and
even, in a key sense, perfect. Moreover, after explaining why grade 3 virtues are
perfect *simpliciter*, he explains that acquired virtues are inherently connected.[23]
Having just noted acquired virtue's deficiency and with that in sight, he refers
to his remarks regarding wholly imperfect virtue, and, emphasizing what distinguishes acquired from wholly imperfect virtues, declares that "*moral virtue*
cannot exist without prudence." With their deficiency foregrounded and without qualification, he nonetheless classifies acquired virtues as, simply, "moral
virtues." Mirroring 65.1 and *DVC* 2 ad 9, he argues that neither moral virtue nor
prudence can exist independently. Without prudence, there is no virtue. While
both wholly imperfect and acquired virtue *alike* fail perfectly to attain virtue's
perfect *ratio*, Thomas says, the one's failure means it lacks something essential

to that *ratio* and is not really virtue, the other's failure does not keep it from being virtue. "Virtues perfect in the second grade, [perfect] with respect to the human good," Thomas concludes, "are connected through prudence, because without prudence no moral virtues are possible, nor can prudence be had if one lack moral virtue" (*DVC* 2).

Original Sin and Pagan Virtue: The Story So Far

We have now seen that I.II 65.1's perfect moral virtue, I.II 65.2's imperfect but true virtue, and *DVC* 2's grade 2 or partly perfect virtue are all (or at least include) acquired virtue, human virtue. Notwithstanding original sin, outsiders can attain this virtue. At 65.2's outset, Thomas refers us to I.II 63.2 as showing acquired virtue's attainability without charity. There, he explains that without grace avoiding mortal sin altogether is impossible and that certain mortal sins are inevitable but that nonetheless one can attain virtue. Acquired virtue, Thomas contends, is attainable without charity by unredeemed, fallen people.[24]

He says the same in *De virtutibus in communi* responding to Augustine's claim that man cannot avoid sin without grace and to the suggestion that therefore virtue cannot be acquired without grace. Acquired virtue "does not make one turn from sin always, but only in most matters," he explains. It does not enable one to avoid every sin: "through the acquired virtues the sin of *infidelitas* is not avoided, nor other sins which are opposed to the infused virtues" (*DV* 9 ad 5). Thomas is obviously dealing with the postlapsarian epoch yet even in view of original sin's effects, he claims that true human virtue, which enables one to turn from sin in "most matters," is attainable without grace.

As the next chapter explains, once charity heals original sin's damage a deeper unity of acquired virtue becomes possible. But even without that, pagan virtue is connected, on the right side of the line separating imperfect virtue from virtue proper. That line is drawn in I.II 65.1, *DVC* 2, and elsewhere and follows from Thomas's very conception of human virtue. It divides true virtue or habits inclining to doing good acts well from imperfect virtue or inclinations to good acts, virtue proper from its furthest and nearest neighbors. Just as there is a wide variety of imperfect virtues, linked by their lack of (or, in the best case, lack of adequate) participation in right reason, so is there a breadth of true virtue. All that is on pagan virtue's side is true virtue indeed, but there remains room for greater degrees of perfection within this state—and with that, greater degrees of connection.[25] Thanks to original sin, there are matters of prudence in which the pagan is hampered where those healed by grace are not. Accordingly, the acquired virtues of the redeemed can be more profoundly connected. But this difference, whatever it concretely amounts to, is one of degree, not kind. It is not a difference that separates virtue from mere inclination, perfect from imperfect, but a difference *within* authentic acquired virtue. For, fully noting original sin's effects, Thomas repeatedly and explicitly declares unbelievers capable of acquired—or, what is the same, connected—virtue.[26]

Vagueness and Virtue, Safety and Boundaries

The time has come to address the vagueness problem we first encountered in considering the distinction within *S-habit* between habit or virtue and disposition, the line dividing perfect from imperfect, virtue from even its nearest antecedent. Consider someone who has pursued prudence and exercised herself well in the matter of all virtues but has not yet attained virtue. While far closer to virtue than someone who has exercised himself in one alone, she falls short because her dispositions lack the stability and endurance proper to habit, failing to produce the good act done well with virtue's consistency, stability, or ease. Certainly, her long-standing and comprehensive efforts give her dispositions a kind of interconnection. Yet, thanks to disposition's lack of adequate consistency in producing good acts done well, this connection—like the disposition themselves—cannot but remain somewhat unstable, loose. Whether we place them in 65.1's or *DVC* 2's category of imperfect virtue or not, Thomas will not regard them as proper virtues for they are not yet virtuous habits. His labeling such things "imperfect virtues" underlines both that category's breadth and the error in regarding the appellation as pejorative. Imperfect virtue, this case reminds, is often morally praiseworthy. It would be foolish and unjust to see the person on the brink of virtue as morally equivalent to one possessed of individual natural virtue. Reducing "imperfect virtue" to individual natural virtue and its near neighbors only tempts us to lower the bar for what counts as true virtue—lest more developed but not yet virtuous dispositions disappear from view. Without doing the work for us, Thomas leaves us room to distinguish among all sorts of imperfect virtues. The door he closes is the one that, blurring the line or dragging virtue down, would refuse to let virtue be virtue.

The achievement of virtue represents the culmination of disposition's gradual transformation into habit's stable solidity. Tenuous connections cohere into genuine unity. Neither "connection" nor virtue appears from nowhere. There are precursors, anticipations. Thomas does not discuss the movement from the immediately prior state to virtue itself.[27] But he repeatedly draws a bright line: where the criteria for good operative habit are met, disposition becomes virtue—no habit of doing good acts well, no virtue. And he elsewhere argues that habit (and so virtue) is a form and so either is definitively present or not.[28] But the question remains of how to understand the division between virtue or habit and the immediately preceding disposition.

How to conceptualize the acquisition—and eventual growth in perfection—of virtue? Consider Timothy Williamson's work on knowledge, which also gives us another way to imagine what it means for virtues, as habits, to be *difficile mobile*.[29] According to Williamson, safety, danger, reliability, and unreliability are modal terms getting at what could or might happen, especially what could or might happen were things slightly different than they are. Imagine, he says, a light ball atop a barely-indented cone and a ball in a deep pit. Both are stable in that they are not moving. But the ball atop the cone is not safe, for it easily could move and even fall. Suppose a huge gust of wind comes along, and neither ball moves. Nonetheless, the balanced ball is in a precarious position, its equilibrium fragile. Had the wind been a bit stronger, longer, or come from a slightly different angle—as it might easily have—the ball would have fallen. In contrast, only a situation radically unlike that which obtains will result in the other ball moving.

The point is suggestive in considering vagueness and bright lines. A bright line separates these balls from a falling or teetering ball—even as the states of the teetering and almost-but-not-teetering balls are otherwise nearly indistinguishable. This line gets at something. But not everything. For in view of *stability*, the balancing ball has more in common with the teetering one than either has with the one in the pit. And if it is safety we care about, the difference between the balancing ball and the one in the pit is more vital or basic than any equilibrium-related similarity. While this difference can shrink as cones shorten and indentations deepen, it generates a line no less bright: a point at which the ball is safe.

For Thomas, virtue concerns safety and reliability. Safety from doing evil, yielding to temptation, choosing sinfully. Reliability in doing good well. Such reliability, he thinks, comes only as a whole character—passions, intellect, and will—is rightly shaped. To the extent they are not—intellect unwise, a single passion unruly, or whatever—the agent lives in danger of falling. Perhaps in some cases where we expect a stumble, the agent does not, but easily he could have. Had things been slightly different—cake moister, woman more attractive, frustration greater—easily he could have yielded. In Williamson's idiom, there is *danger* of some event of type E—doing evil—occurring if and only if in a sufficiently similar case an event of type E occurs.

Given the connection between virtue, safety, and reliability, a ball atop a cone hardly images virtue. Still, that picture suggests how bright lines can avoid arbitrariness (i.e., equilibrium obtains) even while dividing adjacent states that otherwise resemble one another far more (i.e., in terms of danger) than states further along a given trajectory (i.e., more stable equilibrium). Take a more suitable case: a child near a cliff's edge.[30] Say the minimum distance between child and edge necessary to count him safe is three feet. A child three feet from the edge is safe—but barely. He is not safely safe, for the slightest stumble puts him in danger. It does not send him over the edge—that is what it meant for him to be safe to begin with, why safety required three feet. But it puts him in danger, for now he is at risk of falling where he was not before. Part of his initially having been safe is the fact that he can easily return to safety, but part of his having not been safely safe is that he was easily in a position of needing to return. And part of his being in danger is that more or less easily—perhaps in the effort to get back into safety, a panicked scramble, say—he could accidentally fall off the cliff. The last scenario is very unlikely—for were it not, he was not safe to begin with. That is, the initial three-feet calculation must take into account not just how easily he could fall off from *there* but how easily he could fall off from a spot a stumble or so away. To be safely safe is to be far enough in the safety zone that in numerous somewhat different circumstances one still remains safe. That is, it could not easily happen that one would be in danger.[31] To be safe is to be so situated that in numerous somewhat different situations one does not fall—even if, in some, one comes into danger of falling.

For Thomas, the virtuous *reliably* do the good well. They are safe against the possibility of doing otherwise. Virtue makes character such that behavior is reliable and safe in these senses. In a wide range of similar circumstances, one could not easily have failed to do good well. Other things being equal, the wider that range the more perfect the virtue. Growth in virtue—its increase beyond the threshold—mirrors the movement from mere safety to being safely safe (or perhaps one must be safely safe to be virtuous). Yet to be virtuous at all—as opposed to possessed of even the best imperfect virtue—one must be *at least* safe, *at least* reliable (or safely safe). The virtuous person cannot easily behave other than virtuously. Many states resembling virtue are not in fact virtue, for the agent is not yet safe in her disposition to do good well. At some point, as with the child, we reckon her safe—and, Thomas insists, rightly exercise caution. Perhaps at just under three feet, it is still very unlikely that the child could fall—but there remains some chance. Insofar as there does, and especially in view of the consequences, she is unsafe. To be virtuous is to be safe—and just as there is nothing arbitrary about fixing some distance for some child, there is nothing arbitrary in drawing such a bright line when it comes to virtue. Even though immediately prior states are much like the one we regard as safe, they are different in their proximity to danger—in too many situations like our own the result we want to avoid will transpire.

Most parents can judge relatively well whether their child is safe from falling. How do we make such judgments about virtue? Consider native-level fluency. Notwithstanding the progressively higher levels of linguistic ability that precede it, at some point, fluency obtains and is properly ascribed. When there is reason to question whether someone near fluency has achieved it, the judgment is only appropriately made after observing her speak in a wide range of states and contexts and on numerous topics. So it is with virtue. It is only properly ascribed after observing an agent act excellently over time, across varied situations (difficult ones especially), and in multiple emotional states. In both cases, the judges must be highly competent—if not native speakers or fully virtuous than nearly so, or else wise enough to recognize an excellence transcending their own. In contrast, the further from fluency or virtue someone is, the easier to distinguish his state from the ideal, the less wisdom and care required—few struggle to decide whether the unrepentant killer is virtuous, fewer still a Stalin.

In drawing fine distinctions, we depend on the patient judgments of those competent to judge. If these distinctions are worth making, they must serve our purposes. Depending on those purposes, the criteria will be different, the cutoff higher or lower, the dividing line more or less absolute, and so on. The relevant cutoff when hiring a French tutor is different from that for selecting an ambassador. And what suffices in the latter case may not suffice when filling a seat on the *Commission générale de terminologie et de néologie*. The point and success of such distinctions and ascriptions is not a matter of being able to formulate a nonformal, detailed set of necessary and sufficient criteria. Provided *in concreto* we can make the distinction and it serves our purposes, this suffices. The point of a distinction as fine-grained as that between virtue and its immediate antecedent has to do with why we care about the difference between the categories in the first place. We judge the distinction's success and the criteria of application it implicitly presupposes relative to our purposes in drawing it. By examining our purposes to ensure that, and show how, the distinction's criteria of application are sufficiently determinate *given those purposes*, we can diffuse charges of vagueness. If I fear fines for a "heap" of leaves on my stoop, I avoid letting them pile up, sweep regularly, and eschew worry about just how many make a heap.[32] Here, there is no *problem* of vagueness. Consider, then, how Thomas proceeds.

He aims to instruct Dominicans who will hear confession, offer counsel, and otherwise instruct a flock in matters moral.[33] Presumably, the point of distinguishing between virtue and the state immediately prior, or a virtuous person and one almost so, will have to do with the different ways we ought to respond to each and the differences in moral praise and authority each is due. It would be unjust to praise the nonvirtuous more than the virtuous, unwise to grant her more moral authority. And in gathering the wise to deliberate on the most important things—whether some war is just, what constitutes torture, which rights are basic, and so on—surely it would be better to have the truly rather than the nearly virtuous. Considering states further from true virtue, it is both more obvious what is at stake in distinguishing and distinguishing correctly between virtue and what is not and, thanks to Thomas's explication, easier to do so.

Above all, Thomas is concerned that his students draw these more consequential distinctions correctly, and so his teaching conduces to that end. He does not want virtue and imperfect virtue confused at all, but he especially does not want virtue and *profoundly* imperfect virtue confused. Given this concern, when it comes to discussing the category of imperfect virtue he focuses on cases relatively distant, in real terms, from virtue proper. He does so both because confusion here would be most disastrous, and because priests must be able to quickly recognize one possessed of this sort of imperfect virtue so that they can offer her help in cultivating full-fledged virtue and try to prevent her from harming herself and others. He thus explicates this variety of imperfect virtue in detail, lest deeply problematic confusion obtain or those most in need of counsel go without. The linguistic analogy breaks down here, for virtue admits of many imitations; even its most distant cousins can deceive the untrained eye. (Among them, *false* virtues, glittering vices.) Thomas's teaching renders imperfect virtue's distinguishing marks—carelessness about means, negligence in some aspect of moral life, and so on—visible.

The distinction between virtue and its immediate antecedent is child of this more basic, more consequential distinction, an implication of Thomas's central concern. Nonetheless, his insistence that virtue is *habit* and not a mere disposition supplies an actionable line and answers his aims. Knowing that, when confronted with a tough call where it is unclear whether virtue obtains or almost does, what is required is careful observation and no rush to judgment. Only time and attention will tell. Meanwhile, it is less important that this parishioner be correctly labeled, more important that she be encouraged to continue in pursuit of holiness. And the counsel, whether she be virtuous or almost so, will be nearly identical. The safest course, what Thomas's insistence on *habit* as bright line and his near silence on its antecedent elicits, is for priests to continue observing or to assume that it is imperfect virtue. Far worse wrongly to believe virtue obtains and so neglect observation or encourage complacency, than to err the other way, closely observe, and foster the energetic burst that comes when the finish is in sight. What Thomas says—as much as what he does not—fosters such an approach. His pedagogical aims seem to account for the broad, mostly undifferentiated character of his category of imperfect virtue, its emphasis on states furthest from virtue and lack of focus on those closest.

On Being Good and Perfectly Good: Ends, Acts, and Humans *secundum quid*

Early in *DVC* 2, Thomas notes that

> since virtue is that which makes a man good and renders his work good, that virtue is perfect which renders a man's work perfectly good and him perfectly good too. . . . Human acts are made perfectly good by the rule of human acts being reached (by that which attains to the rule of human acts). One [rule] is quasi homogenous and proper to man, namely right reason. The other is the first, transcending measure, which is God. Man attains to the rule of right reason through prudence, which is right reason about matters of conduct, as the Philosopher said in *Nicomachean Ethics* VI. Man attains to God, however, through charity as according to 1 John 4:16: "Who abides in charity, abides in God, and God abides in him."

This is straightforward: perfect virtue renders a person and her work perfectly good either by conducing to a rule and end specified by right reason and "quasi" proper to man, or, through charity, by conducing to beatitude. Strange, however, is the claim that conformity with right reason makes a man and his work *simply* or *perfectly* good.[34] Later he denies that: acquired virtue makes a man and his work only "somewhat" (*aliqauliter*) perfect, perfect vis-à-vis the *human* good. Stranger still is Thomas's reference to reason's end as *quasi*-homogenous and proper to man. "The good of man," he says,

> varies according to various ways of considering him. For there is not the same good of man insofar as he is man and insofar as he is citizen. For the good of man insofar as he is man is that his reason be perfected in knowledge of truth and his lower appetites ruled according to the rule of reason—for man has that whereby he is a man from that whereby he is rational. But the good of man insofar as he is a citizen is that he be ordered according to the city in respect of everything. (*DV* 9)

Thomas cites Aristotle's claim that the virtues of man and virtues of citizen-of-some-polity differ—different polities (and even different roles within them) demanding distinct virtues. Thomas's *Politics* commentary and remarks here indicate that the virtues of man *as man* are the *human* or *political* (in the broad sense) virtues and the good of man *as man* is the life of acquired or political virtue.[35] For now, put aside the complexity of polity-specific virtue and focus on the human or political end and political or acquired virtues.

"The good of man," Thomas says, "varies according to various ways of considering him." Thomas speaks here not of diverse ways of *describing* a single good; he claims, rather, that truly different goods answer to different, true conceptions of humanity. Conducing to these different goods are different virtues. But which way of conceptualizing humanity is the *unqualified* way? Which end answers to *unqualified* humanity, humans considered not according to some capacity or description but *simpliciter*?

Since Thomas characterizes the political good as the good of man *as man*, that could seem the human good. It corresponds to human nature in being attainable by acquired virtues and standing to it, apart from charity, as end. Thus: "The virtues which are in a man insofar as he is a man, insofar as he participates in the earthly city, do not exceed the power (*facultatem*) of human nature" (*DV* 9). Yet, Thomas explains:

> Man is not only a citizen of the earthly city, but is a participant in the heavenly city of Jerusalem, whose ruler is the Lord, along with the angels and all the saints, whether they are ruling in glory and resting in the homeland, or are still pilgrimaging on earth. . . . Man's nature is not sufficient that he be a participant in this

city, he must be elevated to this by God's grace. Thus it is clear that these virtues which are a man's insofar as he participates in this city, are not able to be acquired by him through his nature . . . but are infused in us by a divine gift. (*DV* 9)

Humans are, or are meant to be, citizens of heaven. Beatitude is their end. Thomas's language—*insofar as he is a participant in the heavenly city*—mirrors his earlier remarks about the political end. Rather than showing the political end to be unqualified, his reference to political virtues as virtues of "man as man" speak of man *qua earthly citizen*: humans considered not *simpliciter* but as political animals, in view of the best end naturally attainable.

Certainly, the political end is unique and preeminent relative to other naturally attainable ends. It is humanity's proper end *qua best end attainable without charity*. But it is another thing for it to be the end of humanity *simpliciter*. While not saying which is the end of human nature simply, the passage distinguishes heavenly and earthly ends in virtue of their attainability. And attainability without charity does not, it suggests, tell us what end suits humanity simply. Yes, Thomas believes humans are political animals and regards the natural end as *in some sense* final—*qua* best, most fitting end naturally attainable. But acquired virtue is always only true or perfect *secundum quid*. Infused virtue alone is absolutely perfect and perfects *simpliciter*. The acquired virtues, although truly excellent, conduce only "to a certain happiness (*quamdam felicitatem*) which man is made to acquire in this life by what is properly natural through the act of perfect virtue [that is, acquired virtue] which Aristotle discusses" (*DV* 9 ad 6). Their happiness is only a kind of happiness, *imperfecta felicitas* (I.II 5.3 and 5). A happiness *secundum quid*, attained by a virtue *secundum quid* answers only to the nature of a human *secundum quid*. All this implies something about Thomas's conception of humanity *simpliciter* and its good, about natural and supernatural ends.

Man, Thomas explains,

is able to be perfect in two ways: in one way in respect of the ability of his nature [that is, in its own strength] and in another way in respect of a certain supernatural perfection. *Thus, [in the latter way] man is said to be perfect simpliciter; in the former way [perfect] secundum quid*. Hence there are two virtues of man: one which answers to the first perfection [that is, in accord with his own strength] and which is not complete virtue; the other which answers to his ultimate perfection—and this is the true and perfect virtue of man. (*DV* 10 ad 1)

The political end and its corresponding virtues constitute man's perfection *secundum quid*. Its achievement makes humans perfect not simply but *aliqualiter*.

To consider human nature *simpliciter*, essentially, it seems, is to consider it as ordered to beatitude, the human good simply.

Recall Thomas's initial provocation: that virtue in accord with right reason and virtue in accord with charity alike are perfect and make humans simply good. To consider humans as political animals and their good as the political good is to consider them in a way categorically peerless relative to every non-beatific alternative. This is so because right reason's rule and end are suited to human nature—insofar as it is unaided by grace. They answer to her nature in its natural capacities; but considering humanity naturally, this passage suggests, is not considering humanity *simpliciter*.

The robust flourishing acquired virtue brings is authentic but incomplete: authentic in corresponding to human nature, incomplete in doing so imperfectly. Yet its authenticity, its goodness, must be recognized, Thomas insists. Hence his consistent reference to human virtue and its life as *perfect, simply good*. Their imperfection does not diminish their value. Surpassing excellence is *surpassing* excellence. Thomas's conception of participation means that just as there is no competition between human and divine existence, there is none when it comes to excellence, virtue. The surpassing goodness of infused virtue and its end does not diminish the true goodness and happiness of acquired virtue. On the contrary, the excellence of the ultimate can awaken us to an excellence in the penultimate we might otherwise have missed—their excellence as unique anticipations, arrows pointing beyond themselves.

7 HONEST GOODS

II.II 23.7 CONSIDERS whether there can be true virtues (*vera virtutes*) without charity.[1] Unlike I.II 65.2 or 63.2, the article centrally concerns charity's significance for virtue, especially the difference its absence makes. Citing 1 Corinthians 13, the *sed contra* contends that without charity nothing is of profit. Since virtue should profit one most of all, it continues, "without charity there can be no true virtue (*vera virtus*)" (II.II 23.7 sc). Thomas devotes the corpus, however, to clarifying and decisively qualifying the *sed contra*'s stark claim.

Specifically, he distinguishes first between proximate and final goods, and then between those proximate goods that, by their essence, can be ordered to the final good and those that cannot, false goods. Virtues conducing directly to certain genuine proximate goods are true. But unless such goods are, in turn, ordered through charity to beatitude, these virtues are imperfect. While there can be no *simply true* (*simpliciter vera*) virtue without charity, "there can certainly be true but *imperfect* virtue without charity" (*erit quidem vera virtus, sed imperfecta*) (II.II 23.7). Thomas's argument hangs on three distinctions: between proximate and final goods; apparent and genuine goods; and what is "true simply" (*vera simpliciter*) and what is "true but imperfect" (*vera sed imperfecta*). This chapter elucidates these distinctions and the argument they fund.

Goods, Ends, and Intrinsic Ordainability

Beginning with the first distinction, that between proximate and final goods, Thomas reminds us that virtue, of its very *ratio*, conduces exclusively to *truly good ends*. "Good," he says, "is chiefly (*principaliter*) end, for (*nam*) those things which are unto-the-end are not said to be good unless they are ordered to the end" (II.II 23.7). Good, recall, is chiefly *end*—has that *ratio*—for it is sought, and sought because good. Things are good to the extent that they are desirable, able to elicit pursuit and count as pursuit's terminus. Thomas stresses this good/end connection, which is essential to his distinctions among virtues, since virtue involves consideration of goodness and ends alike. The Latin *nam*, above, can introduce an illustrative example and/or evidence for or explanation of what precedes it. Here, Thomas stresses the good/end relation as it bears on the relation between end and what is ordered to that end.[2] Specifically, when something stands to some end (*ad finem*) as means and that end is desired for its own sake, the means are only desired or called "good" in relation or as ordered to that end (*in ordine ad finem*). In its capacity as means, the goodness or desirability of the means derives from the end. But Thomas does not leave the point there.

"Those things which are for an end (*ad finem*)," he continues, "are not called good unless in relation to the end (*in ordine ad finem*)" (II.II 23.7). Taken alone, this could suggest that anything ordered as means to some end cannot itself be good *in se* but only derivatively, only in relation to the end. Elsewhere, however, Thomas clarifies that some things are good in themselves and can rightly be related to as such, even as they're also ordered to ends beyond themselves.[3] What justly serves as end in one case can serve as means in another. And when it does serve as such a means it does not (necessarily) cease to be and count as good *in se*. Thus, here in 23.7, Thomas speaks of goods short of the ultimate good, beatitude, that are good in themselves, and thanks to their own goodness, they are essentially ordainable to beatitude. Additionally, his very conception of finite goods as having, through participation, goodness truly their own entails that at least some things ordered to an end need not have goodness *only* by being so ordered.

Thomas's comment thus concerns a structural feature of action, end, and desire. The means in some case are *at least* good in conducing to end—whatever *other* goodness they might have. Thomas thus distinguishes between something's being good *per se* and good *secundum quid*: the end is good *per se* and sought in itself; the means is, thanks to the end, at least good *secundum quid*. Surely, we do often regard something good to the extent that it conduces to some end of ours: the fish-oil supplement or doctor-prescribed jogging. And at least in the latter case we might come to regard the running as also good *in se*.

Final and Proximate Goods and Ends

Citing the structural similarity between goods and ends, Thomas claims that the distinction between proximate and final end is paralleled by one between proximate goods and the ultimate good: "Therefore just as the end is two-fold—one final, the other proximate—so too is the good twofold: one final, another proximate and particular" (II.II 23.7). Next, where he earlier spoke of formal categories and structural relations, he now immediately identifies the true final good as beatitude. Another shift accompanies. Before Thomas spoke of end and that which was for (*ad finem*) or ordered to it (*in ordine ad finem*), now, he speaks of two kinds of *ends*: final and proximate.

As proximate, proximate ends are not absolutely final and are thus necessarily ordered to ends beyond themselves. Yet in virtue of being an *end*, they are at least partly desired for their own sake, as some action's end. More than merely *ad finem* or instrumentally good, they are good in themselves. "Intention," Thomas elsewhere says, "considers the end as a terminus of the will's movement" whether or not that terminus be final. As end, a proximate end is just such a terminus (I.II 12.2), something in which will rests (I.II 12.1 ad 4; 12.2 ad 2 and 3). It is non-instrumentally good, a principle of action.[4] In contrast, what is exclusively *ad finem* is no end, no source of rest. Thomas distinguishes two kinds of ends: those desired exclusively for their own sake and those additionally desired because they can be ordered to something further. Referring not just to any end taken as final but beatitude, he distinguishes between *the* final end and those particular ends that can (rightly or wrongly) be pursued *both* for their own sake *and* as a means to the true final end. Every end short of beatitude is proximate, but proximate ends, he stresses, are *ends* no less.

Mirroring the final end/proximate ends distinction is that between the final good and proximate goods. By shifting from what is merely *ad finem* to proximate ends and so proximate goods, Thomas brings into view countless proximate, particular goods, goods rightly valued *in se*. As a proximate end can justly serve as an act's end, so too the proximate good can justly be loved and sought *in se*, even apart from attending to its relation to the ultimate good.[5] The point inheres in the very notion of a genuine proximate *good*. Certain proximate goods are loved wrongly if only loved instrumentally. As chapter 2 showed, by recognizing its goodness as participating God, one can simultaneously love proximate goods for their own sake and for God's, even love God more *in* loving them for their own sake. Thomas thus distinguishes between two goods: the true final good of beatitude and proximate goods, those things other than God that are themselves candidates for just love and pursuit.

⁂

Varieties of Proximate Goods, Varieties of Virtue

Thomas next divides proximate goods: "The secondary and, as it were, partial (*particulare*) good of man can [itself] be divided in two, one, indeed, that is truly good, in as much as *it is in itself* (*quantum est in se*) ordainable to the chief good, which is the final end; the other, however, apparently but not truly good because it leads away from the final good" (II.II 23.7). Proximate goods are either (a) truly good in themselves or (b) only apparently so. We will return to this distinction, but first we need to see how the distinctions so far—between the final good and proximate goods and between true and false proximate goods—fund 23.7's various distinctions among types of virtue.

Since virtue is ordered to the good, we can distinguish among virtues as conducing to various goods. That principle, recall, underwrote I.II 61.5's delineation of five genres of cardinal virtue: human virtues as ordered to the political good, purifying virtues to beatitude, and so on. The same principle obtains here, but the question differs. Only those virtues that conduce to beatitude are simply perfect and true: "True virtue *simpliciter* is that which orders [one] to the chief human good" (II.II 23.7). "Virtue," Thomas cites Aristotle, "is the disposition of the perfect to the best" (II.II 23.7). Charity alone orders man to the best, so no virtue that is true *simpliciter* is possible without charity.

Virtue language is perfection language. And virtues perfect human capacities so that humans achieve good ends in a good way. Simply perfect virtue so perfects a human that she can achieve not just any good end but the best end in the best way. A virtue that fails to do that is necessarily imperfect, for it fails to perfect humans perfectly, in a way that enables them to attain beatitude, the perfect final end. Such virtue, however truly good its end, is imperfect and for that reason and in that way not true virtue *simpliciter*. It is not, because it is not humanity's highest perfection. Only virtues conducing to beatitude are *perfectly* true, for virtue's *ratio* demands it dispose someone in the unqualifiedly best way to the unqualifiedly best end. Such perfection, such virtue, comes through charity alone.

Here, Thomas's Aristotelianism and Augustinianism work hand in hand: his ostensibly Augustinian conclusion that charity's virtues alone are absolutely perfect comes as much on Aristotelian as on Augustinian grounds. That virtues are dispositions of the perfect to the best is an essentially Aristotelian point that, as we saw, Thomas vindicates as Augustinian through the habits treatise and the first article on virtue. For Augustine and Thomas, the final end, known by Scripture, is fellowship with the Triune God, but, in the happiness treatise, drawing on Augustine, Thomas labors to show how this, more than Aristotelian contemplation, fully satisfies *Aristotle's* own notion of happiness (I.II 1–5).[6] Thomas exalts charity-infused virtue as true and perfect *simpliciter* on grounds that are Aristotelian by being Augustinian and vice versa. But what of imperfect perfections?

Corresponding to his distinction between true and false proximate goods, Thomas distinguishes between two sorts of virtue: those which conduce to true proximate goods and are thus true but imperfect and those which conduce to false proximate goods and so are false virtues. "If," he explains, "we take virtue as ordered to some particular end, thus is it possible to speak of virtue without charity—insofar as virtue is ordered to some particular good" (II.II 23.7). We can speak of virtue that, while falling short of beatitude, leads to truly good proximate ends. This virtue can be had without charity because its ends can be. Such virtue, Thomas says, is true but imperfect virtue, *vera virtus sed imperfecta*. And lest we imagine the goods to which this virtue disposes as minimal, insignificant, or removed from the good life's central concerns, Thomas cites nothing less than *conservatio civitatis*, "preservation of the city," the political good, as the sort of a good proximate end to which such virtue can conduce. This, of course, is human virtue. Without charity, Thomas insists again, one can attain virtues ordered to the political and other true proximate goods, the virtues that have concerned us throughout. While not *vera simpliciter*, these *are* virtues, he stresses, true virtues but imperfect—dispositions of the perfect to the second best, imperfect perfection.

There are, as well, dispositions to false proximate goods. These are *false* virtues, semblances of virtue, splendid vice: "If that particular good [to which a person is ordained] is not a true good but merely an apparent good, then the virtue which is ordered to this 'good' will not be a *true* virtue but a false likeness thereof" (II.II 23.7). Citing Augustine, Thomas uses the miser (*avarorum*) to illustrate—the miser's careful deliberation in pursuit of riches is no true prudence, his strict obedience to the law out of fear of repercussion no true justice, his regimen of self-denial no true temperance, his risk of death to avoid financial loss no true courage. The miser's "virtues" are exclusively apparent; as the good is false, so too the virtue.

For Thomas, virtue ordered to true proximate goods is *true* virtue, just not *simply* true. Virtue *secundum quid* is not less than *vera virtus*, but less than *vera virtus simpliciter*.[7] Thomas thus highlights both its continuity and discontinuity with true virtue *simpliciter*: in leading to a truly good and perfective end it is unqualifiedly true; in not attaining beatitude, it is imperfect. Virtue *secundum quid* is true but imperfect virtue, just as true virtue *simpliciter* is true and perfect virtue.[8]

23.7's corpus locates this virtue's imperfection not in deficiency with respect to the political but the beatific end. One might imagine otherwise, that its imperfection concerned some deficiency in regard to the political good. Not so here. Strictly on its own terms this virtue, pagan virtue, is perfect, orienting a person well to the true good of common life. Given the political and human concerns motivating our investigation, it is an imperfection that needn't lessen the Christian's welcome of the pagan and her virtue, even as it may elicit prayer for something still more perfect.

Proximate Goods, True and False

Thomas's distinction between true and false proximate goods raises questions. Consider wealth, for example.[9] Is wealth a true or false proximate good? On the one hand, Thomas uses the miser as an example of someone oriented to a false good, and, in a certain way, it is money that the miser's miserliness orders him to. Indeed, Thomas explicitly identifies money or its possession as the miser's end (I.II 13.4; 16.3). And we need not suppose—and Thomas does not—that miserliness consists exclusively in seeking money *only* for its own sake or taking it as a *final* end. It seems, rather, to involve making money *an* end, which suggests that money is a *false* proximate good. On the other hand, money seems preeminently a proximate good, a good rightly sought for the sake of something else. Thus Thomas himself affirms that it is *right* to seek riches sufficient to lead a life appropriate to one's station (II.II 118.2). Thus, wealth could seem precisely a *true* proximate good, the sort appropriately sought for the sake of some other good. How then are we to understand Thomas's distinction between true and false proximate goods?

While we can't fully treat the question here, given our goal of grasping Thomas's distinction between true but imperfect virtue and false virtue, and, especially, his conception of the former, we need to understand better what it means for something to be a true proximate good. Most simply, the basic distinction between a true (*verum*) good and merely apparent or false (*apparens*) good is one between those ends that are genuinely perfective of human nature and those only apparently so. Elsewhere, Thomas refers to true good as the "good true and connatural" (*verum bonum et connaturale*) (II.II 34.5 ad 3). While all that exists, as existing, is good and thus can be regarded as good, only under certain circumstances is some thing actually good for someone to pursue. The true and false good distinction concerns what is good for humans. And the true good, in this sense, is always "connatural" for a person: in conformity with human nature by perfecting it, conducing to its flourishing and completion (I.II 18.5).[10]

Human action, recall, proceeds under the formality of good. For an act to be human requires that an agent judge her end somehow desirable, for will, as such action's principle, is an appetite for what reason apprehends as desirable. Apart from such apprehension there can be no action (I.II 19.3). Given that will can only desire what reason presents as good, every act, sin included, is chosen as somehow desirable or good. Since the goodness of will's act depends on the goodness of the end and since will can only intend what is somehow good, how is evil action even possible? How, Thomas asks, can an evil end be desired and sinful action undertaken if will can only desire the good (I.II 18.4 ob 1; 19.1 ob 1)?

The category of false good constitutes his answer. An apparent or false good is apparent and false in that, while appearing good, it is not. Of course, as it *is* something, a false good is genuinely good, but whether it is good *for a human* or *the person choosing* is a different matter. "The apparent good (*apparentis boni*)," Thomas explains, "has a certain *ratio* of good, but not, however, the *ratio* of a good that is simply fitting to be desired" (I.II 19.1 ad 1).[11] Necessarily, a false good must be good *somehow* or it could never be the object of will's desire (nor *be* anything). Its falsity consists in its not being good in the *right way*, not truly perfective.[12]

To be truly good, some act's end must not merely have "some measure of good" but the *right* measure, be good in the right way: for a human, just now. What Thomas says of action is every bit as true of action's end: "An [end] having goodness in one . . . way [may] lack it in another. . . . An [end] is not good *simpliciter*, unless it be good in all the [relevant ways], for a single deficiency causes evil, but goodness is thanks to wholeness, integrity" (I.II 18.4 ad 3). To be a true good, an end must be good in all the right ways. Specifically, it must accord with right reason's judgment: reason's considered, correct conclusion about human flourishing (I.II 39.2).[13] Thus, a truly good end might be the glory of God's praise; an apparently good end, the vainglory of foolish people's praise. The first end is truly good because, as end, the reward of God's pleasure in one's life accords with reason's correct judgment about what leads to and constitutes happiness. As for the second, while being well regarded when one deserves it is genuinely good, esteem ought not be sought from fools. Vainglory, taken as end, is a false good (II.II 132.1 and ad 3). It can be intended because of what is truly good in it (e.g., pleasure, perhaps), but thanks to its diverging from what really leads to flourishing, it is a false good, an evil end.[14] In virtue of what is good in some end is it chosen; in virtue of that whereby it contravenes right reason's judgment is it false.[15] So much for this brief rendering of Thomas's distinction between true and false goods.[16]

Money and Misers

In II.II 23.7 matters are complicated by both the proximate/final end distinction and the miser example. It is uncertain whether Thomas's distinction here corresponds precisely to his standard true good/apparent good distinction. Part of the confusion has to do with the miser and the question of his end. Money or possessing money is the miser's end, so Thomas's example suggests that money is a false proximate good (I.II 13.4; 16.3).[17] Yet, elsewhere, he acknowledges money's necessity for this-worldly flourishing: it's an important, often essential means to certain genuine goods. On this view, money clearly is a true proximate good. Considering this text alongside some of Thomas's other remarks about miserliness clears matters up and sheds further light on the distinction between true and false proximate goods.

In 23.7, Thomas says a false good is *false* precisely because it leads away from the final good (*quia abducit a finali bono*). Whatever else a false good is and whatever other circumstances obtain, it is such that simply taking it as end leads one away from the true final good. Are money or other external goods false goods then? Consider someone who takes a job to earn money to support her family or to give alms. Money (or earning money) is her proximate end— and in the activity directed to money's attainment, it is the end—but simply in virtue of having money as her end, she is not led away from the final good. And, recall, Thomas explicitly declares pursuit of money licit provided it be pursued rightly (II.II 118.1).

Unlike vainglory, for instance, "money," just in itself, is no false good.[18] Nor, however, is it a true good. The end specifies human action. "Money" is as much the miser's as the worker's end while, other things being equal, the one pursuit is evil, the other good. The miser's false good, and false and true goods generally, are much more determinate and specific than we might initially think.[19] Thomas's detailed treatment of miserliness or avarice bears this claim out (II.II 118).

Money is what Thomas calls a useful good. The good in money and other external goods, the reason they can be attractive and action-generating, is their utility in securing what is (or seems) valuable in itself, what Thomas calls the "honest good," *bonum honestum* (I 5.6; II.II 145).[20] Money and other external goods are, as it were, intrinsically *instrumental* goods—their genuine desirability consisting in their utility in securing other goods.[21] They are *intrinsically* instrumental because that utility is truly their own. Miserliness involves inordinate desire for money—either (a) desire for money beyond what reason judges necessary for a decent human life (that is, quantitatively too much money) or (b) money regarded as worth pursuing just for its own sake, as an end itself, or pursued even as one's final end.[22] The end of covetousness and of a miser, then, is not just "money" or "possession of money" but "money or the useful *beyond what is in accord with right reason*" and, more narrowly, either "money *beyond what is necessary for living in accord with one's position in life*" (or "the possession of that") or "money regarded as an end in itself" (II.II 118.2 and 3).[23] And in this, we see the necessity of reference to reason in stipulating action's end. Ends are intrinsically normative, for they make reference to reason's judgment about what is good. Ends do not necessarily make such reference in the case of the person intending the end; that is, they may not be intended *under that description*. But in the complete correct description of the act's end there is necessarily a reference to right reason's judgment.[24]

Our concern is not miserliness *per se* but what all this teaches us about the character of false goods. False goods necessarily lead away from the true good—and seeing how Thomas delineates the end of miserliness shows what sort of a thing a false good is and how it could, just in itself, lead away from the true end. Given *this* end—possession of money *beyond what is necessary for one's station*—nothing the miser does in its pursuit, no dispositions toward it, can be good. Those habits that conduce to such ends are false virtues, no matter how good they may seem. They conduce to that which is contrary to human flourishing. A person is the worse for their possession.

Money and other useful goods can partake in the categories of true and false goods alike. Money can be a good end when pursued as a useful good and to a fitting, reasonable degree. It can be a false good and bad end, however, when pursued and loved for its own sake, as choiceworthy for the pleasure and self-satisfaction it can bring to know oneself as wealthy. Two important ways of sinning correspond to these two ways it can serve as end. First, when money is pursued as a useful good, it is possible to seek too much of it, an inordinate amount. Such an act is sinful not (simply) because of money's character or status as end but because it is pursued in an undue way, out of accord with reason. Alternatively, when money is pursued for its own sake, it is an evil end, like adultery or theft.

These two ways of sinning mortally are on display when Thomas explains how angels sin:

> Mortal sin happens in two ways. . . . First, when something evil is chosen—such as when a man sins by choosing adultery, which is evil in itself. Always, such sin proceeds from some ignorance or error, otherwise that which is evil would not be chosen. . . . The adulterer errs in the particulars, choosing this delight of an inordinate act as a certain good to be pursued right now, and doing so because of the yearning of a passion or a habit . . . even if he does not err in regard to the universal principle ['do not commit adultery']. . . . In another way, sin takes hold . . . through one choosing something . . . in itself good, but choosing it in a way that lacks attention to right measure or rule so that the defect making the act sinful is only on the part of choice, which lacks due order, and not on the part of the thing one chooses—so, someone chooses to pray but does not attend to the order established by the Church. Sin like this does not depend on ignorance, but only on the lack of considering the things that one must consider.[25] (I 63.1 ad 4)

Mortal sins occur either when an evil end is pursued—and then it is pursued either as good or, in the case of malice, in recognition of its evil but in light of some good to be gained (I.II 78.1 and ad 2)—or when a good end is pursued unduly. Money, as end, differs from adultery, theft, and the like in that it is *not* an essentially evil end, even as it differs from knowledge, prayer, and the like in that it is not a simply true good. So, while it is not an evil end, it becomes one when viewed as good *in se*. And, while not good *in se*, it can be pursuit's right object, with sin obtaining when more is sought than is right. Most broadly, a false good can be either an evil end regarded somehow as good (e.g., adultery as pleasurable) or a good end conceived and pursued in such a way to make its pursuit evil (e.g., prayer in undue ways).

True Goods and Their Inherent Ordainability

While the true proximate good is true "because considered in itself it can be directed to the principal good, the last end," it is not immediately clear whether the true good counts as true simply because it is ordainable to the final good, or because it is so ordainable *"considered in itself"*—or what, if anything, that distinction even marks. Ordainability to beatitude has something to do with the character of the thing ordained and in the case of a true proximate good, something to do with its *goodness*. It is thanks to a thing's goodness or lack thereof that it can or cannot be ordained to the final good. Take false proximate goods. It was due to their *lack* of the right sort of goodness, their privation, that as ends they necessarily led away from the final good. So, Thomas's remark about the proximate end "considered in itself" concerns that end's *goodness*—the goodness it has—just considered in itself. Something about the thing's in-itself-goodness bears on its ordainability to the final good and, perhaps, its being a *true* proximate good.

Still, it is not yet clear what the relationship is between its ordainability and its in-itself-goodness. Thomas might have stipulated merely that a true proximate good is one that is ordainable to the final end. Instead, he insists that considered *in itself* it be so ordainable. What are we to make of that insistence—and his order of explanation? Given that Thomas is talking about a thing's being good in itself and its being ordainable to the final end, we can wonder whether a proximate end is good in itself *because* it is ordainable to the final good *or* ordainable to the final good because it is good in itself.

Take Thomas's insistence that *considered in itself* the true proximate good is ordainable to the final end. Many ends are such that in themselves they are morally indifferent in their species (I.II 18.8). So, for Thomas, picking straw from the ground is, in itself, morally indifferent—thanks to the moral indifference of that act's end.[26] Its becoming good or bad action, as it necessarily will when actually done by a human (I.II 18.9), will have to do with its being placed in relation to an agent and her various ends. Significantly, because it is an action indifferent in its species it can just as well be referred to a good as to a bad end.

Thus, I might pick up the straw because my neighbor has placed it on the doorstep to signal Jews she will give them safe haven, and I wish them captured. Here, the end and act of straw-picking, indifferent in their species, become evil thanks to my wicked end.[27] Or, I might pick up the straw because it has been carelessly tossed on an art installation and is now obscuring my neighbors' view of the masterpiece. And I might so care for my neighbors because of and through charity. Thus, in this case, precisely because the end of picking up the straw is indifferent it is referable to a good—and indeed the perfectly good—end.

For Thomas, "human end(s) can involve considerable sophistication and possess a detailed particularity" (Pilsner, *HA*, 180). Joseph Pilsner gives the example of even some end as determinate as "passing a particular physiology exam" as still insufficiently specific on Thomas's perspective. Indeed, the means of "studying" that such an end would require are inadequately specific: "After understanding the end better by ascertaining the extent and difficulty of the test material, the student must decide how best to study in this particular case: what study techniques to use, where to study, how long to study, and so forth. In short, the person being tested must proportion his studying (means) so that it favors success on this particular exam (end)" (*HA*, 181).

Recall, no false good is referable to beatitude but necessarily leads away from it. So, in elucidating true proximate goods or ends, Thomas might have said that a proximate good is true insofar as it can be referred to the final end, making such ordainability the sole criterion. Not being false would make a good count as true so that acts and ends morally indifferent in kind could count as truly good. Under certain circumstances, money, then, would count as a true good because referable to beatitude. Yet Thomas stipulates that *considered in themselves* proximate true goods be referable to the final good. The case of specifically indifferent acts and ends shows Thomas cannot be claiming something is good in itself *because* ordainable to beatitude, for morally indifferent ends and action are so ordainable—precisely *because* they are indifferent. But they do not thereby cease to be morally indifferent.[28] Thomas, then, is not saying that ends referable to beatitude are therefore true proximate goods. Nor is he suggesting that being ordainable to the final end either constitutes an end as good *in se* or names what it is for an end to be good *in se*. Ordainability to the final end is necessary but not sufficient for some proximate end to be a true good—but even that is a little misleading.

Honest Good, Good *in se*

Thomas's claim is that for a proximate end to be true it must be good *in se*. Being good *in se* makes a proximate good true and accounts for its ordainability to beatitude.[29] What does it means for something to be good *in se*? Thomas distinguishes three senses in which something can be called or can be good: the pleasant good, the useful good, and the honest or virtuous good (I 5.6). It is the last that concerns us, for it is this kind of goodness that Thomas says is primary, chief (I 5.6 ad 3). The honest good is appropriately desired for its own sake, as an end in itself (II.II 145.1 and 3).[30] The honest or true good is *always* appropriately desired, for the honest good *just is* the good in accord with right reason—its goodness consists in its having a certain desirability thanks to its conformity to right reason's judgment, "a particular beauty from the order of reason" (II.II 145.3).[31] At one point, Thomas remarks that what distinguishes a true from a false good is that the latter is "not fitting to be desired simply" (*simpliciter convenientis ad appetendum*) (I.II 19.1 ad 1). The true or honest good, in contrast, is fitting to be desired simply—in two senses. First, it is fitting to be desired for its own sake, as an end—considered in itself, simply. Second, it is always, unconditionally appropriate to desire it—and this thanks precisely to its necessarily being in accord with right reason.[32]

"Every honest good," Thomas explains, "results from two things—from the rightness of reason and the rightness of will" (I.II 39.2). The two senses in which the honest good is "simply fitting to be desired" are essentially related—it is desirable in itself and for its own sake because it manifests the good of right reason, which is perfective of human nature; and it is fit to be desired unconditionally for that reason as well.[33] To be clear, the pleasant and the useful are good *in se* in the sense that their pleasantness or utility is due to a goodness proper to them, but in both cases that goodness is itself secondary, derivative in relation to something else and as compared to the honest. The useful good is good *as useful* for something else; the pleasant good is good as cause of the senses' (or will's) rest and its being good is just its conducing thereto. It is the honest good that is truly good *in se*, for it is desirable and choiceworthy in itself, apart from its usefulness in relation to something else or even the pleasure it brings in giving will rest. It is the honest good, then, that *considered in itself* or *simply* is ordainable to the final end. Precisely its identity as honest good makes it ordainable considered *in se*.

This point comes out clearly when Thomas addresses an objection in his treatment of the honest good. That objection claims that only the honest good can be truly useful, for only the honest good can lead to the final perfect end. Therefore, it continues, there is no difference between the honest and useful good. Thomas largely accepts the premises but rejects the conclusion. Nothing is "simply and truly useful," he says, that is out of accord with the honest good, for only that which is consistent with the honest good leads to the final end. Though he doesn't put it this way, the honest good is really the *most* useful good for it is necessarily useful in pursuit of the final, perfect good. Not every useful good is honest, Thomas stresses, but every honest good, except God himself, is truly and simply useful (II.II 145.3 ad 3; 145.1).

So, the honest good is the true good, and it is ordainable to the final end just considered in itself, for it already, just in itself, participates in the final good in a way that other goods do not—in virtue of its honesty. It is a *true* good because it is genuinely if not completely perfective. There is, then, an intrinsic, inchoate directedness of the honest to the true final good. Even when the honest good is pursued without being referred to the final good, implicit in that pursuit, thanks to the honest good's very *ratio*, is a kind of openness and even a *quidam,* or "certain," inchoate inclination to the final good. Such openness and movement are latent *apart from the act of referring that good to the final good.*

This is a vital point—both in itself and especially for what it shows us about the *ratio* of true but imperfect virtue. True but imperfect virtue is just that virtue that is well ordered to the true proximate good and is so ordered *apart from reference to the final, perfect good.* In being so ordered, this virtue, like the good to which it is ordained is intrinsically final end friendly, as it were. It is not final end neutral. In possessing it, outsiders are in some real way open to the true, perfect good—and, indeed, experiencing some fragmentary participation therein in a way surpassing that which every human enjoys by simply living and thereby sharing in God's love. The final good is so good, so fully overflowing and abounding that its goodness spills into all things and, in a special way, into honest or true proximate goods and those virtues conducing to them— and, perhaps most importantly, into the lives of the men and women who possess these virtues. In doing so, this Good—as he always is—is at work, drawing all things to Himself. It is no small thing, then, that it is the city's welfare, the common political good, which Thomas names as a true proximate good. The true but imperfect virtues that conduce to that end, that are friendly to and in a fragmentary way participate beatitude, are none other than the political virtues.

How Many Perfections?

Virtue directed to the city's preservation is true but imperfect, Thomas says, "unless it be referred to the final and perfect good" (II.II 23.7).[34] If such virtue is imperfect *unless* referred to the final good, this implies that such virtue can, in some sense, *become* perfect when referred to the final perfect good. True but imperfect virtue, virtue immediately directed to a true proximate good becomes *perfect* virtue when further ordained to beatitude. What is this perfection and how does it relate to the article's earlier claims? And how does this relate to Thomas's insistence I.II 65.2 and *DVC* 2 that political virtue is imperfect precisely because it *cannot* conduce to beatitude?

We take the questions in turn, but whatever the answers, the article's central point holds: There is no perfect or simply true virtue that is not somehow related to beatitude. That holds whether we recognize two sorts of perfect virtues in 23.7 or one. Nonetheless, I believe there are two sorts of perfect virtues in play here—even as both perfections concern beatitude, the perfection open here to true but imperfect or acquired virtue is distinct from that proper to infused virtues.

In characterizing virtue, 23.7 alternately uses the idiom of *imperfect/perfect* and that of *simply true*. Thus, Thomas calls virtue that conduces to the final end "simply true," and calls true but imperfect virtue referred to beatitude, "perfect."[35] One might think that the different terms mark distinct perfections. But 23.7 uses these terms interchangeably. Thus, immediately after employing imperfection language to claim that virtue directed to a proximate good is imperfect unless further referred to beatitude, Thomas states his conclusion to *that* point in terms of the simply true: "Therefore (*secundum hoc*) *simply true* virtue is not possible without charity" (II.II 23.7). Because virtue is *imperfect* unless referred to beatitude, there can be no *simply true* virtue without charity. Perfect virtue just is simply true virtue and vice versa.[36] In 23.7, then, "perfect" and "simply true" are identical, as are "true but imperfect" and "true."

While this language does not show two different sorts of perfect virtue, consider the article's structure. Recall that Thomas distinguishes between three goods or ends and three corresponding sorts of virtues and that only after distinguishing these ends does he distinguish corresponding virtues. As he does, he traces the order of his initial delineation: (A) final good vs. (B) proximate goods, which are divisible into (b1) true proximate goods and (b2) false proximate goods. Corresponding are (A') simply true virtue, (B') virtues directed to proximate goods which are divisible into (b1') true imperfect virtues and (b2') false virtues. Answering to the final end, which he mentions first, is the virtue he mentions first—simply true virtue. Then he distinguishes between two sorts of virtues that relate to the two sorts of *proximate* ends and so on. *By definition*, virtue that concerns the proximate end does not take the final good

as its immediate end but some true or false *proximate* good. The perfection at
the conclusion, the remark in question, is open to (b1'), true virtue immediately related to an inherently proximate good, and it obtains when this virtue
is *further ordained* to beatitude. A true proximate good, Thomas said earlier,
is ordain-*able* to a final end, not ordain-*ed* to it. A virtue directed to a true
proximate good becomes perfect if it and the true proximate good to which it
is immediately ordered are further ordered to beatitude. Where (A'), the perfect virtue mentioned first, is *immediately* related to beatitude (or to something
constituted by its relation to beatitude), the perfect virtue at article's close is
immediately related to a true proximate good that is *in turn* ordained to beatitude.[37] For (b1'), beatitude is not its *proximate* but its *remote* end. Thomas is
thus distinguishing between infused virtues and the acquired virtues as possessed by those who, through charity, have beatitude as final end. Thus, there
are two ways in which a virtue can be perfect or simply true: if *immediately*
ordered to beatitude (or what implicates it) or if *remotely* ordered.

Such remote ordering is not by acquired virtue's own power but through
its use by infused virtue. And the perfection such use confers is not relative
to acquired virtue's own *ratio*, for its proper perfection concerns its own, non-
beatific end. While he offers no explanation, honoring the claim's context and
his commitments, perhaps we can say Thomas imagines this perfection as had
on loan, as it were, by participation in a perfection still higher. As a guide dog
attains a kind of perfection and relation to right reason thanks to the good
human use to which he's put and the participation that use confers, so acquired
virtue attains a perfection through its relation to and use by charity, its remote
ordination to beatitude.[38] If we can, in a sense, count such use a perfection for
the dog, with much better reason may we do so for acquired virtue. For, so
used, it not only shares in and participates what is more perfect, but, informed
by charity, it attains the highest and best use to which it is open and, more,
the very subordination and use to which, more than any other, God would
have it put. And further, as both volitional and rational—indeed as a genuine
perfection of love—unlike the dog, this virtue has in some way a commonality
with, even a share in, that supernatural love which uses it. Even in the natural
order humans relate to beatitude differently than dogs to right reason. While
no perfection relative to its own end, there is nothing higher for acquired virtue
than for it to be used in acts remotely ordered to beatitude in a life directed to
fellowship with God. To the extent that this happens and, if I am right, for that
reason, Thomas regards such use, such informing, a perfection.

Subordination Is Not Inclusion

I've begun now to make good on a promissory note issued in chapter 3. There and elsewhere I have claimed that Christians can possess the acquired virtues alongside the infused moral virtues. This is a standard interpretation, but some say that Thomas believes Christians cannot possess acquired virtues, that, instead, the infused moral virtues replace them—whether by substitution or "absorption"—and/or that anything acquired can do infused can do better. On such readings, acquired virtues are impossible and/or entirely irrelevant for someone with infused moral virtues. Could Christians even possess them, acquired virtues would be redundant and inferior. We needn't address this issue fully, for my central argument concerning pagan virtue in no way hangs on it, but it's worth briefly seeing why acquired and infused moral virtues are compatible.

Acquired and infused moral virtues are distinct species of virtue (I.II 63.4), distinguished not by their possessor's final end but the proximate ends to which they conduce, for in actions or habits, remote ends do not (primarily) specify (e.g., II.II 111.3 ad 3).[39] This point is central to Thomas's explanation of the specific distinction between acquired and infused moral virtues (I.II 63.4 and ob and ad 1) and habit specification more generally (I.II 54.2).[40] For Thomas, the proximate end speaks first and most authoritatively in specification; the remote end offers secondary comments at best.[41] If the remote end did specify, different acts ordered to a single remote end would bear the same species—so, farming and theft to give alms would both be species of almsgiving.[42] When sought *at all* for its own sake (which characterizes acquired virtue's pursuit of common good) the proximate end specifies.

This point figures centrally in I.II 63.4 where Thomas argues that acquired and infused moral virtues constitute different species. Specifically, he imagines acquired virtues as possessed by an agent ordered to the political end as final and infused moral virtues as possessed by someone ordered to beatitude. This difference in final ends, in their capacity *as final ends*, however, does not specify these virtues. Rather, the differences in *proximate* ends does (I.II 63.4 ob and ad 1). Acquired virtue conduces immediately to acts according to right reason; infused moral virtue, to acts dictated immediately by the New Law. Each infused moral virtue is a habit of acting in accord with New Law as immediately applied to that virtue's "proper matter." Since certain acts in each cardinal virtue's domain are necessary for salvation and require grace, God gives such habits to enable them (I.II 64.3 and 4; 54.3).

Virtues belong to distinct species insofar as they conduce to acts proper to a given nature in relation to that nature's end(s) (I.II 63.4; 54.3 and ad 3). Because there are different true ways to view human nature—as king, democratic subject, human *simpliciter*, friend of God—some more fully grasping humanity's *ratio*, there are specifically different virtuous habits.[43] Acquired and infused moral virtues answer to human nature and its ends differently and thereby constitute different species. Thomas makes this point in 63.4, citing Aristotle's distinctions between different species of acquired virtues ordered to different polities, a reference he echoes in his other primary treatment, *De virtutibus in communi* 10 ad 4. "The virtues of citizens are diverse," Thomas explains, "in relation to different polities" (I.II 63.4). Democracies, monarchies, aristocracies, and so on each require different species of virtues for those ruled thanks to their different proximate ends (e.g., "living well as a monarchic subject" and "living well as a democratic subject").[44] That these virtues are specifically different means someone can possess more than one set.

Although Thomas holds that a higher polity "encompasses" a lower polity's good, because their virtues are specifically different, someone with "higher" aristocratic virtue, for instance, who moves to a democracy still has to acquire "lower" democratic virtues, and vice versa (*PC* III.3.8–11). Moreover, someone can possess different species of virtues in accord with different roles. Thomas says a single subject who is both a good citizen and good ruler in a polity can possess two species of justice, one by which he is well ruled, another by which he rules well—and such holds, he says, for all the moral virtues (*PC* III.3.11). Obviously the being-ruled virtues are subordinate to the ruling species. But she who possesses the higher does not thereby possess the lower. Thomas points to subalternate sciences as an example (I.II 54.2 ad 2). Acquiring math neither destroys nor entails musical *scientia*, nor makes acquiring music impossible or irrelevant.

One citizen who is alternately ruler and ruled, with corresponding species of virtue, need not change final ends as her role changes. That the proximate end of the citizen's "being-ruled virtue" is further ordained to a higher end by another principle does not change that virtue's specification. And someone with human virtues does not cease to be ordered to the common good in cultivating the virtues of a ruled citizen.[45] Rather she remains ordered to the common good as remote end and to some subordinate end as proximate. That the end to which some subordinate virtues tend immediately can be referred to some still higher end—as remote—is taken for granted by Thomas and does not change their specification (*DV* 10 ad 4; II.II 32.1 ad 2; I.II 58.6).

In *De virtutibus in communi* 10 ad 4, Thomas deploys just this Aristotelian rubric to explain the relation of acquired and infused virtues for Christians:

> Other virtues [than acquired virtues] are infused with charity. And the act of acquired virtue is not able to be meritorious except by means of (*mediante*) infused virtue. For virtue ordered to a lower end cannot generate an act ordered to a higher end—except by means of a higher virtue. Just as, for instance, that courage which is a human virtue [literally, 'the virtue of a man as a man'] cannot order its act to the political good, except by means of that courage which is a virtue of a man insofar as he is a citizen.[46]

Political courage (higher here)—without destroying the species of human courage (lower here)—*further* refers human courage remotely to its own proximate, higher end by ordering the good that human courage intends to it. Infused moral virtue renders acquired virtue's act meritorious without destroying it. Life ordered to beatitude can include virtues that order one to subordinate goods for their own sake—and still higher virtues ensure, by their work, that one does not seek them *only* for their own sake but for their place in a life ordered to beatitude. One pursues those proximate goods as not only honest (via acquired virtue) but useful (via infused moral virtue), not only worthy of love for their own sake (acquired) but for the sake of something still greater (infused).

Whatever questions remain, the following is clear. For Thomas, a single agent maintaining one final end can possess parallel or hierarchical but specifically different sets of moral virtue. Higher virtues can use lower virtues so that, while remaining themselves due to their proximate end, the end of lower virtues is further ordered to a higher end, the person's final end, say, and lower virtues can somehow be used in view of that end. And specifically different, hierarchically ordered acquired virtues model the interplay between acquired and infused virtues in the Christian life.[47] Such remote referring, thanks to infused virtue, is the perfection open to acquired virtue that Thomas mentions at 23.7's close.

Coordinating the Perfections

In I.II 65.2 and *DVC* 2, acquired virtue seems to be declared imperfect because it is incapable of relating or referring to beatitude, but 23.7's conclusion seems to suggest acquired virtue can be made perfect by remote reference to beatitude.[48]

I believe 23.7's first perfect virtues, infused virtues or those immediately implicating beatitude, correspond to I.II 65.2's perfect and *DVC* 2's simply perfect
virtues, but that 23.7's second perfect virtues, true acquired virtues informed by
charity, do not.[49] Consistent with I.II 65.2 and *DVC* 2, infused virtues are perfect
in a way no acquired virtues, even those informed by charity, can be. What 23.7
adds is the possibility of acquired virtues attaining a perfection those passages
don't consider. 23.7's latent two perfection distinction allows us to harmonize
the passages, maintaining I.II 65.2's insistence that, compared to *any* acquired
virtue, infused virtue is uniquely perfect. Where the other passages focus on
what sets infused virtues apart, 23.7 considers charity's relation to virtues of
whatever kind. Hence its mentioning acquired virtue perfected by charity. 23.7's
perfect acquired virtue is less perfect than infused virtue, for infused virtues
alone implicate beatitude immediately and, in 23.7 no less than elsewhere, they
alone are necessary and sufficient to conduce to beatitude. Without infused
virtue, acquired virtue cannot refer to beatitude even *remotely*. What 23.7 primarily—if obscurely—adds is the distinction between a virtue's proximate and
remote end and, consequently, the possibility that beatitude could become acquired virtue's remote end. The acquired moral virtues do not have to be related
to charity, they can be attained without it—that is 65.2's lesson. But they *can* be
related and it matters if they are—and that is 23.7's lesson.

In I.II 65.1's terms, 23.7's true but imperfect virtues are perfect: as true, they
are necessarily connected. It is unclear whether, in addition to 23.7's true but
imperfect virtues, Thomas would number 23.7's charity-perfected acquired virtues among 65.1's perfect virtues. If so, such charity-informed virtues would be
doubly perfect—perfect in being true or connected (I.II 65.1) *and* perfect due
to charity (II.II 23.7). Regardless, 65.1's perfection does not require or concern
charity; its perfection is a matter of acquired virtue being *true*—the perfection even of 23.7's true but imperfect virtue. There is no reason to think either
(a) that 23.7's imperfection is a matter of disconnection or (b) that I.II 65.1's perfection is a matter of acquired virtue being ordered remotely by charity to beatitude. At no point in I.II 65.1 is connection or perfection a matter of charity's
presence. Problems abound if one assumes perfection means the same thing
across the passages.

Perfect virtue is only attainable through charity and leads to beatitude—
directly for infused virtue; indirectly for acquired. True but imperfect virtue
can be attained without charity. Failing to attain beatitude, it is nonetheless true
virtue because ordered to a true, fitting proximate good, one worth loving for

its own sake and one that participates, in a way the merely useful or pleasurable good does not, in God. In loving and pursuing such good, even as one fails to love and pursue the true final good, one is, at least in that sense, not turned away from beatitude but, in an ultimately ineffectual yet nonetheless real way, turned toward it. For Thomas, such orientation ultimately satisfies neither God nor the heart's desires, but, for all that, it cannot but give a life beauty, goodness, and truth—such as to deserve welcome, admiration, even celebration as the loveliness of the divine good dwells, in some fragmented way, among us.

8 *INFIDELITAS* AND FINAL END CONCEPTIONS

IN II.II 23.7 AD 1, Thomas responds to the claim that true virtue can be had without charity because "some who have not charity do good acts." While there can be truly good acts without charity, such acts and the virtues they give rise to and, in turn, stem from are not perfectly good since not ordered to beatitude. But they are truly good. Attaining true virtue without charity requires doing good acts absent charity: no such acts, no such habits, no true virtues. Given his earlier affirmations of pagan virtue, this insistence on the possibility of truly good acts without charity is unsurprising; already he has declared the fallen unredeemed able to do good without charity, denying that they sin in all they do (II.II 10.4; I.II 100.10).

II.II 23.7 ad 1 offers another angle on pagan virtue by considering action absent charity. "The act of someone lacking charity can be of two sorts," Thomas explains,

> one is according to that with respect to which one lacks charity—as when one does something ordered to that *by which* one lacks charity. And such an act is always evil, just as . . . that act of the infidel *insofar as he is an infidel* is always sin . . . even if he clothe the naked or do something else of this sort *ordaining it to the end of his infidelitas.* There can, however, be another act of one who lacks charity—not according to that with respect to which he lacks charity, but according to some other [that is, other than charity] gift of God he has, either faith or hope, *or even the good of nature* which, as said above, is not wholly destroyed by sin. And in relation to this, without charity, there can be some act good in its kind (*aliquis actus bonus ex suo genere*)—not *perfectly* good, though, because it lacks a due ordering to the final end. (II.II 23.7 ad 1)[1]

The act of one without charity can either be ordered to her lack of charity or to some true good short of beatitude like the good of nature. If referred to her lack of charity, it is evil, even if an act otherwise good *in se*, like almsgiving. If referred to a truly good final end, the act is good but, as not ordered to beatitude, not perfectly so.

At a certain level of abstraction this is clear enough. Yet, what this means concretely is very unclear, especially what it means to refer an act to that by which one lacks charity or how a single agent with (presumably) one last end can do both sorts of acts: some ordered to a true good, some to that whereby he lacks charity. Note that a *single* agent—one *lacking* charity—is capable of both these good and evil acts: good when referred to a final end not contrary to charity, evil when ordered to one contrary to it. So, while no unbeliever can merit salvation or do a perfectly good act, he need not sin in every act. To hold otherwise, Thomas says, is "unsuitable" or "absurd" (I.II 100.10 sc).[2] An unbeliever can do truly good acts—acts morally praiseworthy and imperfect only in failing to be ordered to beatitude. However we interpret 23.7 ad 1, we need to honor these points.

Recall Thomas's two ways of viewing acts: in their species (*secundum suam speciem*) or as individually done (*secundum individuum*) (I.II. 18.8 and 9).[3] Acts considered in their species are considered abstractly, apart from further ends for which they might be done, by whom they're done, and so on. Some acts, like murder, are evil in kind. Simply to know a given act is of this species suffices to know it is evil. Some acts are good in their species—marital intercourse or almsgiving, say—and some neutral, like straw-picking or window-closing. With regard to acts good or neutral in kind, only as actually performed can we know their moral status. An essential part of such determination is the remote ends or final end for the sake of which the act is done—one may give alms for vainglory, shut the window to prevent escape.[4]

For Thomas, every human act is always ordered to some final end (I.II 1.1 and 6). One need not be explicitly conscious of that end for each action, for "the character of the first intention, which is for the final end, abides in every desire [or action] for anything whatsoever, even if one is not actually considering the final end. Just as one who walks the road need not think about the end with each step" (I.II 1.6 ad 3). Elsewhere Thomas gives this point sharper expression, distinguishing two ways in which an agent can relate to a final end: actually (*actu*) and implicitly or virtually (*virtualiter*) (*DC* 11 ad 2 and 3).[5] "Actual" reference demands explicit ordering, placing the final end directly before mind and will in some act: fasting to contemplate beatitude, singing for God. To do this always, consciously ordering each act to one's final end, is not possible for us (*DC* 11 ad 2). Nor, however, is it necessary in order for that act truly to be ordered to some end as final. First intention's imprint stamps all subordinate ends: "Whoever actually intends some secondary [i.e., subordinated] end, intends the final end virtually (*virtute*)—just as a doctor, when collecting herbs, actually intends to make an elixir and likely thinks nothing about health, nevertheless *virtually* (*virtualiter*) intends health, for which he prescribes the elixir" (*DC* 11 ad 2). While explicitly or actually intending to make elixir, the doctor also truly and actively intends the remote end of health—even as, picking through underbrush and swatting mosquitoes, it may be the furthest thing from his mind.[6] Yet not just anything the doctor does, even on his search, is implicitly ordered to health: spying some truffles and planning dinner, he may pick them, thereby abandoning his implicit intention of health, even as he may resume it by continuing his herb searching.[7] And insofar as remote ends of health and eating are themselves subordinate to some more comprehensive remote end of his, like beatitude, both the truffle and herb picking are implicitly ordered to that end. Deciding instead to murder patients and pick hemlock, his picking is not ordered to health or beatitude, actually or implicitly. Implicit reference is *real* reference, *authentic* ordering—actual in that sense—and the ordering to final end that holds for most of our acts (*DC* 11 ad 3). By it or "actual" reference, we order each and every act to a final end. "To virtually refer everything to [some end]," Thomas says, is "nothing other than to have [it] as final end" (*DC* 11 ad 3). To have something as final end and to refer particular acts to a final end is to refer acts to that final end (at least) implicitly.[8]

For acts neutral or good in kind, the last end to which they are ordered always helps constitute them as good or evil.[9] Although feeding the hungry is generically good, if Bob does so in order to seduce an intern, he orders his feeding to an evil end. While feeding and seducing are not essentially related in themselves, they are in intention: the act done, at least partly, as means to that end. And reason's ends, final and otherwise, help specify human acts as good or evil. Final ends help account for our doing some act and so the character of our will and its act.[10]

23.7 ad 1 takes this basic schema and considers the roles of charity, *infidelitas*, and beatitude in determining whether (or to what extent) some act is good or evil. For an unbeliever to act "insofar as he is unbeliever" is for him to refer his act to his *infidelitas* as end. This renders the act evil. Despite its generic goodness, "clothing the naked or some other such act" becomes evil when ordered to *infidelitas* (II.II 23.7 ad 1). The basic point is clear, if not yet what it means to refer something to *infidelitas* as end.

As treating the acts of one without charity, 23.7 ad 1 necessarily concerns acts as done *by someone*, individual acts. Since every such act refers to a final end, 23.7 ad 1 thus considers *final*, not merely remote, ends absent charity, specifically the implications of taking an end other than beatitude as *final*. That final end is either: (a) contrary to charity, in which case the act is evil; or (b) a truly good end that is not beatitude, in which case it is truly good but imperfect. The truly but imperfectly good act must be referred to a true good as its *final*—not merely remote—end, for any other final end would affect its specification. And were that final end not a true good, the action would itself fail to be truly good. The ends 23.7 mentions are thus *final*: "that whereby he lacks charity" or a true good like "his natural good" are sought not merely as remote but final. One without charity can order self and acts to a true good other than beatitude as final and, Thomas claims, in so doing, do truly good acts.

One might think that taking any end other than beatitude as final would make everything so ordered evil.[11] If this were so, the unbeliever's every act *would* be sinful. For each act is ordered to some end as final, and if that end, *taken as final*, be idolatrous or bad, then the act ordered thereto will be sin, no matter the act's generic status. That unbelievers do *generically* good acts is both beside the point in relation to whether they avoid sinning and obvious: Thomas's first example has an unbeliever doing just that, giving alms, and thanks to the final end she orders it to, *sinning*. But there's another act of the unbeliever, says Thomas, one referred not to a final end that makes it sinful but secures it as truly, if imperfectly, good.[12] To declare evil any act ordered to a final end other than beatitude implicitly identifies any aside from that final end as *contrary* to charity.[13] Such a view fails to distinguish between taking as final a true, fitting (*debitum*) good and taking as final something opposed to charity or unfitting. Not just any true good taken as final renders acts or virtues referred thereto good or true. In many cases, taking some true good as final makes it, *for that reason*, false. Made final, the good of one friendship or bodily health is false—neither is a due end (*debitum finis*).[14] Conversely, thanks to its fittingness to human nature and relative universality, the political good, even as attainable without charity's healing, is *debitum finis*.[15] For those without charity, it represents the "minimally good" final end necessary to render acts and virtues ordered thereto imperfectly good. There are certain respects, having to do with rightly relating to God, in which humans unhealed by charity cannot fully attain the political end. Nonetheless, in 23.7 ad 1, Thomas insists that *those without charity* can seek as final some end sufficiently good to render their acts good.[16] This end is attainable *without charity and its healing*. It is not the political end as attainable by integral or charity-healed human nature but the end "in accord with [the] good of nature which is not wholly destroyed by sin" (II.II 23.7 ad 1). This end, where some natural obligations necessarily go unfulfilled, falls short of that attainable by charity-healed nature, yet action and virtue referred to it are truly if imperfectly good.[17]

Compared to the best, this final end and those contrary to charity are, alike, deficient. But as compared to one another, they are vitally different: one charity's preamble; the other its enemy; one (at worst) a *symptom* of *infidelitas*; the other its *cause*. There is unworthiness, Thomas insists, and then there is *unworthiness*. If one's final end is fitting, acts referred thereto can be truly good and habits generating them true but imperfect virtues.[18] While Thomas sees deficiency in these virtues, it is not that of being *false*, but of making final what is relatively but not absolutely so, fitting but imperfect. Only beatitude is pursued as final with perfect justice and making anything else final implicitly entangles one in the defect of ultimately seeking something less. This flaw the truly but imperfectly virtuous share with those ordered to false goods.

Yet, for Thomas, in being ordered to some fitting good as final, an agent is—even in their error—anticipating charity. Thomas refuses to let this pagan's failure have the final word, finding, instead, in the pursuit of the truly but imperfectly good, an unconsummated Christwardness. This ordering is justly called "true virtue," rightly regarded not primarily in terms of commonality with sin but participation in good. The Jesus whom Thomas follows celebrates his goodness wherever it be found, for perfection does not need to deny goodness to make room for itself. Thomas recognizes Jesus as perfecting and transcending, not rejecting, the yearning for goodness, truth, and beauty carved into some souls in the shape of true but imperfect virtues. In seeing such habits as true but imperfect, Thomas, imitating his Lord, says "Yes, *and*" rather than "No." In so doing, he means to give glory to the One from whom they ultimately come.

Infidelitas as End

What does it mean for an act to be ordered to *infidelitas* or "that whereby one lacks charity" as final end? An act cannot be referred to the sheer *absence* of charity, for, strictly speaking, its absence is nothing at all. Rather, as his language suggests, Thomas envisions ordering an act to that *on account of which* one lacks charity: belief(s) thanks to which one lacks charity.[19] Some apparent goods and beliefs about the final end are such that their endorsement is sufficient reason for one not having (received) charity.

One who has received charity loses it by mortal sin and such sin necessarily involves him, in the act of that sin, in pursuing as final some end other than charity's (II.II 24.12; 10.4). But we are interested in the case of unbelievers, those who never had charity to begin with. And further, we are not interested in mortal sin *in general*, since it is clear enough how and why it involves pursuing as final some end contrary to charity and renders acts evil. Instead, we want to understand what it means for an unbeliever to ordain his act to that whereby he lacks charity and, in particular, that whereby he lacks it *qua unbeliever*—what it means for an unbeliever to refer an act "to his *infidelitas* as end," to act "insofar as he is an unbeliever." We also need to account for how a single unbeliever can sometimes refer an act to his *infidelitas* and sometimes to a true good. For, given the inevitability of *infidelitas* without grace, the virtuous pagan *does* at least occasionally refer her act to *infidelitas* as end. How is one agent capable of both acts, sometimes making *infidelitas* final, sometimes something true?

It is not entirely clear how Thomas would have resolved these issues, and the relevant remarks are so scattered, indirect, and diverse that I do not think we can know how he imagined these matters working out. Nonetheless, drawing on these texts and shifting to rational reconstruction, we can formulate at least three interpretive options for solving these puzzles. One of these seems to possess the strengths of the others without their flaws, while also seeming most faithful to the relevant passages and spirit of Thomas's thought alike.

OPTION 1: II.II 10.4, ROMANS 14:23, AND ACCIDENTAL VIRTUE

Call this the "accidental virtue" ("AV") option. It points centrally to a claim in II.II 10.4 where Thomas treats the question posed by Romans 14:23 and a corresponding gloss that says the unbeliever's whole life is sin. 10.4 contends that, contrary to what the passage and its gloss seem to suggest, "*not* every action of an unbeliever is a sin." "Some of his actions," he says, "are good." This confirms 23.7 ad 1's claim that acts ordered by those without charity to some final end other than charity's can be good.

Defending this, Thomas notes that *infidelitas* is a mortal sin, which renders unbelievers unable to do good *in the sense of earning merit*, pleasing God in that way.[20] Merit requires grace, which pagans lack in virtue of *infidelitas*. As in 23.7

ad 1, Thomas notes that mortal sin and *infidelitas* do not "wholly corrupt" (*totaliter corrumpit*) nature. Even those affected by original sin and guilty of *infidelitas* can, through their nature, do true good in accord with it. Their natures remain good and "they are able to do good work for which that good of nature is sufficient." "Even the light of natural reason [as corrupted by unbelief]," he says, "is able to order the intention in relation to the natural good" (II.II 10.4 ad 2). Most simply, *infidelitas* does not make agents incapable of true good. As for the Romans passage and gloss, Thomas says they must be understood either to mean (a) merely that the unbelievers' life cannot be sin-*less* or (b) that "whatever one does *from infidelitas* (*ex infidelitate*) is sin" (II.II 10.4 ad 1). Pagans can do good insofar as they order their act to a fitting final end, but sin "whenever they do some work *ex infidelitate*"—in 23.7's idiom, work "ordained to that *by which* [they] lack charity . . . work ordain[ed] to the end of . . . *infidelitas*" (II.II 23.7 ad 1).

AV proceeds by seizing on the remark: "Just as (*sicut*) one having faith can do some venial or even mortal sin in an act which he does not refer to the end of faith . . . so too can the unbeliever do some good act in that which he does not refer to the end of *infidelitas*" (II.II 10.4). Taking this parallel strictly, AV rightly notes that mortal sin involves a believer in temporarily turning away from and pursuing as final that which is not his true, stable final end. For the believer, mortal sin and its final end are accidental in the sense of being out of accord with and betraying her true final end. It is aberrant and (unless he remain impenitent) nondecisive. This initial point is correct; the next step problematic.

Just as the believer is related to mortal sin, AV claims, so is the infidel related to good deeds. *Infidelitas* is the infidel's true final end as beatitude is the believer's. Thus, the unbeliever may will some *other* good final end. But his doing so is like the believer's willing an evil final end: aberrant. The pagan's final end is *essentially infidelitas*. His departing from it in doing good is a stumble on an otherwise sure-footed march to perdition.[21]

I believe AV misunderstands Thomas's parallel, for it makes pagan virtue inexplicable or impossible. On AV infidels do not just *many* evil deeds, which itself would make acquiring virtue impossible, but many times *more* evil deeds than good ones. AV thus founders on Thomas's affirmation of pagan virtue, for rare good deeds and persistent evildoing cannot produce or sustain virtue.

More fundamentally, however, AV profoundly misconceives the nature of good as compared to evil. Moral evil is always and only parasitic on goodness, the absence of due order. There can be no strict parallel between the infidel's relation to *infidelitas* and the believer's to beatitude, for good and evil are not alike in the way such a parallel requires. They are not principles equally capable of commanding intention, for evil is only desirable insofar as it seems good, and goodness underlies its corruption and disorder. The believer's relation to good is thus unlike the unbeliever's to evil. Further, Thomas repeatedly stresses, while a believer may have no relation to evil, it is impossible for an unbeliever to have no relation to good.

In *Lectura super ad Romanos*, considering Romans 14:23 ("whatever does not proceed from faith is sin") and its gloss, Thomas again parallels believer and infidel: "From [14:23] it seems that, as the gloss says, 'The whole life of unbelievers is sin,' just as the whole life of believers is meritorious, inasmuch as it is ordered to the glory of God" (*RC* 14.3.1140). He does so precisely to reject that perspective:

> The believers' relation to good and the unbelievers' relation to evil *differ*. For the [believer] 'there is no condemnation,' [Rom. 8:28] as said above. . . . But in the unbeliever alongside his *infidelitas* is the *good of his nature*. Thus, when an unbeliever does something good from the command of [right] reason and does not order it to an evil end, he does not sin. (*RC* 14.3.1141)

The unbeliever, Thomas insists, is *not* related to *infidelitas* or sin as the believer to good: first, because a believer might have *no* relation to evil; second, and more importantly, because *always*, along with his *infidelitas* and other sin, is the good of the unbeliever's nature.[22] Otherwise, there would be no *person* to be guilty of sin, implicated in *infidelitas*. Always, therefore, with the unbeliever is his nature's good—which, *as good*, is necessarily greater than the corruption *infidelitas* represents. And, thanks to the presence of that good, he can act in accord with it—in the dual, intrinsically connected senses of having the *power* to so act and having a *good nature* and *reason* by which to *proportion his act*.

"Thus," says Thomas, "when an unbeliever does something good from the command of [right] reason and does not order it to an evil end, he does not sin." He explains 14:23's gloss:

> When it is said in the gloss: 'Every deed which is not from faith is a sin' it must be understood thus: Every deed which is *against* faith . . . is a sin, and if it seems that it is good in its kind (*ex genere*), for instance, if a pagan preserves virginity or gives alms to honor his gods, he sins by this very deed. 'To the defiled and unbelievers nothing is clean—their minds and consciences are defiled' (Tit. 1:15). (*RC* 14.3.1141)

An unbeliever can "only" sin just when he acts *qua unbeliever*, which he does just when he directs his act to *infidelitas* as end, to that which is *contra fidem*.

Thomas illustrates: "If a pagan preserve virginity or give alms *in order to honor his gods* (*ad honorem suorum deorum*), he sins by the very fact of his doing so [i.e. doing this for *that reason*]." Doing something to honor one's *gods* shows what it concretely means to order action to *infidelitas* and thus sin. More generally, if still loosely, ordaining action to *infidelitas* is ordering action to false beliefs about or concerning God. There are numerous complexities to consider in due time, but note now Thomas's use of the plural *deorum*, gods. That God is one is something knowable without revelation. As we will see, false religious belief and the rejection or suppression of what one can or ought to know about God constitutes *infidelitas* (II.II 10.1 ad 1). Referring one's act to *infidelitas* means referring it, somehow, to such beliefs.

10.4's parallel, then, concerns the variance in final ends across acts for a single agent, *not* the particular ends intended. As a believer can sin mortally and thus intend *in that act* a final end other than charity's, so can a pagan intend different final ends across various acts. And while the mortally sinning believer contravenes her otherwise stable final end, it is wrong to assume *infidelitas* is the unbeliever's stable final end. It need not be, Thomas reminds, because of the character of the good and its difference from evil.

Moreover, if one who intends beatitude can, despite its matchlessness, step away and intend as final something contrary, how much more can the unbeliever will the good *according to* her nature? It is more mysterious how a believer could do evil than how an unbeliever could do good. The very differences in the cases underline his point: if one ordered to beatitude can temporarily intend an end *contrary* to her nature, much more can the unbeliever act *according* to her nature's good. Thomas stands the objection on its head—really, it is the unbeliever's intending *infidelitas* as end that is more difficult to explain than her intending the true good. The believer's ordaining action to beatitude and the unbeliever's seeking the good befitting her nature are what we ought to expect; it is the reversals that should surprise. Thomas takes the twisting path he does because of the Biblical passage with which he must begin. But evil, for Christian theology is always more difficult to account for than good. If the reverse seems true, that is a clue something has gone awry.

OPTION 2: *SOLA RELIGIO* AND *INFIDELITAS*

The second or "*sola religio*" ("SR") interpretive option notes that, with one exception, each time Thomas gives an example of an act being referred to *infidelitas,* it is an act *charitable* in kind.[23] Almsgiving is the only act mentioned in II.II 10.4 and that around which the Titus commentary's treatment centers (*CT* 1.4.43).[24] 23.7 refers to clothing the naked and feeding the hungry, species of almsgiving (II.II 23.7 ob and ad 1). And the Romans commentary mentions almsgiving and preservation of virginity, an act of charity and one closely related thereto.[25]

For SR, these examples show what it means to refer action to *infidelitas* as final and how to distinguish such acts from those not so referred. Only in specifically religious or charitable actions, SR claims, does the unbeliever have *infidelitas* as end and thus necessarily do evil. While SR offers an elegantly simple rubric for discerning whether an unbeliever is referring to *infidelitas* as final and sharply limits the number of cases in which she counts as doing so and thus doing evil, it is implausible.[26]

First, Thomas holds that specifically religious acts—like almsgiving—can be done for nonreligious ends (II.II 32.1 ad 2). An unbeliever could give alms for the political good, for instance. Moreover, specifically *nonreligious* acts, of courage, say, can be done for religious ends, ordained to *infidelitas*.[27] Further, SR presumes that *infidelitas* as an end can be neatly and easily separated from the unbeliever's comprehensive conception of the final end: sometimes the unbeliever acts for *infidelitas*, sometimes for another end, and deciphering which is as easy as asking whether or not an act is specifically religious. Religious beliefs, it imagines, are readily cordoned off from a person's other beliefs about the final end and human flourishing. But this neglects two points essential to Thomas's perspective: that every human action is ordered to some final end that (lest the agent be, or be driven, mad) need be at least relatively stable; that religious beliefs are an essential, constitutive part of most people's conception of their final end. The convergence of these two features make it difficult to understand how we can answer the question of whether *infidelitas* is implicated in one of an unbeliever's actions. This because each action intends some end as final, usually that specified by the agent's relatively stable conception of the final end, and because that final end itself involves beliefs about the divine. What is more, due to the good of her nature, the unbeliever has very many true beliefs about the final end. As much as her false religious beliefs, these correct beliefs constitute her conception of the final end. And when she acts for that end, these correct beliefs move her, her individual acts are ordered to them too. Since *infidelitas* as well as many, many more true beliefs *together* constitute her conception of the final end, in some act where the unbeliever acts for that end, how do we determine whether the act is good or evil, ordained to *infidelitas* or not?

While SR disintegrates in light of Thomas's understanding of final ends and the role of religious belief in conceptions thereof, it does make one thing clear: an interpretation that would render Thomas's theory applicable to real cases must propose a way to concretely distinguish action for *infidelitas* from action for good ends. SR bequeaths that priority, even as we must avoid its artificial simplicity. And from AV we should inherit a right emphasis on the divided-ness of heart that follows from *infidelitas*, while refusing its implausibly and unfaithfully harsh stance. In proposing a way forward we are doing what, as far as I can tell, Thomas did not. His texts set limits without offering resolution. He lays down that when *infidelitas* is end the act is evil but does not tell us how to know when it *is* end or what precisely it practically means for it to be. Take his example of doing something in order to honor the gods, an end he says is *infidelitas*. Does this mean acting for that reason alone? For that reason along with others? And what if some of the other reasons are good reasons—stemming from true conceptions of the final end? What Thomas and we need is a way of distinguishing those of an unbeliever's acts referred to *infidelitas* as end and those referred to the true good that is faithful to his commitments. Depending on how this question is answered, whether we suppose *infidelitas* is implicated in few or many of her actions and in what way, the pagan is capable of either extraordinarily few or very many good acts.

OPTION 3: COMPLEX FINAL ENDS AND VARIETIES OF SALIENCY

A person's conception of her final end is complex, multifaceted, and relatively comprehensive. It is a conglomerate of more or less explicit, well worked out, and well held together beliefs about what constitutes happiness. It specifies the conditions that a person believes would constitute genuine human flourishing if realized. While conceptions of the final end can be expressed abstractly and simply as in "the final end is fellowship in virtue with God," such a formulation is merely shorthand for a host of complex, essential, detailed beliefs that together stipulate just what "makes up" that end, what, for example, someone means by "fellowship in virtue with God." Taking beatitude as final "requires not only that we accept, in general (*in universali*), 'that God be loved above all things,' but that in *this* very act of choice and will we direct ourselves to some determinate, particular choiceworthy thing" (*DC* 6 ad 15). A final end, for Thomas, is determinate and specific enough to conduce to particular choices here and now, to rule certain things out and require others. Thus, in taking "fellowship in virtue with God" as end, a person has numerous beliefs about who God is, how he's known, what's involved in "fellowship" and "virtue," how the final end relates to subordinate ends, how its constitutive features relate to one another, their relative importance, and so on. Further, a person has beliefs about these beliefs and their relations—how, whether, and in what ways, they are connected, from whence their authority derives, which are non-negotiable, which less essential, and so on. Call the set of all these beliefs a "final end conception" ("FEC").[28]

An FEC belongs to a person insofar as it is practical knowledge, insofar as it is or is intended to be action-guiding. This set of beliefs is practical in that it terminates in action. In holding an FEC, a person is oriented to the end specified by her FEC as the final good: *good* in that she regards and volitionally relates to it as worth acting for, desirable, choiceworthy; *final* in that she regards it as non-instrumentally good, most desirable, choiceworthy, and comprehensive, such that all other good is somehow included in it, related to it, and finds its own goodness most fully explicable in relation to it.[29] She seeks to attain that end above all, tending toward its realization as much as she can in all her action, so that any account of those of her human acts that she does not regard as departing from that end will eventually have to make reference to that end in order for them to be correctly and fully understood.

While her acts may be intelligible apart from such reference and while some of her acts will be opposed to or diverge from that end, no explanation of those acts not so opposed or divergent will be complete (in the sense of explaining them as *her* actions or the precise actions they are) without reference to her final end. And even those acts opposed to or diverging from her final end will be most fully grasped as her actions, in relation to her as agent, when understood as being so opposed or divergent. Her agency's unity depends fundamentally on her FEC, and that unity comes most clearly into view in its light. A person takes some final end as her own when she intends its realization in her life through her behavior, beliefs, attitudes, stances, abstentions, actions, and so on and orders her life and conducts herself with its achievement in view, regarding that achievement and the object thereof as the highest, most desirable good. An FEC is a person's when that person takes the final end stipulated therein as her chief good.

Every person's FEC contains at least some false beliefs.[30] For Thomas, even Christians with the most accurate conception of what constitutes fellowship in charity with God still do not (fully) know God's essence and almost inevitably will hold some mistaken notions about matters not contained within the *articuli fidei*.[31] Human finitude, sin, propensity for error, God's hiddenness in this life, *sacra doctrina*'s complexity, and the relations among dogma collaborate to guarantee that at least some (and likely many) false beliefs pollute even the most sophisticated believer's FEC. More obviously, the non-Christian holds a mix of true and false beliefs about the final end. For Thomas, many of these false beliefs will concern religious matters that impinge on the FEC, even though some of the pagan's final end–related beliefs about religious matters may be true. For now, leave aside the content of these beliefs, the senses in which they count as false, and various complexities that obtain for those who ostensibly do not hold religious beliefs or have them in their FEC.[32] What we need to see just now is that a person's FEC contains a host of true beliefs, many false beliefs, and some false beliefs about religious matters. Given that Thomas believes every human act is ordered to a final end, how should we understand the act of such a person when ordered, as it typically is, to this final end?

On one AV-like account, every such act would be sinful, for in referring to her final end, such acts would implicate the false religious beliefs contained therein. Only when a person took some other end as final could she do good. But such an account suffers all AV's flaws: by making good action rare and inconsistent, it simply cannot square with Thomas's affirmations of pagan virtue, much less his conception of the priority of good over evil.

What we need is an account that honors all the following of Thomas's commitments: (1) every human act is ordered to a final end, (2) most are ordered to a person's relatively stable FEC rather than some other end temporarily taken as final, (3) almost everyone's FEC contains religious beliefs, (4) acts referred to *infidelitas* or false religious beliefs as final are evil, and (5) outsiders are capable of good action with enough consistency and frequency that they can possess true virtue. Given these five commitments, we need an account on which an agent can intend her stable FEC without necessarily being guilty of referring her action to *infidelitas* in doing so. Even as her FEC includes false religious beliefs, it needs to be the case that sometimes in ordaining an act to her final end an agent is implicated in ordaining her action to *infidelitas* and sometime not. And it needs to be possible that most of the time she is not.

The best way I can see of holding all these criteria together is to maintain that in ordaining an act to her final end, a person need not count as ordaining it to all (or each) of the particular beliefs that together constitute her FEC— even as she does count as ordaining the act to her final end. Put differently, each member of the set of beliefs comprising the FEC need not be implicated in every act ordained to the FEC. While we can understand the final end as a monolithic whole, we need not so understand it when it comes to understanding how it guides particular acts. Or, rather, what it is for this FEC to be sought and viewed as such just *is* for it to serve and be considered in its capacity as principle of action.

An end is a principle of action. In the case of the final end, it is not necessarily the case that the final end in its entirety or all of one's final end-constituting beliefs serve as principles for each of one's acts directed to the final end. More precisely, that the set considered as a set serves as a principle or counts as doing so is (a) thanks to some particular constitutive member(s) so serving and (b) does not imply that each member of the set in its capacity as the particular belief that it is serves as a principle. Not all of one's beliefs about the final end, then, are necessarily implicated or actively engaged in one's acts directed to the final end. So, while one is pursuing or referring one's action to the final end, it need not be that in doing so all the particular commitments that constitute the whole conception are relevant in the decision to undertake the act in question. Thus, one counts as pursuing one's final end in some act in any instance where one or more of one's beliefs about the final end in their capacity as final end–type beliefs is action-guiding.[33] Thus, even when only one such belief is salient with respect to some act, one still counts as referring one's act to one's final end. One counts as doing so, for one is ordaining one's act to the final end, only in this case less than all of one's beliefs about what constitutes that end are salient for this act. Some one or more of one's other final end constitutive beliefs could be other than what they are without their affecting one's decision in this particular case.[34]

It makes sense that to a significant extent *not* all of one's FEC-constitutive beliefs would be salient in decisions about particular acts. Surely, in some cases, the choice between two actions is indifferent from the perspective of a wide-range (or large percentage, as it were) of one's FEC. This "portion" of one's FEC could just as well serve as principle for either, both, or neither of these actions. In other words, from the standpoint of those beliefs, it is of no matter whether one does D. Instead, only one or a few, among many others beliefs, are action-guiding just now, principles of this particular action. In such an instance, one refers one's action to the final end but one's doing so just *is* one's being guided by these particular beliefs in their capacity as FEC-constitutive beliefs. Only one or a few such beliefs that go into making up one's final end actually account for *this* action. And, when it comes to drawing the sorts of distinctions Thomas wishes to make between the ends for which unbelievers act, these beliefs rather than every other are those to which one refers one's actions.

For example, say Christopher Hitchens's FEC includes beliefs about the good of literary productions and protecting the weak along with beliefs about the destructiveness of all religious belief. Hitchens writes an article on democratic struggles in Lebanon. He does so partly in view of his FEC—in particular, the good of literary production or of protecting the weak. In writing this piece he pursues the good of literary production and/or that of protecting the weak as partly constitutive of the vision of flourishing his FEC stipulates. While his anti-religious commitments help comprise his FEC, in the case of this article, they play no role, are no principle. Indeed, were they absent and his FEC otherwise identical he would have written the same article for the same reasons. On my proposal, for Thomas, Hitchens would count as ordering his action to his final end, and in particular to the good in accord with his nature (since literary production and protecting the weak are such goods), *but* not as ordaining it to his *infidelitas* as end, even as *infidelitas* is partly constitutive of his overall conception of the final end. That his FEC can be characterized as atheistic—even militantly atheistic—does not entail that all his acts referred thereto are "atheistic," for his FEC is not *only* atheistic, not only his atheism, but also, and even much more, good in accord with his nature.[35] And to the extent that this act depends not on his atheism but those dimensions of his FEC that are good, this act is not sin. His writing this article will be a good, albeit imperfect, act.

With respect to those beliefs that help constitute one's FEC but are not relevant in one's choosing some particular action, one does not count as referring one's act to those beliefs (in the relevant sense) because they are not salient for one's choice of this particular act. Certainly, they have a kind of salience insofar as they are part of one's FEC—and this in two senses. First, in the sense that they help comprise the set which, *qua* set, is, thanks to other set members, salient. Additionally, the kind of salience they have *tout court* is a sort of latent or at-the-ready salience. As partly constitutive of the FEC, they are *always* salient in the sense that they are always *candidates* for being salient. This is part of what committing oneself to them, giving them a place in one's FEC, means— they are always candidates for proving salient in such and such circumstances. They are, as it were, *preapproved* reasons to act: at the ready to play the role of principle of action should one choose to deploy them (e.g., "I will write this article to show those Muslims the error of their ways") or should circumstances arise in which they are implicated (e.g. "That Christian is trying to evangelize my friend!").[36] And they are not merely preapproved reasons for acting, but they specify a set of possible actions and particular reasons for acting that are partly constitutive of one's vision of human flourishing. This sort of conditional or weak salience, however, is different from the active or strong salience some belief or beliefs have just when they serve as principle for a particular action.[37] And, only this active or strong salience allows us to speak of the action being *referred* or *ordained* to the particular end or belief serving as principle in a given action.[38]

On this view thanks to her FEC, a person is primed by the beliefs that constitute her FEC to will such and such in such and such circumstances—and in *that* sense all of a person's FEC beliefs are engaged in or "salient" for each action even as they only come into play or are truly salient in certain circumstances. And only when they do come into play can it be appropriate to speak of the action being *referred* or *ordained* to them in particular. All this to say, we ought not understand an agent who ordains an act to his final end to be referring his act to each and every belief that constitutes his FEC. Of course, there will be beliefs about the connection of the nonsalient belief to other beliefs and about the necessity of the nonsalient belief as a constitutive part of the final end. But that is just to say that whatever this belief is, it is among his beliefs *about the final end*. And that helps account for why in the case where just one or a few beliefs are strongly or actively salient, we are nonetheless correct to speak of an agent ordaining his action to the *final end* even as this particular belief or these few beliefs and no other final end–related beliefs are action-guiding in this case. In other words, it is precisely in respect of the (perhaps very) relative unity of someone's FEC, her beliefs about the connection and ordering of the commitments constitutive of the FEC, that even as only one or more beliefs are strongly salient for some action, the other beliefs and the FEC as a whole count as being referred to. That there are these beliefs about connections between commitments, a conception of how (or functional faith that) it "all hangs together," explains the sense in which it is right to say and actually true that the act is referred to the FEC—and not just to whichever belief or beliefs happen to be strongly salient.[39] At the same time, that these other beliefs are only indirectly or collaterally implicated—implicated by being connected to the strongly salient belief and part of the FEC—accounts for why they do not count as being referred to in the relevant sense, the sense that would make it the case that *infidelitas*, say, was being referred to as final end.

Take Thomas's proscription of baptizing children against their pagan parents' will (II.II 10.12). Recall that he appeals to the parent's natural right to raise his child in his religion. Here is a pagan whose *infidelitas* is partly constitutive of his FEC. Surely, beliefs concerning childrearing are informed by religious commitments and have a place in his FEC. Putting aside nuances related to religious instruction, the parent's childrearing, Thomas says, concerns natural justice and can be in accord with natural justice when this child is raised well. The child-raising or many acts thereof can be *good*—because in accord with natural justice—*and* they are referred to the parent's final end. Indeed, if we can imagine *any* acts as regularly referred to one's stable FEC, as deeply implicating one's vision of human flourishing, surely it is acts of parenting, so numerous, all-pervasive, and wide-ranging. Both *infidelitas* and child-raising–type beliefs are part of the pagan's FEC, but his child-raising acts can be in accord with natural justice and so good even though he refers them to an FEC that itself includes *infidelitas*-type beliefs.

Or say Hitchens has some beliefs in his FEC about the high place of intellectual activity, especially literary production, and about its connection to the badness of religious belief and the importance of undermining it. In the case where he writes the article solely in view of the good of literary production as partly constitutive of his FEC, where literary production–type beliefs alone are strongly salient, his beliefs about the connection (or relation) of that good to the good of undermining religious belief are implicated. They are implicated insofar as he refers his action to his literary production beliefs as partly constitutive of his FEC, under their formality as final end–type beliefs. In doing that, he orders himself and his action to them, as having a place in his FEC and so as related in some way to all the other beliefs that together constitute that FEC in its totality. Just so it is true that he is ordaining his action to his FEC and not just to literary production as an end in itself or as some merely proximate end. In this sense he is referring his action to his FEC. While his literary production–type beliefs are strongly salient—the reason and way in which his FEC is action-guiding just now—his *infidelitas*-type beliefs concerning religion's badness are implicated as connected or somehow related to those beliefs. But they are not implicated or salient in the strong sense that would make him count as referring his action to them as end, not salient in the sense that his literary production–type beliefs are. They are not, for, in this case, their absence from his FEC would not have caused him to act otherwise.[40] They are not principles: undermining religious belief was not his intent, and he would not regard his action as having failed if this literary production turned out not to undermine religious belief (although he might regard it a happy accident if it did).

In all of this, what I am trying to suggest—and what Thomas seems to demand or imply—is that one can order one's action to one's final end even as one is not ordering one's action (or ordering it directly) to some particular aspect or subset of one's FEC beliefs. I have tried to sketch a plausible way we can work this out. Recall that we are trying to hold together the seemingly incompatible commitments that mark *Thomas's* thought: that FECs are comprehensive and always or nearly always include religious beliefs; that every human action is referred to a final end and usually to a person's relatively stable FEC; that, nonetheless, in referring acts to her FEC, sometimes a nonbeliever counts as referring her action to her *infidelitas* and sometimes to a good in accord with her nature. The proposed solution honors all these commitments and tries to do so in a reasonable way. Whether we endorse this particular solution, it is at least clear that Thomas wants to hold these criteria together. And if there is some better way to do that, all the better. For now, however, this is one plausible way to work out Thomas's inchoate vision.

Mixed or Multiple Strongly Salient Ends

However this works, an agent must be able to refer his action to his FEC in such a way that his action is *not* referred to one or more aspects of that FEC. Two sorts of cases are easy to parse: those where *infidelitas* has no bearing at all on some action and those where *infidelitas* alone among FEC beliefs is strongly salient. Such actions are good and bad, respectively. When in view of his FEC Hitchens writes a book exclusively to undermine belief in God, say, Thomas holds this act to be evil. When in view of his FEC he writes solely to further tolerance, say, the act is good. Many acts, however, are done for multiple reasons. That is to say, in many instances several of a person's final end beliefs bear on or are implicated in her doing some action. And it is certainly possible that in some circumstances both truly good ends and ends of *infidelitas* are implicated.

Thus, Hitchens writes a book both to undermine belief in God and to further tolerance, or a Muslim prays both to honor God and Muhammad as seal of the prophets. How might Thomas evaluate such actions? Further, it is often hard to know just which FEC beliefs are salient for some action. Even if someone tells us, "Ultimately, I give these alms to honor Jupiter," or "Ultimately, I preserve virginity to honor the gods," and it seems she is truthful, we can still wonder whether that settles the matter—maybe other dimensions of her final end are in play that she is not mentioning or perhaps she would do the act just now for some other reason.[41] More likely, the agent will tell us nothing at all. How ought we to understand those actions? Given that we often lack reliable access to an agent's intentions with respect to the final end in some act, we need a strategy for evaluating such cases that reckons with our ignorance.[42] These ostensibly separate questions—concerning acts done for mixed ends and the puzzle of intention where the final end is concerned—are interestingly related. As we will see, the principles that ought to govern our understanding of actions for "mixed" ends can help guide us in situations of ignorance about an act's relation to the final end.

There are at least two basic interpretive options concerning mixed ends. We could suppose that *any* active involvement of *infidelitas*, no matter the other ends implicated, renders the act evil. Or we could suppose that, at least in some cases, the involvement of good ends renders the act good, causes it not to count as ordered to *infidelitas*. The first of these options falls prey to the problems that led us to reject both SR and AV: it either ends up divorcing the believer's religious commitments from his FEC or makes it impossible to perform good action with enough consistency to attain virtue. I propose a version of the second option that nonetheless honors a key commitment of the first as most faithful to Thomas.[43]

Strong and Weak *Infidelitas*

In that spirit, we can first distinguish between two varieties of *infidelitas*—a distinction that while novel to Thomas is relevant for the way I think he would want to classify various acts arising from *infidelitas*. While Thomas distinguishes among varieties of *infidelitas*, he does not distinguish between *infidelitas* that is actively anti-Christian or anti-theist, and *infidelitas* that merely involves an agent in believing things that are untrue or contrary to Christianity. He simply classifies both as "resistance to faith before it has been accepted" (II.II 10.5 and 6).[44] The distinction I wish to draw concerns *infidelitas* and agents that are *within* this category. It is between (a) *infidelitas* as intentional, active condemnation or suppression of Christianity (or monotheism insofar as it overlaps with Christianity) and beliefs related thereto and (b) *infidelitas* as commitment to religious belief that is incompatible with or contrary to Christianity (or monotheism insofar as it overlaps with Christianity) and so incidentally opposed to it, lacking the character of active opposition.[45]

The distinction is perhaps clearest at the level of action. There is action rooted in *infidelitas* that is essentially and directly opposed to Christianity—action that *attacks* beliefs or positions associated with Christian belief. And there is action rooted in *infidelitas* that, while contrary to or incompatible with Christian belief, is not intended as an attack on Christianity—action that only incidentally opposes Christian belief. Call the former, "strong *infidelitas*," the latter, "weak *infidelitas*."[46] The defining mark of strong *infidelitas* just is its oppositional or combative character, its belief about the good of suppressing or defeating Christianity. Strong *infidelitas* generates or involves the intent to combat and overturn Christian belief. Weak *infidelitas* does not. From this difference in intention (along with the action intention generates) we can work back and specify a difference in the material commitments of each kind of *infidelitas*. Now, in drawing this distinction we have defined the *infidelitas* proper to non-Christians: it involves adherence to beliefs, whether in the form of affirmations (e.g., belief that Muhammad is the seal of the prophets, that Jesus was an angel, that there are many gods) or denials (e.g., belief that there is no God, that Jesus is not God, that humans have no souls, that there is no afterlife) concerning religious matters that are contrary to Christianity or *articuli fidei*. Believing, for example, that God is one would not implicate one in *infidelitas*, but believing that he is not Triune would.[47] We will say more below, but for now, further distinguishing strong from weak forms illumines the concept of *infidelitas*.

Concretely, the strong and weak *infidelitas* distinction is one between, say, writing a book to undermine Christian faith and writing a book to edify adherents of some view incompatible with or opposed to Christianity. While the latter case is opposed to Christianity in that it propounds a perspective that if true entails Christianity's falsity, it does not constitute a direct attack on Christian faith in the sense that the former does. It opposes Christianity only incidentally. Of course, should that book also include anti-Christian polemics, so that in promoting its view it also attacks Christianity, then we have a direct attack—strong *infidelitas*. Or, if it aimed to convert Christians, then it has the relevant character of opposition even if it might lack the aggression or mean-spiritedness, say, of the book seeking to discredit or mock Christianity.

Suppose a Muslim prays to honor God and Muhammad. His seeking to honor Muhammad (but not his seeking to honor God) is opposed to Christianity in the sense that it involves him in believing things incompatible with Christianity's truth; however, his praying for Muhammad's sake is no *attack* on Christianity.[48] The *infidelitas* implicated in his praying is weak not strong. It does not generate action aimed at suppression of or direct opposition to Christianity even as it involves him in believing doctrines incompatible with Christianity. Should he pray that God destroy Christians, however, the prayer is an attack and is rooted in *infidelitas* that is not merely incompatible with but directed against Christianity. Likewise, should he pray that God convert Christians, then his prayer has the character of attack in the relevant sense, even though that character is gentler than that of the other prayer. What unites the two—and distinguishes them from the prayer prayed to honor Muhammad but without negative reference to Christianity—is precisely their oppositional, direct engagement with Christianity, whether that involve desiring to see Christians persecuted or converted. The focus is not merely endurance and flourishing in one's religion or being faithful to it, but additionally the vindication of one's faith over and against Christianity. In this, I do not mean to elide the stance of the person who wishes to see Christians destroyed with that of one who wants them converted. There is a world of difference here. But I have my eye on a different point, in respect of which that distinction is not relevant. When it comes to the question of *infidelitas*, its role as principle in action, and the consequences of its serving that role, what matters is not the opposition's intensity, motive, or spirit, but simply whether it is direct and intentional. Strong *infidelitas*'s defining feature just is its direct, intentional opposition to Christianity. Surely, Thomas would regard as evil any action for which strong *infidelitas* was principle—no matter the other ends implicated. Insofar as strong *infidelitas* is salient, this alone constitutes an act as referred to it in the evil-making sense.

This is the sense in which AV grasps something true for Thomas. It is incredible to imagine Thomas not regarding action for which strong *infidelitas* is salient as wrong, as ordered to *infidelitas*—whatever its other ends. How could he see an action that aimed to destroy, suppress, or overcome Christianity as other than sinful? Whether we might prefer a Thomas who did so, he would have little to do with the Thomas of history or even the spirit of Thomas's thought.[49] We cannot pretend Thomas does not say what he does about *infidelitas*-directed action—and surely if any action counts as so referred it must be this sort. This interpretation may seem to saddle Thomas with a negative stance toward non-Christians. But appearances deceive. Drawing this weak/strong *infidelitas* distinction and forwarding this perspective are actually the first steps in advancing the maximally charitable view that can still claim to keep faith with Thomas. In particular, this weak/strong *infidelitas* distinction makes room for ascribing to Thomas the view that actions with final ends that include *weak infidelitas* among them might still count as good—notwithstanding their connection to *infidelitas*.

Before sketching that possibility, note that the weak/strong *infidelitas* distinction has some textual cachet. Throughout the faith treatise, Thomas stresses that *infidelitas* has the character of sin in virtue of its *contrarietas* and *retitor*, opposition and resistance, to faith (II.II 10.1 and 5). Precisely resistance and opposition to Christian faith give *infidelitas* the *ratio* of sin. And the more that resistance and opposition the more it has sin's *ratio*. Thus, Thomas initially distinguishes between *infidelitas* that is mere absence of faith and *infidelitas* that is opposition to faith, where that means, at least, that one has heard the Gospel and not believed (II.II 10.1 and 5).[50] It is the latter *infidelitas* that has sin's character, he says, and that "perfects" the *ratio* of *infidelitas*, fulfills its definition. Additionally, when he later explicitly treats the *infidelitas* of "pagans and Gentiles," of those who have heard but not believed the Gospel, he ranks their *infidelitas* the least grave of the sinful sort (II.II 10.6). Heresy, because it involves resistance to the faith after its having been accepted, is the gravest form of *infidelitas*: "*Infidelitas* has the *ratio* of fault, more from that which resists faith than from its not having it" (II.II 10.6). It seems reasonable to say that the more there is of resisting and opposing the faith in *infidelitas*—since this is what makes *infidelitas* sinful in the first place—the more sinful that variety of *infidelitas*. Just this sort of thought allows Thomas to rank the gravity of various forms of *infidelitas*. My weak/strong *infidelitas* distinction takes his resistance-related distinction and draws it within one of these categories of *infidelitas*. Clearly, Thomas holds that the more *infidelitas* has of resistance, the more sinful it is. Honoring this, I have drawn a relatively bright line between (1) intentional and direct opposition and resistance or strong *infidelitas* and (2) indirect and incidental opposition and resistance or weak *infidelitas*. While going beyond Thomas, this seems fully in keeping with his thought.

With that distinction in hand, I would suggest that in cases where an agent refers her action to weak *infidelitas* and to some true, good aspect of her FEC, we ought to take Thomas to regard such action as good. We should see him as viewing such action not as referred to weak *infidelitas* (or at least not referred to *infidelitas* in an evil-making way) but as referred to the good in accord with the agent's nature, ordered to *that* aspect of the FEC. While someone could argue that, weak or strong, *any infidelitas* with strong salience renders that act sinful, I suggest the contrary. Doing so makes Thomas more capacious without, I think, betraying his basic commitments. Further, it seems likely that very many of an unbeliever's actions would be directed *both* to weak *infidelitas* and some true good. Certainly, it appears, very many more actions would be so directed than ordered to strong *infidelitas*, either alone or with some good— this thanks to strong *infidelitas*'s essential Christianity-regarding character. If pagan virtue is possible, as Thomas says it is, it becomes increasingly difficult to see how it could be attainable if an unbeliever's acts count as evil *just in virtue of her unbelief*. This point argues for regarding actions ordained both to weak *infidelitas* and some truly good end(s) as good acts, as not referred to *infidelitas* in the evil-making way.

It is noteworthy that in II.II 23.7 when Thomas gives an example of true but imperfect virtue, he cites the case of virtue directed to the common political good as final. Since this end makes virtue directed thereto true but imperfect, it must make action so directed good but imperfect too. But for Thomas, the political common good involves religious commitments and practices. Any political common good he can imagine involves citizens engaging in religious practices and holding religious beliefs. Thus, insofar as the political common good holds a place in a person's FEC so too does realization of the religious activities that partly constitute it. As Thomas knew, for many, among these religious beliefs will be some false beliefs about which God or gods ought to be honored in political life, how, by whom, and so on. Yet, unless we imagine, implausibly, that in speaking here of virtue referred to the political good Thomas has in mind virtue referred to that good as flawlessly, perfectly conceived (i.e., as it would be by unfallen humanity), then we have here an instance of virtue—and by extension action—referred to some final end that includes but is not entirely constituted by false religious belief. The person acting for the political end, for whom that component of her FEC is strongly salient for some act, frequently acts as well for false religious ends that are also strongly salient: many of her acts will have in view the religious dimensions of the political good alongside the nonreligious dimensions. But she does not count as thereby doing evil, for her virtue is true.

This suggests that just in virtue of weak *infidelitas* having strong salience in some act, that act does not necessarily count as evil. In this case, presumably, it would not count as evil precisely because of the role the political good—and all the many *true* beliefs the agent has about it—play in the action. Many beside the false religious beliefs suffice to generate the action, and presumably, the agent would still do the act even if he did not hold the false religious beliefs about the political good that he does. Thus, the act does not count as being referred to *infidelitas*—or not in the evil-making sense.

Whether such textual arguments are decisive, they are at least suggestive. Chiefly, I prefer this reading for the way it balances Thomas's various commitments—his desire to recognize *infidelitas* as sin and its pursuit as leading away from true good, on the one hand, and, on the other, his insistence that evil never corrupts good entirely and his explicit claims that unbelievers cannot only do good works but attain true but imperfect virtue. Why might the presence of weak *infidelitas* alongside truly good ends as that to which some act is ordained *not* render the act sinful? Why should the presence of truly good ends make that difference when ordering an act to *infidelitas alone* (weak or strong) makes it sinful? Here, my response actually intersects with the epistemological puzzle I raised earlier.

In most cases, we will have little or no idea what an agent's intentions are with respect to the final end in some act. Even if we could question her at length, doing so would be impractical and rude. Yet those who live in community with others who do not share their religious beliefs need to have some sense of the quality of one another's character, of how reliable, just, and trustworthy their neighbors are, and, in making these determinations, some way of accounting for the moral significance of their neighbors' religious convictions. They need to go about life without the intrusion of questioning someone about her final end in some action, much less the suspicion and distance that questioning and its stance would embody.

The presence of some good end alongside the end of weak *infidelitas* ought to make a difference, ought to make the action count as good notwithstanding the involvement of *infidelitas*, if and because that good end itself suffices to explain the action. Thus, in act *B*, when some good aspect of the FEC is intended alongside weak *infidelitas*, *B* ought to count as good if the intention of the truly good end itself suffices to generate *B*, suffices as its principle. That good end *is* so sufficient when, even in the absence of the salient weak *infidelitas* alongside it, the agent would still undertake *B*.[51]

Thus, take the Muslim who prays out of love for God and to honor Muhammad. The former end is good in accord with his nature; the latter is a form of weak *infidelitas*. Say that in just these circumstances this believer would have prayed simply due to his love for God even if he had not had any desire or thought of honoring the prophet. Put differently, his weak *infidelitas* played a role in generating the action, it was strongly salient, but it was not *necessary*

for his so acting; his love for God was itself sufficient to generate the action just
now. On my proposal, this act counts as good thanks to the truly good end it
pursues, notwithstanding the salience of weak *infidelitas*.[52] His other truly good
ends suffice to explain and generate the action, even if it so happens that the
end of weak *infidelitas* is implicated too. Because these truly good ends *suffice*
to generate the action, I suggest we see Thomas as regarding it as good.[53] Thus,
some act ordered to weak *infidelitas* nonetheless counts as good if and only if
some good aspect of the FEC to which the action is also ordered itself suffices to
generate the action. And it does suffice when the *absence* of *infidelitas* as an end
for the act would not result in any difference in whether the act was done.[54] This
way of putting the point clarifies a possible ambiguity. It should be clear that so
long as weak *infidelitas* is not *necessary* to generate the action, and some good
and also intended component of the FEC suffices to do so, that the action counts
as good.[55] But, as we will see, that very reasoning suggests that even if weak
infidelitas is *sufficient* (but not necessary) to generate the act then, provided the
good intended aspect of the FEC is also sufficient, the act still counts as good.

In contrast, if some Muslim prays to honor Muhammad and to honor
God, but the former end is *necessary* to generate the action so that if he were
not seeking to honor Muhammad he would not pray in these circumstances,
then this act would count as sin. It would because he would count as ordaining his act to *infidelitas* in the relevant sense—any involvement of truly good
ends would not suffice to serve as principles of the act. Ordination of an act to
infidelitas is always problematic for Thomas, for it involves an agent in being
directed away from the true end. On my interpretation, however, that evil is
outweighed or swallowed up by the parallel intention of a truly good end that
itself suffices to generate the action. In stipulating that the good end be sufficient to produce the action, I have specified that it be at least as action-genera-
tive as the end of weak *infidelitas*. This by no means suggests that in other cases
where an agent is ordaining action to good and bad ends that the bad ends can
be offset by the good ends and thus render the action good. On the contrary,
I am suggesting that this possibility is peculiar to the case of weak *infidelitas*.
It is a unique feature of *weak infidelitas* that it might be offset or trumped, and
it obtains only because the sinfulness of *infidelitas* itself consists precisely in
resistance to the faith—which is resistance to the true final end. Such resistance
is precisely what makes it sinful. Yet in the case where a good end is pursued
as well and itself suffices to generate the action, in a vital sense the true final
end is *not* being resisted. Even as thanks to *infidelitas* one is caught up in some

resistance to the true final end, because it is *weak infidelitas*, that resistance is itself incidental, indirect—and so relatively weak. Moreover, this resistance is not even necessary to generate the action. Further, thanks to one's being *directly* ordered to a truly good end that *does* suffice to generate the action, one is explicitly ordering oneself to an honest, fitting good. In such cases, as one does the specifically good act ordered to a truly good end, the sense in which one is actually resisting the ultimate good seems minimal.

As for the epistemological question, just here the connection emerges. Yet we now move into much more speculative waters: it is harder to know what Thomas might say about these matters. Nonetheless, in his spirit, I suggest a principle of interpretive charity that dovetails with the perspective outlined above—even as it moves in a still more capacious direction. Assume what will often be the case: that we lack certainty about the role weak *infidelitas* and good facets of a person's FEC are playing in generating some act. I propose that in cases where we can reasonably view some other final end than weak *infidelitas* as playing a role in generating some action, we do so and count the specifically good act so ordained as good. Put differently, unless we have good reason to suspect that *only* weak *infidelitas* could generate or serve as principle for some act, we ought not to regard that act as ordained to weak *infidelitas*, as evil.[56]

This perspective moves beyond that sketched above: it asks us to regard an act as good whenever it seems reasonable to hold that some truly good FEC-type belief plays a role in generating the act, regardless of the role of weak *infidelitas*. Confidence that a good FEC-type belief helped generate the action should lead us to regard the act as good, even if it is open to doubt that the good end sufficed to generate the action or seems possible that weak *infidelitas* was necessary. I move in this more capacious direction primarily in view of Thomas's pervasive commitment to charity in relating to outsiders but also in view of both the significant ambiguity that would attend almost any real-life case of the sort we are considering and the principle that condemning the innocent is always worse than acquitting the guilty.[57]

Thus, say we observe some pagan preserving virginity and know that in his context some do so to honor the gods, others to chasten their desires so to better equip themselves for just living, and others to do both. Provided there is not decisive evidence that his end is honoring the gods alone, we ought to assume his end is just and count his action good.[58] On this "innocent until proven guilty" model, an unbeliever's specifically good acts are regarded as good—as referred to a good end—unless and until there is decisive evidence to show that his final end in some act is weak *infidelitas* alone. This "alone" is key: only when there is decisive evidence that weak *infidelitas* alone is the end, ought we to regard the act bad.[59] An extension of this charitable epistemological principle, or its application to a different case, concerns weak and strong *infidelitas*: when ascribing *infidelitas* we ought to presume it is weak unless we have decisive evidence that it is strong. In short, *infidelitas* counts as weak until proven strong.

Thomas's insistence that unbelievers can possess virtue seems to demand this robust, thoroughgoing charity—the more of a pagan's acts are vitiated by *infidelitas*, the less likely *any* pagan could be virtuous. More profoundly, though, my elevation of charity finds precedent in Thomas's constant insistence on the priority of good to evil: in *res* and *ratio*, good always has precedence over evil. Evil is only explicable in terms of a relation to good. My proposal extends this commitment.

Evil, according to Thomas, never corrupts entirely—especially not the good of human nature. Any human's FEC *just in virtue of her being human* will necessarily be far more true than false, far more good than evil. Statistically speaking, far more of anyone's acts will be oriented toward or implicate truly good aspects of their FEC than false ones—especially for one like the virtuous pagan who is prone to acts good in kind in the first place. We thus have a better chance of getting the interpretation right, understanding our neighbor correctly, if we see her as pursuing some truly good facet of her final end until shown otherwise.[60] This holds even for those whom we judge to do relatively *more* evil actions—we ought first to look for some flaw in the other conditions relevant to constituting an action as morally good (including proximate and relatively remote ends) *before* we look to their FEC. This interpretation also coheres, I think, with the outworking of charity that Thomas commends wherein one presumes the best rather than the worst of others, that more rather than less goodness endures in someone's heart.

A Christian slowness to judge another's heart is perhaps less a refraining from assessment than a slowness to condemn (Matt. 7:1–5). Put positively, it is a willingness and hopefulness to find in another, as much as one can, the beauty and goodness of God's image pervading and thriving notwithstanding sin. Even more, it is the hope of discovering the Spirit's work, the beginnings of Christlikeness, transformation, re-creation. It is readiness to find God's grace beyond the walls of the church, perhaps especially, in the hearts of those who do not *yet* know him and do not *yet* knowingly love him, but are, thanks to his work in them, already *in via*, already known, already loved.

Those Who Have Not Heard:
Infidelitas as Punishment, *Infidelitas* without Sin

The following pages consider those who have not heard the Gospel, among whom (alone) a distinct variety of *infidelitas* can obtain, one which Thomas categorizes more as "punishment" than sin. Because their *infidelitas* is marked not by resistance to the faith but merely its absence, their *infidelitas* "has not the *ratio* of sin" (II.II 10.1). *Infidelitas* in this sense denotes absence of Christian faith. If any of these are condemned, Thomas says, it is not because of the *sin* of *infidelitas* but something else (II.II 10.1). And treating Romans 10:14, "How shall they believe [in] Him of whom they have not heard?" which he also cites in *Summa theologiae* II.II 10.1, Thomas declares this *infidelitas* non-sinful in the Romans commentary: "From this it is clear that not every unbelieving person is excused from sin, but those who have not heard," and he cites John 15:22: "If I had not come and had not spoken to them they would have no sin [but now they have no excuse for their sin]" (*RC* 10.2.842).[61] "Is it possible," he asks, "that those to whom [the Gospel] has not come, for example those who were raised in the wilds, are excused from the sin of *infidelitas*?" He responds: "To this it must be said that according to the pronouncement of the Lord in John 15:22, those who have not heard the Lord himself or his followers, are excused from the sin of *infidelitas*" (*RC* 10.3.849). This may suggest that "hearing" requires encountering Christianity through a believer faithful in practice and doctrine—not a conquistador, say. If so, many are those who have not heard.

Here and in II.II 10.1, Thomas argues that in the absence of hearing the Gospel *infidelitas* lacks sin's *ratio*: one cannot resist what one hasn't heard, and it is resistance that constitutes *infidelitas* as sin. Regardless, those innocent of the sin of *infidelitas* would bear no sin for referring their acts to it. But even if such action is no sin, we can still ask whether it is *good*—for it is one thing to hold that a good act ordered to *infidelitas* of this sort is not sinful; another to hold, that a Muslim, say, who has not heard the Gospel does *good* in doing something for Muhammad's sake.

WHAT *INFIDELITAS* IS

Whether it involves resistance or not, *infidelitas* is constituted by particular commitments: denying the truth of various Christian (or monotheistic) claims and/or holding substantive religious commitments incompatible with Christianity. These include beliefs like "this world is all there is," "Buddha is divine," "we are all part of God," "there is no God," "Jesus is not God," and so on. For those who have heard the Gospel, holding these beliefs counts as sinful *infidelitas*; resistance gives it the *ratio* of sin, but the *infidelitas* itself consists in beliefs that implicate one in such resistance.[62] When such beliefs are part of a person's FEC and necessary to generate some act, that act is sinful. But consider an Aristotelian monotheist or Muslim who has heard the Gospel but adheres to a vision of God that as far as it goes is true, compatible with Christianity, but lacks key affirmations. And take the case of such a one referring an act not to something he affirms that Christians deny or denies that Christians affirm, but just to that vision of God insofar as it is compatible with Christianity. Does this constitute *infidelitas*?

It might seem to, for holding to this incomplete vision of God in the face of the Christian alternative could seem a kind of resistance. But I do not think that is how Thomas would conceive it. This vision of God is, as far as it goes, true and in accord with reason.[63] It is precisely reference to such a truly good but imperfect end that makes some act *imperfectly* good. For reference to this end to count as reference to sinful *infidelitas* and so as sinful would be an instance of double jeopardy, faulting a person twice for the same sin. For Thomas, the flaw in this vision of God is already registered just in virtue of it and action referred to it being imperfect. To count it again as constituting resistance, sinful *infidelitas*, is unnecessary and mistaken. Indeed, we can just as well view the maintenance of such belief in the face of Christianity as *agreement* with Christianity. For this vision of God is not in discord with Christianity and, in itself, reference to it involves no resistance. Still, the Aristotelian monotheist who has heard the Gospel is differently positioned than Aristotle himself. How does Thomas register that difference and any resistance it involves?

The difference in culpability between Aristotle and the Gospel-rejecting Aristotelian cannot be a matter simply of the latter's ongoing adherence to a vision of God that is, after all, entirely compatible with Christianity—one Thomas calls a preamble to faith.[64] That vision does not become false, nor loyalty to it become sin, in virtue of its being shown incomplete through charity's advent. Put differently, the Aristotelian monotheist who converts need not repent of this vision any more than one possessed of true but imperfect virtue need mortify his virtue.[65] Instead, both need to see how charity transforms these good but imperfect visions and virtues—and undergo that transformation. Pursuit of this vision of God is, like the pagan's pursuit of justice, good but imperfect; even in the face of refusal to convert, the pursuit does not in itself constitute sinful *infidelitas*. Really this question duplicates that of whether one sins simply in virtue of not taking the perfect end as final, of whether having nature's good as final end constitutes sin.

Still, unlike Aristotle, the Gospel-aware Aristotelian is entangled in resistance, sinful *infidelitas*—not, however, through holding his theistic beliefs or believing his end the true one.[66] He is entangled in virtue of his believing distinctively Christian claims about God to be false. And, more profoundly, in virtue of the pride-generated commitments that rule Christianity out of consideration (II.II 10.1 ad 3; 10.2 and ad 2). As Thomas has it, thanks to this pride he refuses to convert, balks at mystery, and dismisses revelation. Commenting on 1 Corinthians, Thomas says of these Gentiles who regard the Gospel as foolishness that

> because of their lack of wisdom they reckon it impossible for God to become man and to suffer death according to human nature . . . shameful that a man would undergo crucifixion. . . . Pursuing wisdom, they want to judge every doctrine put before them according to the rule of human wisdom. . . . [Thus] the word of the cross is foolishness to them . . . because it seemed contrary to . . . human wisdom that God would die and that a man just and wise would willingly take on the most wretched death. . . . [But the reason] something divine appears foolish [is] not because it *lacks* wisdom but because it *far surpasses* (*superexcedit*) human wisdom. Men are accustomed to reckoning foolish whatever surpasses their understanding or experience (*sensum*). . . . God led the faithful to saving knowledge of himself by different things, things not discovered in or through creatures' natures, and thus things reckoned foolish by the worldly, who consider the nature of human matters alone. (*CC* 1.3.50, 57, 58, 62, 55)

While Thomas traces the cause of *infidelitas* to pride, which is proper to the will, *infidelitas* itself is in the intellect as subject (II.II 10.2 and ad 2).[67] Resistance or sinful *infidelitas* is not pride *per se* but those particular beliefs that cause one to regard the Gospel as false. The Aristotelian who has rejected Christianity is thus entangled in *infidelitas* through those convictions in virtue of which he refuses to belief Christianity's claims, or even to entertain their possible truth. Beliefs such as "nothing transcends human reason," "the reception of knowledge through revelation is servile and beneath humanity," or "God cannot communicate with creatures," implicate him in resistance, sinful *infidelitas*.[68] Actions ordered to these beliefs (and not, as well, to true ones) are sinful.

SHEER ABSENCE

Consider *infidelitas* that has the character of *pura negatio*, sheer absence, that lacks the *ratio* of sin.[69] What could it mean to refer something to this sort of *infidelitas*? In one sense, this absence is just lack of Christian faith, nothing, and so no end. *Infidelitas* is not lack as such, however, but lack of due truth about religious matters.[70] Such lack can take the form not only of that which should be present but is not, but that which should not but is. *Infidelitas* in this sense denotes not just that absence of truth that is nothing, but the absence of truth that is false belief.

The pre-Christian, ideal Aristotelian participates in *infidelitas* in that her belief about God lacks truth that Scripture discloses. Her *infidelitas* really is the sheer absence of truth, not something to which she can refer action.[71] In contrast, the Hindu or Muslim participates in *infidelitas* in the additional sense of having false views that she ought not—the absence of due truth that is a substantively false religious belief (e.g., that Muhammad is the last prophet, that "idols" are gods). As it is not pride or resistance *per se* that constitutes *infidelitas* in the Gospel-refusing Aristotelian but the particular beliefs in virtue of which she does not believe, so too here, it is not "absence" *per se* that constitutes *infidelitas* but the absence of due belief that is false belief. It is easy to see how such a belief could be the principle of an action. When it is, because this *infidelitas* lacks the character of sin, that action is not sinful.

Return to the Gospel-ignorant Aristotelian monotheist. Certain of his beliefs are entirely consonant with Christianity and his actions referred to those beliefs are truly but imperfectly good. But matters are more difficult when it comes to *infidelitas* consisting in false religious beliefs. Can Thomas regard it good when a Gospel-ignorant Muslim gives alms for the memory of Muhammad or an unevangelized Hindu fasts to honor a god? Answering this question requires us to consider briefly Thomas's complex notion of the suppression of the truth.

SUPPRESSING THE TRUTH

In II.II 10.1, Thomas notes that while it is not in human nature's power to have Christian faith, neither is it in human nature to "fight (*repugnet*) his inner instinct" (II.II 10.1 ad 1).[72] Man, he claims, is inclined to some belief in the divine just by his nature, and the suppression of this belief is contrary to human nature and so has sin's *ratio*.[73] The truth-suppressor is guilty of sin—and suppression is possible whether one has heard the Gospel or not. This concept of "suppression" thus offers a way to think about guilt and sin in the context of *infidelitas* *before* and *apart* from hearing the Gospel. Suppression (in certain forms) is the pre-Gospel analog of resistance; it has the capacity to make various pre-Gospel religious beliefs sinful.[74] But who counts as suppressing the truth?

Thomas identifies two types of suppression and suppressors. First, the Aristotelian who in addition to his true monotheistic beliefs has various false religious commitments related to an overconfidence about what reason shows—convictions of the sort that would lead him to reject Christianity as "foolishness." *Qua* Aristotelian, he just is a highly skilled theoretical reasoner, able to do what few can: arrive at the truth about God knowable by reason. For such a one to go on, against reason, and form false religious beliefs—beliefs of the sort that would give him a *prima facie* bias against or skepticism toward Christian truth—would be blameworthy. If he can reason well enough to arrive at religious truth, he could avoid such errors.[75] Embracing such falsity involves a suppressor in going beyond what his own reasoning actually shows and consequently disposing himself to reject Christianity. Like *infidelitas*, this involves a disordered will: some defect of love, commanding and conducting his intellect in problematic ways. "The will's contempt," Thomas explains, "causes the intellect to dissent" (II.II 10.2 ad 2).[76] Because this false religious belief is vincible, he is blameworthy for it. Those beliefs that comprise this error constitute suppression: a variety of *infidelitas* that, notwithstanding its being possessed by a person who has not heard the Gospel, is nonetheless sinful.

For Thomas, someone like Aristotle, who believed in and worshiped the God vaguely known through reason, would, to that extent, not be guilty of suppression (II.II 81.1 and 7).[77] Conversely, if Aristotle himself failed to be a monotheist, he would be guilty of sin, suppressing the truth, because, given his rational powers, he was capable of reaching it. On that basis, we might think all who fall short of something like Aristotelian monotheism count as thwarting the truth, guilty of suppression. But this is not so. Thomas insists that the vast majority of people are simply unable to follow the arguments that establish the existence of reason's God and, in fact, rightly depend on the teaching of "the wise" (*sapientes*) for most of their religious knowledge (II.II 2.6). Revelation of truths about God in principle knowable through reason is necessary precisely because so few can discover them—and even those who can, do so only with "much time and many errors" (I 1.1). Such people are not to count as *morally* or *spiritually* flawed in virtue of the weakness of their theoretical reason, their incapacity for a certain *scientia*. How can one suppress what, try as one might, one has not the capacity to know? It is thus contrary to what Thomas says to suggest that all those who fail to arrive at Aristotelian monotheism count as suppressing the truth.

So which of a person's false beliefs are implicated in or are the fruit of suppression and thus candidates for being sinful? The answer Thomas would give, I think, is both agent-specific and universal. And it leads us to Thomas's other, much less developed notion of suppression. Thomas believes every human has a religious inclination (*interior instinctus*). His remarks on this inclination are few, scattered, and ambiguous, but he imagines everyone as internally disposed to form some (ideally) true beliefs about God's existence and character and to worship him.[78] Both this pathway of belief formation and its fruit differ from the theological *scientia* of the *sapientes*: *interior instinctus* trades in belief rather than knowledge, is even more error prone, and yields still vaguer conclusions.[79] More even than natural theology, its paltry fruit depends on experience, capacities, and context—and so has natural theology's defects and more besides. Given the majority's appropriate reliance on the *sapientes* in matters religious and the extent to which the deliverances of *interior instinctus* depend on what seems possible and plausible given someone's experience, capacities, and collateral commitments, Thomas would distinguish suppressing (*repugnet*) the instinct from honoring it but arriving at false religious beliefs.[80] Put otherwise, honoring will look materially different across individuals, epochs, and cultures: amidst a polytheistic culture and doing his best not to suppress his inclination, one arrives at polytheism; another, with greater theoretical capacities, arrives at monotheism. And we can easily imagine the latter, thanks to her capacities, putting in less effort to reach truth and in that sense being less praiseworthy (or more blameworthy) than the polytheist. Lacking the *ratio* of resistance, to follow *interior instinctus* to false religious views is a different matter than suppression and its guilt. Suppression seems less—or even not—a matter of false conclusions, but an effort to thwart the very inclination that would lead there, to kill or deny one's longing for the sacred, the holy.

It is hard to know how Thomas would hold all these variables together: If a "common" person is raised as and remains a polytheist does her polytheism count as sinful fruit of truth-suppression? What about a Muslim? The overwhelming textual evidence suggests that the truth of monotheism is something to which very few can reason. Treating the Biblically paradigmatic case of truth-suppression, Thomas refers to the *wise* alone (*RC* 1.6, esp. 113). And his brief remarks on the *interior instinctus* suggest the majority's failure to arrive at true religion is both frequent and rarely due to suppression. In Thomas's spirit and a charitable mode, I would propose that someone only count as "suppressing" in just those respects and beliefs in which she falls short of what, given her context, upbringing, and capacities, is the best she can do in terms of reasoning and reflection. If that "best" is polytheism, say, or Islam, and that is where she arrives, then she is not guilty of suppression. More capaciously still, perhaps the vast majority only count as suppressing insofar as they seek to deaden themselves to the religious impulse, neutralize any sense of or love for the sacred.

If this honors Thomas's insistence on the difficulty of these matters, the inadequacy of most to confront them successfully, and the importance of context and capacities, we must also honor his insistence on the universality of the religious impulse. Here, it is difficult to imagine Thomas regarding those, especially *sapientes*, who believe in no goodness or reality transcending the human as not involved in suppression—even allowing for the full range of contexts and upbringings humans face and the full gamut of capacities. Atheism, at least in its most familiar forms, marks the terrain where I imagine Thomas believes some suppression is necessarily implicated. Of course, atheism was so foreign to him that our curiosity grossly outstrips anything he says.[81] Couple that with the central role of anthropological observation in his theorizing, especially his meditations on the *interior instinctus*, and great caution is required. He certainly thinks human existence and experience are such that everyone is oriented to a mystery and goodness transcending not only herself but the natural world. This religious impulse should lead to awe, honor, worship, and, especially, gratitude before that reality. He thinks the denial of this goodness—of this impulse to hope and rage that is felt most intensely at life's edges, to long that beauty, goodness, and truth are not accidents of culture but have a source uniting them, worthy of devotion and love, who will account for and defeat evil—involves a choice to suppress or ignore the heart's desires, a failure to receive the goodness of existence as *given* and to confess its horrors as too often our own doing.

A less familiar atheism, that of "religious naturalists," those atheists who affirm a value that is transcendent in the sense of being sacred and inviolable, who take as their final end "fellowship in virtue with all that is," and regard piety and gratitude to all the sources of existence as essential virtues, poses a more complicated case. While Thomas himself almost certainly regards all atheism as implicated in suppression, if he inhabited our world, observing and interacting with such individuals and examining their experiential and evidentiary data, it is unclear to me that he would regard religious naturalists as different in kind from other, more traditional religious believers who also hold false beliefs. Why should Thomas regard the religious beliefs of polytheists, say, as different in kind from those of religious naturalists?[82] In both cases, there is a more-or-less good faith effort to honor the religious inclination and read creation's book to see what it says about the sources of existence. The conclusions reached in each case are false, Thomas would insist. But if suppression is implicated in either, it is implicated in both. Instead, the defect seems one not of trying to ignore or suppress the evidence or deliberately defying the internal inclination toward worship and gratitude, but of drawing false conclusions. If this is so, it would follow that the religious naturalist needs to be evaluated, like the polytheist, individually, with attention to her capacities and context.

Religious naturalist and religious believer alike affirm a common religious inclination and impulse—regarding some things as intrinsically and profoundly valuable, sacred, and worthy of a devotion approaching worship. This commonality rather than their different verdicts about the sources of these gifts would be seen as salient. Whether a religious naturalist were guilty of suppression would be a matter of examining her particular conduct and capacities. The more familiar atheist, though, who casts aspersion on or denies the inclination that her religious naturalist cousin seeks to give its due, would almost certainly remain guilty of truth suppression for Thomas.

Regarding the sinless *infidelitas* of those who have not heard, Thomas notes that "if any among them did what was in himself to do, the Lord would make provision for him according to his compassion by sending them a preacher of the faith, just as he sent Peter to Cornelius and Paul to the Macedonians" (*RC* 10.3.849). The remark implies that when the Gospel is unheard, whether there is *infidelitas* depends on one's conduct in relation to one's capacities and context.[83] Here, Thomas speaks of God sending preachers. But the more basic point has to do with God's mercy more generally in relation to human pursuit of divine truth—his charity in looking charitably upon our efforts at charity.[84] And we can imagine such mercy taking forms other than the sending of preachers: among them the suspension of condemnation for certain varieties of *infidelitas* or the classification of certain convictions as not constituting it.

Perhaps, then, the person who does what she can to find the truth about God—and nevertheless ends up with false beliefs, even the belief that there is no God—but holds that there is some goodness and value worthy of religious devotion is not guilty of suppression.[85] Suppression, on this reading, is more a matter of conduct than conclusion, more a matter of the way one relates to one's religious inclination than whether one successfully traces it to its true source.[86] It may thus be possible to be faithful to Thomas's spirit—perhaps even the Biblical witness that informs it—while regarding religious naturalists innocent of suppression.

BUT CAN THEY DO *GOOD* ACTS?

Provided they are not guilty of suppression, those who have not heard the Gospel are not guilty of sin in virtue of their *infidelitas*. To be clear, whether someone is guilty of suppression is not something I have tried to answer fully here. Surely, though, the answer has much to do with a person's conduct in relation to the religious inclination. And this gives us a rubric for thinking about whether and how some variety of pre-Gospel *infidelitas* might or might not be sinful. It also provides us a way forward concerning the goodness of acts referred to false religious beliefs that do not bear the *ratio* of sin, of resistance—whether Thomas can consider it good, not just *not sinful*, when our Gospel-ignorant Muslim gives alms for Muhammad's sake or our unevangelized Hindu fasts to honor a god.

On my reading, he can in virtue of the agent's conduct in pursuing religious truth. Granted their falsity, these beliefs, let us say, represent the agent's good faith effort to know and love God, the result of attempting to follow the path that, when all goes well, terminates in religious truth. This at least gives us some way to account for how these ends can count as good. For Thomas, the acts such ends generate must count as either good or evil. Given his insistence that the Gospel-ignorant person does not sin in her *infidelitas*, viewed charitably and thanks to their etiology, these false religious ends have more the *ratio* of good than evil—or at least ought to be so regarded. Generically good action that is referred to the sort of *infidelitas* that itself lacks sin's *ratio* must be good, therefore the end of *infidelitas* in such cases must itself be good. This account, which points us to the agent's effort and, in so doing, draws on Thomas's comments regarding God's mercy, gives us some reasonable explanation for how this *infidelitas*, this false belief, could count as a good end. It is thanks to the agent's efforts, yes, but, far more deeply, it is thanks to the mercy of God. Continuing his remarks about God's mercy to those who do what they can: "But, nevertheless, *that* they do whatever is in them to do, namely, turning themselves to God, is itself from God who moves their hearts to the good: 'Turn us, O Lord, to you, and we will be turned!'(Lam. 5:21)" (*RC* 10.3.849).

Infidelitas, Distinctions, and Charity

In sum, for those who have heard the Gospel, the following obtains. If *strong infidelitas* has strong salience, the action is evil, no matter what other ends may have strong salience: if Bob clothes the naked to convert them to atheism or out of hate for Christianity, then even if love for the neighbor is also strongly salient and, counterfactually, would suffice to generate the action absent the involvement of his strong *infidelitas*, the act is evil. If *weak infidelitas* has strong salience, then the action is evil if the weak *infidelitas alone* has strong salience, if no other of the agent's good ends would suffice to generate the action in its absence. If one or some other good end(s) *would* suffice, the action would count as good. Thus, if a Mormon prays with the only final end of honoring Joseph Smith, the act is evil. If the prayer is also undertaken to honor God and that end would have sufficed to generate the action in just these circumstances, the act is good. For those ignorant of the Gospel, specifically good action referred to *infidelitas* that lacks the *ratio* of resistance, which is not implicated in suppression, is good—even if referred to that end alone. So, the unevangelized, non-suppressing Buddhist who gives alms for Buddhist religious reasons does good. Where the *infidelitas* in question is somehow tied to suppression, I believe we can draw another strong/weak *infidelitas* distinction. This strong *infidelitas* has the same hostile, aggressive spirit and activist bent as the other sort of strong *infidelitas*, but is directed not against Christianity but the preambles of faith and/or the *interior instinctus*. Like the evangelized's, this weak *infidelitas* lacks strong *infidelitas*'s directly combative character, but encompasses the possibility of a weaker, less direct suppression that may be (and may render the false beliefs it generates) blameworthy, sharing with the other weak *infidelitas* something of resistance.[87] Unlike that *infidelitas*, which has no connection to suppression, it is not absolutely sinless. With that distinction in place, the rubric for assessing action is the same as that for those who have heard the Gospel.

Thomas does not consider these complex cases, explain when and how exactly *infidelitas* counts as an act's end, or how we ought to understand cases where multiple ends are pursued. I have tried to honor his charitable impulses and his insistence that sinful *infidelitas* renders action referred to it sinful. My suggestions regarding how we ought to understand the conjunction of weak *infidelitas* and another good end go beyond what he says, but so does nearly anything on the subject. Some may contend that if any *infidelitas* has strong salience for some act then that act is evil, but that seems contrary to Thomas, in spirit and letter alike, failing to honor his charitable impulses or the texts that display them. Additionally, given the epistemological difficulties that obtain in relation to acts and final ends, I believe the uncharitable interpretation meets an insuperable difficulty—either it will lack a consistent way to interpret or assess actions in light of its commitments, eventually proffering interpretations that are at odds with or unsupported by its assumptions, or it will, of necessity, veer toward an interpretation on which most of the unbeliever's actions do implicate *infidelitas* and are evil. Neither option is attractive.

My resolution to the epistemological challenge carries forward the charitable impulse with a doubly charitable "innocent until proven guilty" principle. First, only ascribe strong salience to *infidelitas* if no other of the agent's good final end-type beliefs can explain the action. Second, if *infidelitas* is definitely strongly salient, assume it to be *weak infidelitas* unless one has good reason to regard it as strong. I belief this suggestion best unites Thomas's insistence on the possibility and reality of pagan virtue, the fact that every human act is ordered to some final end, and the fact that religious beliefs are involved in almost everyone's relatively stable FEC. This interpretation does justice to the textual evidence in Thomas's treatments of the question of whether the nonbeliever can do good and how. And, to bring things full circle, it holds together II.II 23.7's claims that it is possible for a nonbeliever to refer her act to *infidelitas* as end and so sin, and possible for her instead to refer it to a good in accord with her nature, making it truly but imperfectly good. What is more, it provides a concrete account of just how an outsider, one without charity and somehow entangled in *infidelitas*, can attain virtue that is true because referred to a truly good end. Virtue that conduces to a final end that is truly good can, if informed by charity, be remotely referred to beatitude. In being possessed of such virtue, an outsider is caught up in the goodness of God, becoming a person ready to receive divine grace.

III ETHICS AS A WORK OF CHARITY

9 SIN AND THE LIMITS OF VIRTUE

THIS AND THE CONCLUDING CHAPTER consider the implications of sin and grace, respectively, for Thomas's vision of pagan virtue. Together, they show the depth of his commitment to an Augustinian view of the pervasiveness of sin and the primacy of grace in his conception and welcome of pagan virtue. For many, an Augustinian desire to register sin's destructive grip leads to a portrait of Thomas as hostile to outsider virtue. While such readers are right to insist that Thomas thinks sin matters for pagan virtue, they are mistaken in their notion of how it does. For Thomas, postlapsarian humans cannot avoid the sin of failing to fulfill the natural obligation to love God above all (I.II 109.3).[1] In healing this, charity enables acquired virtue to conduce most perfectly to the natural end, attaining a perfection otherwise unreachable after the fall and distinct from that had through charity's referring such virtue remotely to beatitude. Thus, with respect to the natural end, there is a difference in the acquired virtue attainable with charity and without, a blemish in even the most perfect pagan virtue. Notably, Thomas himself hardly mentions this difference, devoting his energy instead to affirming pagan virtue and distinguishing pagan and Christian acquired virtue alike from their disconnected, inherently imperfect antecedents. Nonetheless, treating sin's place in Thomas's account of pagan virtue, this chapter details that distinction. Our brevity mirrors his.

What the Difference Is Not

Consider first what the difference between pagan and Christian acquired virtue is *not*. As we've seen, absent evidence and despite Thomas's claims, some have thought it a matter of connection: pagan virtue is disconnected; the acquired virtue of Christians is not. While correct that acquired virtues are not most perfectly possessed or most perfectly ordered to the natural end without charity due to fallen humanity's inability to love God above all, this perspective wrongly imagines that this entails disunity.[2]

But possession of authentic virtues and their connection rise and fall together. And Thomas places pagan virtue firmly on that line's true, "connected" side. Of course, virtues grow in unity as they become still more perfect. But whatever pagan virtue's deficiency relative to what charity's healing enables, for Thomas, pagan virtue is true "connected" virtue. Indeed, this difference so little concerns Thomas that he never even spells it out, exclusively treating pagan and Christian acquired virtue together. In the idiom of I.II 65.1's and most of the virtue treatise, *both* are perfect.

Another misguided effort to name the difference between pagan and Christian acquired virtue holds that for Thomas the end to which virtuous pagans are ordered can only be directed away from or against God. Pagans either cannot be ordered to a true but imperfect final natural end like the political good in which God is imperfectly loved, or, even if they can, this end is evil, false, and directed away from God. So, "anyone who lacks . . . charity is ordered *away from the last natural end*" (*AA*, 300). "There can be no ordering to the natural end without an ordering to the supernatural end" (292). Instead, nonbelievers who seem to be ordered to the imperfect natural end are necessarily and irreducibly ordered to *self* as final (295–96, 298).[3]

This approach, in which the incapacity to love God above all, which we will see follows from original sin, is equated with the inevitability of taking self as final end or of idolatry more generally, runs afoul of Thomas's affirmation of pagan virtue and capacity to do good, and his insistence that fallen humans can order themselves to the natural end, even if that end is deficient in respect of perfect natural love for God. Indeed, this perspective really amounts to the denial of pagan virtue altogether—and even the unbeliever's capacity to do other than sin. On top of the evidence we have already seen, we find still further confirmation that such a view is mistaken in Thomas's treatment of *timor servilis*, servile fear (II.II 19.4–6).

Servile fear is distinguished from other varieties of fear by its unique object—God's punishment by which he would lead the wayward back (II.II 19.1, 4, 5, and 2 and ad 4). For us, the key point comes in Thomas's denial that charity drives out servile fear (II.II 19.6). Servile fear, he says, is rooted in love of self. What is feared is something contrary to one's good, one's love. Servile fear and self-love are twin concepts: loving one's good and fearing its loss are two sides of a common coin. Asking about charity's relation to servile fear amounts to asking about its relation to self-love. For Thomas, there are three ways in which self-love/servile fear can relate to charity. Self-love can be opposed to (*contrariatur*) charity—so, one might take oneself and one's private good as end. And it might be ordered to or enclosed in (*includitur*) charity so that one love oneself for God's sake—which is only possible for those possessed of charity, not our pagans. But it is the third possibility that concerns us.[4]

Someone can love himself, Thomas explains, in a way that is "distinct from," not informed by, "charity but not contrary to it" (II.II 19.6). On this third way, "someone loves (*diligit*) himself according to the *ratio* of his own good, but not so that this good of himself constitute his [final] end." "In like manner," Thomas continues, "some neighbor can be loved with a love other than charity (which is rooted in God), provided that the neighbor is loved under the formality (*ratio*) of kinship or some other human condition that is nevertheless referable to charity." Thomas here holds out the possibility of a non-idolatrous self-love and love of neighbor *without charity*. What is more, he holds out the possibility of such love as non-idolatrous on the basis of these loves being referred to some final end *other* than charity, a final end itself *both* non-idolatrous and, more, positively *in se* referable to charity's end.[5]

Thomas envisions, without charity, the possibility of neighbor-love and self-love not contrary to charity but referable to God. And this on the basis of self and neighbor being loved as ordered to a non-idolatrous final end—a "human condition . . . referable to charity" (*conditionis humanae, quae tamen referibilis sit ad caritatem*). Certain penultimate final ends, recall, are intrinsically referable to charity and, under certain circumstances, non-idolatrous when taken as final. When one loves self and neighbor on account of such goods, one loves them in a way referable to God. Here, in speaking of self-love Thomas seems to refer explicitly to the case of a person loving herself for her own sake—yet without taking her own good as her final end.

That is significant in itself against the suggestion that self-love apart from charity is bound to be idolatrous or ordered away from God: loving oneself, *even for one's own good*, need not entangle one in the idolatry of taking self as final end. But Thomas's subsequent comments are even more significant. If one can love neighbor well apart from charity, in view, say, of a common political good that is referable to charity, then one can love oneself in that way and for that end too. And when one does, one acts and loves not contrary to charity but in a way referable to beatitude, ready—without repentance for this love *qua* love—to be taken up into Christian life. Indeed, Thomas echoes the point in the charity treatise. Arguing that humans are bound by charity to love God more than self, he notes that "even through the political virtues . . . sometimes, citizens sustain loss of property and injury to their persons for the sake of the common good" (II.II 26.3).[6] He mentions as a noncontroversial aside the possibility of a person sacrificing his possessions and even his very self for the sake of the political good. It is the virtues, he says, that enable this. This is something that "is observable," "clear" (*apparet*). The remark underlines the prior chapter's point that, failing to take beatitude as final, a pagan need not plunge into idolatry, much less take herself as final end. Instead, she can be ordered by acquired virtue to the political end, and in being so ordered love herself rightly if imperfectly. When one without charity takes certain fitting (*debitum*) but penultimate goods as final and loves finite things, including self, as ordered to those ends, one does not thereby count as idolatrous. Instead, one loves and lives in a way that poses no obstacle to charity's end. One can love neighbor and self nonidolatrously. One can move, claims Thomas, toward acquiring true—if finally imperfect—virtue.

The Difference *in abstracto*: I.II 63.2 ad 2

Recall that with respect to beatitude, the difference between the virtues of those possessed of charity and those who are not is relatively clear. First, only infused virtue is simply perfect virtue, for it alone orders directly to beatitude. Before or after the fall, it is unattainable without charity. This is not a difference sin makes, but a function of what even prelapsarian humanity can and cannot attain of its own strength. Second, for those possessed of infused and acquired virtue, charity can make a difference in acquired virtue by ordering it mediately to beatitude. Apart from matters to do with original sin and its effects, there is a perfection belonging to acquired virtue only when conjoined with charity.[7] These two differences—between infused and acquired virtue in respect to their ends and between acquired virtue possessed with charity and had without it—mark differences in the virtues attainable with and without charity. But neither of these has to do with acquired virtue's ability to conduce perfectly to the natural end.

The difference that concerns us results from sin and does involve the political end. Charity *elevates* nature so that by grace beatitude is attainable and, even in this life, that end is participated in a fragmentary, proleptic way. And charity *heals* human nature, so that original sin's damage is or begins to be undone and human nature can, by nature, achieve all it could prior to the fall. Charity thus matters for acquired virtue on two levels: by in-forming it so that it is re-motely referred to beatitude—used in its pursuit (*DV* 10 ad 4); and by healing humans so that acquired virtue can (in principle) conduce perfectly to the in-herently imperfect end proportionate to human nature.[8] The difference original sin makes for acquired virtue is precisely at this latter level: without charity, ac-quired virtue cannot conduce perfectly to the imperfect, political end (I.II 63.4).

While charity never heals without elevating or elevates without healing, we can observe and speak of these effects individually. Regarding some virtue's act—say, acquired religion's display of piety where God is loved perfectly above all else—we can recognize it as an outworking of charity's restoration, for it enables perfect action directed to God *qua* natural end. It is an act or virtue that, pre-Fall, could have been done or had by nature without charity. And we can imagine another or the same act or acquired virtue, insofar as it is referred *mediately* to beatitude. And we can characterize it as, in that respect, transcend-ing nature, of charity. For Thomas, even in relation to the natural end, acquired virtue possessed with charity differs from acquired virtue possessed without it, due to the postlapsarian incapacity of humans without charity to fulfill the natural obligation to love God above all. It is here, as Thomas has it, that the difference between pagan virtue and the acquired virtue of the Christian lies.

Notably, the only place where Thomas explicitly discusses sin's conse-quences on acquired virtue is in I.II 63.2—precisely as he *defends* the claim that acquired virtues can be attained by fallen humans without grace. There, Thomas considers objections concerning the consequences of original and ongoing sin for human moral capacities without charity, especially passages like Romans 14:23, which seem to declare it impossible to do good—much less attain vir-tue—without grace. Just where Thomas explicitly raises the issue of sin's conse-quences, he affirms that while infused virtue cannot be had apart from charity, acquired virtues can. The passage clarifies that whatever the imperfection or limits sin imposes, these neither render acquired virtue unattainable nor pre-vent pagan virtue from being true acquired virtue, the very sort attainable by healed humanity. Indeed, Thomas himself never distinguishes—or even hints at a distinction—between pagan and Christian acquired virtue *qua* acquired virtue.[9] Any deficiency does not divide authentic human virtue from disposi-tion or something less but, insofar as it registers at all, constitutes a shortcom-ing within true human virtue. All this is especially clear here: Thomas simply notes that certain sins are unavoidable without grace, declares acquired virtue entirely compatible with this, and registers no difference whatsoever between this virtue and that attainable by healed human nature. We need not rehearse our analysis of I.II 63.2, but I.II 63.2 ad 2, which speaks most directly to our focus, is worth recalling.

Citing a Scriptural passage to the effect that sin cannot be avoided without grace, the objection Thomas faces claims virtue is unattainable without grace (I.II 63.2 ob 2). Responding, Thomas notes it is true that mortal sin is incompatible with infused virtue but stresses that "actual sin, *even mortal sin*" is not incompatible with acquired virtue (I.II 63.2 ad 2). Mortal and other sin, he says, is compatible with acquired virtue for an act is not habit's contrary. It would require an opposing habit of sin to destroy an acquired virtue. "This distinction," Brian Shanley notes, "makes it possible to reconcile Aquinas's" and, we might add, *Scripture's*, "claims about the inevitability of mortal sin with the thesis of the reality of acquired moral virtue" (*APV*, 557). "Therefore," Thomas explains, "although without grace man is not able so to avoid mortal sin that he *never* sin mortally, nevertheless, he is not prevented from being able to acquire a habit of virtue—by which he refrains from evil deeds *even in most cases, and particularly from those things which are most contrary to reason*" (I.II 63.2 ad 2).[10] Thomas has in view fallen humanity's nature without grace's healing: it is for such fallen human nature that mortal sin cannot be avoided without grace.[11] Thomas is not speaking of someone who has lost charity through mortal sin, for such loss does not undo baptism's healing. He refers, rather, to one who has not known redeeming grace at all. Such a one, he says, can attain acquired virtue, notwithstanding her sinful nature and even though certain mortal sins contrary to the theological virtues are inevitable for her.

Rightly noting that in I.II 88.2, Thomas "distinguishes sins that are against the love of God (e.g., blasphemy and false oaths) from sins that are against love of neighbor (e.g., homicide and adultery)," Shanley claims that, "without grace and the theological virtues it is impossible to avoid the first kind of mortal sins. But it is possible . . . generally to avoid the second category of sins because these acts are opposed to reason. Presumably a person would not need grace either to recognize the wrongness of actions of this kind or to avoid them for the most part" (*APV* 558). But Thomas never says this, and, moreover, it seems false that original sin would entail blasphemy or false oaths, for instance—which, for Thomas, are as contrary to reason as sins against neighbor. A standard by which blasphemy but not theft counts as "against reason" is alien to Thomas. For an account of the sin he does think inevitable without charity we must turn to I.II 109—to which Thomas himself directs us in concluding 63.2 ad 2.

The Difference *in concreto*: I.II 109.3

As noted, pagan virtue's defect concerns the inability of fallen humans to love God above all things. This love, natural and within prelapsarian human power, must not be confused with the love of God that constitutes charity, for which even unfallen humanity required grace (I.II 109.3 ad 1). "In the state of integral [i.e. unfallen] nature," Thomas explains, "no gift of grace added to nature was needed for naturally loving God above everything . . . but in the state of corrupt nature, even for this, man needs the help of healing grace" (I.II 109.3). Failure to love God in this way is failure to attain perfectly the end of humans considered as political animals—for that end involves ordering all things to God in his capacity as source and goal of all goodness and existence (I.II 109.7 ad 3). Loving God "above all things" requires not just loving God more than all else, but relating to all things as coming from God and so as having their goodness in virtue of their gifted-ness, their constitution as participations in him. In that way, in loving whatever one loves, one loves God. Without grace, this is not entirely possible for fallen humanity. While someone could arrive at this vision of the cosmos without grace, Thomas might allow, she could not so enact this vision so as always to love and live in this way.

For Thomas, "even if fallen man rationally recognizes the existence of God as source and end of all goodness and being, he cannot . . . effectively make God the ultimate end of his life . . . that knowledge cannot lead to the consistent volition of God as ultimate good apart from grace" (*APV*, 570, 571).[12] That God is and be this end is necessary for humans fully to achieve natural happiness. To the extent that God is *not*—or not perfectly—this end, the lives and virtues that conduce to the otherwise fitting and right political end are imperfect in a way over and above (or within and beneath) the inherent imperfection of strictly all acquired virtue and this-worldly happiness.

In 109.3, Thomas notes that thanks to will's corruption by original sin, instead of loving God above all, humans "follow a private good (*bonum privatum*) unless healed by the grace of God" (I.II 109.3).[13] This could seem to suggest that without charity, humans can only seek a narrow, self-interested good. Were Thomas saying this, it would contradict all we have seen him say about pagan virtue, and even the capacity of unbelievers to do good. Recall, then, that God is here being loved *qua* natural end and listen to how Thomas characterizes God *qua* natural end just a few lines earlier as he explains that everything naturally loves God above all: "Every single thing, by natural desire or love, loves its own proper good *because of the common good* (*bonum commune*) *of the entire universe, which is God* (*quod est Deus*)" (I.II 109.3). Where "common good" sometimes refers to the whole complex of the political good, here it refers to God alone. In declaring humans directed only to a "private good" (*bonum privatum*), Thomas is not suggesting that humans can only pursue themselves or things equally problematic as final ends. Rather, any end but God—including the political end wherein he is loved imperfectly—is here *bonum privatum*.[14] Any good or end—no matter how inclusive, comprehensive, public, or genuine— is private if it excludes God or, including him, does not perfectly make him chief.[15] Thus, one who takes the good of the earthly city and his neighbors as final end, for instance, counts as pursuing a private good here. So too one who accords God a place—even the highest place in his final end conception—but fails effectively and rightly always to relate all things to him.

While I.II 109.3 most precisely specifies the limits of fallen human nature and so the limits of pagan virtue, surrounding articles complete the portrait. In 109.2, Thomas asks whether man can do any good without grace. It is here that he distinguishes between integral, or unfallen, and fallen human nature. Fallen human nature, he says, cannot do the "whole good" (*totum bonum*) proportionate to it (I.II 109.2).[16] And I.II 109.3, recall, spells out in just what respect fallen human nature is deficient in relation to the political good. I.II 109.2 further notes that fallen nature is "not totally corrupted so that it be deprived of the whole good of nature." "It is," he says, "through the power of its nature, able to do some particular good—such as building homes, planting vineyards, and such like things" (I.II 109.2). This can sound rather minimal—as though, all said, fallen human nature cannot do very much at all. However, just above Thomas has used the distinction between achievement of acquired and infused virtue to sketch the limits of integral human nature: the limits of integral human nature are coincident, he says, with the limits of acquired virtue. He needs, however, still to distinguish integral from *fallen* human nature. But the category of acquired virtue has been "used up," as it were: having already deployed it to mark integral nature's limits, it would be rather complicated to again use that category in some modified, qualified form to describe the limits of fallen in distinction from integral nature. Doing so would risk making the article overly confusing and its central concern—the integral/fallen nature distinction—unnecessarily blurry. Besides, it is elsewhere and earlier in the *Summa*'s curriculum that Thomas treats the question of pagan virtue, and there he devotes the space necessary to elucidating just what sort of virtue can be achieved without charity.

More importantly, the context shows that it is actually incorrect to understand this portrait as minimalist or negative. The list—"building homes, planting vineyards, and such like things"—is actually duplicated and expanded later, in I.II 109.5, where Thomas considers whether man can merit eternal life without grace.[17] That article's basic contrast is between human nature as elevated or not elevated by grace.[18] Having explained that beatitude is beyond unaided humanity's power, he explains that "without grace man . . . is able to do works conducing to a certain *connatural human good*, such as 'to work in the field, to drink, to eat, to have friends, and other similar things'" (I.II 109.5).[19] This is the same list, slightly expanded, from the same source, as appeared in 109.2. But here, it is used *precisely to gloss man's connatural good*. The list, in other words, is meant to fill out that in which the connatural human good consists. Far from being minimalist, for Thomas, it refers synecdochically to the rich complex of human relationships and activities that constitute natural human life. These things—friendship, work, the table—are the sorts of things humans can do without grace—and when possessed of virtue, the sorts of things they can do with excellence. So, when Thomas earlier cites this list to explain what fallen nature can attain, it is incorrect to read it in a negative, minimalist way, for only paragraphs later, it glosses the connatural human good, what human nature *as such* can achieve apart from grace.

The natural duty to love of God above all things is the single natural obligation Thomas declares impossible for fallen human nature to fulfill without healing grace, the one mortal sin that is inevitable for postlapsarian humanity (I.II 109.3). This failing impinges most sharply, of course, on the virtue of religion, that virtue concerned, most simply, with giving God right worship *qua* natural end (II.II 81.1). While the question (81) and treatise on religion (81–100) are very complex, resisting facile summary, our focus on pagan virtue allows for brevity. For, even supposing Thomas held the virtue of religion unattainable without charity's healing due to the pagan's incapacity to fulfill the natural duty to love God above all, his numerous, explicit affirmations of pagan virtue remain: the pagan, necessarily lacking the virtue of religion (on that interpretation), still counts for Thomas as possessed of virtue. That is, the damage wrought by religion's absence as a virtue is not such to render pagans incapable of authentic, "connected" virtue.

Yet we need not hold that Thomas does deny that the virtue of religion can be had without charity. Indeed, the most comprehensive examination of Thomas on the virtue of religion that I know of contends that Thomas *does* allow for a true but imperfect virtue of religion apart from charity's work and notwithstanding the inability of fallen humanity to love God naturally above all.[20] While rightly noting that "the limit and distortion of worship" effected by original sin in relation to natural love of God limits moral flourishing, Jared Staudt argues that "an imperfect virtue of religion could precede faith [and charity]."[21] Enabling its possessor to "recognize . . . the One, Creator God and the necessity to worship Him," it could even prepare the way for faith by "remov[ing] obstacles such [as] idolatry or irreligion."[22] If Staudt is right—and there is good reason to think he is—even at the point where we would expect its damage to be most debilitating, the incapacity to love God above all does not foreclose the possibility of a virtue of religion. Pagan virtue's blemishes need not involve the absence of the virtue of religion but merely its imperfection.[23]

How one settles this matter, of course, is inextricably related to the question of how exactly to understand Thomas's claims in I.II 109 concerning the incapacity to love God above all: Does Thomas mean to deny that pagans can *ever*, even momentarily, love God above all or merely that they cannot do so with *perfect* virtue's stability?[24] We cannot settle these issues here. Nor need we, for we have seen in great detail both Thomas's robust affirmation of pagan virtue and its deep rootedness in his thought. And this reality is something any attempt to synthesize the interrelations among religion, original sin, and pagan virtue will need to face.[25]

Lament and Hope

While it should come as no surprise that "public reason" Thomists neglect how Augustinian Thomas is in his view of sin, it could seem odd to fault hyper-Augustinians on this point: How could Thomas take sin more seriously than to reject pagan virtue as so much splendid vice?[26] Yet, following Augustine, for Thomas sin is most pernicious and relevant not as it exists "out there," but "in here," not in another's but in one's own heart. The hyper-Augustinian rejection of pagan virtue tends precisely to externalize sin and its dangers—so that it is almost exclusively outsiders whom Thomas regards as subject to *superbia* and *libido dominandi*. More, hyper-Augustinians often depict the Christian as at perfect peace, struggling neither for virtue nor against sin, while declaring Aristotelian virtue violent and martial.[27] For Thomas, however, in this life the redeemed "remain corrupted and encumbered (*infectio*) in the flesh which is enslaved to 'the law of sin' (Rom. 7:25). A certain darkness of intellect lingers too . . . [so that] we are unable to fully know what would be best for us" (I.II 109.9).[28] The flesh even of those with charity rebels against the spirit, and the Christian suffers "attacks of fleshly impulses" to such an extent that she must ever beseech God lest she not persevere in grace (I.II 109.10). For all, says Thomas summarizing Augustine, are subject in "this present life to many evils which cannot be avoided, to ignorance in the intellect, to inordinate desire in the appetite, and to much suffering in the body" (I.II 5.3).[29]

In I.II 109.8, Thomas paints what is, perhaps, his bleakest portrait of fallen human nature without charity. Only now are we really in a position to hear these words for the lament, the groaning for grace, the cry "Come, Lord Jesus!" that they are.[30] And we are so positioned precisely because we have seen as well Thomas's celebration and welcome of pagan virtue along with his considered, precise articulation of its limits, marked by the incapacity to love God above all. While that sin and its inevitability do not preclude pagan virtue, render it untrue, disconnected, or any such thing, they suggest that its achievement—indeed, just as much, the achievement of *any* acquired virtue—will be, as it so obviously is, too rare. This sin means that pagan virtue—true and worthy of love and praise though it is—wears its beauty, like all human virtue, with a scar.

Nothing Thomas says here is inconsistent with what we have seen so far, but in these words we hear, amidst his welcome of pagan virtue and affirmation of the good of nature, how fully committed he is to the Augustinian and, indeed, Scriptural portrait of humans as creatures in desperate need of healing, grace, and rebirth. This strain comes through all the more strongly, for really, the article is not primarily concerned with the brokenness and frailty of fallen human nature, but much more with the frailty even of unfallen humanity—moreover, even of *redeemed* humanity. To hear the article rightly, then, is to hear it as centered, foremost, on the profound need of grace—a need that saturates all human existence, from beginning to end. Grace, gift, is what—at every step—makes that existence possible.

Thus, Thomas considers whether without grace humans can avoid sin—a question that, at its deepest level, asks about disintegration, alienation, the threat of human self-undoing of God's good creation. It asks just where and who humans are and can be without grace. Its answer, in the first place, is nowhere and nothing. While humans could avoid sin prior to the fall, Thomas says, "nevertheless [they] could not have done this without God's help to preserve them in the good—[indeed,] had God's help been removed, even [their] very nature[s] would have fallen back into nothingness" (I.II 109.8). In one sense, the claim is not unfamiliar. Threaded throughout his work is the insistence that humans can only act and be thanks to God's gift of creation and first movement of the will. Yet, on another level, it is remarkable in its forcefulness, its rhetorical power and, more profoundly, its substance. The point here is not merely that God is will's efficient cause and the Creator, but that, as such, his sustaining, active help is always and everywhere necessary to constitute humans as creatures. Without God's help, humans, he says, are nothing. The emphasis is on the fact that nature itself, *esse* and *bonum* as participated by creatures, are ever dependent on God's sustaining love. Nature, human nature included, is only stable as God loves it into being so—it is neither itself nor anything at all without God's help. The radical, unceasing character of human dependence on God's goodness, even apart from issues to do with sin, is the note Thomas sounds at the article's inception. We are what we are by the grace of God. With this beginning, he makes altogether clear his desire to lift up and celebrate grace, God's inherently undeservable and gratuitous self-giving love—and to do so not as something belonging to the redeemed only, but, in this sense, to all humanity. In this respect, all, he insists, is by grace.

From there, he moves to consider sin's power even in the life of the redeemed. Before glory, he says, while grace gives man power to avoid mortal sin entirely, it does not give him power to avoid venial sin. It does not, for it extends to the healing of mind but not passions. The lower passions are only fully healed, only brought into absolute obedience, in heaven.[31] And even there, Thomas reminds, "even in the state of glory, when grace will be completely perfect," even then, "man will need [God's] help." Human dependency on God's self-giving, unmerited love is unceasing, stretching from creation eternally forward. Only after explicating the inevitability of sin even for the redeemed—and only in comparison to their case—does Thomas touch on the capacities of unhealed humanity. Just as in the case of the redeemed sin flows from the lack of appetite's perfect obedience to reason and will, in the case of those unhealed by grace, sin flows from the lack of due order that pertains in virtue of their reason's lack of perfect obedience to God. As lower appetites need be subject completely to reason in order to avoid all sin, much more does reason need be subject fully to God—but this does not obtain for fallen humanity. "Before human reason is repaired by justifying grace," Thomas explains,

> man is able to avoid individual mortal sins—and for a certain time. For it is not necessary that someone be continually involved in actually sinning. But that he be without mortal sin for a long time is not possible. . . . Man's reason not being

[fully] subject to God, many disorders occur in its very act. For when the heart of man is not so confirmed in God that it wills not to depart from him to pursue any good or avoid any evil [that threatens], many things happen which in order to obtain or to avoid man falls away from God by breaking his commands—and thus he sins mortally. (I.II 109.8)

The heart not entirely fixed on God above all—finding in him the fullness of all goodness, loving him above all else, ordering all things to him—will at times, even if exclusively in matters to do with failing to love him above all else, depart from him by pursuing false goods. The failure to love God above all else will, at times, manifest itself in the choice of that which is not genuinely choice-worthy and in a way that constitutes mortal sin. This is the defect of all outsider virtue—what distinguishes it from the acquired virtue of Christians and what entails that its life and happiness always fall short of the perfect natural good.

Awaiting Redemption

How, then, do we reconcile such a portrait of sin's effects with virtue's attain-ability—for anyone? The question asks for a longer answer than can here be given. Still, we can say an initial word. While Thomas would, like Aristotle, stress the rarity of acquired virtue, more profoundly, I think he seeks to honor what he regards as both Scriptural and anthropological evidence: in Word and world there are both wicked and virtuous who know not Christ. For theologi-cal reasons—among them the goodness of creation, the destructive power of sin, the faithfulness of God—Thomas affirms both the possibility of virtue without charity and the ubiquity of deep brokenness. Thomas would suggest, I think, that Scripture calls the believer to live in a God-trusting tension of dual affirmation.

And, there is, I think, another way to honor such passages—neither erasing nor prioritizing them, but letting them stand as stark, necessary reminders of the horrendous reach of sin in this time in between, spurs to recall the cost, necessity, and meaning of redemption. Thomas would not have us welcome pagan virtue by minimizing the reality of sin and necessity of grace. What more trenchant reminder could there be of sin's awful, loathsome weight than such proclamations—protruding and inexplicable, interrupting and awaiting resolu-tion, like the very disease they name? And yet, like that self-same reality, de-fanged, robbed of pretentious and pretending finality, denied the final word. Instead, overshadowed and overcome—if not yet perfectly so—by God's "Yes" in Jesus Christ, in and through whom, we find, in the midst of death, life. After all, as Thomas himself reminds, "Whatever good we do—whether shunning sin . . . or doing the good—*totum est a Deo*" (*JC* 3.3.496). It is all, pagan virtue included, from God.

If Thomas's view of sin is more Augustinian than many have thought, it is the concluding chapter's wager that he is more Augustinian still in his commitment to the superabundance of God's self-giving love, its power and promise even where we might despair of discovering it. For Thomas, all—outsider virtue included—is gift. And that gift is everywhere to be found. Thomas's words, concluding 109.8 and following on the heels of his lament against the havoc of sin, beckon us forward: Not just in Eden, he says, but "this day too, whatever a man wills, that is given. But now, that a man will the true good—this he does by the grace of God" (I.II 109.8 ad 3).

10 THE OTHER FACE OF GRACE

MOST INTERPRETERS SEE THOMAS as either welcoming pagan virtue in-sofar as he follows Aristotle and betrays his theological commitments or as denying it thanks to his rejection of Greek philosophy and fidelity to Augustine, Scripture, and Christ. Either way, Thomas—and those who would follow—must choose between essentially incompatible options. At the heart of this book has been a different claim: Thomas welcomes pagan virtue as true and authentic, not in spite but because of his Augustinian commitments. In so doing, he strives to be Augustinian by being Aristotelian and vice versa, honoring each, forsaking neither, as he constructs a genuinely transformative synthesis. This effort, moreover, is itself driven by Augustinian charity—Thomas *enacts* the very welcome of the pagan and his virtue that he commends. His ethics, in other words, as proposal about outsiders, way of doing moral theology, and, more, way of being in the world, is a work of charity.

Augustine *or* Aristotle

For all the weight made to hang on the key passages concerning pagan virtue, interpretive efforts—if not corresponding claims—have been limited, even as the rival parties remain locked in a dispute underwritten by their shared assumptions. Recall how things usually go.

In *Theology and Social Theory*, John Milbank endorses what he takes to be Augustine's rejection of pagan virtue—a rejection he ascribes to Aquinas too.[1] For Augustine, "[pagan] virtues were hopelessly contaminated by the celebration of violence" and were always only virtues of "resistance and domination" (*TST*, 289, 394). "Augustine and Aquinas are in essential agreement," he claims, "there can be no true fulfillment of natural justice and natural peace without reference to the Church and the workings of grace" (230). Pitting Aquinas with

Augustine, against Aristotle and pagan virtue (363–67), "Aquinas," he insists, "explains that there is no *vera virtus* without *caritas*" (233).[2] As for showing this to be Thomas's view, a single note cites "II.II 23.7." Elsewhere, Milbank's outlook is bleaker still: "After the Fall, humans . . . became *incapable of obeying the natural law*: Aquinas is quite clear, we cannot do any genuinely 'natural' good" (*TA*, 39, my emphasis).[3] Thomas himself, however, explicitly entertains that possibility—and rejects it repeatedly: precisely the natural (as opposed to supernatural) good *can* be done without charity (e.g. II.II 10.4).

Referencing I.II 93.6, Milbank declares: "There are only two categories of people for Aquinas: the fallen wicked and the engraced good" (*TA*, 124). Actually, 93.6 finds Thomas explaining that "in no human does [sin] so rule that the whole good of nature is corrupted." "For that reason," he continues, "an inclination to doing those things which are in accord with the eternal law remains" (I.II 93.6 ad 2). So long as this capacity is neither obliterated nor sin so heaped up to prove an insurmountable obstacle, it is possible to obey natural law, to do good.[4] Milbank, however, claims Thomas as ally in his "assault" on Aristotelian naturalism and denial of the pagan's ability to do good (*TA*, 21).[5]

Bonnie Kent's "Aristotelian" Aquinas, in contrast, can seem to neglect what Thomas has to say about sin and its effects or to portray him as regarding the supernatural good as altogether irrelevant to political life. While opposing hyper-Augustinians, she shares their assumption that Thomas, especially when it comes to pagan virtue, must decide: Aristotle or Augustine, philosophy or theology.[6] His affirmation of pagan virtue, she stresses, forsakes Augustine; his elevation of beatitude abandons Aristotle. Following one then the other, he "reflects his respect for [both]."[7] Kent says nothing about sin's effects on acquired virtue and appears to hold that even among those without charity they conduce perfectly to the natural end.[8] Their only defect concerns beatitude.[9] Charity heals no deficiencies but merely adds (or not) to this life's happiness. She does not register that for Thomas this life's happiness is, even on its own terms, in vital ways unhappy. Is it any surprise when Augustinians respond to her charge that their Thomas is only "superficially Aristotelian" by declaring her Aquinas Pelagian, even non-Christian?[10]

Alasdair MacIntyre offers something distinctive, Aquinas pursuing a transformative synthesis.[11] Yet, when it comes to pagan virtue, the vision fades: Thomas is Augustinian *instead* of Aristotelian. Aristotle is not only shown deficient on non-Aristotelian grounds, but Thomas makes no effort even to demonstrate his proposal's Aristotelian character.[12] "Just as and because justice is continually the victim of the vice and sin of pride," MacIntyre insists, "so justice cannot flourish, *cannot indeed . . . even exist as a natural virtue, unless and insofar as it is informed by the supernatural virtue of caritas*" (*WJ*, 205, my emphasis). Without charity, "natural" or acquired justice is not merely imperfect, but "cannot even exist." Recognizing Thomas's commitment to virtue's unity, MacIntyre regards not merely justice but *all* acquired virtue unattainable without charity (197). That Thomas takes this stand is meant to portray how "radically defective" he views aspects of Aristotle's account of human life and teleology (205). He "follow[s] Augustine *rather than Aristotle*," so forsaking Aristotle that his "virtue" is no virtue at all (204).[13] "The Augustinian understanding of fallen human nature is used to explain the limitation of Aristotle's arguments" (205). Rather than trying to show how Augustine's insight is at least compatible with Aristotle's thought, that it *not* be is just the point.[14] In support of his claims, MacIntyre refers, without elaboration, to II.II "23–44" (205).[15]

The dominant interpretive assumption about Thomas on our topic, this either/or between Aristotle and Augustine, recognition and fidelity, is mirrored by the choice many Christians feel they face in confronting pagan virtue. It's the choice posed by figures like the ones above as they move from interpreting Thomas to giving him a contemporary voice.

The hyper-Augustinians would have Christians regard most if not all their non-Christian neighbors not only as without virtue, but incapable of attaining it. They offer the church a way to speak in its own voice but to pagans and their virtues leave it saying only "no." Particularity's price is distance, suspicion, and denial. On the other hand, the "Aristotelians" welcome outsiders and their moral excellences but bequeath Christians a deracinated vision and secularized vocabulary where final ends and realities of grace and sin hardly or don't even figure. Among the "Aristotelians," there's a strange convergence between new natural lawyers and certain liberal theologians. Both imagine the way through difference is by its denial, either insisting on the universality and transparency of self-evident basic goods or beginning and ending with the sensibilities of politically correct "spirituality" or interest group Christianity. Each cloaks a different set of values in the shroud of what everyone knows. What they hold in common is the assumption that religious particularity, in politics and friendship, can only foreclose and destroy.

If grace and Christian commitment are necessary for authentic flourishing here and now—if they make some real difference in the goodness of one's life— then recognizing the outsider's virtue can easily seem a betrayal, an implicit confession that, at least in this life, grace and the grace-giving God are not so important. To welcome pagan virtue, on this view, is to exalt the wisdom of man over the wisdom of God, to conform to the spirit of the age rather than the truth of Scripture. It is a tired variation on Pelagianism, a quintessentially "secular" betrayal. Conversely, to reject pagan virtue can seem the most pernicious fundamentalism, moral provincialism, and fideist denial of reason and reality. How, one can ask, does it exhibit love of truth, much less love of neighbor, to refuse to recognize—or worse, to portray as vice—the virtue so clearly evident merely because its possessor does not confess Christ? To live between these options is to subject oneself to a dissonance more than cognitive but existential and spiritual. So, many pick a story: the non-Christian neighbor's care for a dying parent or special-needs child is just another manifestation of pride and self-love, Isaiah's "filthy rags"; the difference between Christianity and other religions does not really make a difference, determinate theological convictions about matters beyond justice and politics are so many "orchidaceous extras." Caricatures though these may be, for many, the dominant alternatives boil down to something not so different from these, the ready-made solutions for navigating the challenge of difference. Christians must choose: theology or justice, character or common good, church or world. Some might complain that contemporary theologians have not done enough to expand the options.

If I am right, Thomas has something to offer—not merely in his prescription for theologizing pagan virtue but in his example. Part of seeing that is grasping how his welcome of the outsider and her virtue is an instance of his being Augustinian by being Aristotelian and vice versa, and recognizing too how not just the welcome but the mode of achieving it is fundamentally driven by his Christian convictions. Precisely his commitment to charity leads him not only to welcome pagan virtue but, more than that, to construct a way of doing so that, in its very form, itself *performs* that welcome.

Charity, Not Scholasticism: Aristotle *and* Augustine

"Those who use philosophical teachings in *sacra doctrina* by rendering them obedient to faith do not *mix* water with wine but *transform* water into wine" (*BDT* I 2.3 ad 5).[16] In so describing his synthesis, Thomas underlines both its transformative and directional dimensions. He strives to transform dichotomy and competition into a richer, synthetic unification of Aristotelianism and Augustinianism. And he seeks to make *Christian* wine—a vintage more profoundly Augustinian in its views of sin and grace than we might imagine. He seeks, in short, to be Augustinian by being Aristotelian and vice versa—and he does so for Christian reasons. We saw in chapter 2 how the *Summa*'s shape as *sacra doctrina*, an authentically Aristotelian yet inescapably Christian *scientia*, bears witness to this dynamic. Yet the very structure of each article does the same.

While not alien to Christian theology, the dialectical model of attending to and questioning received opinions on a given matter that marks the *Summa*'s articles is an Aristotelian inheritance, on display in *Nicomachean Ethics* and the *Politics*.[17] For Aristotle, the candidates for inclusion in the table of authorities are primarily Greek philosophers or Athenians. For Thomas, however, his trust in the Spirit leads him to listen with anticipation to those who know neither Scripture nor Christ. An essentially Aristotelian model of dialectical inquiry is, for Augustinian reasons, populated with non-Christian voices—chief among them Aristotle's. And that distinctively Aristotelian model is itself embraced on Augustinian grounds.

Aristotle and other non-Christians are not merely given voice, but driven by his commitment to charity and an expectation that God is drawing all things to himself, Thomas expects and works to discover the truth in their claims— that is each article's labor. Alien voices not only count as authorities worthy of answer; he presumes they will actually contribute to our wisdom. In every case where, through drawing a distinction, some truth can be found, charity demands the distinction be drawn. Thomas regards it a kind of failure if he cannot find the truth in the claims of Aristotle, Maimonides, and the like even when those claims seem contrary to Christian truth. Charity seeks the good wherever it may be found; its philosophical face is the drawing of distinctions to discover the wisdom in the voices of all those who seek the truth. Yet, this very distinction-drawing, like the dialectical model, is itself a distinctively Aristotelian form of inquiry. In Thomas's hands, however, this Aristotelian swerve only deepens the pedagogical, pastoral shape of his text.

Materially, charity's interpretive work eventually leads to the attribution of greater and greater presumptive authority to those who time and again are found wise. As Aristotle himself is, repeatedly, discovered to speak truth, his voice is accorded progressively more credence and respect. It becomes increasingly important that on any given issue his position be given its due, and it becomes increasingly problematic if his position on some subject opposes Christian claims.[18] If he is so often right, possessed of such wisdom, it seems unreasonable—and more, uncharitable—to dismiss him as simply wrong even on those matters where he appears to contradict the faith. And so, in those cases, one strives with special rigor to find the distinctions and interpretations that manifest the insight or wisdom in the very claim that initially seems, from a Christian perspective, beyond redemption. For the truly Christian perspective becomes one in which almost nothing is beyond redemption. In so pursuing charity, one ends up being simultaneously Christian and Aristotelian.

Speaking for many Augustinians of his day, Thomas's Franciscan contemporary Bonaventure, with an eye to Aristotle, warned instead that philosophy would turn the wine of Scripture into water—a perverse undoing of the Cana miracle, the very corruption of theology (*Hexaemeron* 19.4). Indeed, most theology masters in Thomas's era regarded Aristotle with suspicion if not outright hostility. To give him a central voice in *sacra doctrina* was futile at best and dangerous at worst. Moreover, at least since Lombard's *Sentences* some 100 years earlier, the overwhelming tendency had been to regard pagan virtue as false. "And even were it more than splendid vice," ran the thinking, "what had pagan virtue, Aristotle's virtue, to do with the *church*? With *theology*?" [19] Such was the climate in which Thomas welcomed Aristotle, pursued his synthesis, and affirmed pagan virtue.

Thomas did so as an act of spiritual pedagogy and fidelity to his Lord. He undertook his synthesis not for the sake of "being Christian and Aristotelian" but for the sake of being Christian—because charity demands no less. Through this process, a system takes on the flavor of its authorities, in Thomas's case, Aristotle. For Augustinian reasons, Thomas is Aristotelian, profoundly shaped by Aristotle's commitments and insights. But precisely charity's work leads to this elevation of Aristotle: Aristotle *because* of the Gospel. Thomas avoids choosing between Aristotle and Christianity and instead finds a way at each step, not just in sum, to choose and integrate both so that: an Aristotelian account of habit can, on Aristotelian grounds, admit the possibility of Augustinian infusion; an Augustinian definition of virtue can be shown properly, even ideally, Aristotelian; Christian *sacra doctrina* can satisfy Aristotle's vision of *scientia*; and pagan virtue can be welcomed in a way that honors priest and philosopher. Thomas's Aristotelianism comes not at the expense of his Augustinianism but through it. Charity cannot forsake itself. It must, rather, find a way in which its "yes" to the outsider, to Aristotle, is, as well, a "yes" to itself.

For *sacra doctrina*, recall, ethics is an expression, a facet, of concern with God; it has the place it does in the *Summa* because it has the place it does in journeying to and with Christ. The same is true of Thomas's pervasive, untiring engagement with Aristotle. If the *Summa* is unimaginable without Thomas's engagement with Aristotle, it is because, for Thomas, the Christian life in this age is itself unimaginable without the impulse to welcome and befriend the outsider, and in that way to imitate an outsider-loving Lord. Aristotle is Thomas's outsider *par excellence*. There is no question whether Thomas welcomes his virtue. He does so thanks to his commitment to Christian charity. Even if we said that Thomas only recognizes in Aristotle intellectual virtue, the path that leads to this recognition is nearly the same that leads to his welcoming the *moral* virtue of outsiders, the virtue that concerns us, and nearly the same too as the path he commends to his brothers and sisters in Christ. For just as charity demands of Thomas an openness to Aristotle's insights, a distinction between the relatively wise and foolish among outsiders, and, eventually, a recognition of the preeminence of Aristotle's wisdom even over that of many Christians, so too does it demand such openness to and recognition of the pagan and her virtue, a distinction between those outsiders who are virtuous and those who are not, and even the possibility that the moral virtue of some outsiders may well surpass that of all but a few Christians. The path of interpretive charity, in writing the *Summa* or living in the world, leads to a distinction between the relatively wise and just outside the Church and the relatively foolish and vicious there. The failure to make such distinctions is a failure to love neighbor and God. Just as charity leads one to recognize that on many matters apart from the *articuli fidei* Aristotle is wiser than nearly all Christians, so too it leads one to the recognition that the fallen heathen might well be more truly courageous in defending the vulnerable from unjust assault, more devoted to leading a temperate life in the face of temptation, more skilled at giving prudent counsel and choosing wisely about the most difficult matters, or more excellent in doing justice in love than most Christians would be. In all this the Christian finds reason to thank and praise God. If I am right, Thomas is not only Aristotelian in his Augustinianism and vice versa, but he is so thanks to his unswerving commitment to charity—his expectation that the ravages of sin cannot in this life completely destroy the goodness of God's gift in creation and his conviction that love's work is to search out and welcome that goodness wherever it can be found.

Thomas is hard. He is hard both because of the multitude of his distinctions and his fluency with multiple profoundly rich and disparate traditions. This is especially so when it comes to his considerations of pagan virtue—where authorities clash and distinctions abound. Yet the deepest difficulty we encounter, if I am right, is not finally the dizzying maze of a mind enamored with technical reason, encumbered with prodigious learnedness, and gifted beyond nearly all of us; it is, rather, the difficulty of charity. His countless distinctions and endless authorities are so many acts of justice transformed by love. If most of us find that Thomas sometimes asks of us more than we can easily bear, perhaps it is because love—the love that expresses itself in the courageous willingness to find wisdom in the would-be rival and the toiling patience to hew friendship by means of distinction—does not come easily. Thomas is hard because charity is hard.

Fraternal Correction: Love's Secret Work

In all this, I do not mean to suggest that Thomas never departs substantially from his authorities. At times we find him refusing some claim—even if it comes from Aristotle or, indeed, Augustine. The standard stories assume as much—and count his handling of pagan virtue a cardinal case. That Thomas sometimes rejects a position is obvious, and, in some cases, he makes this disagreement explicit (I 76.1). When such negations amount to a refusal to fall below justice or abandon truth in the name of false peace, this can express charity.

Yet, especially when treating Augustine or Aristotle, Thomas will sometimes silently correct, devotion to charity shaping his departures.[20] Hardly letting us know he is doing so, he will edit, omit, or swerve a claim toward truth. Often, few will be in a position to notice the departure or its significance.[21]

Recall Thomas's substitution—"It would be better if [Augustine] had said *habit*" (I.II 55.4). That is the extent of his criticism—if we can call it that. Thanks to his way of putting things, the modification seems merely verbal. One can pass by without registering it as a change, much less correction. We saw earlier how Thomas vindicates the substitution on Augustinian grounds. He could hardly do more to honor Augustine. And yet, for Augustine, habit is not virtue's first language. Many would say its primary place in his thought is negative, a matter of sinful self-possession. Assume that reading is correct and, more, that Thomas held or at least registered it.[22]

If so, there is a sense here in which Thomas corrects Augustine. But he does not present it as such, reject what Augustine says about habit, or call attention to the departure's significance. Least of all does he leave us thinking that he judges Augustine to have erred. Instead, he corrects in the most unobtrusive way possible.

He does so out of charity. He wants Augustine's best insights realized, not to expose his shortcomings publicly and risk scandalizing weaker brothers. For Thomas, ethics under the sign of cross and empty tomb is best parsed in terms of virtues, and virtues are types of habits. Augustine is right, he thinks, to understand ethics in terms of will, grace, and love but mistaken if he thinks doing so is fully salutary without further conceiving these loves in terms of habits. The church will be impoverished and Augustine's richest thoughts fail to reach their apogee, if we follow him in eliding sinful habit and its pathologies with habit as such.

On Thomas's view, one way to characterize Augustine's error in regard to habit is as a failure to draw sufficient distinctions—a failure of charity. Thomas is loath to do the same: not merely in regard to habit but in relating to Augustine himself. If Thomas passes along Augustine's (alleged) antipathy to habit, he would be guilty of active scandal, knowingly leading brethren into error (II.II 43.1).[23] Yet, if he corrects Augustine, the danger of scandal is, if less obvious, equally great: seeing Augustine stumble may lead the weak to fall. In the paradigmatic Biblical case—eating meat offered to idols—the problem is not with eating but lack of concern for those whom one can expect it to spiritually trouble (II.II 43.1 and ad 4; 1 Cor. 8; Rom. 14). Even "what has the *appearance* of sin, must always be refrained from on account of love of neighbor" (II.II 43.2).

If one can act without endangering weaker brothers but endangers them nonetheless, one manifests the lack of charity proper to scandal (II.II 43.2 sc). In correcting Augustine, Thomas must take care lest some be "spiritually swayed from the good," tempted to pride, scorn, or despair (II.II 43.5). Fraternal correction thus acts *per secretam*, in secret (II.II 33.1 ob 2, not denied; 33.4 ad 2). When it comes to correcting Augustine or Aristotle, for Thomas, their good and that of his students are intimately linked.[24] The very concern that makes correction necessary—that neglecting it would endanger someone's soul—also demands care for their spiritual health when it comes to *how* one proceeds:

> Just as the doctor brings health if possible without amputating some limb, but if that prove impossible, amputates the least necessary part that the life be saved; similarly, one who wants to correct [his] brother, ought, if possible, correct such that . . . his reputation be preserved. For this is profitable . . . because with one having being dishonored, others are dishonored [too] . . . and others are provoked to sin from a single sin becoming public. (II.II 33.7)

Thus, out of love for Augustine and those who might falter, and seeking for Augustine's wisdom to reach its consummation, Thomas follows the Gospel injunction, going in private to issue correction. The same impulse that leads him to correct, leads him to do so *per secretam*.

Perhaps nowhere is this clearer than in his departure from Augustine's apparently explicit rejection of pagan virtue. There, in charity, honoring what he thinks Augustine's deepest currents, Thomas distinguishes where Augustine seems not to, proceeding as though Augustine had been dividing infused from acquired, perfect from imperfect all along, as if Augustine had never proclaimed the falsity of pagan virtue, only the absolute supremacy of infused (I.II 63.2; 65.2). This, then, is Thomas's way: in negation as much as affirmation, refusal as much as synthesis, to construct an ethics that remains—before neighbors far and near—a work of charity.

Augustinianisms and Hyper-Augustinianisms

Some—Augustinians especially—worry about certain aspects of Thomas's thought. Yet, notwithstanding the profound coherence I've tried to display, one should not assume that following Thomas on pagan virtue entails following him everywhere, much less that departing on some matter entangles one in inconsistency or infidelity. The point is one Thomas himself demonstrated with each of thousands of objections and responses: we should not assume that going with someone on X entails going with him on Y. Nor, if we embrace his style of synthesis and notion of fraternal correction, can we assume that even if the figure in question thought it did, that disagreeing (or reconceptualizing things so that it did not) amounts to betrayal or abandonment. To imagine otherwise would be very anti-Thomist indeed.

Suppose we distinguish three varieties of Augustinianism corresponding to each of the three criteria for an ethics for the church the introduction outlined. Being Augustinian on the first involves the forceful rejection of any sort of Pelagianism, the celebration of the abundance and priority of God's grace, and the recognition and lament of the ubiquity and destructiveness of sin. The second species entails recognition of the church's unique importance for formation. While affirming what R. A. Markus describes as Augustine's celebration of "Christian mediocrity," his anti-perfectionist welcome of flawed, ordinary Christians, it holds out lively hope that even now God will transform his people through the church and its grace-imbued practices.[25] A third species views church/world relations through the lens of Augustine's affirmation of enduring created goodness, his vision of the entire cosmos—above all our own deepest longings—as beckoning us ever to the creational Word from whom all things come and in whom alone we can find our rest. There are many other ways of being Augustinian, but these are three vital ones.

We can further imagine different varieties of *hyper*-Augustinianism corresponding to each of these distinct criteria, different ways of getting them wrong on their own terms or in relating them. The variety of hyper-Augustinianism that I have referred to and rejected throughout is constituted by the rejection of pagan virtue. Whether rooted in a distorted vision of the primacy of grace and ubiquity of sin, a conviction that the church is the *only* site of true moral formation, or neglect of creation's enduring goodness, it downplays or denies the vital difference between the vicious and relatively virtuous pagan, the unjust and imperfectly just—distinctions essential to loving the neighbor and seeking the common good. For this species of hyper-Augustinianism, not to be informed by charity is exclusively to be informed by sin, not to worship the Triune God is only and in every act to worship oneself.

Yet even those who are hyper-Augustinian in this or another sense may hold other commitments Thomas would welcome, such as a robust vision of the church's role in formation. And, although following Thomas on pagan virtue rules out commitments entailing its rejection, his account may even be compatible with other varieties of hyper-Augustinianism than the one that has concerned us. Thus, even if believing the church is the *only* site of true moral formation—a distinct variety of hyper-Augustinianism—may also push one toward rejecting pagan virtue, the hyper-Augustinianism that has concerned us, it need not *entail* it—provided one conceive of *church* or *pagan* with sufficient creativity.

This book's primary contribution to an ethics for the church has been to address the question of pagan virtue and to do so in a way that shows the integrity and interdependence of that answer with Thomas's Augustinian vision of grace and spiritual formation. I have also tried to show something about the *way* such an ethics ought to proceed, to commend Thomas's practice of ethics as a work of charity.

By now, I think it could hardly be clearer that Thomas articulates a brilliant and careful vision of virtue. And this book, especially part one, has unfolded the multilayered, reciprocal connections between that account and his welcome of pagan virtue. As for grace and sin, both chapter 2 and my ongoing efforts to show the charity-imbued character of his welcome have meant to reveal a similarly integrated relation between that welcome and his devotion to the first Augustinian commitment. This and the preceding chapter make that case still further. At the very least Thomas's insistence on the utter incapacity of pagan virtue for salvation clarifies that his welcome has nothing to do with any sort of Pelagianism. Far from contravening the Augustinian commitments I have sketched, his welcome deepens, depends on, and expresses them. Thomas's account of pagan virtue is not merely compatible with these varieties of Augustinianism; it represents their robust integration.

Pagan Virtue as a Work of Charity

There is no question that Thomas counts infused virtues primary; they alone are perfect and true *simpliciter*, the prime analogue in relation to which acquired virtues are *secundum quid*. In this, Thomas is supremely and obviously faithful to Augustine. But, even in this most Augustinian commitment, he is no less loyal to Aristotle, no less welcoming to the outsider. Thomas exalts infused virtue, in part, *on Aristotelian grounds*. It is a properly Aristotelian insistence—and one which began the treatise on the virtues and which it echoes throughout— that a virtue is the limit of a power (I.II 55.1 and 3). And revelation, the *articula fidei*—which, as first principles delivered from above, fully satisfy the criteria for Aristotelian *scientia*—disclose that the limit of our powers is not, as we might have suspected, the virtues and life that attain the political good, but the virtues and life that attain face-to-face fellowship with Father, Son, and Holy Spirit. That and that which conduces to it, a limit and virtue attainable by charity alone, are truly the limits of our power. That can only perfectly be a virtue for Aristotle which conduces to the perfectly final end, the utmost limit of a power, and thus the claim that the infused virtues are the most perfect virtues is at once a profoundly Augustinian and Aristotelian claim, one in virtue of being the other.

In explaining just how this can be, how that which can only be attained through a gift of charity can nonetheless be regarded as the limit of *our* power, Thomas again relies on and satisfies Aristotle. He uses Aristotle to show how perhaps the most important Aristotelian worry about Augustinian commitment can be answered in a way that is simultaneously faithful to each. How or in what sense could something count as the limit of our power that, in fact, surpasses our power? This question seems to point to an insuperable gulf between the figures. In claiming that a human's perfect final end, true and absolute happiness, is beyond a person's power to attain, Thomas could seem at his most non- or even anti-Aristotelian, subordinating Aristotle to Augustine in just the way so many suppose. Such a claim seems to depart definitively from Aristotle, for it seems to reject a principle as close to the heart of Aristotelian moral philosophy as any: his function argument.

On that argument, the human good is identified by determining the distinctively human function. And that in turn is determined by the nature of the human, namely, what that nature can achieve, what is suited to fulfill it. Aristotle explains:

> Just as for a flute-player, a sculptor, or an artist, and, in general, for all things that have a function or activity, the good and the 'well' is thought to reside in the function, so would it seem to be for man. . . . As eye, hand, foot, and in general each of the parts evidently has a function, may one lay it down that man similarly has a function apart from all these? What then can this be? (*NE* 1.7)

Aristotle goes on to delineate the proper function of humans by considering human nature and what is fitting to it. Determining the function, the good, is, for Aristotle, a matter of looking at human nature and what is suited to it as its perfection. It is easy to see how, in light of this, Thomas might be thought to abandon Aristotle in claiming that the perfect human good is one that transcends a human's power to attain, and the perfectly true virtue one had by divine gift alone. Such claims seem to fly in the face of the function argument: what cannot be attained by humans could hardly be the human function, what is beyond a power cannot be its limit. If something transcends the capacity of human nature to attain and is, in that sense, not that nature's function, then it becomes hard, if not impossible, to see how it could possibly be that nature's end.

Thomas addresses this very issue. And although he does not explicitly use the language of the function argument, precisely that is at play when he articulates and responds to an objection in I.II 5.5. The article asks whether man can achieve happiness by his natural powers. While Thomas notes that imperfect happiness can be had by a human's natural powers, he explains that perfect, final happiness cannot. The objection concerns the paradoxical question of how some end could be both specified by nature and, at the same time, beyond it, how some limit could be at once ours and unattainable without charity. "It seems that man can attain beatitude by his natural powers," the objection says, "for nature does not fail in necessities—and nothing is more necessary to man than that by which he attains the last end" (I.II 5.5 ob 1). The objection is a permutation of the function argument: How, it asks, could some end simultaneously be specified as final by a creature's nature—suited to it—and not also be attainable by that nature? How could something be humanity's end that humans have not power to achieve? That "nature does not fail in necessities," seems to entail that for any end to count *as end* for some creature, any limit *as limit*, it be attainable by that creature. Thomas is, of course, committed to beatitude's finality yet the objection raises the worry that since "nature does not fail in necessities," there is a problem. Either the supernatural end *is* final and nature does fail in the most necessary of things, namely a creature's capacity to attain its end, and thus there is a profoundly problematic mismatch between human nature and its end, a mismatch that would raise insuperable Aristotelian questions about the sense in which this "end" of beatitude is really even an end at all. Or the supernatural end is *not* humanity's final end, and a—maybe *the*—central Christian claim is shown entirely unacceptable, even incoherent, by Aristotelian lights. It is significant that Thomas does not explicitly mention Aristotle in formulating the objection, even though it could hardly be more obvious that he stands in the background and even as it represents a point at which his thought seems irreconcilable with Christianity. All the more significant is that Thomas does mention him explicitly in the response: he has Aristotle himself deliver the argument's concluding line, the puzzle's resolution.

Thomas's way forward shows not only the depth of his commitment to welcoming the pagan Aristotle, but the transformative, reconciling character of his synthesis. Thus, Thomas begins his response by agreeing with the objection's central claim, that nature does not fail in necessities, least of all in the most necessary. His solution is that perfect happiness is in a vital sense within a creature's power. It is so because a creature has the power to turn to God for the help necessary to attain that final, perfect end.[26] And—and this is absolutely key—reproducing a line directly from Aristotle, even including the citation, he writes: "What we do through our friends (*per amicos*), we do, in a sense, ourselves."[27] Aristotle's function argument holds for the supernatural end precisely because of *Aristotle's* conception of friendship. Since what we do by our friend, is, in a sense, done by ourselves, what we do through friendship with God, we do ourselves. The proper function for human beings, then, beatific happiness, is, by Aristotelian lights, attainable by human power in a sense that satisfies the function argument. Moreover, Thomas's choice to cite Aristotle directly in the response but not in the objection, serves to underline, for reader and listener, his fidelity to Aristotle.

Yet, in all this, he remains unswervingly loyal to Augustine: First, in his unbending, anti-Pelagian insistence that the supernatural end is, essentially, beyond the power of human nature to attain: without grace it cannot be had, full stop. Second, in his insistence that it is *God* who attains this end for us: it is only thanks to an Aristotelian conception of friendship that something that is—in a way satisfying to the most stringent anti-Pelagian—not done by us but by someone else, nonetheless counts *for Aristotle* as being done by us. For, on Aristotle's conception of friendship invoked here, the idea is not that something done with a friend's help or cooperation counts as done by us—that would leave us with some sort of semi-Pelagian doctrine. Rather, the notion is that certain things our friends do count, thanks to our friendship, as being done by us. And finally, in that it is precisely in and through *friendship with God* that we are saved—and here the Aristotelian and Augustinian join in a profound unity. This unity is made possible because the truth about friendship that Aristotle hits upon has its origin and source in God—is one in kind with the truth known by Augustine—and known, in both cases, though by different modes, because God has revealed it. Aristotle hits on a feature that marks the most primordial friendship of all, that between Father, Son, and Spirit. The mystery of friendship, of oneness and diversity in action, has its origin in God's friendship with himself. Our friendships, more, our friendship with God, and chiefly God's immanent fellowship, is marked by the mystery of a unity that maintains the integrity of the persons even as the action effected immediately by one is, in a real sense, always also the action of the others.

Thus, at just the point where the stakes are highest and disagreement seems most insuperable, just where we might imagine Thomas would be least Aristotelian and most Augustinian, loyal to the one at the other's expense, he shows himself unfailingly committed to both. With Augustine—and bringing Aristotle along—he insists that only infused virtue, to the exclusion of virtue without charity, is absolutely perfect and true *simpliciter*. And it is exclusively infused virtue that Thomas insists Augustine denies to outsiders (e.g., I.II 63.2).

Charity's Bounty

Thomas bequeaths Christians a way of welcoming pagan virtue that does not merely refuse to compromise fidelity, but, more profoundly, makes recognition of and hospitality toward outsider virtue another way of knowing the Father, loving the Son, and discerning the Spirit. Not only can one greet pagan virtue as authentic without falling into Pelagianism or sacrificing a robust commitment to the necessity and supremacy of grace, but more than that, one can, in the very act of recognition and welcome, celebrate the goodness and faithfulness of a God whose work of creation participates enough of his goodness that it is not completely overcome by sin. For those both without and within the church, Thomas's charity-driven devotion to good-seeking and distinction-drawing offers instruction for confronting challenges of difference. Thomas shows how sympathetic use of "outsider" resources, a relentless hermeneutics of charity, and an unbending commitment to the richest life-affirming dimensions of one's own tradition, can fund an ethics that does justice to insiders and outsiders alike.

But Thomas's efforts yield more than inspiration and formal guidance. His accounts of virtue and habituation, strong and weak *infidelitas*, final end conceptions and their roles, and much else besides are resources for charting a way toward welcoming outsiders. Perhaps most importantly, the wedding of an expectation of goodness and beauty beyond the walls of one's communities with a patient willingness to open oneself up to the threat of difference and to devote oneself to the toil of careful analysis represents a substantive contribution to our own efforts to cope with difference. For Thomas's way with texts suggests a way with the lives and communities of those we call outsiders.

The simplicity and ease of drawing one distinction—same and different, insider and outsider, friend and enemy—is often bedfellow of scapegoating, enmity, and violence. Thomas would have us distinguish—and distinguish again. Interpretive charity belongs not just to the reading of texts but, with far more consequence, to our life together. To search for and find the good in others requires not only more and better distinctions than the simple insider/outsider binary, but that, in our relationships, whatever may divide, we be slow to unqualified negative judgments and ready to make the distinction that, without being untruthful, finds what is lovely if it is to be found. Thomas additionally suggests the importance of discerning which distinctions matter most and a concomitant openness to the possibility that a difference in religious commitment—over whether there is a God or gods, whether he has a Son, whether there is heaven or hell, and so on—may be less consequential for our common life and achievement of the political good than a difference over whether we love justice, pursue the good, and recognize at least some values as sacred. It's not that such religious convictions themselves are unimportant. To the contrary, it's such convictions, in all their detail, that, as Thomas has it, impel—and find expression in—welcome of and friendship with the stranger. Thomas teaches and even shows that the disruption particularity brings can be one that troubles indifference, spurs alliances, and provokes works of justice. It would be a shame—or worse—Thomas reminds us, if we fail to build a friendship, political or otherwise, because of our inability to know the right distinctions to make or because of a lack of the practical wisdom and love to make them well. To embrace such charity, whatever our traditions, is not to refuse to name evil and injustice. It is, rather, a readiness to find and repent of evil at home first, to forgive the unjust when they seek it, and to ally with others different from ourselves in pursuing the good. As Thomas would remind, charity and its distinction-drawing work have a powerful prophetic voice. Among the categories it names: perpetrator and victim, master and slave, evildoer and innocent.

Creation as Gift, Creation as Grace

I have claimed that on the topic of pagan virtue with respect to his views of both sin and grace, Thomas is more Augustinian than many suppose. "That a man will the true good," we heard Thomas say at the close of the last chapter, "this he does by the grace of God" (I.II 109.8). Seizing on this and other scattered comments some might say that even acquired virtue is, finally, a gift of charity. I leave that argument for others to make.[28] But there is a different and not unrelated point the remark calls to mind, whether Thomas is making it here, and one that Thomists and Christians of all stripes, I hope, and perhaps others too, in their own ways, might welcome.

For Thomas, all that we have and all that we are is gift: unmerited, unsought, irreplaceable. Unmerited because there is no just claim—no claim at all—that we can make prior to our existence. Unsought for there is no self to undertake the seeking before God gives it to us. Irreplaceable because each human being uniquely bears the sacred image of the Triune God. Whatever the merits of his other claims, about this de Lubac is surely right: for Thomas, God gives the very possibility of our receiving, making us something that we might be given anything else.[29] Even on an entirely mundane level, to be a capable of virtue, much less to have it, is first to have been the recipient of love and gift. It is to have others do for oneself and on one's behalf that for which one can take no credit. Persons of virtue, Timothy Jackson notes,

> do not just happen; they must be 'built up,' to use the Pauline phrase. We all
> depend on the kindness of strangers—initially our parents . . . or their surro-

> gates—to be fed, materially and spiritually. If we do not receive an uncondi-
> tional and unearned care early on [then apart from a gift of divine grace], we
> [can] never [even] grow into responsible agents. . . . Love [and the life of virtue]
> is a passive potential that must be sparked from without by an initially gratu-
> itous care. . . . Persons must be cultivated as and by lovers, and without [that]
> care . . . life itself[, much less virtue,] is not possible.[30]

"The benefit," Emerson concurs, speaking in a different register, from different
convictions, "overran the merit the first day, and has overran the merit ever
since. The merit itself, so-called, I reckon part of the receiving."[31]

Regularly, and throughout II.II 109, Thomas speaks of the absolute dependence of all human existence and all human willing on the gift of God given in
creation. That we are or will good at all is a gift of love. "If God's help to preserve
him in the good had been removed," we heard Thomas say earlier of Adam,
"even his very nature would have fallen back into nothingness" (II.II 109.8). "It
is," says Thomas citing Philippians, "God who works in us both to will and to
complete" (I.II 9.6 sc). To be sure, humans exercise choice in what they regard
as good and, as I.II 109.8 says, what they will is given to them. But of necessity
they are *moved* to good, of necessity they are drawn by will to the universal
good—which is God himself (I.II 9.6). That this should be the case, that will
should be moved at all and moved only to what a person regards as good, is
gift. Without it, "man cannot will anything" (I.II 9.6 ad 3). What Thomas says of
intellect is no less true of will: "To know any truth whatsoever," to will any good
whatsoever, to achieve any virtue whatsoever, to love any beauty whatsoever,
"man requires Divine help, that the intellect," the will, the heart, "be moved
by God to its act" (I.II 109.1). "Every truth spoken by anyone is from the Holy
Spirit as infusing the natural light, and moving us to understand and speak it,"
far more every good done by anyone is from the Holy Spirit as giving the will
its power, effecting its first act, ordaining it to universal good (I.II 109.1 ad 1).
"Human nature," Thomas continues, "requires the help of God to will or do any
good whatsoever" (I.II 109.2).

In making these remarks, Thomas repeatedly considers and contrasts the
work of charity with the work of creation. What is easy to miss is that even
as he stresses the special way in which the will's movement to beatitude is an
act of charity, he insists no less that even the *natural* movement of intellect,
will, and self are gifts, grace. Such a claim makes certain readers nervous. But
it is Thomas himself who makes it. "Even natural gifts themselves," he insists,

"can be called 'graces' inasmuch as they are given to man by God without any prior human merit" (*De veritate* 24.15). Even natural gifts, even creation, is, by Thomas's light, grace.

In these questions concerned with the role and necessity of charity in redemption, Thomas characterizes as gift, as grace, the very natures to which redemption comes. Part of his argument is that creation, no less than charity, is gift, that humans can no more will good without God's help than they can redeem themselves. Creation and providence are, to be sure, different acts of God's self-giving love than charity, and Thomas is careful to keep them distinct. But he is also keen to stress that they *are acts of God's self-giving love*. When he asks whether man can wish or do any good without grace, his solution, when considering the natural good is not, as we might expect, to say that this is willed or done without grace. Rather, while distinguishing the natural and the supernatural good, the operation of nature and the operation of charity, he characterizes the operation of nature as *itself* dependent on God, itself an act of grace. Thomas answers that the good done by nature, the achievement of acquired virtue, is itself by grace: no good whatsoever can be willed without God's aid (*auxilio*) (I.II 109.2). Such virtue is had without *amor supernaturalis*, supernatural charity, but not without *auxilio Dei*, God's help (II.II 136.2 ad 3 and 2).[32] "The mind even of unfallen humanity," Thomas says, "is not so much master of its act that it does not need to be moved by God—much more man's will after the fall" (I.II 109.2 ad 1). Man's will, he says, "is moved by a . . . principle above [it], namely God" (I.II 109.2 ad 1). And just here, even as he stresses the gratuitous character of all willing and doing good whatsoever, he explicitly cites Aristotle, reaching even into the *Eudemian Ethics* in his relentless effort to show that this too is no betrayal of the outsider.

Charity does not depend for its status as gratuitous on a draining or erasure of nature's gratuity, just as the preeminence of ultimate goodness does not require the deflation of subordinate goods. That man will the good, that man will *at all*, is grace, gift. No less is God the author of the good we do by nature, the one to whom all praise and credit are due, than is he author of the good we do by charity. And so, in a sense different than might be expected, humans are *given* what they will, they determine themselves in relation to their conception of the good, but *that* a man will good whether natural or supernatural, that is by grace—whether the grace that is nature or that which is charity: "what a man wills, that is given. But now, that a man will good—this he does with the help of grace" (I.II 109.8 ad 3).

Grace and Virtue

A perfection, a virtue, is a completion, a bringing to fruition what has already begun. In the case of acquired virtue, the trajectory on which it works is natural virtue, something had by nature—something handed down from above, begun through creation by God. Acquired virtue does not bring its own inception—it receives and works on a trajectory that precedes it and without which it is in no way possible. The willing of good in the process of habituation is gift, but more, that there even be natural virtue to perfect by such willing is gift as well. Grace begins and ends acquired virtue, enclosing it at each step. The movement on which acquired virtue builds is God-given and God-directed, an initial creature-defining ordering to the true good, the final end, the Triune God. And so, acquired, not just infused, virtue, the virtue of the outsider not just the virtue of the Christian is, finally, gift, finally grace. For creation, both in the orientation of natural virtue and acquired virtue's more determinate willing of the true good, is sustained and perfected only by and with the help of God. It is nothing without him. To will the good—whether in a single act or, habitually, with the acquired virtues—is always already to be moved by God, not necessarily with the distinctive movement of charity, but with the movement of his love, of which charity is but another, more fully unveiled, face. To refuse the outsider's virtue is, for Thomas, no less than to deny and turn away from the goodness and glory of God, to fall under the woe spoken against those who would call good evil. To welcome the virtue of the outsider is to welcome the work and presence of the Word in and through whom all things are made and made anew. It is to behold, as through a glass darkly, another no less glorious, no less wondrous, face of grace.

NOTES

INTRODUCTION

1. Aristotle regards many, even most, people as incapable of virtue (e.g., *Politics* I.2, 5, and 13). I do not treat Augustine's account of pagan virtue and, so as to deal with the more difficult case, proceed as though he rejects it. I would be happy to see his views shown to be more generous. Jennifer Herdt summarizes the predominant, "negative" interpretation, *Putting on Virtue*, 45–71. James Wetzel, "Splendid Vices and Secular Virtues," and T. H. Irwin, "Splendid Vices," offer more positive readings.

2. Hauerwas and Charles Pinches, *Christians among the Virtues*, 157.

3. Elsewhere Milbank contends: "Thomas Aquinas explains that there is no *vera virtus* without *caritas*" (*TST*, 233).

4. Shanley, *APV*, 553; Kent, "Moral Provincialism."

5. The concluding chapter distinguishes several varieties of hyper-Augustinianism, but my concern throughout is with hyper-Augustinianism considered as the rejection of pagan virtue. There is irony in linking "Aristotelian" to "public reason," but "Aristotelian" here stands not for Aristotle's particular commitments but, metonymically, for "philosophy" or "reason" as counterposed to "theology" or "revelation"—what Aristotle represents *qua* commitment to be guided by reason alone. Aristotle, John Cooper contends, "made philosophy the . . . only authoritative, foundation and guide for the whole of human life . . . only reason, and what reason could discover and establish as the truth, could be an ultimately acceptable basis on which to live a life," *Pursuits of Wisdom*, 6. The "public reason" stance represents one *specification* (however substantively non-Aristotelian) of this commitment.

6. Smith, *Radical Orthodoxy*, 243 (the bracketed phrase, including emphasis, comes directly from Smith's remarks a few lines earlier).

7. For Milbank the alternatives to Christianity are postmodern nihilism or the retrieval of Greek paganism, both of which are rooted in the embrace of violence (*TST*, 261–62, 288–89). And see Smith's summary, *Radical Orthodoxy*, 241n.35.

8. While Milbank regards properly antique virtue as no longer attainable, contemporary re-appropriations are equally contaminated by celebration and worship of violence (*TST*, 327–67, esp. 328–31, 366–67). "In my view," he says, "[we] must . . . retrieve the account given by Augustine in the *Civitas Dei*" (391). That critique, which specifies that

Rome's "virtue is not virtue . . . its justice not justice," that it is "fundamentally sinful," that its "peace . . . is only apparent," and that its "notion of virtue itself reduced to the pursuit of glory and pre-eminence," applies to contemporary non-Christians (391–95).

9. MacIntyre echoes this view throughout his work: *WJ*, 1–11, 326–48, esp. 342–48; *TRV*, 193–94. He identifies himself as an Augustinian-Thomist Christian, which tradition he says denies pagan virtue (*TRV*, 140; *WJ*, 205; *After Virtue*, 23–35). None of this is to suggest that he advocates hostility, see Luke Bretherton, *Hospitality as Holiness*, 97–100 and 9–33.

10. Hauerwas, *Christians among the Virtues*, 63, xiii.

11. Ibid., 27.

12. Hauerwas, *Peaceable Kingdom*, 6–7.

13. In *Peaceable Kingdom* itself, Hauerwas insists that Christians not only can but *must* find non-Christians who "manifest God's peace better than we [Christians] do" (101). More recently, he has stressed: "That I go to church does not mean I think that Jesus is only to be found there. It just means that he has promised to show up there in a manner that can help us discern how he shows up in other places" (Hauerwas, *Radical Ordinary*, 105). Samuel Wells suggests that Hauerwas's hope that "strangers . . . be welcomed as a gift" is at the core of his theology, Hauerwas, *A Community of Character: Toward a Constructive Christian Social Ethic* (Notre Dame, IN: University of Notre Dame Press, 1981), 10; Wells, *Transforming Fate into Destiny: The Theological Ethics of Stanley Hauerwas* (Eugene, OR: Wipf and Stock), 1–2. Milbank's de Lubacian reading of Thomas and emphasis on gift and participation can suggest a conception of grace as always at work outside the church, so that there are none without it (and so none incapable of virtue): "The church *like grace* is everywhere," Milbank, *Being Reconciled: Ontology and Pardon* (New York: Routledge, 2003), 138, my emphasis. And see, e.g., ibid., 66, 113–18, and 138–61. Smith *chastises* Milbank on this point (*Radical Orthodoxy*, 257). MacIntyre sometimes seems to imagine virtuous individuals who are neither Christian nor even religious (*WJ*, 342).

14. Provided it be distinguished from Rawls's usage, the term "public reason" is one that key figures have warmly appropriated: "The attractions of the term . . . have not been much diminished for me by . . . Rawls," says John Finnis, it "seems to me quite a good phrase for summarily conveying the gist of . . . political thought as expounded by . . . Aquinas" (George, *Natural Law and Public Reason*, 77). Footnoting that remark, Finnis cites the entirety of his *Aquinas* (94n.5). Robert George characterizes his own efforts similarly (4). "Public reason" Thomism texts include: Germain Grisez, Joseph Boyle, and Finnis, "Practical Principles"; Robert P. George, *Natural Law Theory*, especially Boyle's "Natural Law and the Ethics of Traditions"; Grisez, *Way of Jesus*; Budziszewski, *Written on the Heart*. Some might include Ralph McInerny, *Ethica Thomistica*.

15. See, e.g., Finnis, *Aquinas*, 109n.24; McInerny, *Ethica Thomistica*, 119–20; Boyle, "Natural Law," 15.

16. "There are," Boyle says, "moral principles which all mature human beings can know, the naturally known principles which are written on the human heart . . . These principles . . . are accessible to all . . . In fact, it understates the matter to say that these

principles are *knowable* by all. Aquinas seems to hold that they are actually known by all . . . who have the concepts prerequisite for human action," "Natural Law," 11, and see, e.g., 20–21. For Boyle virtues help one apply natural law principles successfully and act accordingly, 13–14.

17. Finnis, *Aquinas*, 105.

18. Ibid. Grisez's work, however, does attend to particularly Christian moral life.

19. In letting "Augustinian" stand metonymically for Thomas's Christianity, I am *not* suggesting his theology is exclusively Augustinian—it is Dionysian, Damascene, and much else. Nor am I suggesting that Augustine and Aristotle were the only authorities among whom Thomas negotiated. Rather, there were positions that Thomas and others took to be those of, respectively, Augustine or Christianity and Aristotle. Some of these were seen as incompatible, leaving it unclear whether or how they could coexist in a single vision. On these dimensions of Thomas's context, see Bonnie Kent, *Virtues of the Will*, 5–19, 23, 34, 246.

20. Very imperfect exemplars of prophetic Thomism might include some members of the school of Salamanca (such as Vitoria) and certain missionary Dominicans (such as las Casas) *only* to the extent that they (a) resisted Spanish imperialism and (b) did not neglect the importance of virtue in such efforts. Roger Ruston, *Human Rights and the Image of God* (London: SCM Press, 2004), Annabel Brett, *Liberty, Right, and Nature: Individual Rights in Later Scholastic Thought* (New York: Cambridge University Press, 1997), and others have explored (a), but save G. Scott Davis's "Conscience and Conquest," there is relatively little on (b).

21. See respectively, e.g., I.II 65.2 and II.II 39.4 ad 1. While there are other terms Thomas uses to refer to all or certain non-Christians (e.g., "sinner," or *peccator* (II.II 32.9 ad 1); "unbeliever," or *infidelis* (II.II 10.3 ad 3); "Muslim," or *Saraceni*, (*CC* 15.5.965)), despite their difference, all refer to pagans in the salient sense—for, in the passages relevant to us, all refer to fallen humans without charity.

22. Karl Rahner's conception of "anonymous Christianity" is probably the most well-known development of the notion of implicit faith (*Foundations*, 311–21). Following *Lumen Gentium*, many interpreters have focused on Thomas's conception of implicit faith drawing primarily on scattered remarks in the treatises on faith and baptism (e.g., II.II 2.5, 6, and 7; 10.4; III 68.2, 69.4). See, e.g., Thomas O'Meara, *Thomas Aquinas*, 235–41. Many who think Thomas rejects pagan virtue hold that some ostensible pagans, those with implicit faith, can attain authentic virtue.

23. The question of outsider or "pagan" virtue is nearly always treated as the question of what virtue (if any) Thomas believes attainable without charity. The possibility of implicit faith is regarded as a separate topic; I do not treat it. Throughout, whether speaking of Thomas's views or his interpreters', I mean by "outsiders" and "pagans," "non-Christians without charity." Thus, I describe those who believe non-Christians can attain virtue only through implicit faith as denying pagan virtue. Perhaps someone will say that when Thomas claims postlapsarian humans can attain true acquired virtue without charity, he in fact imagines such people as having implicit faith and so having charity after all. While such a claim contradicts what Thomas explicitly says as he refers

precisely to the achievements of fallen humans *without charity*, if *per impossibile* it were true, I am less concerned to deny that these outsiders secretly have charity than to elucidate what Thomas says they can attain *despite their not being Christians*.

24. While Thomas considers at relatively greater length postlapsarian human capacities apart from charity, his remarks on implicit faith are few, complex, and brief and his concern there is *merit* and *salvation* not human virtue.

25. Some elide the issues of pagan *capacities* for virtue with that of pagan *theories* of virtue. While our central focus is the former (which is what I mean by "pagan virtue"), we will also see that Thomas's way with Aristotle's *theory* of virtue is one important dimension of his welcoming stance on pagan virtue.

26. Communities and cultures are necessary for understanding individuals but on questions of pagan virtue attention to the concrete neighbor is essential.

27. These particularities matter but, other things being equal, are not such to render Thomas's reflections on pagan virtue irrelevant for non-Christians, at least not *prima facie*.

28. Flannery O'Connor, *Mystery and Manners: Occasional Prose* (New York: Farrar, Straus & Giroux, 1974), 112.

29. There are several ways in which this book's argument could be expanded. One is in regard to supplemental matters of Thomistic interpretation and disputes in the exegetical literature; another is in regard to unfolding my remarks on Augustinianism, hyper-Augustinianism, and the argument's implications for them. So as not to make this book overly long, in the former case, I am making that material available in articles and/ or online at my website. The latter topic is the subject of my next book.

CHAPTER 1

1. Solomon Grayzel, *CJ*, 241, and cited in Steven Boguslawski, *TAJ*, 33n.41. I am indebted to Boguslawski's discussion and bibliography.

2. Jeremy Cohen, "Functional Classification," 104 and cited in *TAJ*, 20.

3. Ibid.

4. R. W. Southern, *Western Society*, 283.

5. Fergus Kerr, *After Aquinas*, 4.

6. Ibid.

7. R. E. Houser may be right, however, to see Ibn Sina rather than Ibn Rushd as informing *De principiis naturae*, "Avicenna and Aquinas's *De principiis naturae*, cc. 1–3," *The Thomist* 76.4 (2012): 577–610.

8. As few as one out of ten Dominicans had that opportunity (Torrell, *Aquinas's Summa*, 9). And see Leonard Boyle, "Setting of the *Summa*," esp. 19–22, 26–31.

9. It was issued 23 times between the twelfth and fifteenth centuries (*TAJ*, 31).

10. Solomon Grayzel, "Papal Bull," 262. Cohen concurs (*FJ*, 242–43).

11. And see Cohen, *FJ*, 242.

12. For all we know Albert may have opposed the undertaking or found the texts acceptable.

13. Giacomo Todeschini, "Franciscan Economics," 111–12.

14. Ibid., 112.

15. Further, on Peckham's formulation rulers stand to benefit economically from maintenance of the status quo, whereas Thomas makes it economically problematic for a ruler to allow usury.

16. Ibid., 102.

17. Ibid., 105.

18. Thomas's primary apologies for mendicant life, *Contra impugnates Dei cultum et religionem* and *De perfectione spiritualis vitae*, mention Jews rarely and only in reference to Scriptural passages. Jews do not figure in the arguments.

19. Boguslawski affirms John Hood's defense of Thomas against criticisms like Cohen's but argues that by attributing to Thomas mere preservation of the Augustinian status quo, Hood does not fully recognize the degree to which he is a friend to Jews (*TAJ*, 3–4). Hood contends against Cohen that "Aquinas presented the received view of Judaism and the Jews in an unusually coherent form" (*Aquinas and the Jews*, xii). That received view is the "dualistic view of Jews and Jewish history rooted in the New Testament and the teaching of the Church Fathers" wherein the Jews are both the "chosen people of God who had received the Law" and "in some sense guilty for murdering Christ" (xii). "Aquinas," Hood says, did not "*pace* Cohen . . . work to alter [this tradition] *in any significant way*" (xii, my emphasis). Recognizing Thomas's relatively tolerant stance, Hood strangely attributes this to a "fundamental cleavage between his theological views and his social teaching," where he imagines the former would tend toward *intolerance* (87).

20. See *TAJ*, Chapters 4–5, esp. 92–101, 105–8.

21. See, e.g., Torrell, *STA*, 251–56.

22. His evidence is a remark from the late fourteenth century by Petrus Marsilius who, amidst a glowing account of Raymond, claims he had Thomas write *SCG*. But, for reasons like Mark Jordan's, most hold that we should not trust Marsilius's account (*Rewritten Theology*, 90–94). Torrell summarizes the broader historical debate on *SCG* (*STA*, 104–7). Though some think it was written in view of evangelizing *Muslims*, none of the more than a dozen scholars Torrell discusses hold Cohen's view.

23. Again, his only evidence is Marsilius's remark. There's no reason to think the two shared such affinity. On top of Thomas's proscription of persecution: (1) It's unclear that he devotes *any* energy to conversion efforts; (2) Where Raymond founded schools of linguistic instruction for missionaries and facilitated Christian-Jewish disputations, there is no evidence that Thomas did so.

24. Cohen reads the passage differently in various texts: Cf. *FJ*, 124, with *LL*, 372–73, and *CK*, 89.

25. Without explanation or acknowledgement and even as it remains almost exclusively negative, Thomas's role in Cohen's story varies somewhat even within Cohen's work—his profound responsibility for novel anti-Judaism and increased persecution occasionally qualified, but then reaffirmed. Thus, without noting his departure from *FJ*, Cohen admits it's "questionable" whether Raymond solicited *SCG* yet still says it may "embod[y] Thomas's concurrence with [him]" about Jews (*LL*, 372). Or claiming *FJ*

made only "brief, passing mention" of Thomas, without noting he's doing so, Cohen first tempers some of *FJ*'s claims (*LL*, 365–68)—but then largely resumes and even darkens its story: Thomas blurred the distinction between contemporary Jews and heretics (388) and suggested that they "smack[ed] of heterodoxy" (374) and had "consciously forsaken" Biblical Judaism (388–89). For Thomas, like Raymond and his ilk, Jews "resemble heretics, deliberate unbelievers" (388, 362–63). He "echoed the ideological basis for their . . . anti-Judaism" (389) and whatever protections he *explicitly* advocates "the Jew who emerged from his . . . theology challenged the very rationale for" toleration (388). *CK* largely lacks even *LL*'s qualifications. Given this, fully settling Cohen's position(s) on Thomas would be difficult. Since our interest is not primarily in interpeting Cohen himself but in Thomas's relation to Jews and anti-Judaism, I engage Cohen's negative portrait of Thomas as a useful type and without trying to square it with his rare qualifications—which I doubt can be done. Still, in case it can, I'm happy for my claims about Cohen's view/narrative to be taken as claims about "the view/narrative most of his claims authorize," or even "a view/narrative of Thomas as anti-Judaizer built on Cohen's work." Should it turn out that Cohen does not hold the view most of his claims express, all the better. But establishing that would require retracting arguments and rhetoric present as recently as *CK*.

26. Joseph Shatzmiller, *Deuxième controverse*, 54, and cited in *CK*, 90.

27. And see, e.g., *LL*, 339–40, 352. Such rhetorical moves further belie Cohen's rare qualifications about Thomas's role.

28. The original commentary dates at latest from 1265–68. While it was likely later revised, it's unclear what this would have meant. On the difficulties in dating *CC*, see Daniel Keating, "Aquinas on 1 and 2 Corinthians," 127–28.

29. Thomas held Chrysostom nearly as highly as Augustine. When, with Paris in its splendor before them, a student once said "Oh, to be Lord of this fine city!" Thomas replied, "I'd rather have Chrysostom's homilies on Matthew," James A. Weisheipl, *Friar Thomas*, 121–22.

30. Discarding his fuzzier *scientia/cognitio conjecturalis* distinction, Thomas uses *ignorantia affecta* as a more precise concept for parsing the leaders' awareness and harmonizing his authorities. *Ignorantia affectata* is real ignorance arrived at dishonestly. So, despite strong suspicions, Harry avoids asking Sally if she's married lest he learn what would require him not to sleep with her. Given its sinful origins, this ignorance aggravates culpability. It's the same point he made in *CC* but a new idiom. Cohen's impeaching claim that it's a "puzzling idea," "whittl[ing] away at the essential difference between ignorance and intention" neglects the context of Thomas's need to reconcile Biblical texts and improve upon *CC*'s murkiness (*CK*, 82). A page earlier, Cohen himself notes that the *Sentences* had raised the difficulty of how envy and ignorance could coexist (81).

31. Cohen nowhere notes that Thomas is depending on and wrestling with these sources (the closest he comes is *LL*, 374). Instead, Cohen depicts him as "departing" from Anselm and Abelard, whom Thomas never mentions in this context and rarely engages at all (*LL* 339; *CK*, 82). Nor does Thomas engage Augustine's teaching on the topic, whom Cohen says Thomas "take[s] issue with" (*CK*, 81) and who himself charac-

terizes the Jews as "blinded in their hearts" by pride (*DCD* 18.35), perverse and full of malice (15.35), impious and brutal (3.14), and guilty of crucifying Jesus for showing the kingdom's spiritual nature (5.18).

32. One can even read the notion of *ignorantia affectata* as helping him maintain this structure.

33. Were Cohen's point merely that Thomas was representative of his time, he needn't show such causality, but from *FJ* to his 2007 *CK* he depicts Thomas as "[breaking] new ground" (*CK*, 82), pushing things "in a radically new fashion" (81), and "overturn[ing] the Augustinian tradition" (82)—in short as contributing to the changes in anti-Judaism and persecution that he documents (e.g., 89).

34. Boyle, "Setting of the *Summa*," esp. 40; J.N. Hillgarth, "Who Read Aquinas?"

35. Boyle, ibid., esp. 39–40; Hillgarth, ibid., esp. 47–49. The *Tertia Pars* "accounts for only about 18 percent of all the extant manuscripts of . . . the parts" (Boyle, "Setting Revisited," 13).

36. Leonard Boyle, "*Summa Confessorum*," esp. 50–53, 60–62; "Setting of the *Summa*," 43–45.

37. Based on my study of *Summa confessorum*, especially as aided by Bartholomew of San Concordio's fourteenth-century index thereof, *Summa de casibus conscientiae*— a major, widely used manual in its own right. Neither in treating Jews (*SC* I.4; *Scc* fol. 90vb-92rb), infidels (*Scc* fol. 84vb-85ra), homicide (*SC* II.1; *Scc* fol. 71rb-73va), Christ (*Scc* fol. 190va), nor even *ignorantia* (*SC* III.33.16–19, fol. 152va-153rb; *Scc* fol. 75va-b) and its relations to guilt and *ignorantia affectata*—where *SC* mentions Laban's deception of Jacob and the most natural place to cite the Jews as an example—is 47.5 mentioned.

38. *SC* I.4, esp. Q.4, fol. 10vb. And see *Scc* fol. 92rb, which, asking "whether children of Jews or pagans can be baptized against the parent's will," cites *Summa theologiae* II.II 10 as saying "it is not licit."

39. This is a subdivision within the category of those whose *infidelitas* is characterized by resistance to or rejection (*renitendo*) of Christian faith as opposed to sheer absence of faith (II.II 10.1 and 5). Chapter 8 treats *infidelitas* in detail.

40. In considering Jews to have faith *in figura*, Thomas understands the Jews, in one sense, as following Jesus as Messiah, at a distance. See Bruce Marshall, "*Quasi in Figura*," esp. 482–84.

41. While conceding II.II 10.11's Augustinian character (*LL*, 367), Cohen misses this connection and Thomas's absolute distinction between Jewish and heretical *infidelitas* (373–89).

42. Christians with insecure faith may not undertake disputations. Whether that holds for non-Christians, he does not say. Given his commitment to addressing the strongest objections, surely he would want disputants to engage the wisest non-Christians.

43. Thomas is not suggesting that all or many non-Christians try to corrupt the faith of Christians.

44. Thus, the faith of the simple who live where there are no unbelievers is firmer

"because they have heard nothing different from what they believe" (II.II 10.7). Sensitivity to this dynamic informs his article on social interaction (II.II 10.9).

45. Disputations could alienate unbelievers if Christians performed poorly or acted unjustly or uncharitably.

46. On avoiding scandal, II.II 10.10 and 11. On evangelization through daily interaction, II.II 10.9. Not all disputations were forced; some Jews were eager to dispute.

47. John Bowlin shows how Augustine's "sentiments about just and unjust coercion are [largely] our own" and that Augustine tries to justify coercion "precisely because [and insofar as it] satisf[ies] these sentiments" ("Justifying Coercion," 68). In this respect, Thomas follows Augustine closely.

48. Thomas's remarks that "even if [Christians] were to defeat [unbelievers who persecute Christians] and hold them as prisoners of war (*captivos*), they would leave them in freedom whether to believe or not" (II.II 10.8) does not authorize domination, for: (1) The remark concerns prisoners of war not the entire populace; (2) Even a just war today would raise difficult questions about the reconstitution of the defeated society. In Thomas's day, with its weaker institutions, limited technology and resources, and greater difficulty in achieving security, the question of reconstituting a just order was at least as complicated; (3) The remark stresses that even those who *are* held prisoner must be left free in their religious beliefs.

49. Vitoria, *Political Writing*, 223–30. Whether Thomas would follow Vitoria here is uncertain. He does think some religious groups may be coerced to repent (e.g., Christian heretics) or be suppressed (e.g., witches).

50. While some faiths may involve commitment to blasphemous doctrines and their propagation, this reverts to the question of what constitutes blasphemy and implicates matters that are addressed in chapter 8.

51. The logic of Thomas's argument may suggest that he would allow unbelievers to possess any political office short of the highest provided they were subject to a still higher Christian ruler. A non-Christian's possessing a Christian servant exemplifies the kind of case Thomas intends to forbid, but he allows Christians to be employed by unbelievers (II.II 10.10 ad 3). Regarding authority his concern is at least twofold: (1) to preserve the faith of Christians who might fall away under non-Christian authority (e.g., II.II 10.10 ad 3; 10.9); (2) to prevent the faith from being scorned, through such falling away or through scandalizing unbelievers. Thus, while the Church can free Christian servants of even those Jews not subject to its temporal rule, it must not do so lest it embitter Jews toward the Church and diminish the possibility of conversion.

52. Human law for Thomas *just is* a participation, a partial realization, of God's eternal law, of which Divine law, revelation, is another face.

53. For Christian and non-Christian rulers alike, just rule requires pursuit of the common good. Failure to do that vitiates the ruler's authority and entails that such rule is not even *ex iure humano*, whether "already established" or not.

54. Southern, *Western Society*, 73.

55. *Hostibus* can denote either "strangers" or "enemies"—my translation retains the ambiguity.

56. Thomas regards non-Christian worship as, in some ways, sinful, and his explicit grounds for tolerating *non-*Jewish rites is that not doing so might cause worse evils. This pragmatic approach seems at odds with his principled proscription of compulsion in II.II 10.8, for surely he imagines nonbelievers will *practice* their faith. With others, that article imagines nonbelievers *as worshipers* alongside Christians. Nor does he there cite performance of rites as "impeding the faith"—which exclusion would be odd if he so regarded them. Perhaps: (1) By *ritus*, Thomas refers here not to regular worship but public celebration. The former is permissible, but whether the latter is depends on prudential consideration. (2) Non-Christian rites are almost always allowed because Thomas judges the harm of prohibition as nearly always greater.

Whether Thomas regards Jewish rites as mortally sinful for Jews is disputable. I.II 103.4, where some say he declares Jewish performances mortal sin, may rather concern centrally—even exclusively—Christian adherence to ceremonial law. Its examples (exclusively) and arguments (primarily) refer to Christians, and read otherwise it seems to contradict II.II 10.11. Marshall claims 103.4 and 10.11 are Thomas's "official" and "unofficial" views, respectively (*Quasi*, 482). Even granting that distinction, why regard the place where Thomas explicitly considers ongoing *Jewish* adherence to the Law his "unofficial" view and the place where Jews may not even be in view his "official" one? Reading 103.4 as treating Christians eliminates the need for such distinctions, especially depending on how we conceive the relation between (a) what a Christian intends and signifies by keeping ceremonial law and (b) what a Jew intends and signifies. The shape and structure of their intentions vis-à-vis Jesus are distinct. Even if a Jew's law-keeping presupposes rejection of Jesus, it is not clear that, as compared to a Christian, her obeying the law constitutes (i) as direct a claim about Jesus (or whether it constitutes a *direct* claim at all), (ii) whether it is as much entangled in falsehood, or (iii) whether it is essentially dependent on beliefs about Jesus (or to the same degree). That an act (also) signifies *X*, even if one foresees this, needn't entail that one either *intends* to signify *X* or acts in order to so signify. Chapter 8 has implications for this topic. For his part, Cohen considers neither the relation between these passages nor such complexities (*LL*, 367, 387–89).

57. Nancy Turner, "Jews and Judaism," 96.

58. Southern, *Western Society*, 191.

59. David Burrell, "Aquinas and Islam," 72.

60. Torrell, *Aquinas's Summa*, 82–83.

61. Burrell, "Aquinas and Islam," 74.

62. Primarily through Maimonides, through whom Thomas may have encountered Asharite "occasionalism" (see, e.g., *SCG* III 97.15; *DP* 3.7).

63. Louis Gardet, "*La connaissance*," 149, and Burrell, "Aquinas and Islam," 74.

64. Thomas claims that Muslims believe resurrection or heaven consists in having *uxores, et voluptates, et delicias corporals*—wives, bodily delights, and luxuries (*CC* 15.7.1000; 3.937, 5.965), and "Muslims are promised rivers of milk and honey, Jews land, but Christians the glory of angels" (*De decem praeceptis* 3 corpus).

65. William distinguishes *Tartari* who belong to the Khan kingdom from "pure pagans who are without law" and "have no city, only huts in the woods" (*Itinerarium*, Ch. 16,

204). Roger Bacon and Mathew Paris, contemporaries of Thomas, attended to Tatars (e.g., Bacon, *Opus Maius*, 1:385; Jeremy Catto, "Ideas and Experience," 3).

66. This pertains even for some Christian commitments, e.g., certain notions of sin might lead some to consider the cultivation of virtue to be prideful.

67. Each is my own rendering. Variations on the former appear in Fabian Larcher's online translation, on which Holley Taylor Coolman, "Romans 9–11," relies, and in 1999 ("*non en partie come jusqu'à maintenant, mais tous universelement*") (p. 407) and 1869 French translations. Variations on the latter appear in Boguslawski (*TAJ*, 97) and Hood (*Aquinas and the Jews*, 77–78). Context offers evidence for each, but even on the more "universalist" renderings, the temporal scope Thomas has in view and whether he means strictly every Jew both remain unclear.

68. Coolman assimilates Boguslawski's more qualified affirmation (*TAJ*, 97) to her own and does the same with Hood, who actually rejects her universalism (*Aquinas and the Jews*, 77–78; Coolman, 104–6). Does Thomas think leaders whom he blames for Jesus's death or resurrection-denying Sadducees will be saved? Would he make that claim so casually and briefly? Lines later, clarifying Paul's comment that God will "have mercy on all," he explains: "his mercy [will] find a place among every race (*genere*) of men . . . not . . . all men individually." This holds for every "race [of men] and not for [all] the individuals thereof" (*RC* 11.4.932). Context suggests he's referring to Jews here too: a preceding, parallel "all" refers to "every *genus* of men, Jews as much as Gentiles" (932).

69. Wyschogrod, "Jewish Perspective," 161.

CHAPTER 2

1. See I 5 and 65.1 ad 2. On evil see Herbert McCabe, *God Matters*, 25–38.

2. I italicize "esse" only when referring to the concept *esse*.

3. Complexities abound in relating *ens* (being) and esse, but the two are interchangeable here. On their relation, see Lawrence Dewan, *Form and Being*, esp. chapter 4 and 190–96, and John Wippel, *Metaphysical Thought*, 110–24. Other complexities that needn't trouble us concern the esse/ens/good relation in regard to mathematical items (I 5.3 ad 4).

4. *Ratio* is a complex term that can mean, e.g., "faculty of reason" (I 1.1); "formality" or "mode of knowing" (I 1.1 ad 2; 1.3 ad 2); or "concept" (here and I 5.2). Here, Thomas juxtaposes *ratio* to *res* and speaks of good's *ratio* as consisting in desirability.

5. It's a different, more complicated matter if *no one* applies that concept to him. Such distinctions needn't intervene for Thomas here, for God always knows himself as desirable.

6. For Thomas, some instances of goodness do depend, in part, on human practices (I 103.4 and 7).

7. Their difference in *ratio*, however, precludes their always being used interchangeably (I 5.1 ad 1).

8. This is how to understand Thomas's claims about good's *ratio* or "very nature" (*ipsa natura*) as desirable, perfect, etc. (e.g., *SCG* I 37). These aren't proper definitions, disclosures of good's essence; they *cannot* be.

9. The Leonine edition has *enuntiaverunt* rather than Corpus Thomisticum's *enunciaverunt*. Here, the difference is negligible.

10. That's not to say we can't know particular goods—an Islay whisky or Wilbur poem—directly and as good. We have in view, recall, the essence and definition of goodness as such, as identical with esse. Ultimately all good is an effect of the divine Good: in being generated by God (I 5.5 ad 2) and in having its goodness made good in virtue of the divine Good (I 6.4).

11. Here he's not trying to prove that good *exists* but that it and esse are identical. On I 2.3, see Kevin Hector, "Apophaticism in Aquinas," and Brian Shanley, *Treatise on the Divine Nature.*

12. There's a distinction between each seeking its own perfection and each seeking perfection as such. More on this below.

13. Within these parameters a creature's freedom varies according to its kind (I 18.4). A dog may or may not chase mail carriers but none sends letters.

14. The mode of perfection against which an individual creature is judged is determined not by its *individual* capacities but those of its species. Thus, even if some individual's capacities were such that it could never achieve its species' perfections (e.g., it was blind or caged), because of those incapacities it would count as imperfect vis-à-vis its mode of perfection. The very judgment that it has *incapacities* is an implicit recognition of its imperfection vis-à-vis the species ideal. We can also consider a creature's perfection with respect to its individual capacities or those of similarly imperfect creatures (e.g., blind Rex vis-à-vis other blind dogs). But those conceptions are neither what Thomas means here nor (usually) in describing creatures as pursuing their perfection.

15. There are, however, degrees of perfection *across* different species: the most imperfect animal is, *qua* animal, more perfect than the most perfect plant.

16. These points apply as much to the *absence* of a natural feature or capacity (e.g., sight) as to the presence of something *extra* (e.g., an extra limb).

17. In seeking it species ideal, X will be seeking the good it can actually attain. A three-legged dog, say, seeks its species ideal but in a way inflected by its lacking a leg.

18. For "Thomas-like" perspectives addressing contemporary epistemic, evolutionary, and other challenges, see Michael Thompson, *Life and Action*, and Micah Lott, "Elephant Seals."

19. "Good" is one of very few terms Thomas says is predicated primarily and essentially of God.

20. That doing so helps is more than incidental. While *perfectum* signifies "[any] thing not lacking in actuality," including God, etymologically, Thomas says, it originally concerned *made* things (I 4.1 ad 2).

21. Considered not as *painting* but as *material object*, it is no more in act than a bad painting: both are in potency to use as wrapping paper.

22. Maximal potentiality does not entail maximal capacity for actuality. "First matter," matter with no determinate form, has maximal potency but since it can always be acted upon (e.g., given some form) it *always* stands in potential to countless other ways

of being and thus could never be the most actual thing (I 4.1). In contrast, a horse *qua* horse has less potentiality than pure matter thanks to its form, which limits the change it can undergo while remaining a horse. "Limits" make creatures more perfect than first matter by reducing their potency.

23. Thomas also makes this case on the basis of God's self-subsistent existence, his identity as the one whose existence is entirely from himself and for whom essence (who he is) is identical to existence (that he is). Since every perfection is (at least) some mode of existing, of *being* this or that, the self-subsistently existent one has all perfections of existence (I 3.4; 4.2).

24. Complexities abound here. Thomas says God gives esse *and* a patient to receive it (*DP* 3.1 ad 17). He holds that: (A) nothing exists outside of existence and everything exists as participating esse (e.g., *DP* 7.2 ad 9); *and* (B) esse is distinct from form, matter, substances, even as each only *exists* as sharing in esse. (B) reminds that while nothing exists "outside of" esse, more and other than esse exists: that is, there's something more and else to be than esse. Esse is necessary but not sufficient for *thinking* what there is and for what there *is*. What *exists* is at *least* esse, but forms, for example, are not esse itself but receive it and so, while not *existing* apart from it, they are logically but not temporally its recipient, contracting it to a *particular* existence. Logically, they receive esse, not as making it more actual but as being actualized *by it*. While I emphasize (A) here, especially Thomas's claim that esse is more actual and formal than form itself, I don't deny (B), on which, see Dewan, *Form and Being*, chapter 11, and Stephen Brock, "Harmonizing Plato."

25. Forms determine even spirit—making this angel Raphael, that one Gabriel.

26. Houses and material substances have esse *by* their form as principle (e.g., I 75.6; 77.6) but it is thanks to esse, as still more formal and as had by forms, that existence comes through forms. If someone held wooden letters to spell *cat*, and we count the letters as matter, their order as form, and their being so held as esse, we glimpse both the connection and distinction between form and esse: this "person gives form as well as actuality, and gives actuality by giving form" (*Form and Being*, 198).

27. And see I 19.6 and *DP* 7.2 ad 9.

28. *Ens*, as distinct from esse, is the first knowable, but the difference is irrelevant for our point.

29. We *can* grasp that *X* exists *then* what it is, as when we make it out in the dark, but this is not his point. Hearing "sound" (without knowing what it is) is saliently like hearing speaking: in both cases we hear sound-of-a-certain-sort. The knowable *is* esse-of-a-certain-sort, and whatever we know, we are knowing esse-of-a-certain-sort. These epistemological points follow from what Thomas holds about what actually *is*.

30. Every perfection is not *only* or *simply* esse, but every perfection is *at least* esse. For example, form itself is a perfection (I 14.6) and not *simply* a perfection of esse. But insofar as form exists it is *at least* a perfection of esse. It can only give the distinctive perfection it gives as it shares in esse. The parenthetical qualification pertains throughout.

31. God authors not only esse but subjects like forms that (logically, not temporally) receive it. Only God's esse has nothing *whatsoever* added. On God's esse, see Brock, "Harmonizing Plato," esp. 480–84.

32. We might instead grasp the position of striker simply through the concept *striker*. While that involves understanding the striker's relation to other players and the game itself, mastery of the concept *soccer* entails grasping still more concepts (e.g., soccer's relation to rugby).

33. And: I 15.2; 22.3; 84.2 and ad 2. These ideas encompass individuals and accidents (I 14.11 and 14) and do not exist outside God's knowledge (I 15.1 ad 1).

34. They not only preexist in him but do so more perfectly—for they are not other than his self.

35. On the preceding four sentences see too: I 15.1–3; 19.4; 44.3 and ad 1; 46.1.

36. This is *not* a point about our judgment but about what is the case.

37. God does not understand the creature *by* its idea; its idea *is* his understanding (I 15.2 and ad 2). Further, that God has some idea of something less perfect than himself does not mean that the idea *qua* idea is imperfect. What the idea is *of*, is one thing; the act of thinking it, something else.

38. This resemblance is unlike that between two new baseballs; new and used baseballs; parent and child; or even animal and rock (I 4.3).

39. Thus: "there is one goodness of all things; and yet many goodnesses" (I 6.4). God is the one goodness or good-maker, but each creature has its own goodness *qua* existent.

40. And: I 2.3; 19.1; 19.4; I.II.1.2.

41. Even interpreters as estimable as Ralph McInerny can veer toward this two-tier Thomism, *Ethica Thomistica*, 114–22.

42. Thomas, we'll see, means to overcome such reason/revelation, Aristotle/Augustine dichotomies.

43. Mark Jordan is surely right when he notes that the *Summa* is "the best single work in which to watch [Thomas] construct theological teaching page by page" ("Theology and Philosophy," 236).

44. Readers as diverse as Leonard Boyle, "Setting of the *Summa*"; Michel Corbin, *Chemin de la théologie*; James Weisheipl, *Friar Thomas*; Otto Pesch, *Theologie der Rechtfertigung*; Frederick Bauerschmidt, *Faith, Reason, and Following Christ*, esp. 41–82; M. D. Chenu, *Nature, Man, and Society*; Eugene Rogers, *Aquinas and Barth*; Gilles Emery, *TT*; Rudi te Velde, *Aquinas on God*; and Fergus Kerr, *After Aquinas*, regard Thomas as pursuing *sacra doctrina* in *ST*. For further bibliography, see Matthew Levering, *Scripture and Metaphysics*, 23–38.

45. This, Eugene Rogers's fundamental claim, Fergus Kerr praises and defends as "not a very daring move to make" (*After Aquinas*, 64).

46. Thomas's language makes the link between the two *prooemia* clear: using a purpose clause (*ut* + subjunctive) and echoing the initial *prooemium*'s language, he frames the investigation of *sacra doctrina*'s identity and scope explicitly in terms of keeping *ST* within the limits articulated in the work's *prooemium* (*ut intentio nostra sub aliquibus certis limitibus comprehendatur*).

47. Due to their practical, contingent character ecology and some other sciences I

use as examples do not technically count as *scientia*, but given our aims we can safely treat them as such in what follows.

48. For Thomas, *scientia* is both "invented" and "discovered," his conception implying neither Cartesian dualism nor modern foundationalism (Rogers, *Aquinas and Barth*, 24–30). I owe the ornithology focus to Rogers, *Aquinas and Barth*.

49. Elsewhere Thomas distinguishes between Scripture and *articuli fidei*, but in question one, at least when discussing this issue, he uses the terms as synonyms (cf. I 1.8).

50. It takes God so understood as object; that's not to say it knows his essence (I 1.7 ad 1).

51. "It is GOD," says Yves Congar, "who reveals himself in all of this sacred history of which Christ is the focal point . . . According to this fashion and in this measure . . . here below he reveals to us *who* he is—by telling us of the one with *whom* we have this relationship," "Christ in Economy," 8, cited in William Henn, *Hierarchy*, 112. And see, Congar, *Meaning of Tradition*, 86.

52. See, Rogers, *Aquinas and Barth*, 18, 58–59.

53. Put aside for now the Jesus/Word distinction.

54. The name must denote a real, not merely rational, relation (*DP* 9.9 ad 7). It must designate "that relative property which distinguishes and constitutes the person and which is identical to the person itself" (*TT*, 192).

55. See, e.g., I 34.1 and ad 2; 34.2; 34.3 ad 4; 42.2 ad 1.

56. If (a), this refers to an act common to the Divine nature but rightly appropriated to the Word thanks to his personal property (e.g., I 39.7 ad 3).

57. The Son/*sacra doctrina* relation can also be parsed in terms of Jesus's identity as *begotten Wisdom* cf. I 1.6 (*sacra doctrina* as wisdom/*sapientia*), 39.7 ad 2, and 34.1 ad 2. Seeing *sacra doctrina* as *scientia* does not exclude seeing it as wisdom too—not for Thomas at least! For Thomas, *sacra doctrina* as *scientia* is not *Konklusionstheologie*, indifference to the principles (Jesus and Scripture) themselves. That view elides *sacra doctrina*'s incapacity (and refusal) *qua scientia* to demonstrate the *authority* and *truth* of its first principles, with indifference to elucidating, investigating, and examining those principles or failure to respond to objections to them. It focuses on *scientia*'s deductive to the neglect of its *principled* character. *Principles* are what *scientia* is about, *and* principles virtually contain *scientia*. *Sacra doctrina* is no less interested in Jesus and Scripture than chemistry in elements or the periodic table. On *sapientia*, see Mark Johnson, "Sapiential Character," but 88n.10 understates somewhat *scientia*'s interest in its principle.

58. This holds differently in creation/providence than in redemption.

59. Jesus *himself*, Incarnate Word—in his "totality"—*is* the first principle, unlike a bird or oak, say, which is not *itself* a principle but the outworking of a form internal to and distinct from it. That's why we can coherently ask what Jesus's ontological outworking is.

60. Rogers, *Aquinas and Barth*, 18.

61. On "more universal" see Rogers, *Aquinas and Barth*, 48–53. On theology and philosophy faculty relations, see, e.g., Bonnie Kent, *Virtues of the Will*.

62. I put aside complexities concerning *sacra doctrina*'s status as wisdom and rela-

tion to the gift of wisdom (I 1.6 ad 3), which bear on whether unbelievers can do *sacra doctrina* and on Christian knowledge of God apart from *sacra doctrina*. (See, e.g., *CNE* 2.4.9, where Thomas compares the moral philosopher who fails to act well to the ill who, while hearing the doctor, don't takes their medicine.) In paralleling *sacra doctrina* to infused virtue, I thus focus on *sacra doctrina* as infused virtue's *learned* speculative complement, even as the best Christian life would add the *gift* of wisdom as speculative analog to infused virtue—and that even if the believer lacked *sacra doctrina* (II.II 45.4).

63. As *developed* and not having God as object, acquired virtue differs from natural love of God.

64. On this "through," see *TT*, 195–209.

65. And see, e.g., I.II 58.2 ad 1; *SCG* IV.13 and 42.

66. See *TT*, 168–72.

67. And see *SCG* IV.20.

68. Thomas uses *Metaphysics* V here (*TT*, 54).

69. There is a *logical* procession of Son from Father, and Spirit from both, but no temporality here and certainly no primordial Good above, before, or other than Father, Son, and Spirit, the one God.

70. And see *TT*, 72–74.

71. I *Sent* d. 26 2.2 ad 2, cited in *TT*, 357.

72. And see *TT*, 179.

CHAPTER 3

1. Thomas's commentary on the *Nicomachean Ethics* concerns virtue but does not constitute his teaching in quite the same way as these texts.

2. In *ST*, that question comes fourth, after three articles on habit. It comes second in *DV*.

3. Numerous influential and diverse treatments of Thomas's ethics—including treatments focused on his conception of virtue—all but ignore his treatment of habits: e.g., Jean Porter, *Recovery of Virtue*; John Finnis, *Aquinas*; John Bowlin, *Contingency and Fortune*; Denis Bradley, *Twofold Human Good*; and Ralph McInerny, *Ethica Thomistica*.

4. Servais Pinckaers, "*La vertu*." And see, e.g., Daniel Nelson, *Priority of Prudence*, 72–76.

5. See, e.g., Marcel Mauss, "*Les techniques du corps*," *Journal de Psychologie* 32.3–4 (1936); and Pierre Bourdieu, *Outline of a Theory of Practice* (New York: Cambridge University Press, 1977).

6. Other features are inessential given our interests or are treated later.

7. Within a given capacity, habits require the coordination of multiple variables themselves capable of different adjustments (I.II 49.4). For our purposes, the point needn't concern us.

8. I put aside complexities posed by certain intellectual habits like "understanding" (*intellectus*) (II.II. 49.2).

9. More precisely, they do not bear them just *in themselves*, apart from the way

they might be coordinated with other capacities to form together a more comprehensive capacity.

10. This does not violate the consistency criterion mentioned below but allows us to proleptically refine it. That criterion entails that *soul*, in which the habit resides *essentially*, be able consistently to perform the operation corresponding to the habit. Lance maintains that even as his body fails to comply.

11. While we can envision a habit and acts directly opposed to self-absorption, such as a habit or acts of self-neglect or appropriate self-regard, it is difficult to imagine an act or habit *opposed* to bicycling. This point traces a distinction between two sorts of operative habits, moral and nonmoral ones.

12. More literally but less clearly: "A habit is a disposition according to which what is disposed is well- or ill-disposed either to itself (i.e., its nature) or to what it is ordered to as end."

13. And see, Joseph Pilsner, *HA*, esp. 70–140.

14. Thomas actually identifies color as vision's formal object, but that detail does not concern us here.

15. A power need not be sufficient to effect an operation: there's no operation of hearing, e.g., without sound.

16. More than mere inclination for what is perceived as good, will's operations are complex, varied, and involve interchange with intellect. See, David M. Gallagher, "Will and Its Acts."

17. Every operative habit is a habit of the soul but not every habit of the soul is operative. Grace is subject in soul, effecting a transformation in relation to soul's nature not immediately related to operation (I.II 50.2; 110, esp. 110.4). This qualification applies in what follows.

18. If the habit's immediate subject were the creature itself, the habit would be immediately related to the *creature's* nature, precisely because the creature's nature was its subject.

19. More on this qualifier—"immediately"—below.

20. Or if we elide various senses of "nature." Properly, human nature is not merely soul but soul-and-some-matter. So understood, this would show that by relating to soul (not soul-and-some-matter), bodily habit is related to its subject's (the body's) nature, *not* the creature's. However, here, Thomas uses "nature" more loosely so that (a) soul can (at least) seem to count as a human's nature (e.g., I.II 50.2 ad 1), and (b) considered as *form*, soul is both body's and creature's nature. I follow Thomas's usage.

21. See, e.g., I 75.5; 76.1, 4, and 7; *Sentencia libri De anima* 2.1.15–16.

22. While body just is matter-informed-by-soul, we can nonetheless consider it in isolation (as matter so informed) or in its relation to soul, to which it is not identical. It's the latter Thomas has in view.

23. Aristotle, Thomas notes, does not say health is habit *simpliciter* but *as a habit* (I.II 50.1 ad 2). On one formulation bodily "habits" are, due to their changeability, not habits but dispositions (I.II 49.2 ad 3). Nonetheless, Thomas often calls them "habits."

24. It's in this sense that *difficile mobile* does not divide species (*DM* 7.2 ad 4).

25. For clarity, I reverse Thomas's order of presentation.

26. After drawing I.II 49.2 ad 3's distinctions, Thomas says "this (*hoc*) seems more consonant with Aristotle's intent." While (1) immediately precedes the remark, it's not certain whether he means (1) vis-à-vis (2) or both vis-à-vis the notion of disposition as habit's genus, for he proceeds by citing Aristotle's point that bodily determinations that become actually *difficile mobile* are called "habits" while easily lost *scientia* is called not habit but "disposition." The example shows the essential connection of *difficile mobile* with the term and *ratio* of habit and the link between its absence and disposition. His point supports (2) as much as or more than (1), so he may mean to suggest the priority of *both* to the notion of disposition as habit's genus. Whatever he's claiming about *Aristotle's* intent, nothing in I.II 49.2 ad 3 suggests Thomas is not himself endorsing (2), the essential link between *difficile mobile* and habit, or the corresponding terminology. His subsequent account presupposes as much, and he elsewhere explicitly endorses (2) (e.g., *DM* 7.2 ad 4, 7.3 ad 4). Indeed, *DM* 7.2 ad 4 not only endorses (2) but seems to *deny* (1), and *DM* 7.3 ob 4 ascribes (2) to Aristotle. I.II 49.2 ad 3 links *difficile mobile* to habit; its absence to disposition: in marking and naming the division within the species habit and between that species and disposition, *difficile mobile* is essentially linked to habit's term and *ratio*. What lacks *difficile mobile* is, at best, habit only specifically.

27. While opinion (*opinio*) can change as quickly as what it's about (e.g., that Sam's doing *D*; now he's not), it is an *S-habit* (but not a virtue, for it's related to falsity and truth alike) (I.II 55.4; 57.2 ad 3; *CNE* 6.3, esp. 2). And it's an *S-habit* rather than *S-disposition* just because it's a determination of *soul* rather than *body*. While not (usually) *difficile mobile* itself, it's subjected in what is. The point illustrates well how mere membership in *S-habit* entails next to nothing about a determination's *actual* stability. Perhaps opinion is an inherently imperfect *S-habit*, a disposition that, due to its radically changeable cause, never stops being one, never becomes habit. Against that stands a sort of true opinion, presumably stable, that Thomas likens unto but says falls short of prudence (II. II 47.12 ob 1; *PC* III.3.11). And see I.II 51.3.

28. In both cases, different entailments follow from correct application of the species term than from the perfect-member term. Still, rationality relates differently to the human species than *difficile mobile* to *S-habit*.

29. This is why when it comes to *species* division he turns to and depends on the subject's identity, mediating the matter of changeability through that. Vagueness is incompatible with what specification demands; relying on subject avoids it. In contrast, given his aims a division within *S-habit* between habit and disposition that is both determinate and characterized in terms of a perfect/imperfect rubric can bear the challenge of vagueness.

30. This "mere disposition" is not the same "disposition" denoting the genus in which habit is species. Habit is disposition but not mere disposition as humans are animals but, through reason, not mere animals.

31. In both cases, the adjectives, *complete* and *inchoata*, are distributive, modifying both *scientia* and virtue: *dispositiones quae sunt . . . nondum perfecte, sicut scientia*

et virtus inchoata. Quod autem dicit secundum speciem, includit perfectas dispositiones, quae dicuntur habitus, sicut scientia et virtus complete. While Thomas quotes Simplicius (on Aristotle's *Categories*), he is articulating his own position, interweaving Simplicius's remarks, and melding Aristotle's different treatments in *Metaphysics* V.20 and *Categories* 8. Throughout I.II 49.1 and 2 Thomas draws from these authorities, even as he articulates his own distinct position.

32. This *inchoata scientia et virtus* seems not to be that initial, strictly natural orientation that goes by the same name and on which habit builds as principle. The clearest evidence is Thomas's characterization of them here as "in preparation and propensity not yet perfect," not yet arrived at habit, which implies they are substantially *beginnings* of habit, imperfect *S-habits*. In contrast, I.II 51.1 says natural virtues are *not* properly beginnings of habit. And see I.II 74.4 ad 3.

33. Complexities obtain for infused virtue, which one mortal sin banishes. We can't address the matter fully here, but note: (1) this is due to their unique dependence on charity as cause, which is in salient respects unlike the cause of acquired or non-supernatural habit; (2) Thomas's clarity that this is *not* the case for acquired virtue; (3) his citation of and attempt to honor Aristotle in treating infused virtue's loss (I.II 71.4); (4) the possibility of a sense, unique to charity, in which it is *difficile mobile* in virtue of its cause (e.g., stable by its cause's nature, easily lost only accidentally) (*DV* 1 ad 10). See too I.II 65.3 ad 2.

34. As will become clear below and especially in the next chapter, *S-virtue* is simply *S-habit*, our (2) above, that meets a few additional conditions. That is, it is likewise a determination of soul rather than body that admits of a *difficile mobile* division between mere disposition and habit/virtue. What those additional conditions are we'll see shortly, but for now we can safely treat the two terms together.

35. More precisely, any half-decent orientation of will, appetitive power, or, in the case of prudence, mind.

36. Osborne, *AA* and *PIV*, esp. 49–50, 53–54.

37. This is his central claim in two articles. In *AA*, he says that those without charity can have "only habits or dispositions for performing good acts" and that this is what Thomas means by the "true virtue" that can be had without charity (*AA*, 301). Such "true virtues" lack connection for Osborne, are "very imperfect" (294), and fail to make one live "a virtuous life" (294, 283), yet he also speaks of them as consistently producing good acts (299, 301), which is incompatible with his insistence on their disconnection and which entails their essential and profound instability. His later *PIV* "corrects" this, stressing the radical instability and inconsistency of these dispositions and their acts (*PIV*, 49, 53, 44, 46, 58).

38. Osborne's *PIV* details neither Thomas's changeability-related distinctions between *S-habit* and *S-disposition* nor that within *S-habit* and can seem to waiver on these points (e.g., cf. *PIV* 44, 48, 55–57). It can seem to elide "belonging to *S-virtue*" and "attaining virtue/habit's *ratio* in the sense of not missing something *essential* to it" so that its "true" seems to refer to both indiscriminately or simply to the latter. But *PIV*, 53 and 57 acknowledge the difficulty.

39. He calls it only "imperfect" virtue (e.g., I.II 65.1). The only time he calls some-

thing "true but imperfect virtue" (II.II 23.7), he's referring, we'll see, *not* to mere disposition, but an authentic, inherently unified habit of virtue, imperfect only as compared to charity-related virtues. And see I.II 65.1 where, citing Gregory, *vera*, true, is applied only to virtue proper, in distinction from disconnected, imperfect virtue.

40. One might wonder whether Phelps's habit is specifically different from the novice's. Vitally, whether it is or not, the professional's habit does not stand to the novice's as habit to mere disposition, authentic virtue to disposition thereto. Supposing they are specifically different (likely not Thomas's view), the novice's habit would not be an imperfect version of the professional's but simply a different habit. Supposing they are not (likely Thomas's view), the novice's habit is imperfect in relation to the professional's *while still being on the habit-side* of the habit/mere disposition divide. This is a different (and different sort of) perfect/imperfect distinction than the division within *S-habit* between habit and disposition; it is a division *within* the habit slice of *S-habit*. On this distinction, see I.II 66.1. In the case of swimming, cycling, and so on, the analogue to mere disposition—to an imperfect *S-habit*, an imperfect habit in *that* sense—would be the case of the person who struggles just to swim, ride, etc. Notwithstanding their differences, novice and professional alike, due to their determinations' *at will*-ness and *difficile mobile*, stand together on the habit-side of the line dividing habit from mere disposition.

41. The glutton's sensitive appetite obeys his standing judgment about the goodness of eating *lots* of food, and his appetite obediently hungers even after it would have stopped had he not so corrupted it.

42. The final qualifying phrase honors the fact that sensitive powers are only obedient to reason to some degree and do not need will to use them in order for them to operate. Thus, these powers can obey reason through will's use of them, but do not need will to effect their exercise in order for them to operate.

43. Stephen Brock, *Action and Conduct*, 183.

44. Concerns about circularity are addressed, e.g., in Eleonore Stump, *Aquinas*, 278–84. Such concerns stem from taking Thomas as answering the question "How is action as such possible?" rather than answering, about some act, the moral psychological question "What happened?"

45. The will's "application of its own power of using to a use cannot be a separate act, prior to the use; this would lead to an infinite regress in the will's use of itself. In causing one of his powers to act, the human agent is simultaneously causing himself to do so" (Brock, *Action and Conduct*, 183).

46. Bonnie Kent sees Thomas's emphasis on will in relation to habit as departing from Aristotle's notion of habit ("Habits and Virtues," 116–30). Yet, will's connection to habit, I've argued, seems inevitable given habit's relation to operation, on which Aristotle insists. Thomas's emphasis here thus follows, in part, from honoring Aristotle's commitment to the habit/operation relation.

47. When animals have such quasi-habits, often they do by having undergone the *use* we call training—they have been *used* by us. But it is *not* because Tucker acquired

tricks by being trained that they fail to count as habits; many human habits are similarly acquired but still count as habits.

48. This is Brock's language. The steed who, seeing the newborn antelope underfoot, refuses to move despite her mount's urging seems to refrain from exercising her quasi-habit of obedience. Thomas ascribes such cases to the "estimative (*aestimativa*) power" of animals—that by which we explain migratory flight or a squirrel's nut-gathering (I 78.4). For Thomas, these things are done by nature. So, the horse remains unmoved not through refraining from *using* her quasi-habit, but because the "estimative power" trumps it: an instinct that a "habit" of training has yet to (and perhaps cannot) reach.

49. Taking hair-growth medicine is an act of use but not of growing the hair. The healthy person who runs a race does not directly use her habit of *health* but of movement—health stands to *usus* here as the knife's sharpness to the act of cutting (itself an act of *usus*).

50. Here, I count fluency as the bright line separating habit from its antecedents.

51. "Natural virtue" as I, following Thomas, use the term should not be confused with acquired virtue—which some label "natural virtue" in order to distinguish it from infused or "supernatural" virtue.

52. Chapter 4 treats the more complicated case of prudence.

53. Thomas here seems to call these inclinations "principles of common law," although elsewhere, e.g., I.II 63.1, he declares such principles cognitive, subjected in intellect, which precludes their being the inclinations themselves. Perhaps, (a) he's using the phrase more broadly here and/or (b) he regards appetitive counterparts (e.g., I.II 23.7 ad 4) to the cognitive principles as themselves counting as or worth calling "practical principles." The alternative, that he's paralleling (1) the relation of principles to intellect to (2) some unnamed X in relation to appetite, is grammatically and contextually dubious.

54. I treat natural virtue–related exegetical questions that arise in comparing I.II 63.1 and 51.1 elsewhere.

55. In claiming that Christians and non-Christians share a species of virtue—acquired virtue—I am taking a stand on a somewhat controversial interpretive matter. This book is not the place to make my full case, but I give a sketch in chapter 7, even as various claims intervene between now and then. To be clear, however, *this issue swings free from the question of whether Thomas affirms pagan virtue and from my case that he does.* It touches on those claims only insofar as I compare the virtues attainable by pagans with the acquired virtues of Christians who possess them. Readers who deny that Christians can possess acquired virtues will reject that comparison, but nothing in their position on which virtues Christians can possess requires them to reject my reading of Thomas on pagan virtue.

CHAPTER 4

1. Thus: (1) I.II 55's *prooemium* promises consideration of virtue's essence (55), subject (56), and division (57–62), and 57's *prooemium* clarifies that examination of intellectual and moral virtues (57–61) will precede theological virtue (62), a nonhuman virtue. As we'll see, 61's last article reminds that "we have been talking about [*human* virtue] up

to this point" (I.II 61.5). While prior articles occasionally mention particular nonhuman virtues or use them as examples (e.g., 56.3 refers to faith; 57.1 to charity), direct treatment of nonhuman virtue, including its relations to human virtue, only begins at Question 62, *after* 61.5's introduction of the division. 61.5's remark thus stands as closing bracket to Thomas's central focus on human virtues. Its point—and mine—is not that he *exclusively* considers human virtues in the intervening articles but that (a) he *at least* has them in view at each point, even as many remarks also apply to nonhuman virtue (e.g., most of 56's consideration of where virtue is subject), and (b) his generic references to *virtue* encompass human virtue. (2) Having said that *virtue's* essence is 55's focus, in 55.1–3 Thomas explicitly treats *human* virtue. (3) Throughout 55–61.5, he regularly uses *virtue* as a synonym for *human virtue* (e.g., I.II 55.2; 55.3 ob 1 and the corpus's last line; 56.4). After 61.5, *virtue* sometimes refers exclusively to nonhuman virtues (e.g., I.II 62.2 ad 3), but until then in no case does it exclude *human virtue*. (4) With the section's declared focus on *virtue*, 58.3 nonetheless exclusively considers "whether *human* virtue is sufficiently divided between moral and intellectual," neither mentioning infused cardinal virtues, which admit of that division, nor explaining why theological virtues do not (I.II 58.3 ad 3). He delays addressing these matters until *after* 61.5—in I.II 63.3 and 62.2, respectively.

2. My subsequent remarks on intellectual virtue mostly exclude prudence.

3. In I.II 55.3 ad 2, Thomas speaks of a power's perfection that is not virtue and "even directly contrary to [right] reason." Such habit is perfect *qua completion* but is not a *good* completion and so not virtue.

4. Arts are operative, *not* bodily, habits. The operative/bodily distinction should not be confused with that between speculative (*speculativus*) virtue (e.g., *scientia*, liberal arts) and art. The latter distinction is *within* operative habit (I.II 57.3 ad 3). Whether Thomas considers art an intellectual virtue is a bit ambiguous (cf. *speculativus* and *intellectualis* in I.II 57.3), but I refer to *all* good nonmoral operative habits, speculative and artistic, as intellectual virtues.

5. All powers have a *naturalis inclinatio*, natural movement "internal" to them independent of will—intellect toward truth, for instance, or sight to seeing (I 78.1 ad 3). But, apart from will's involvement, this natural movement is *not* movement of agent *qua* agent. They are elicited operations not (necessarily) commanded by will (I 81.3 and ad 2; 81.2; 80.1 ad 3). And see Brock, *Action and Conduct*, 168–174.

6. See I.II 56.3 and 57.4. They do not bear on our claims, but complexities obtain concerning the sense in which intentional error counts as product of artistic or intellectual virtue. Cf. I.II 57.3 ob and ad 1.

7. We are concerned with virtue here as *principle*, not *object*, of action. See n.10 below.

8. Nor do they bear on the goodness of the *end* to which one puts them, on which more below.

9. I am indebted here to Brock, *Action and Conduct*, 160–186, esp. 184.

10. For Thomas, one cannot hate the truth *per se*, but one can (perversely) hate particular truths for reasons extrinsic to their identity as truth *simpliciter* (e.g., as disclosing something one hates) (I.II 29.5). Matters are complex, but the essential point is twofold:

1. We are here considering *scientia* not as body of truths but as *habit* and, when used by will, principle of intellectual operation. Thus, one's orientation to *scientia qua* habit can be, accordingly, different from one's orientation to *scientia* considered as "set of particular truths," and different still from *scientia* considered as truth *simpliciter*; 2. It will always be a matter of *will* how one orients oneself to *scientia qua* habit, for *scientia itself* does not bear on its own (good) use; it enables intellect to operate when *will commands*. Only *qua object* of will, not *principle*, might it (thanks to any affiliation with truth) "contribute" to its use (i.e., by *being* desired), but this is not the right sort of contribution. So, notwithstanding the natural desire for truth, while *scientia* may differ from other intellectual habits vis-à-vis "relatedness-to-truth," this does not matter in this context.

11. Hatred or love might lead to acts that affected her possession of *scientia*, but *hatred* or *love* is principle here—*not scientia*.

12. Even the person who does not know geometry can wish she did: vaguely sensing the proofs' elegance and her teacher's joy in them, she imagines having the habit as her teacher does. She has a notion of the *scientia* and longs to exercise it, but cannot.

13. Geometric *scientia*, *qua* habit, actualizes potency and puts the intellect in "act" in that sense, the sense *having* a habit necessarily does, but that is a different matter than *using* the habit.

14. Doing action habitually as compared to non-habitually but well adds at least a certain ease-related pleasure attendant to the action entirely apart from one's *stance* toward that pleasure. Bo has an overeating habit: when overeating, he feels, thanks to habit, a pleasurable ease. But he may despise that natural feeling of ease, in what he regards an unnatural action. He may also despise even the food-related pleasures of filling his belly. All of this raises questions about pleasure's phenomenology but surely we can distinguish the pleasurable ease habit brings willy-nilly from either one's judgment of or stance toward that pleasure (e.g., a shoeshiner is ashamed at how easily he shines shoes) or the pleasure the habit enables (e.g., the same shoeshiner feels the ease of action but does not find the shining itself pleasurable). Regarding the latter, we can imagine a runner who, willy-nilly, thanks to her running habit feels the natural ease of habit in her running but, because of an injury, does not find pleasure in the running itself—this, even if she loves running.

15. Of course, there *can* be mutually reinforcing relations between intellectual virtue and love. Often love grows in proportion to increasing excellence. Apparently, Wayne Gretzky, even at three, would watch entire hockey games on TV and weep when they ended. Presumably, this love drove him to pursue his hockey habit and presumably, the more excellent he became, the more in hockey he found to love and enjoy. Yet there is no *essential* connection between intellectual virtues and inclination to their use or love for the activity they enable: Gretzky-like skill does not entail Gretzky-like love; nor Gretzky-like love, Gretzky-like skill. But when skill and love do reinforce one another, they sometime produce performances that set new standards of excellence for a given practice.

16. And principles in the sense in which an end or object can counts as such.

17. Taken abstractly, intellectual virtue's operation is good—as opposed to vice's. But *actual* operation and human action always occur in a context involving means, ends,

circumstances, etc. And an act's goodness is a matter of that act as *actually* done. Nothing can make an intrinsically evil act good, but any defect in ends, circumstance, means, etc., renders an act evil (I.II 18.8 and 9; Pilsner, *HA*, 234–36).

18. And if she is not using it here, other things being equal, she likely does not *have* it. Thomas treats "false virtue" elsewhere (e.g., II.II 55), but note that if a soldier in an evil cause appears to exercise courage, because these deeds are evil, necessarily virtues cannot be their principles. Because these habit *can* be so used, they are not virtues. In speaking of "false virtue," it's important to distinguish between (1) bad habits or vices that might appear to be virtue (e.g., II.II 47.13's "false prudence"), and (2) habits that fail to be entirely good or dispositions prior to virtue that nonetheless may be mistaken for virtue (e.g., II.II 47.13's examples of imperfect prudence, and some of II.II 123.1 ad 2's examples).

19. Someone might object that such propaganda is not really art and thus that artistic virtue is not used here. Yet for Thomas art concerns the capacity to make things well, not the ends for which one makes them or their moral qualities—which are matters of the will and moral virtues. For an artist coerced into producing propaganda, at the level of *making*, the same skills are in play as in her uncoerced work. What is not in play is a connection of the art to her moral vision. But *that*, Thomas reminds, is not artistic but moral virtue. Conversely, the artist who leaves fascism to join the resistance may have ideological work to do, but she won't need to relearn how to paint.

20. Brock, *Action and Conduct*, 160–86. A concept becomes increasingly determinate for us the better we understand the various relations of inference (of entailment and exclusion) that follow from its application. On the point in Hegel, see Robert Brandom, *Tales of the Mighty Dead: Historical Essays in the Metaphysics of Intentionality* (Cambridge, MA: Harvard University Press), 178–209.

21. Most precisely, one is primed to so desire it. For, one can regard something under the formality of good and thus be inclined toward it, but with an inclination that, apart from various factors, is not to pursue it *here and now*. In such cases, one's will is engaged in "simple willing" (*simplex voluntas*) (I.II 18.5; 21.4).

22. See, e.g., McInerny, *Ethica Thomistica*, 3–11.

23. Interdependence with moral virtue distinguishes prudence from *synderesis*, an intellectual virtue of understanding practical principles, on which moral virtues depend but which does not itself depend on them (I.II 58.4 and 5; II.II 47.6). Prudence's uniqueness is partly due to the interrelation between practical reason's and will's acts, such as counsel (*consilium*) and choice (*electio*), a formally volitional operation of reason (I.II 14.1 ad 1) and formally rational act of will (I.II 13.1), respectively.

24. Along with all virtues of appetitive parts and those specially related thereto, like prudence. While my focus, with Thomas, is on human moral virtue, none of this suggests he thinks theological and infused moral virtues are not virtues *simpliciter*, only that he also here regards human virtues as such.

25. "These sort (*huiusmodi*) of habits" he says, "are called virtue *simpliciter*." The pronoun's antecedent is virtues that make their possessor and her work good—and, behind that, the preceding sentence's examples: "justice or temperance . . . and the like."

That all this at least *includes* the human species of these virtues is clear, for: (1) The corpus begins with Thomas referring to and drawing on what he "said above" in I.II 55.1, 2, and especially 3 about virtue, which explicitly referred to and concerned human virtue. Nothing intervenes between the opening line and these remarks about virtue *simpliciter* to suggest human virtue has dropped out of the picture. (2) When he explains how intellect too "can be subject of virtue *simpliciter*," he cites prudence as an example, glossing it as concerning *recta ratio*, right reason (I.II 56.3). If he meant to exclude human prudence and speak only of nonhuman or infused prudence, he would surely gloss it in terms not of conformity to *right reason* but *lex/regula Divina*, Divine law/rule, for infused prudence conforms to *that* and in the key discussions of infused prudence Thomas refers to that, usually *in explicit contrast* to right reason (e.g., I.II 63.2 and 4). These distinct rules distinguish the species. (3) I.II 56.1 and the article after 56.3, 56.4 (esp. ad 1), explicitly frame their remarks as concerning (or at least including) *human* virtue. 56.3 and 4 concern whether virtue can be subject of, respectively, intellect and passions. To claim that 56.3 excludes human virtue would implausibly have Thomas unconcerned to show that human virtue could be subject in intellect, then immediately showing that it can be subject in the passions. (4) There is nothing in 56.3 or its context to suggest he is excluding human virtue. More, the passage falls squarely in that portion of the virtue treatise focused on human virtue, where generic references to *virtue* include human moral virtue (see n.1).

26. "Intellect," too he explains, "according as it has an ordering to will, can be subject of virtue *simpliciter*," and he cites prudence as an example (I.II 56.3). And see *DV* 7.

27. Ralph McInerny, *Disputed Questions on Virtue*, 41.

28. This is true too of Thomas's use of *simpliciter*, at least in this context. Thus, at I.II 57.3 ad 1, drawing the same distinction that occupied I.II 56.3, he says intellectual virtues that lack a special relation to will "fall short of the perfect (*perfecta*) ratio of virtue." Here, he uses perfection and simplicity language synonymously. He does the same later when he declares human moral virtue in relation to infused virtue to be, in a different sense, less than perfect, less than virtue *simpliciter* (I.II 65.2).

29. And note its direct contrast to malice/vice "*simpliciter*" (*CNE* 7.1.10).

30. I.II 56.3 establishes that human moral virtue *is* unqualified virtue, virtue *simpliciter*; I.II 61.1 explains that the term *virtue* means human moral virtue. If we thought 56.3 were merely making 61.1's linguistic point, that it did not address what virtue *simpliciter* was, then we'd need to understand I.II 65.2 in that way too. There, with the same language of virtue *simplicter dicta* and virtue *secundum quid*, or "according to something," Thomas says that infused virtue is virtue *simpliciter* and human moral virtue is virtue *secundum quid*. The task of reconciling 56.3 and 65.2 awaits; my point here is that this feature of the two texts is shared such that what holds for the one on this point necessarily holds for the other. That is, either they both make merely a linguistic point along 61.1's lines *or* they both make a deeper point about what virtue *simpliciter* is. The context of each and Thomas's usage elsewhere indicate the latter. Still, should someone hold that 61.1 is making not a linguistic but substantive point *à la* 56.3, that claim would support my more basic point.

31. Thus, Osborne declares it "dangerous to use only one text to delineate the many

states of virtues for which Thomas provides an account" (*PIV*, 48–49) and faults others on this front (40), yet he himself neglects texts like I.II 49.1–2 that he sees as essential for his own claims (49).

32. Similar complexities lurk in *DV*: "If the last part is omitted," he says, Augustine's definition fits every human virtue (*virtuti humanae*) (*DV* 2).

33. Thus, I.II 63.2 and 4 identify the phrase as peculiar to *infused* virtue's definition.

34. Mark Jordan claims that one result of Thomas's theological emphasis is that he "must rework the notion of habit that he has constructed so carefully in I.II Questions 49–54 using Aristotle and Aristotle's interpreters" ("Theology and Philosophy," 238). It is unclear just what he means. I have argued that Thomas constructs his account of habits to vindicate infused virtues as habits. He reworks Aristotle's account but does so by carefully constructing his own and using Aristotle to do so.

35. Stressing the difference between Augustine's and Aristotle's "competing," "very different" definitions of virtue ("Theology and Philosophy," 238), Jordan portrays Thomas as faced with a "contest" (236) that he resolves "only by subordinating Aristotle to Augustine" (237). And he regards it as "puzzling" (238) when, after concerning himself with the Aristotelian definition in I.II 55.1–3, Thomas adduces Augustine's definition in I.II 55.4, which Jordan declares "much more . . . theological" because it mentions divine infusion (238). Yet what it means for Thomas to be engaged in theology or to consider acquired virtues "as if from above" (238) is not a matter of explicitly mentioning God, and certainly not a matter of his devaluing acquired virtue (240–41)—as even Jordan's own more accurate earlier remarks suggest (235–36). And while Jordan rightly sees the reliance on Augustine's definition as *prospectively synthetic*, part of efforts building toward I.II 61.5 and later texts, he does not consider the extent to which it meets synthetic aims both more immediately and, retrospectively, in relation to the habit treatise—those I highlight here.

36. On the definition's role in the period, see, e.g., Stanley Cunningham, *Reclaiming Moral Agency*, esp. 49–56 and 159–61, as well as his extensive bibliography.

37. Proponents include, e.g.: John of St. Thomas, *Cursus Theologicus*, 17.2; Garrigou-Lagrange, *Three Ages*, 67–70; and Jacques Maritain, who claims Thomas denied that non-Christians could achieve "connected virtues" (*Science and Wisdom*, 138–61). Osborne's *PIV*, n.19 and n.23 offer further bibliography.

38. Chapter 6 addresses worries about how one can become virtuous if having any virtue requires having them all.

39. And: I.II 17.1; 57.6. Prudence makes intellect not only reason well about action, but actually *command* well—to "order," as it were, the will to "do *that* thing" (I.II 58.5 ad 3).

40. And: I.II 58.3 ad 2. Prudence also presupposes principles such as "do no evil" that are naturally known through *synderesis* (II.II 47.6 ad 1), the intellectual habit of understanding practical principles (I.II 57.2; 58.5).

41. This intimate, reciprocal relation between practical reason and will—so intimate that Thomas speaks even of choice as an act of reason (I.II 57.5) and prudence as presenting an end (I.II 66.3 ad 3)—helps account for prudence's numbering among *moral* virtues despite not properly being one or a habit of desire. Because it deliberates about

what to *do*, and because its operation terminates in a command for will to effect, it is numbered among the *moral* virtues (I.II 56.3). Will's orientation continues to play a vital role in each decision along the way to some end. Thus, if Bob is just he wills to invest the estate justly rather than in the heroin market. For each such end, prudence must decide well about the means. See Gallagher, "Will and Its Acts," 78–79 on the point that "each person is always caught up in any number of [chains of ends]," so that the same act may serve as a means to multiple ends or the end with respect to one act of deliberation may stand as means with respect to another.

42. See Bowlin, *Contingency and Fortune*, 2–54, 167–212.

43. That is, they perform one of their respective operations—inclining toward food or spirited defense of wounded pride. These appetites "cause" hunger and anger not by triggering something else—their very movement *is* hunger and anger (or the feeling thereof).

44. And see Bowlin, *Contingency and Fortune*, 34. The parenthetical qualification is key: Thomas knows bodies do not always obey reason/will or do so immediately. As chapter 3 showed, for Thomas, such cases are still importantly different from that of the passions' disobedience.

45. We needn't suppose Thomas thinks one goes over these things explicitly. Also, a genuinely *practical* syllogism begins with *desire*: I find myself *wanting* the cake, and that desire terminates in action because I am oriented by *will* toward a perceived good as end. This is distinct from what G. E. M. Anscombe calls an "idle syllogism," *Intention* 2nd ed. (Cambridge, MA: Harvard University Press, 2000), 59–63.

46. This is the case of the incontinent man (*DM* 3.9 ad 7).

47. Passion does not *overcome* reason, but "trumps" it in the sense of preventing it from issuing the erstwhile good command. See n.41 and n.49.

48. Thomas uses this example to make a different point.

49. The distinction between my anger causing me to do it (or playing a role) and my truly being blinded by rage mirrors that between a crime of passion and what the law calls "temporary insanity." For Thomas, the only cases in which sensitive or irascible appetites truly *overcome* a person and are themselves principles of action are cases of madness and insanity. In such cases, anger, lust, or whatever does not cause a bad *choice*; rather, one makes no *choice* at all—will is bypassed. The act thus fails to count as human and is not something just in itself for which one can appropriately be held *morally* responsible. I could, however, be morally blameworthy, if it were my fault that I were the sort of person who could be so overcome. And see Bowlin, *Contingency and Fortune*, 34–35, 42–48.

50. One may do right accidentally, but in such cases one lacks (or fails to use) the virtue of justice, for, not knowing the right determinate good through prudence, one fails to love it stably.

51. For Thomas, there cannot be a habit that *consistently* causes the right thing to be done that is not a habit of acting *with* right reason—a unified virtue.

52. Thomas deploys this illustration for different purposes.

53. For Thomas, this shaping is not done exclusively by one's power: one always works on a self already and still being shaped by numerous forces.

54. On Thomas's differences from Kant here, see Brock, *Action and Conduct*, 139–49.

55. For Thomas, this goodness of conformity to *rectam rationem* is necessarily perfective of and truly good for—and thus satisfying for and truly desirable to—the agent. Action with right reason conduces to human flourishing, happiness. It delights the will. Its failure to do so shows the agent is not (or not yet) virtuous. For Thomas, unlike Kant as typically read, *conformity with right reason* as a reason for acting is in no way counterposed to *happiness* or *fulfillment* as a reason, so that one could act for what is in accord with right reason and not act for what will make one happy. The Thomistically virtuous discover, correctly, that happiness comes through action in accord with right reason—that such action is the specification or material content of happiness. Acting for right reason is not different than acting for one's happiness; it is a *way*—the *right way*—of acting for happiness.

56. I am indebted to John Bowlin for conversation on this point.

57. In this passage Thomas parallels passion's contribution and the body's, but the broader context of I.II 59.4 and 5 indicates that he is not implying the necessity of bodily integrity for possession of virtue.

58. Vice too brings a kind of unity, but one ordered to false good, bad action done wholeheartedly. On this Harry Frankfurt and Thomas might agree, *The Reasons of Love* (Princeton: Princeton University Press, 2006), 98–99.

59. The various appetites will at least imperfectly participate reason—and so function as principle(s)—in *some way*, regardless of reason's good or bad character.

60. Thomas alternately depicts rational and appetitive powers as: (1) together, a single principle (as above); (2) agent and instrument (as here). For our purposes here, we can treat them together.

61. Seeing the inherent and necessary unity of the virtues and their particular interdependence may tempt us to wonder whether or in what sense each is distinct. "The subject of a virtue," Thomas reminds, "is that power whose act the virtue is ordained to rectify" (II.II 58.4). Whatever particular power a virtue perfects, *that* is its subject, regardless of the role that power or virtue plays in someone's unified act or operation.

62. See, e.g., *DV* 9.

63. For Thomas, this is the grain of truth in the notion (false on his view) that passions can guide intellect or agent to moral truth. And see Bowlin, *Contingency and Fortune*, 51–53.

64. And, again, as we'll see, virtue can be perfect in the sense of disposing all those subjects as *fully and completely as possible* to the best end attainable. This state is only attainable, Thomas holds, through charity.

65. It is one thing, e.g., for some dog to live up to the *perfect definition* of a dog (e.g., a perfect definition of an imperfect dog), another thing for a dog *itself* to be perfect, for it to live up to a "perfect definition of a perfect dog." Thomas's argument works only as a version of the latter: human moral virtue is cardinal because "what is perfect is more

principle than what is imperfect" and for the virtues *themselves* to be cardinal what must be perfect is not merely their *ratio* but their attaining it.

66. The Benziger edition incorrectly renders *purgatorias* and *purgati animi* as, respectively, *perfecting* and *perfect*.

67. Glossing *social* as *human*, he describes purifying virtues as "between social—which are *human* virtues—and exemplar" (*inter politicas, quae sunt virtutes humanae*).

68. Occasionally, but not here, Thomas distinguishes between the "virtue of man *qua* good man" and "the virtue of man *qua* citizen," between human and political virtue (*DV* 10). That distinction is not relevant here, for here: (1) he's referring to a single species of virtue, using *political* and *human* synonymously and interchangeably; (2) he's referring to human virtue *not* the political virtue that sometimes names something distinct, for (a) the definition answers to human virtue and (b) otherwise the parallelism with *purgatorias* and *purgati* would disintegrate.

69. With Thomas, I refer here to *grace*. Context indicates he's using grace as synonymous with charity here, but even if he intended a distinction it wouldn't obstruct my point: all charity is a form of grace; insofar as there's a distinction, grace is the broader category.

70. I.II 61.5 describes human virtue as *virtutes prout in homine existunt secundum conditionem suae naturea*, or "virtues as they exist *in humans according to the condition of their [rational] nature*," and I.II 63.2 speaks of *virtus hominis ordinatur ad bonum quod modificatur secundum regulam rationis humanae*, or "virtues of humans *ordered to the good which is determined according to the rule of human reason*." The passages refer to one thing: virtue that inclines to the good that does not exceed but accords with human nature.

71. Recall that habits conduce to a determinate proximate end and different proximate ends demand and specify different habits.

72. See, e.g., II.II 132.3 and 1 ad 2, which cite *DCD* 5.14. Coming chapters, especially the last, help show what we can now only glimpse: how, in this transformation and throughout, with synthetic brilliance and deep devotion to charity, Thomas is striving to honor Augustine. He does so especially through fraternal correction that honors the Bishop's spirit and through a commitment to the reality of sin and the necessity of grace.

73. If he had, then in abandoning the capacities of fallen human beings as the subject in common between objection and corpus, he would have almost certainly had to maintain that he and Augustine were talking about the same sort of virtue.

74. I.II 63.2 ad 2, which chapter 10 treats, constitutes still further evidence that fallen humanity is Thomas's concern. Addressing the compatibility of committing mortal sin with acquisition and maintenance of human virtue, it reinforces that Thomas's affirmation of virtue's attainability without charity concerns fallen humans.

CHAPTER 5

1. The former group includes, e.g., Shanley, *APV*; Kent, *Virtues of the Will*; McKay, "Prudence and Acquired Virtue"; Herdt, *Splendid Vices*; Mark Jordan, "Theology and Philosophy"; the "none at all" group includes Milbank, *TA*; MacIntyre, *WJ*; John Inglis, *Spheres*; the "disconnected," Osborne, *AA* and *PIV* and see chapter 4 note 37.

2. Osborne characterizes as a "misreading of this passage" and "misinterpretation of

Thomas's moral thought" the suggestion "that without charity one can possess acquired moral virtue that is perfect because it is connected with the other moral virtues through prudence" (*PIV*, 53).

3. Chapter 6 treats I.II 65.1 and this interpretive claim.

4. We put aside the difference charity makes for those who have the acquired virtues as well. This imperfection/perfection distinction swings free from that issue.

5. The scare quotes throughout remind that connection is proper to virtue *as such*.

6. Osborne is speaking of acquired prudence: (1) because there *is* no question of whether those without charity can possess *infused* prudence (they cannot) and (2) because the preceding sentence refers first to acquired virtues being "connected through *acquired* prudence" and then, reiterating the point, he drops "acquired" and refers to the acquired virtues being connected through "prudence."

7. Osborne faults others for thinking "even the [acquired] virtue of prudence can be possessed without charity" (*AA*, 301).

8. Osborne supposes that I.II 65.2 teaches that acquired prudence cannot be had without charity (e.g., *AA*, 291–92). Yet his later *PIV* claims that he has "never held or implied this position" (*PIV*, 57) and argues for the attainability without charity of "imperfect acquired prudence," a loosely held, narrowly delimited disposition to reason correctly that fails to connect the virtues. Such prudence, however, lacks right reason's character, an *essential* component of virtue's *ratio*.

9. It is possible but unlikely that I.II 65.1 concerns moral virtues in general and not acquired virtues alone. Nothing is at stake for my argument in this since 65.1's points would hold for acquired virtues regardless. I proceed as though 65.1's explicit focus is on acquired virtues, explaining my reasoning in another note and the next chapter. Also, even if some earlier texts concerned moral virtues *generally*, their points would necessarily hold for acquired virtue.

10. Why the "other"? Prudence is distinguished from the (other) moral virtues because it is subjected in intellect rather than appetite.

11. Given his reference to what he stated above, I believe he is speaking of acquired virtue, but since he wants to make a point about prudence and moral virtue *as such*, it's irrelevant for our purposes whether the sentence explicitly concerns acquired virtue.

12. For now, mirroring Thomas's diction at this juncture of the argument, I refer to the "prudence" related to charity without labeling it, but we will see shortly that he is referring to infused prudence. The parenthetical "acquired" honors the fact that the initial point applies to the prudence/moral virtue relation as such.

13. Used inclusively, "moral virtue" includes prudence; used narrowly (the usage when there is talk of interdependency between moral virtue and prudence), it refers to appetitive virtues alone. Initially he uses the phrase inclusively when he refers to moral virtue's attainability without charity. Thus, the articles "above" to which he refers (e.g., I.II 63.2) as showing moral virtue's attainability without charity also show that prudence is essential to virtue's *ratio*, and they number prudence among the moral virtues. In contrast, the narrower use is on display whenever he characterizes moral virtues and prudence as interdependent. This actually underlines his inclusion of acquired prudence in

his affirmation of acquired moral virtue's attainability without charity, for 65.2 presumes prudence's necessity for the possibility of any moral virtue at all.

14. His vagueness may be deliberate, emphasizing that completely unqualified prudence requires charity, even as acquired prudence, imperfect but true, does not.

15. If infused prudence depended on *acquired* moral virtue then for anyone to have infused virtues, she would have to possess acquired virtues too.

16. Given what has preceded—an argument in which points about prudence *as such* are extracted from points about *acquired* prudence—I doubt we can know which.

17. Even if we hold that PNC generates a *scientia* of logic, logic is both not *identical* to speculative reasoning and a notably formal *scientia*. PNC does not *generate* speculative reasoning.

18. I later argue that II.II 23.7 holds forth a charity-dependent perfection for acquired virtue, but not the perfection that is proper to infused virtue.

19. More precisely, the highest good proper to its species: political good for acquired prudence; beatitude for infused. In what follows, I speak of prudence in general, but note well this difference in special matters and that, given beatitude's more comprehensive character, infused prudence attains the *ratio* of prudence as such (insofar as we can speak of such a thing) better than acquired prudence, hence its perfection.

20. See Bowlin, *Contingency and Fortune*, 22–34 and Pilsner, *HA*, 149, 162–64.

21. When the scope is too narrow, the determination falls short of virtue and is a disposition to a virtue, one of I.II 65.1's imperfect virtues.

22. The qualification is vital, as chapter 7 shows. This point is not to be confused with the incorrect claim that in being well-ordered immediately to a more comprehensive end one is necessarily well-ordered immediately to subordinate ends.

23. Such linguistic laxity extends to I.II 65.3, which: asks whether charity can be without the "moral virtues," but its corpus addresses *infused* moral virtue; says infused moral virtues are connected through "prudence," meaning *infused* prudence; and, in ad 2, contrasts infused moral virtue, as 65.3's topic, with *acquired* moral virtue.

24. They can be related to it in *some* way, we'll see: through a higher virtue's mediation they can be directed remotely to an end that, strictly speaking, surpasses it (e.g., *DV* 10 ad 4). II.II 23.7 indicates that acquired virtues are more perfect when had with charity than without, but this is a different perfection that 65.2's.

25. Excepting the happiness attainable even now through the foretaste theological virtue affords. Chapter 6 touches on some of the complexities raised by infused moral virtues, which I consider more fully elsewhere. Given our focus, it suffices simply to note that infused moral virtues pertain to avoiding sin and attaining beatitude, not *in se* to full realization of the political good and its imperfect happiness. See, e.g., II.II 47.14.

26. This defect, we'll see, concerns loving God supremely, a natural duty that, due to original sin, requires charity's healing work for one to fulfill (I.II 63.2 ad 2; 109.2–4).

27. Even supposing acquired virtues were a broader genus of which political virtues were part (which is not the case here for Thomas), that would not undermine my central interpretive claim here.

28. The imperfect and perfect distinctions of I.II 65.1 and 65.2 are clearly different. And 65.2's imperfect virtue is (or at least is included in) 65.1's perfect virtue.

CHAPTER 6

1. The alternatives aren't exclusive; the point, rather, is that habituation-rooted dispositions are *included* in the category of imperfect virtue.

2. The person close to achieving true virtue exercises herself in all the activities of the virtues but has not yet done so sufficiently. The person *in via* exercises herself rightly in some ways but in other ways, to the extent that she acts differently than the virtuous, somewhat wrongly or, at least, nonvirtuosly.

3. As *ex assuetudine*, such inclination is due to a *process* of habituation without or in addition to roots in individual nature.

4. We can distinguish further between: (a) some broader habit, *an implication* of which is inclination to good courage-related deeds; and (b) a narrower habit, bearing especially on courage-related matters, but producing not a *stable* disposition to *good* deeds in this realm but only a more-or-less successful inclination. For our purposes, this distinction is irrelevant: neither is a habit of doing good deeds.

5. It is properly called an *inclination* to do good deeds in respect to its instability and inconsistency. If there is a *habit*, it is not a habit *of doing good deeds* but of acting a certain way, one manifestation of which is the inclination to do good deeds in certain circumstances. *Qua* habit it is not productive of good deeds for it is equally productive of bad ones. An inclination resulting in good deeds may result from or partly constitute the habit but, unlike virtue, this orientation is not altogether constitutive of it.

6. Hypothetically, someone with imperfect virtue could have a *habit* of doing good acts is if she had a habit of unfailingly following a perfectly prudent person's counsel. But this would not be a habit of doing good acts *well* because these acts would be done in this dependent, non-virtuous way (I.II 57.5 ad 2). Regardless, Thomas says nobody could successfully obey such a person without possessing prudence herself (*DV* 6 ad 2).

7. I.II 65.1's claims about moral virtues' inherent unity hold for acquired and infused moral virtue alike. Treating infused moral virtue, 65.2 invokes 65.1's argument. It's unclear whether Thomas presents 65.1's argument as (a) about *acquired* moral virtue, or (b) moral virtue of both species. Regardless, in (a) the argument implicitly holds for moral virtue generally, and in (b) by being about both (or moral virtue generally) it necessarily holds for acquired virtue too. (a) seems more likely given: (1) the mention of and comparison to disconnected virtue, to which there is no analog within infused species, (2) reference to arguments "stated above" that concerned acquired virtue, (3) citation of Cicero as an authority. I refer to 65.1 as explicitly about acquired virtue, but it is irrelevant whether this is correct.

8. II.II 47.13 divides prudence into false, true but imperfect, and true. I believe 47.13's divisions don't map readily onto 65.1's and that its category of simply "true" virtue refers exclusively to infused prudence, for: (1) true prudence here seems to lead to beatitude; (2) 47.14 centrally concerns infused prudence yet calls it *prudence*, while calling acquired prudence *acquired prudence*. Either 47.13's "true but imperfect" category

includes both 65.1's perfect and imperfect virtues, or else its categories are not exhaustive and simply exclude 65.1's perfect virtues. The only sense in which 47.13's "true but imperfect" prudence is *true* is vis-à-vis false prudence, effective reasoning in pursuit of evil. 65.1's virtues, perfect and imperfect alike, are *all* true in that sense. They are all members of *S-virtue*, distinct from false virtue. Thus, 47.13's *true* implicates neither 65.1's perfect/imperfect distinction nor my claim that only 65.1's perfect virtues fully attain virtue's *ratio*. 47.13's virtues are imperfect by not conducing to beatitude; in *that* sense, so are even 65.1's perfect virtues. In that way, 47.13's "imperfect" is more like I.II 65.2's imperfect than 65.1's; yet, in their narrowness, 47.13's *examples* of imperfect virtue fit 65.1's imperfect virtue, *not* 65.2's. Perhaps 47.13's examples belie the full breadth of its "true but imperfect" category, so that 65.1's perfect virtue is included: the political end of 65.1's perfect virtue is imperfect vis-à-vis beatitude, yet categorically more universal than 47.13's cases of business and sailing. Both Angela McKay and Osborne consider II.II 47.13 ("Prudence and Acquired Virtue," 549–52; *PIV*, 57–62). Osborne claims its "true" prudence refers to *both* infused prudence and the acquired prudence attainable only with grace, and that its "true but imperfect" prudence is only the *profoundly* imperfect variety his *PIV* says pagans can attain. McKay and Osborne both leave many questions unanswered *and* take 47.13 as an exhaustive account of the types of prudence open to "sinners." There's no need to do that. Osborne's take on its "true" prudence runs afoul of the *single* object, the *totius bonum finem vitae* that 47.13 declares its end. Acquired and infused prudence have *different* specifying ends (I.II 63.4). Yet, explicating "true" prudence, Thomas refers there only to *one* end of life.

9. Is not this prudence false rather than merely imperfect? It would be false were it ordered to brothel-running as end, but it is ordered directly and exclusively to my good, liberality-related ends and in relation to those ends *alone* I am prudent. It's a measure of its imperfection that this prudence fails to rule out brothel-funding.

10. I have retained the Latin's ambiguity where, arguably, it's unclear whether it is prudence or moral virtue that Thomas says is a "choosing habit."

11. More precisely, only infused virtue with charity can do it *immediately*. II.II 23.7 indicates that acquired virtue *possessed with charity* can be *mediately* directed to beatitude.

12. How does this passage relate to I.II 65.1 in regard to prudence's exclusion here, particularly given the possibility of imperfect prudence among 65.1's imperfect virtues? Suggesting that all of 65.1's imperfect virtues are without imperfect prudence is almost certainly incorrect since 65.1's imperfect virtues include deliberately acquired dispositions. Two possibilities suggest themselves: (1) To view *DVC*'s gradations as non-exhaustive and its wholly imperfect virtue as an especially imperfect subcategory of 65.1's imperfect virtue, which as a broader category, includes imperfect prudence toward its more developed end. 65.1's imperfect virtue is thus not encompassed in *DVC*'s gradations, for they are not included in *DVC*'s true but imperfect connected virtue. (2) To see the prudence which *DVC*'s wholly imperfect virtue is denied as true, acquired prudence. Here, wholly imperfect virtue *can* have or include 65.1–type imperfect prudence, for *DVC* characterizes prudence as "reaching the rule of right reason," which neither 65.1–type imperfect prudence nor wholly imperfect virtue do. This reading makes wholly imperfect virtues coextensive

with 65.1's imperfect virtues. Thomas distinguishes wholly imperfect virtue from grade two because the former can be used evilly and thereby fail to attain virtue's *ratio*. This suggests that (1) or (2) is correct and rules out the inclusion of 65.1's imperfect prudence in *DVC*'s grade two. That grade two is connected and, in *DVC* 2's description, identified with the presence of *any prudence at all* seems to push for (2), as does *DVC* 2 ad 9. I proceed as though (2) is correct but there is no problem for my broader argument if (1) is.

13. Closer still to genuine virtue would be someone who, having exercised herself in *all* matters to do with virtue, is on the brink of having the habits but needs still more exercise.

14. Speaking of "acts of virtue" (*actus virtutis*) (*DVC* 2 ad 9), Thomas means here not acts done *from* virtue, but acts that are good. For example, Thomas refers to a person who has a vicious habit "breaking forth in a virtuous act" (*prorumpat in actum virtutis*) (II.II 78.2 and, e.g., I.II 105.3 ad 1). In other cases, he means an act produced *by* a virtue (e.g., I.II 58.1; I.II 66.2).

15. We are dealing with the case of someone at the end of the imperfect virtue spectrum close to real virtue in the sense that the deeds in question are done *prompte*—promptly. In regard to quickness, she is like the virtuous and unlike the continent who only act relatively slowly and laboriously. She is unlike the virtuous or continent person in that those people do the right thing for the right reason.

16. This point reminds us that Thomas is not simply putting forward an abstract schema disconnected from real experience but is observing human behavior and trying to account for it.

17. While Thomas speaks here of someone acting *well* (*bene*) in anger matters, we should not confuse this *well* with the "good works done *well*" that distinguishes virtue from imperfect virtue. Notwithstanding the *bene*, his point is just that this anger-restraining habit *lacks* relation (or sufficient relation) to right reason, and the works it produces are *merely* good, *not* good works done well. He uses *bene* for grammatical not substantive reasons. Nor is this case identical with that at I.II 58.3 ad 2. Here Thomas discusses *moral* virtue; there perfections of *rational* capacities, perseverance and continence, which he says are *not* perfections of sensitive faculty.

18. Since anger and irascible passions relate to sensitive passions—guarding the goods sensitive passions desire—even apart from matters particular to prudence's corruption, someone with lustful sensitive passion will tend to get angry at or fear the wrong things anyway.

19. Doing this with some consistency would be the work of imperfect food-related prudence.

20. Thus: "The principles of morals are interconnected to such an extent that through a defect in one follows a defect in the others—say, if one were defective on the principle *concupiscence must not be indulged*, which pertains to sensible desire, then sometimes indulging concupiscence, he would do harm and thereby violate justice" (*DVC* 2 ad 4). We can imagine moral life as comparable to a *single* unified *scientia* with multiple principles, like geometry—the violation of one impacting the whole. Insufficient prudence in one matter is insufficient prudence *simpliciter*. But see too n.26 below.

21. How, if this is so, could one ever get this disposition of doing good works of one virtue in the first place? Presumably, by being more productive in one's deliberate cultivation of that disposition than one is destructive by one's neglect. The idea, however, is that while in the short run, one might outrun one's neglect, eventually and inevitably that neglect catches up—overtaking and destroying or damaging one's previous success. Many are the crusading, ostensibly incorruptible politicians eventually entangled in injustice or scandal.

22. And see *DV* 6 regarding the proper good.

23. *DVC* 2's argument concerning the connection of acquired and infused virtues, respectively, follows I.II 65.2's general structure. Specifically, Thomas first argues for the connection of moral (and in this case, acquired) virtues through prudence and then addresses the way charity connects the infused virtues. While not explicitly referring back to prudence as 65.2 did, the substance, citing charity's principle-supplying role, is similar. The parallel reinforces my points about 65.2 concerning the importance of distinguishing between the two stages of Thomas's argument for the unity of infused virtues: beginning with a structural point about prudence and acquired or moral virtue and applying that point more broadly to infused virtue's case.

24. In I.II 63.2 ad 2, his explanation centers on the fact that it is not an *act* that is contrary to a habit but another *habit*: not *several* mortal sins are contrary to a habit of virtue but a habit-constituting *multitude*.

25. See, e.g., I.II 66.1, *DVC* 3, and especially *DVC* 2 ad 7 and ad 18 regarding breadth/depth distinctions.

26. Such points need to shape our reading of passages like I.II 65.1 ad 4, where Thomas says that reason cannot "in any way be called right reason, if it be defective in any principle whatsoever." This can seem to suggest that any error whatsoever—such as that which follows for prudence from original sin's damage—vitiates right reason altogether, which would imply the *impossibility* of pagan virtue. While the remark's immediate context itself belies that claim, we should also allow his explicit, repeated affirmation that pagans *can* possess acquired virtue to govern our grasp of what he means there. Right reason, in fact, admits some error, without ceasing to be *right*: "Virtue's *ratio*," says Thomas, "demands . . . one attain . . . *near* (*prope*) [right reason's] mean," not that mean as a perfect, indivisible point (I.II 66.1 and ad 2; and see, e.g., *CNE* 2.6.5; *Commentaria in Physicorum* 6.1.7; and esp. II.II 33.2). That room for error extends at least as far as the negative consequences that original sin entails. The alternative is to hold that Aquinas contradicts himself when he says things like this or to deny what I.II 65.2 and many other passages clearly affirm about pagan virtue. Neglect of this point may undergird many readings of Thomas as denying "connected" pagan virtue.

27. Thomas claims virtue is caused by acts at once virtuous and vicious: "The acts preceding virtue are . . . virtuous in respect to that which is done . . . but not in respect to the mode of acting, because prior to the acquisition of a habit of virtue a man does not do the acts of virtue in the way in which a virtuous man does [them], namely promptly, with pleasure, without wavering, and without difficulty" (*DV* 9 ad 13). This state remains distant from virtue, even as it presumes right reason's partial participation and the exer-

cise of all rather than just some virtuous acts. To my knowledge, no recent pagan virtue "minimalists" suggest that this antecedent is what outsiders can attain but characterize pagan virtue as something radically more deficient (e.g., restraining anger) (see n.25).

28. See I.II 54.4, 54.2, 54.1 and ad 1, as well as chapter 3.

29. Timothy Williamson, *Knowledge and Its Limits*.

30. Ibid., 125.

31. Ibid.

32. See, e.g., Jeffrey Stout, "A House Founded on the Sea: Is Democracy a Dictatorship of Relativism?" *Common Knowledge* 13.2 (2007), 392–93.

33. See esp., Boyle, "Setting of the *Summa*."

34. Thomas uses *simpliciter* and *perfecte* interchangeably here to modify virtue and the good it produces. For simplicity, I use "perfect."

35. That political virtue is the virtue of man *qua* man is also clear since Thomas contrasts infused virtues or virtues of man *qua heavenly citizen* with virtues of man *qua* man and glosses the latter as virtues of a human as an *earthly citizen* (*DV* 9). We must distinguish human/acquired/political virtues from the more narrowly political or polity-specific virtues that pertain to particular polities and roles therein. Political/acquired virtues answer to man *qua* man, *qua* political animal. When Thomas refers to polity-specific virtues, he (confusingly) (a) calls them political virtues or virtues of a man as a citizen, and (b) calls human or political virtues *virtues proper, moral virtues, virtues of a man as a man*, or the like. Usually, he refers to human/acquired/political virtue as political virtues and their good as the political good but, having noted the distinction, we should not think he is referring to the narrowly political virtues in those cases. And see *PC* III.3, esp. 6–7.

CHAPTER 7

1. That virtue's unity is I.II 65's focus while charity is II.II 23's may explain some of their differences.

2. On the illustrative usage, he depicts the good-end connection by noting that in the case of something ordered to the end, it is in respect of its being so ordered that it is desirable, good. On the explanatory use, good has the *ratio* of end because when X stands to end Y as means, X counts in that regard as good.

3. See, e.g, I.II 56.1 ad 2 and II.II 47.2.

4. Or so regarded: not everything taken as good is truly good *hic et nunc*.

5. Justly but not perfectly. More on this complex point below. For philosophical explication, see Robert Adams, *Finite and Infinite Goods*, 131–76.

6. And MacIntyre *TRV*, 137–38; Bowlin, *Contingency and Fortune*, 40–44.

7. Following Thomas's standard usage, "virtue *secundum quid*" here refers to *human* virtue, not (or not merely) some lesser, more qualified virtue (e.g., polity-specific virtue).

8. The link between the *simpliciter/secundum quid* idiom and the *true and perfect/ true but imperfect* idiom is clearest in the corpus's final lines and II.II 23.7 ad 2. In ad 2, Thomas says no *simpliciter vera* virtue is possible without charity, but in the corpus says that virtue directed to a proximate good is "true but imperfect" unless further ordained

to beatitude by charity. And he immediately notes that "therefore, there is not simply true virtue without charity" (II.II 23.7). Thus, *vera virtus simpliciter* is *vera perfecta* virtue—and true but imperfect virtue really is true virtue, *vera virtus*, just not true virtue *simpliciter*.

9. We needn't distinguish between wealth *qua* state and *qua* materials necessary for that state.

10. Here *all* that is perfective of humanity, even beatitude, is included in and counts as *connaturale*: "That is good for each thing which is fitting (*convenit*) according to its form" (I.II 18.5). *Qua* human nature's one perfect end, beatitude is justly called connatural.

11. And see II.II 55.3.

12. E.g., thanks to its species (e.g., a thieving act) or the way it is desired (e.g., inordinately) or the aspect under which it is desired (e.g., a strictly useful good desired as an end *in se*).

13. And/or it must accord with Scripture.

14. See Pilsner, *HA*, 67–69.

15. Excepting complexities related to malice, Thomas disallows that one intends false goods *as* false. But intention concerns the *facts* not just an agent's description: e.g., praise *from sinners*. See Pilsner, *HA*, 87–91, esp. 89.

16. See II.II 34.5 ad 3; 55.3; *De veritate* 25.1 ob 8 and ad 7; *DM* 3.12 ob 7 and ad 1; 12.2.

17. Ends can be things, actions, and/or states of affairs (e.g., money, a city's right order, participation therein).

18. Vainglory as end is the praise of *these* people, say, where these people are foolish.

19. And see Bowlin, *Contingency and Fortune*, 93–137.

20. She who loves money *per se* is more numismatist or hoarder than miser.

21. Avarice concerns all external goods as useful. It immoderately seeks material objects *qua useful*.

22. This inordinateness can involve seeking quantitatively too much *or* finding in money/its possession too much pleasure. The "avaricious man delights in considering himself as a possessor of wealth" (II.II 118.6). Thomas imagines someone seeking money as final end (I.II 16.4), but doing so is not necessary for being a miser (II.II 118.1 and ad 2 and 3; 118.3 and 4).

23. Or pleasure in money (II.II 118.6).

24. The miser doesn't regard his end as "beyond right reason's measure" but in desiring the particular end he does desire (e.g., $40 trillion), he desires wealth beyond that measure. Right reason's judgment is implicated in constituting indifferent actions (e.g., straw-picking) *as indifferent*. Useful, pleasant, and honest goods alike are necessarily determinate enough that taking them as ends either conduces toward (other things equal) or away from the final good. As specifying action, they must be sufficiently determinate that just having them as end suffices to denominate an act as good or evil (*considered abstractly*, since that end's relation to other ends bears on the morality of the act as performed).

25. Lucifer disregarded God's right rule. Best to read Thomas's example in that light—not misspeaking the Lord's Prayer, say, but praying wicked things.

26. The act has straw-picking as end and something other than moral goodness explains the will's attraction thereto (I.II 18.8 and ad 2).

27. "Picking it up" is proximate end vis-à-vis the remote end of getting the Jews captured and something to which the means of stooping and grabbing as opposed to spearing with pointy cane is ordained as means.

28. Ends/acts neutral in kind only take on moral good's *ratio* due to *another* end/ good to which they are related. If we understood an end more determinately (which I doubt Thomas would allow unless we *also* held a more basic, neutral end, such as straw-picking, as ordered thereto), so that we characterized an end as "earning-money-to-care-for-my-family," then it would have moral good's *ratio* precisely thanks to a relation in which the neutral end/act (e.g., "money") stood to some *in se* good (e.g., "maternal duty"). In themselves, they just are *neutral*.

29. A true proximate end is ordainable *because* good *in se*; its ordainability is no *additional* criterion.

30. The honest good is not identical with the final good. Desiring X for its own sake comports with also desiring X as useful, and every honest good but God is *also* useful (II.II 145.3 ob and ad 3).

31. Since constituted to perfect themselves by acting with reason's correct judgment about good, the good so ascertained will be most desirable for humans.

32. That is only an honest good which is choiceworthy *hic et nunc* (I.II 39.2). The honest good is what reason rightly judges good and will rightly desires here and now. Taken *in abstracto*, sorrow is not desirable *in se*, not an honest good, but it is when reason rightly judges another true good threatened and when will rejects that evil (I.II 39.2). Thomas speaks interchangeably of true good and honest good (e.g., II.II 35.1).

33. "By natural appetite, a man is inclined to desire a proper good (*proprium bonum*), but since this is varied in multiple ways and the good of man consists in numerous things, *it is not possible that there could be in man a natural appetite to these determinate goods given all the conditions that need to be filled for some good actually to be good for him*—for this varies widely in relation to the diverse conditions of persons, time, location, and so on. And for the same reason natural judgment, which is uniform, does not suffice for knowing this good. Therefore, by reason, which compares among different things, it is necessary for a man to discover and judge the proper good—as all the conditions determine it and insofar as it is to be known right here and now" (*DV* 6). Arguably "public reason" Thomists run together (a) natural virtue/inclination to natural goods with (b) goods discovered, here and now by right reason and for which a person *actually* acts, goods sufficiently determinate to be action's principles. (a) is natural but not sufficiently determinate to be the end of some act and just so cannot supply the goodness requisite to make action good, the good that "public reason" readings need; (b) is good but not natural in the way they want. Their appeal to the self-evident character of "basic goods" leans on the natural virtues that, while ordering to goods generically true, are not determinate enough to act for here and now. Insofar as one can act "for them," they are too generic to vouchsafe an act's goodness, a goodness only reliably secured through reason's case-by-case success.

34. *Si vero illud bonum particulare sit verum bonum, puta conservatio civitatis vel aliquid huiusmodi, erit quidem vera virtus, sed imperfecta, nisi referatur ad finale et per-fectum bonum* (II.II 23.7). There are two interpretive possibilities here. On (A), Thomas has two species of virtue in view: one ordered to a true good but not further ordered to beatitude; another ordered to that true good and ultimately to the final good too. The former is acquired virtue, true but imperfect; the latter, infused moral virtue, true and perfect. On (B), Thomas imagines acquired virtue becoming perfect in a new way and doing so thanks to a new relation in which it stands to beatitude. Remaining the self-same virtue, specifically identical, it attains a new perfection by being *additionally* re-ferred to beatitude. I endorse and pursue (B), for: (1) The sentence's grammar cannot sus-tain (A). *Virtus* is surely *referatur*'s subject. (Even were *verum bonum particulare* subject, the claim amounts to the same: for virtue to be referred to perfect good, the particular good must be and, hence, the virtue.) The claim can only be that virtue ordered to a true good can *become* perfect if that virtue/good is *further* referred to beatitude. The "unless referred" (*nisi referatur*) construction with no new subject indicates that whatever is *now* referred to beatitude is *already* also ordered to some particular good, otherwise there is no stable, self-same subject to be referred to beatitude. (2) If infused moral virtue were in view, it would need to be ordered immediately to a different good than acquired virtue's, not the same one only further referred to beatitude. Infused and acquired virtue share a common *matter* (e.g., order in irascible appetite) not a common *good*. Infused moral virtue isn't acquired virtue plus ordination to beatitude. (3) In 23.7, whenever Thomas depicts the relation between virtue or good and its proximate end, he uses a form of *or-dino*. Here, however, he speaks of true but imperfect virtues *referred* (*referatur*) to beati-tude, which on (B) is their *remote* end. While there's no inherent difference in the terms, it's plausible that Thomas might mark the distinction between immediate and remote ordination here by using these two terms: *ordino* for immediate ordination and *refert* for remote ordination. Elsewhere, Thomas analogously tweaks his language to underline a distinction (e.g., *materia* in *BDT* II 3.2 co. 5, and see Pilsner *HA* 140n.185). (4) That Thomas has (B) in mind is further suggested by 23.8, where he explores how charity can serve as *every* virtue's form, directing each to beatitude, without causing any to lose its specific identity, a question (B) raises. (5) The article's overarching logic suggests (B): if (B) is incorrect, 23.7 implies a question—how *should* we think of acquired virtue that is further ordained to beatitude?—that it fails to answer. Further, Thomas elsewhere clearly says acquired virtue *can* be so ordained (*DV* 10 ad 4). On (B), we have at least one place where he tells us how to think of such virtue: as perfect. So, even if (A) or a variation on it is correct, in endorsing (B), I explain a view Thomas clearly endorses elsewhere; (B) adds only the title *perfect* to this virtue, so referred. Whether (A) or (B) is correct, this perfection is *not* the growth in perfection proper to acquired virtue that charity's healing brings. And this remark is *not* referring to acquired virtue becoming or being replaced by infused moral virtue: infused virtue is a different species.

35. Or, if this is not acquired virtue, whatever virtue this is.

36. This helps avoid misreading II.II 23.7 ad 2: there is no "*simply true*" justice with-out charity, but there is *true* justice without charity.

37. Infused moral virtue does not have beatitude itself as immediate *object* but orders its *matter* immediately thereto. It has the same matter (e.g., sensible pleasure) as its acquired counterpart but not the same proximate end (e.g., sensible pleasure as immediately related to beatitude vs. sensible pleasure as immediately related to political good). *For simplicity's sake, in speaking below of infused virtue as immediately or directly ordered to beatitude this is what I mean.* The parenthetical qualification should be understood. And the choice has more than simplicity to commend it: While charity alone has beatitude as object, other infused virtues relate immediately to it by having ordination to it implicated in their object. And since I mean to emphasize the *remoteness* of acquired virtue's ordering to beatitude, not its *accidental* character, speaking of infused as *per se* related to beatitude would obscure the contrast.

38. This virtue would alternate between such perfection and imperfection depending on whether it was further ordained to beatitude. Or we could imagine it as stably perfect insofar as its possessor was *habitually* ordered to beatitude and thereby inclined to so remotely refer her acquired virtues. Likewise, we can imagine Rex the dog as variably perfect or imperfect in this sense as in or out of master's use. Recall that this perfection differs from perfection proper, which concerns virtue's *ratio* and does not so vary. Note too that such ordination and perfection rise and fall with charity's possession, which effects an ordering of will on which they depend. Despite major differences, faith offers a model (II.II 4.3 and 4). Charity is accidental to faith (II.II 4.4 ad 2), effecting a change not in it but in its subject (ad 4), which change nonetheless perfects faith by making and keeping it living (ad 3). Unlike acquired virtue, lifeless faith is no virtue and the perfection charity effects is proper to its *ratio*. Still, the perfection charity gives acquired virtue is also due to a new ordering of will, which ordering is not already encompassed by the preexisting order that is acquired virtue (or faith) and which does not change that order itself, even as the new ordering has implications for it. For faith, that prior ordering is in intellect; for acquired virtue, will and appetite. In both cases, however, and in senses befitting the change it effects vis-à-vis what they are, charity brings perfection so long as it is present and thanks precisely to how it effects will's order independent of and accidental to the already existing order. I'm grateful to Steve Brock for dialogue on this issue.

39. Any specification from the remote end *adds* a species to that which the proximate end provides (*HA*, 217–38, 242–46; Rogers, *Aquinas and Barth*, 174–80).

40. Any differences between act specification and habit specification don't bear on our concern, for habits are specified, in the relevant sense, by the proximate end of the acts to which they dispose.

41. See, e.g., *HA*, 220–22.

42. Ibid. And see, e.g., *DV* 12 ob and ad 1; 10 ob 9; II.II 111.3 ob and ad 3.

43. The king's monarchic-ruling virtues are good habits answering to human nature considered in one true way; the citizen's monarchic-subject virtues are good habits answering to his nature in another way.

44. I focus here on virtues of *ruled* citizens and use "democracy" to refer to what Aristotle and Thomas call "polity" (*politia*) (*Politics* 1279a36–40; *PC* III.6.3).

45. If that were so, being a virtuous citizen of some *good* polity would be incompatible with being a virtuous person! Being a virtuous citizen would mean forsaking human virtue—making a subordinate end final.

46. In some polities human/moral virtues are not identical to the ruler's virtues. Here, the latter are higher.

47. And see II.II 32.1 ad 2 and I.II 58.6 on higher virtue commanding lower to do their proper act so that *both* are exercised.

48. *DVC* 4 may also make this point.

49. II.II 23.7's true but imperfect virtues are *DVC* 2's grade 2 virtues: true (23.7) and perfect (*DVC* 2) but not simply so. It's unclear whether 23.7's charity-perfected acquired virtue fits on *DVC*'s schema.

CHAPTER 8

1. "Good in its kind" here must be distinguished from its usual usage which names acts taken abstractly as opposed to acts as actually or individually done (I.II 18, esp. 2 and 7). For here: (1) He treats *individual* acts—"acts of someone lacking charity," which must be actually done acts—and distinguishes between two sorts of individual acts, those ordered to *infidelitas* as final and those ordered to some true, non-beatific good as final. Any distinction in goodness must therefore concern the goodness of actually done acts. This also rules out any claim that the distinction here is between the individual act and the act taken generically; (2) Were he merely claiming pagans could do acts good in kind, his very distinction would dissolve, for the first case he cites is that of a pagan *doing an act good in kind*, almsgiving, which is rendered evil by its final end. That an unbeliever can do a generically good act is assumed—as the case of the pagan *giving alms* demonstrates; (3) Acts only generically good could never suffice to produce virtue (or, while remaining *generic*, even be *done*); (4) Acts good in kind are not appropriately counterposed to acts perfectly good, as here conceived—only *actually* done acts are candidate for reference to beatitude and, *as done*, will already be ordered to an end as final and thus never sufficiently specified as "generically good"; (5) II.II 10.4, *RC* 14.3.1140–41, and other texts, which 23.7 ad 1 mirrors, claim that pagans do not sin in all they do. But avoiding sin requires doing not merely an act good in kind but ordering it to a due final end. Remarks below further substantiate these points and this reading.

2. While the remark immediately regards mortal sin, Thomas holds the point for sin as such: not every act of the infidel is sinful, mortal *or* venial. "Absurd" is the Benziger edition's translation.

3. See Pilsner, *HA*, 234.

4. A remote end is any to which some act is ordered beyond its immediate end. The final end is the last of the remote ends.

5. One can also relate to it habitually (*habitu*). Habitual ordering, however, concerns agents not acts, habits not reference of act to end. One has habitual ordering just because and insofar as one has habits disposing to certain ends. Thus, one is habitually ordered to some end even while sleeping, doing nothing (*DC* 11 ad 3), or, save charity's case, acting *against* habit's end.

6. Thomas also imagines obtaining a donkey for pilgrimage (*DM* 2.5 ob 11, not denied).

7. He imagines a walk to church that begins ordered to vainglory but, after a change of heart, ends ordered to God (*DM* 7.3).

8. What about one's final end when first deliberating about the final end? It will at least presuppose something this determinate (and in fact true) as final: that the good life involves deliberating about what that life's end ought to be. For Thomas, human nature abhors a final end vacuum. An increasingly determinate conception of the final end, he holds, coincides with movement to full responsibility. We can unpack ongoing deliberation on the model of Neurath's raft: such deliberation will itself always presuppose some more or less determinate FEC or facets thereof. In relation to the final end, there's no neutral ground, as it were, from whence to undertake that deliberation.

9. See Pilsner, *HA*, 234–38, 61–66; II.II 58.6; 23.8; 11.1; I.II 18.7; *CNE* 5.3.4. While acts evil in kind are always evil, remote ends matter in assigning blame: stealing to save a child differs from stealing out of greed. T. H. Irwin's "Splendid Vices" neglects the final end's role in an act's or virtue's moral character (120–23).

10. His point coheres with our intuitions. The killer who treats his family well solely to conceal his chief end of murdering his victims is not praiseworthy for his apparently good family-related actions. He has undertaken them—regarded them good—just for their role in helping fulfill his murderous aims. We do not say of him, "Well, he was a good father, we really ought to give him credit for that." We do not, because it seems that any fathering was ordered to concealing his crimes. If, instead, he regarded his family as good *in se* aside from its role in concealing his killing, then, insofar as familial acts were pursued for the good familial end, we might consider them, to that extent, good. And, by Thomas's lights, we would need to suppose as well some alternate final end governing his behavior in such acts than that governing his murderous ones.

11. This seems to be Pilsner's view (*HA*, 235).

12. Thomas contrasts acts "according to that with respect to which he lacks charity" with acts "according to some . . . gift of God [aside from charity]." The parallel and the distinction in acts it funds work only insofar as Thomas has *final* ends in view in both cases.

13. Some cite I.II 89.6 to claim that someone's final end is, necessarily, either self or God, but: (1) If self were the *only* end someone without charity could make final, such people could do no good at all; (2) II.II 19.6 indicates that self need not be final end apart from charity.

14. Whether unfitting final ends and those contrary to charity are coincident (e.g., whether some true good that by being made final is idolatrous and, *qua* idolatrous, should be regarded as contrary to charity), such final ends are alike in rendering sinful acts ordered thereto. I thus speak indifferently of them in what follows.

15. See I.II 109.2 and 3; 63. 1 and 2 ad 2; 5.3 and 5. Other sufficiently fitting ends include, e.g., metaphysical contemplation of God (I.II 5.3 and 5) and love of God above all things (I.II 109.2 and 3).

16. II.II 23.7 ad 1 may *also* consider believers who have lost charity but have been healed (II.II 23.7 ob 1).

17. To the objection that virtue is unattainable without grace since certain sins cannot be avoided without grace, Thomas responds that "the sin of *infidelitas* is not evaded through acquired virtue" (*DV* 9 ad 5). He assumes many without charity are entangled in it *and* that it is compatible with possessing acquired virtue.

18. And see I.II 109.4 and 100.11.

19. Cf. II.II 6.2 regarding lifeless faith.

20. Pleasing God and earning merit denote the same thing here. II.II 10.4 ad 3 does *not* negate the article's claim but classifies Cornelius as doing a different sort of good— the kind that earns merit—and being a different sort of "unbeliever," one with implicit faith.

21. See, e.g., *AA*, 295–96. A version of AV imagines infidels with two coequal final ends: infidelitas and common good. My criticisms hold for that option, and, more, it self-destructs by disintegrating the believer/infidel parallel. They also hold for another version still, which, despite Thomas's never doing so, claims venial sin and its flawed relation to beatitude as model for the pagan's good acts in relation to her final end. The comparison fails on its own terms. (Note that tensions mark Thomas's analysis of venial sin: cf. the earlier I.II 88.1 ad 2 and 3 and *DM* 7.1 ad 3 and 4 with *DC* 11 ad 2 and 3's later claim that habitual reference *fails* to fulfill charity's precept that all acts refer to beatitude, that actual or implicit reference is necessary in a believer's act. 88.1 and *DM* lack *DC* 11's notion of virtual/implicit reference, which helps fund its contrary claim that charity's precept demands actual, *not* habitual, reference and which undermines their claims concerning the venial sin/beatitude relation. The earlier texts either elide implicit with habitual reference or lack the distinction.) Thomas holds that in venial sin that act's final end cannot be other than beatitude, lest one makes final an end other than beatitude (I.II 88.1 ob 2 and 3, ad 2 and 3), which is mortal sin for believers. So, she implicitly acts or tries to act for beatitude as final and in one sense *does*, lest she sin mortally (*DC* 11 ad 3), for she cannot have something else or against beatitude as final. Yet what she does cannot truly be ordered to it, like our doctor implicitly intending health but wrongly and culpably picking sage, which neither furthers nor destroys health. He orders (or tries to order) his will to health in the act, but the ordering *fails*, even as he's *trying* to intend health. In any case, the good/evil asymmetry, however, guarantees that all this is essentially unlike the pagan's good acts or acts of pagan virtue. Additionally, between venial sin and beatitude there's an *inherent* incompatibility. Because of a defect in the very act, it *cannot* be referred to beatitude. Idle words can't lead to heaven as sage can't produce health. There's nothing like this with pagan virtue, no mismatch or inherent deordination between good individual act and fitting final end to which the pagan refers it.

22. See too, e.g., *CC* 1.3.49–50.

23. Thomas distinguishes between the material act of a virtue and that action done *virtuously*. Almsgiving is charitable in kind, but may be done other than *through* charity,

just as an *act* of justice, say paying one's bills, can be done without the virtue of justice (II.II 32.1 ad 2).

24. Cornelius's almsgiving is II.II 10.4's only concrete action. Notwithstanding 10.4 ad 3's further distinctions regarding Cornelius, in the *sed contra*'s context where he mentions almsgiving, Thomas treats Cornelius as a stand-in for unbelievers: precisely as a conclusion from the passage declaring Cornelius's alms God-pleasing, Thomas says that some of the *unbeliever's* acts are good.

25. "Preserving virginity" (*virginitatem servet*) isn't an act of charity but involves perpetual chastity in order to contemplate divine things (II.II 154.1, 4, and 3 ad 4).

26. This particular interpretation is representative of a family of interpretations linked by their effort to tie Thomas's conception either to particularly religious action or entirely to divorce religious ends from the unbeliever's conception of his final end more broadly.

27. Contra Thomas, SR also conflates religious with charitable acts. See, e.g., II.II 32.1 ad 2.

28. More precisely, "*some* beliefs about these beliefs," for certain beliefs about these beliefs might not be proper to the FEC—say, certain beliefs about the reliability or source of various beliefs (e.g., Bob believes *B* about the final end and believes that he believes *B* because of something that happened when he was a child, but he regards his belief about that event's role in his holding *B* irrelevant to the final end). Other beliefs about beliefs might be proper to the FEC itself (e.g., Todd holds that the final end is partly characterized by believing particular beliefs to be certain thanks to their having been revealed). In talking about "beliefs about beliefs" we can also refer to distinct issues of our cognitive or volitional orientations toward given beliefs: how important we believe them, say. So, actually taking some end as final involves orienting ourselves to that end and beliefs about it in a certain way, one facet of which may involve holding beliefs about our beliefs. These beliefs may differ from the substance of the conception taken as final. Happily, we can leave these complexities aside.

29. Thomas might say that a value pluralist's FEC has, *qua conception of her happy life*, the relevant unity: that of a *single* life notwithstanding the (on her view) non-harmonious character of the goods internal to it.

30. And perhaps some false beliefs about connections among beliefs, e.g., thinking anarchy necessary for realizing political liberty. On the account forthcoming, such falsity is not relevantly distinct from falsity in one's FEC generally.

31. Such errors are not proper to faith (II.II 1.3) but will still belong to a person's FEC—which, in this life, is not identical to faith or faith's object. For Thomas, faith itself admits no error but someone's FEC and orientation thereto are not exclusively *ex fide* (II.II 1.3 ad 2). One can even be mistaken about what is *ex fide* (e.g., that Moses wrote Exodus) (II.II 1.3 ad 2; 2.6). Also, for Thomas conceptions of God are not idolatrous or false just by being *human* conceptions. Only if a Christian falls into heresy, which involves not only holding false beliefs about essential matters but knowingly holding them contrary to Church teaching and/or refusing to correct them, could such false beliefs in her FEC cause actions referred thereto to be evil.

32. By "senses," I have in mind complexities that obtain in relation to Thomas's desire to distinguish between different kinds of error he thinks are involved in the distinct acts of *infidelitas* that the following illustrate, belief that: God is not a Trinity, there is no God, Muhammad is the seal of the prophets.

33. To speak of them in their capacity as "final end–type beliefs" is to distinguish between the possibility of acting for some end *E* where *E* is seen as partly constitutive of the final end as opposed to merely as a means to it. Thus Bob could pursue an act thanks to some end *E* but that end *E* can be regarded as and serve as a principle in its role as partly constitutive of his FEC or not (e.g., simply as a means thereto). Supposing the belief "This is my *final* end" or one saliently like it is part of an FEC, one option *not* open is to suppose that someone is innocent of idolatry/sin only if *that* belief is *not* implicated in some act ordered to her end—for whatever role that *belief* may play, necessarily she still orders her act to the FEC-specified end *as final end*, in that *mode*. And from the standpoint of idolatry that would be saliently similar, equally culpable. Also, here and throughout, I have in view implicit and actual ordination to the final end. Most reference to the final end is implicit but, recall, this concerns its place in immediate consciousness, *not* the particularity of its role as principle, in respect to which implicit and actual reference are identical.

34. This need not count against the possibility of the final end's (or FEC's) integrity, its constitutive features (or beliefs) being more-or-less well held together or interconnected—unless in each case the interconnection took the form of a narrow variety of interdependence such that a change in one feature (or FEC-constitutive belief) entailed a change in the presently action-guiding feature (or belief) in just the way that would change its role as principle in this particular action. Even if some features (or FEC-constitutive beliefs) are so related, it is doubtful very many would be.

35. For all this, Hitchens may be *habitually* ordered to the atheistic dimension of his FEC and thus have what Thomas would consider bad character.

36. There is no *necessity* here: one may or may not decide to act or to act for the reason the circumstances seem to implicate. Aside from the demands imposed by Thomas's commitments, there is also textual precedent for such consideration in his notion of *velleity* (I.II 13.5) and his remarks on habitual ordering where, e.g., he elucidates Abraham's chastity in terms of how he *would* have lived if unmarried (*De perfectione* 8). Indeed, it's tempting to use Thomas's notion of habitual ordering to make my points, but habitual ordering is not the ordination of particular acts. Still, since virtue can embed ordination to some FEC, if by a habit's *use* an act were ordered to the *entire* FEC even as only certain beliefs were salient, this might work. Yet ordination to the FEC as a whole, non-salient beliefs included, could not be *merely* habitual—or else one would not truly be ordering the act to any other than the given *salient* end as final. Could this be sustained, it would be still another way of unfolding the points above and further rooting them in Thomas's text.

37. I refer occasionally to weak or conditionally salient beliefs as "non-salient" and to strongly or truly salient beliefs simply as "salient."

38. Or it is the only kind that, when implicated, makes an act good or evil as the case may be. We might *say* that other FEC beliefs are referred to in some action even

though they are not strongly salient, but if so, we should be clear that actions are not referred to them in the good- or evil-making sense. The set *considered as a set* can count as having strong salience in virtue of one or more particular members having strong salience in their capacity as FEC-type beliefs. But this does not authorize the inference that some member of the set just in virtue of its membership itself has strong salience in a given action.

39. About those who have given little thought to their happiness, Thomas might point to something like an implicit, functional moral faith and very relative integrity of vision born out by the coherence manifest in the person's agency itself.

40. If their absence would have, that implies that his literary production beliefs were dependent on them, in which case those anti-religious-belief commitments would have been strongly salient. Caution is needed here, for acts are specified by their ends, and so there is a sense in which any change in end affects act specification and, in that sense, constitutes a change in action. Thus, a change in the FEC would in that sense constitute a change in action specification. It suffices to note, however, that precisely what we are up to is untangling what it actually *means* for an FEC to play a role as principle in (and help specify) an action, and that involves us in considering the FEC not only in its role as set but in view of its constitutive parts—and while the set would change in this counterfactual, the relevant end in virtue of which it serves as principle would not, and it is in that sense that the action would not change.

41. Perhaps we think it could be hard for an agent to know how various facets of her FEC are in play in some case. This raises questions for Thomas's perspective but not ones peculiar to our topic.

42. The mystery concerns the agent's intention of the *final* end. Frequently, there is no such mystery about an agent's intention with respect to proximate ends.

43. Such fidelity rules out two possibilities. One argues that acts can have a mixed character, being, in different respects, both morally good and bad. So, writing a book to promote peace *and* attack Christianity, is mixed: good insofar as one intends the former, bad insofar as one intends the latter. Thomas rejects such a perspective, for essential to his vision of act specification is the belief that moral good and evil divide human acts essentially. Some acts can be more evil than others and good acts can be imperfect, but good and evil are distinct species and his theory disallows mixed action in the proposed sense (I.II 18.5; Pilsner, *HA*, 61–69). Another option claims that the single book-writing action is actually two—one evil and one good. But this is equally implausible for Thomas (*HA*, 9–17). This is distinct from *DM* 7.3's walk to church where ends *change* and thus there are multiple acts.

44. Provided we refer to those who have heard the Gospel and put aside Jews and heretics, both of these varieties of *infidelitas* are together classified by Thomas as "resistance to faith not yet accepted" (II.II 10.5 and 6).

45. Hereafter, I omit this parenthetical qualification.

46. We can wonder whether strong *infidelitas* as here defined is blasphemy (II.II 13). If so, since blasphemy itself is a species of *infidelitas* for Thomas, the collapse of strong *infidelitas* into blasphemy would represent no challenge to my claims. But I believe that

for Thomas blasphemy is most properly in the purview of Christians and others who believe in God and that there is imperfect overlap between what counts as blasphemy and what counts as strong *infidelitas*.

47. For Thomas, as I explain below, I do not take it that, having rejected Trinitarianism, ongoing belief that "God is one" is identical to the belief "God is not a Trinity" or that in serving as principles the two beliefs have the same import. The former, I argue, does not entangle one in *infidelitas*; the latter can entangle one in weak or strong *infidelitas*. In other, *different* cases where ongoing commitment to the truth of *P* is now understood to entail commitment to the falsity of *Q*, knowing that some entailment follows from some commitment no more necessitates that one acts *for* or *on account of* that entailment (the falsity of *Q*) in acting for the commitment than it follows that one intends some consequence merely because one foresees it.

48. The honoring of Muhammad could be a matter of the prayer's liturgical form.

49. Would we prefer a Thomas who did so? Acts rooted in strong *infidelitas* aim to *destroy* Christianity—that which Thomas believes essential to full flourishing. Would we ask people not to consider wrong acts intended to *destroy* what is most essential to their own conception of flourishing? To ask an atheist not to regard a Christian's effort to discredit atheism as morally flawed? Thomas's stance is one many might embrace in the face of acts ordered to destroying their own conception of flourishing. Still, regarding such action as wrong does not entail: that the *person* is irrational or evil; that all or most of her acts are; that it is legitimate to coerce or restrain her.

50. This distinction is *not* that between strong and weak *infidelitas*. Unbelievers not actively opposed to Christianity do not thereby fall in the "mere absence" category. While those who have heard nothing (*qui nihil audierunt de fide*) can fall in that category, Thomas categorizes those who have heard something even if they are not aggressively opposed to the faith as resisting the faith and falling in the "sinful" *infidelitas* category: "either the faith is *resisted* not yet having been received, *and such is the infidelitas of pagans or Gentiles*" (II.II 10.5). Non-Christians who have heard the Gospel count as *resisting* (*renitor*) the faith. But only insofar as that *infidelitas* plays an active role in action does it prove morally relevant.

51. Recall, the weak salience/strong salience distinction divides ends *not* directly relevant to action generation from those that *are*. It does not concern necessary or sufficient conditions for action generation. Whether some end is necessary or sufficient to generate an action or neither necessary nor sufficient but still generative (the various distinctions at play just here), all these options are distinctions *within* the category of the strongly salient. Only strongly salient ends are in view here.

52. Matters can get complex here insofar as the prayer's form will likely be one prescribed by and following after Muhammad—and in that sense might seem to make weak *infidelitas* necessary for the act: if he did not believe in Muhammad's prophethood he would not pray in this way and so, in a sense, acceptance of Muhammad's prophethood is implicit in the praying. This is true as far as it goes. Yet without separating the prayer's form from its content, we can distinguish between use of the form *qua* way of honoring the Prophet and use of the form *qua* way of rightly worshiping the one God,

even as we recognize these will come bundled for this believer. What is necessary for us, however, and suffices to implicate a good end, is just that the praying, in every respect, seeks to honor and love God. *Per impossible*, if the believer came to think his praying honored God but was indifferent in regard to the Prophet, he would continue doing it. The same points would hold across any number of different religions and their particular practices. Consider too someone who gives Baal-worship a place in her FEC, where she thinks she's worshiping the god so named by her fellows but conceives of and acts for Baal in ways actually suited to God. Without plumbing all the complexities, insofar as she's actually worshiping/acting for God, her confusion about the name needn't mean we take her acts/end to implicate Baal. For us, she is saliently like others with imperfectly true religious beliefs: her generically good acts ordered to her end insofar as it is true and good are good.

53. As not "referred to *infidelitas*" in the problematic sense.

54. The counterfactual language serves a purely diagnostic role here. It is *not* the case that some counterfactual or conditional determines the act's morality. Rather, they reveal what is *actually* the case about the matter at hand—a fact about the agent's intentions here and now. That Sue would still do *D* just now in the absence of weak *infidelitas* tells us that weak *infidelitas* is not *necessary* for the generation of the act *as actually done now* and that her good end in fact suffices for its generation. It is not what she *would* do that determines the act's moral status, but what she *does* do—which the conditional helps reveal.

55. This means that for cases in which weak *infidelitas* and some good end are each necessary but only co-jointly sufficient, the action is not good. In such cases, without the resistance there is no act.

56. Withholding judgment is also possible, but: (1) We are dealing with and considering pronouncing evil an act that has everything to recommend it as good—including what we reasonably take to be an intended good dimension of the FEC—save the possibility that *infidelitas alone* was necessary and sufficient to generate it; (2) It is in the nature of the case, I think, that full assurance will rarely be forthcoming, for we would await certainty as to whether the intended good aspect of the FEC sufficed to generate the action, but it is unclear whether more time would even give such clarity; (3) The very act of withholding judgment is costly—for insofar as the agent detects this stance, it seems likely to be interpreted as suspicion, a negative rather than neutral stance, and to that extent likely to short-circuit friendship or even generate hostility; (4) And see note 41.

57. There is an assymetry between (a) the Christian/pagan relation, in view here, and (b) the Dominican/lay Christian relation discussed in chapter 6, where spiritual and pedagogical aims recommend erring on the side of not prematurely ascribing virtue. Further, in (a) it is *exclusively* in regard to *infidelitas* that this pagan's act or virtue is possibly flawed.

58. What might constitute clear evidence? Perhaps observing consistent disregard for justice across other acts.

59. The first principle of charity dictates we regard good those actions where we

know weak *infidelitas* is implicated provided we *know* some truly good additionally intended end would suffice to generate the action. Joining that principle to this epistemological one suggests that if we do not *know* but suspect that both weak *infidelitas* and some true good are salient for an action, we ought to regard the act good. This principle of epistemic charity has not just its generosity to recommend it. See Donald Davidson, *Inquiries into Truth and Interpretation*, 2nd ed. (New York: Oxford University Press, 2001), 137; Bjørn Ramberg, "Post-ontological Philosophy," in *Rorty and His Critics*, ed. Robert Brandom (Oxford: Blackwell Publishing, 2000), 351–69.

60. We are concerned with acts where the *only* question as to their full goodness is whether they are referred to *infidelitas* alone. Moral goodness in action is far more difficult to achieve than a mostly true or good FEC. Such an FEC is necessary but not sufficient for good action.

61. While Thomas speaks of their being excused from the sin of unbelief, we can read the point more fully in line with II.II 10.1: they are excused from this sin in that they are not guilty of it, for a necessary condition constituting it *as* sin, namely resistance, does not obtain.

62. All the better for my account if it is hard to imagine someone referring acts to such ends.

63. Here, it is this we have in view as end and principle. The *absence* of Trinitarianism, say, is not serving as principle—and simply *qua* absence cannot.

64. We have in view Aristotelian monotheism *qua* reason's deliverance—and so as excluding errors.

65. The former may need to abandon beliefs that reason alone could not settle on which she took some position (e.g., the eternality of the world), but she will not need to *repent* for such beliefs.

66. The belief that the end is final is a *symptom* of the resistance rather than *constitutive* of it. He is correct that contemplation of God is final end, only he fails to grasp, *inter alia*, that this takes the form of friendship with God. Those commitments that result in his not recognizing his end as less than final constitute *infidelitas*.

67. While sinful, this pride is not peculiar to *infidelitas* or unbelievers. It is not had in virtue of *infidelitas* and need not produce it. It corrupts action in ways relevantly similar to other sin. Since its corrupting role is not peculiar to outsiders *per se* and thus not our explicit concern, I put aside further consideration.

68. When such beliefs are held by one who has not heard, they have the character of being false but not of being *infidelitas*. False beliefs about God that Thomas would regard as stepping beyond what reason knows about divine nature will likely be connected to the beliefs mentioned. For Thomas, reason's disclosure about God is never incompatible with revelation.

69. I render *pura negatio* as "sheer absence" not "pure negation" because Thomas is speaking of those who have not heard, and "pure negation" seems to denote the refusal of faith.

70. This account parallels Thomas's conception of sin (I.II 71 and 75–78): the analog

to his account of *infidelitas* as resistance is certain malice; the analog to *infidelitas* as absence, evil generally.

71. It is unclear whether Thomas would have us characterize the Aristotelian's true but incomplete beliefs as themselves constituting *infidelitas*. Given his treatment of the virtue of religion, I believe he would not (II.II 81). However, in a way it does not matter for our aims because even if he did, this *infidelitas* would lack sin's character and be true, good, so reference to it would be good.

72. He likely has in view internal resistance to the *Gospel* but his point is inherently broader.

73. I leave aside exploration of a point he develops in *RC* where "suppression" presupposes true knowledge of reason's God and names first the thwarting of this knowledge whereby one refuses to let it lead to due worship. Given the will/intellect interdependency, this volitional defect leads to a darkening and/or corruption of knowledge so that one overestimates what one knows of God and/or identifies him with created things. Looking forward, Thomas traces internal darkening to "ascribing blessings to self," crediting self not God with the gifts one enjoys. This might be a way to distinguish "pure" atheists from religious naturalists who share with believers gratitude and piety to sources transcending the self (*RC* 1.7.129).

74. Thomas may even regard resistance as a form of suppression (II.II 10.1 ad 1).

75. Recall, Thomas traces his defect ultimately to a moral and spiritual failure to act in accord with the truth he did know. Of course, such a one is no less on the hook epistemically.

76. These remarks immediately concern *infidelitas* but the same dynamic of the will badly commanding the intellect pertains in suppression.

77. Mere belief is not sufficient to avoid suppression; worship is required. And he believes some ancients worshiped God (II.II 81 and 82).

78. Interestingly, he does not cite Romans 1 (nor, usually, other Biblical texts) to support this.

79. The instinct seems to produce a sense that there is a source and sustainer of the universe and life. Thomas's most developed explication, still ambiguous, is likely *Collationes Credo in Deum*, 2 and 3. He may have wayward Christians in view in noting that "many frequently" tend toward idolatry, superstition, and polytheism (2). If so, how much more would non-Christians so tend and, given the compassion and charity that mark his comments, how much more would he extend and have Christians extend such grace toward them? His sermon tries to induce a Christian humility born of recognizing human frailty, commonality with idolaters, and our utter dependence on God. See too III 60.5 ad 3.

80. He seems to imply the distinction, identifying intellectual weakness and inordinate relations to true goods (i.e., family and human authority)—neither of which bears suppression's *ratio* of unnaturalness—as the human sources of idolatry and polytheism (*Collationes Credo in Deum* 2).

81. He does imagine those who reject providence: I 22.2; *Scriptum super Sententiis* I. 3.1.2 co.

82. On some quasi-apophatic readings of the "five ways" (e.g., Victor Preller's), the *praeambula fidei* might overlap significantly with the religious naturalists' beliefs. I'm skeptical about such readings.

83. We leave aside the matter of Thomas's stance on preparation for grace, which Joseph Wawrykow, e.g., contends is itself regarded as grace's gift, "Grace," *Theology of Thomas Aquinas.*

84. I owe this turn of phrase to Jeff Stout.

85. Some false beliefs (e.g., that God is evil) surely count as suppression for Thomas.

86. What of New Age thinking, Scientology, or occultism, to take very different examples? Perhaps in cases like these Thomas would regard many of the basic commitments to be morally or rationally suspect even for those unskilled in theoretical reasoning, so that such commitments were blameworthy. Distinguishing false from authentic spirituality and blameworthy (rationally unconstrained) from good-faith (considered, rationally careful) efforts to honor the religious inclination would allow Thomas to open the door widely without treating willingness not to thwart religious inclination as the only relevant question in these matters. Not all "spirituality" is spirituality.

87. This allows for the possibility of an unevangelized person to be spiritually accountable for some of his false religious beliefs: e.g., by failing to do what he might or exercise enough care (or, at one extreme, to be involved in some suppression) without being implicated in the effort fully to shut down the *interior instinctus* or to directly reject the truth known to reason. Most simply, it avoids the "nuclear option" of the full-fledged charge of suppression while not itself exhibiting a disregard for truth or justice that would elide, say, a good-faith effort that terminated in idolatry and a half-hearted effort that did so.

CHAPTER 9

1. I leave aside for now whether this means: that humans can *never* so love God; cannot do so in, e.g., a perfect, unfailing way taken as necessary to fulfill the command; or something else. More below, but, as here, I usually refer to this incapacity without qualification.

2. Osborne, e.g., takes this view (*AA*, 297), reading I.II 65.2 as implying the dependence of acquired prudence and virtue's unity on infused prudence and/or charity (289–94, esp. 291–92).

3. And see *PIV*, 56. This would make even Osborne's pagan "virtue" impossible. For Thomas, recall, humans intend a last end in whatever they do, and intending a bad final end, such as self, makes an act evil. If self is someone's final end most of her actions will be directed thereto as final. Even if she occasionally does good acts directed to some *other than her stable, evil final end,* she could never do so with even the minimal consistency necessary to acquire an Osbornian disposition.

4. That Thomas's claims hold for pagans is implicit in the article's very structure. To ask whether servile fear can *remain* (*remanere*) *after* charity comes presupposes a possible *prior* presence. More, Thomas's third way suggests, and may have in view, pagans, those who lack charity. Recall that one of his formulations, drawn from Hebrews, for

assessing the spiritual lives of those outside the faith is whether they believe in God and that he rewards those who seek him (e.g., II.II 2.8 ob 1). Such belief implies that one also believe this God punishes sin, including that of failing to seek him. Also, servile fear does not require that one describe or know fear's object as "God's punishment," only that it actually *be* God's punishment.

5. Even if venial sinners are somehow also included here, pagans certainly are, for this love is not ordered to beatitude.

6. Thomas does not explicitly say (or deny) here that he has in view those without charity, but his argument suggests that he does. He wants to make this point: If folks can, do, and ought sometimes sacrifice themselves for the common good, love it more than self, how much more ought they to love God through charity more than self. If these politically virtuous were also informed by charity then (unless something has gone wrong) it follows that their order to the political good is itself already ordered to beatitude, in which case the example would beg the question, remaining subject to the very challenge it meant to address. Its most effective version—which coheres with its "How much more then" structure—concerns those *not* ordered to charity who still love some good end more than self.

7. This is the perfection Thomas seems to refer to at II.II 23.7's close and imply in, e.g., *DV* 10 ad 4.

8. The qualification is important: charity's possession entails directedness to beatitude as final—none with charity is oriented merely to the natural end of natural love for God as final.

9. The qualification is necessary in virtue of the distinction answering to charity's referring acquired virtue remotely to beatitude.

10. The "by which" phrase is not introducing a qualification of acquired virtue, as though this were "acquired-virtue-by-which-one-is-able-to-abstain." Rather, it describes acquired virtue's work in this case. Thomas says *"per quam"* where *quam*'s antecedent just *is* acquired virtue.

11. For believers, mortal sin breaks the unitive relation with God charity constitutes; those without charity cannot experience such a rupture. Yet they can commit a sin mortal in kind (I.II 88.2), and in so sinning are still more alienated from God. An actual sin's status as mortal depends on the act's species, which species require not that an agent have charity but that the act's object be inherently contrary to charity.

12. Shanley continues, "For the knowledge of God to make a moral difference in a person's life, grace is required" (*APV*, 571). This differs from his earlier claims and seems incorrect. Thomas's claim is not that without grace knowledge of God can make no difference to moral life, but that God cannot (stably) be *ultimate end*—with all that entails—without grace. For Thomas, beliefs about and love for God can matter for moral life without charity, but God cannot be (always) loved above all. Thus, someone could love God and give God a central place in her FEC such that her true beliefs about and love for God enhanced her behavior. What Thomas rules out is that God could effectively be (consistently) loved *above all* by such a person without grace. More on these parenthetical qualifications below.

13. Benziger wrongly adds a possessive pronoun so that the will follows "*its* private good."

14. Thus, at article's start, Thomas refers readers to what he said earlier concerning the angels' natural love for God: there too he portrays God as the *bonum universale*, universal good. *Any* good other than God, even that order to which suffices for virtue, is merely a private good, not *the* common good.

15. In equating "private good" with self or a self-centered good, Shanley understands pursuit of any genuine but incomplete end as evidence of charity: since charity is necessary to pursue any non-private end such pursuit entails charity. He reads I.II 89.6 as claiming that at the "age of reason" one chooses between self as end or God or (more likely) some other more comprehensive good and that the choice of any due end is thanks to charity (572–74; O'Brien, "Commentary"). His point holds if a person perfectly loves God above all things.

16. Illustrating what good integral nature can achieve, Thomas says it can achieve such things as "the good of acquired virtue." Given the further comparison between integral and fallen human nature, this could seem to suggest that fallen nature cannot achieve acquired virtue. But even aside from his affirmations of pagan virtue, note: (1) his point is to suggest the limits of *integral* nature by comparing the "good of acquired virtue," which integral nature can achieve, to "the good of infused virtue," which it cannot. Given his concern precisely to sketch integral nature's limits, that cannot be anything other or higher than acquired virtue's good; (2) Both in I.II 109.2 and its context, he's concerned to distinguish integral from fallen nature. As in I.II 109.3, the concrete difference in the capacities of each concerns love of God above all. Undoubtedly, the perfect good and perfect possession of acquired virtue require such love, without which one lacks some of acquired virtue's good. Thus, we should take the remark to concern acquired virtue's *perfect* good, which only integral nature can attain, acquired virtue in 109.3's sense.

17. Shanley notes that this list, present in both of articles, derives from an authority, but his claim that it "reflect[s] Aquinas's use of traditional sources *rather than his own thinking*," is problematic: it is one thing whether X comes from a "traditional source;" another whether X reflects Thomas's thinking (*APV*, 568, my emphasis). We have no reason to think this list does *not* reflect Thomas's thinking. We have reason to think a minimalist interpretation of it incorrect.

18. It is not clear whether in speaking of this unelevated human nature he is referring only to integral or both integral and fallen nature. Either way, he makes the point I am after.

19. Literally, "certain good connatural to man" (*aliquod bonum homini connaturale*).

20. R. Jared Staudt, "Religion as a Virtue."

21. Ibid, 234; 289. On the limit, 217–24; on the affirmation, 293–94, 299. While affirming pagan virtue as true but imperfect, Staudt does not say in what precisely this imperfection consists (283). While a few remarks may be overly negative (226–27; 294), those above seem accurate.

22. Ibid., 289.

23. Consider for instance, that it is *Cicero* whom Thomas cites as the sole authority in the religion treatise's first article, which concerns what religion is (II.II 81.1)—a point Staudt notes too (Ibid., 186–87).

24. While Thomas's affirmation of pagan virtue remains regardless, some interpretive options for the natural love/virtue of religion relation include: (a) imperfect virtue of religion + impossibility of ever loving God above all (the virtue's imperfection could consist in failure *ever* to love God above all, though this would seem to make *no* virtue rather than an imperfect one, so this seems most unlikely); (b) imperfect/occasional love sufficing for imperfect virtue of religion; (c) impossibility of love *or* virtue of religion; (d) occasional/imperfect love not sufficing even for an imperfect virtue of religion.

25. Suppose someone showed that Thomas (a) denies even an imperfect virtue of religion without charity and (b) that this is incompatible with or contradictory to his affirmation of pagan virtue. Still, it remains that (1) the pagan virtue affirmation endures, giving us reason to see Thomas as, perhaps, simply inconsistent; (2) such an outcome could constitute an invitation of the sort detailed below to live, by faith as it were, in the tension; (3) those committed to prophetic Thomism would have reason to prioritize Thomas's affirmation to pagan virtue and seek a way to reconstruct his approach to religion.

26. In *Aquinas*, Finnis never even mentions infused moral virtue, scarcely mentions sin, and seems to imagine neither as figuring significantly in one's capacity to realize this life's happiness.

27. For Milbank, e.g., Aristotelian virtues are "agonistic," rooted in "conflict and conquest" (*TST*, 337), mere "victory over . . . passions" (393), that "reduce[s] to . . . self-control" and "only ends war by war" (367); for Christians even now it seems, virtue brings ideal, perfect peace without and within (392–94, 364–67).

28. I am indebted to Benziger's handling of *quid nobis expedit*.

29. And see Bowlin, *Contingency and Fortune*, 138–44.

30. A remark in a Scripture commentary paraphrasing a Chrysostom quote from Thomas's early *Cantena Aurea* represents his most negative sounding pagan virtue comment. Elsewhere, I explain why the remark does not represent his considered or mature position, but reading such passages as lament avoids the error of ignoring them altogether.

31. And see I.II 109.9.

CHAPTER 10

1. *TST*'s second edition, Milbank says, has been "modified . . . to ensure that it is more in keeping with [his] original intentions [and] current thinking." This involved removing "exaggerations of the differences between Augustine and Aquinas" (xxxi-ii).

2. *TST*, 364–65; 412–14. Milbank occasionally speaks of Aquinas making claims about "natural [i.e., acquired] virtue" but criticizes Thomas at such points for being "too Greek" (31, 414). Apparently conceding that Thomas has a conception of acquired virtue, he seems to believe Thomas regards this virtue as false (412).

3. Milbank's evidence consists in one note citing three passages: I.II 65.2, I.II 93.6 (the only one he remarks on), and I 94.3, which describes Adam's prelapsarian knowl-

edge. While his "any genuine 'natural' good" is ambiguous and may relate to his de Lubacianism, his notes suggest we should read him as denying the possibility of even good acts without charity (*TA*, 124–25).

4. The damned have sinned so much that the natural inclination to good is "blocked" from generating good action, but even if such wickedness could be achieved in this life, it is not proper to unredeemed humanity as such (I.II 85.1 and 2).

5. Whether Milbank regards Thomas as seeing no one as without charity, in I.II 65.2, 63.2, II.II 23.7, 10.4, and elsewhere, Thomas describes *himself* as considering what postlapsarian humans can do without charity.

6. Kent does not see Thomas as correlating these figures alone.

7. Kent, *Virtues of the Will*, 28.

8. Ibid., 27, and "Habits and Virtues," 122–23, 125.

9. Cf. Irwin's view, "Splendid Vices," 122–23.

10. Kent, "Moral Provincialism," 276, and see Shanley, *APV*; Osborne, *AA*.

11. Thus, he notes that on happiness Thomas invokes "Aristotle . . . against Aristotle in the interest of Scripture and of Augustine . . . because Thomas was trying to be a better Aristotelian than Aristotle" (*TRV*, 137). And see *TRV*, 120–24; *WJ*, 1–11, 146–208, 400–3.

12. And see *TRV*, 140–41.

13. And see *TRV*, 140.

14. Referring to a "retrospective vindication" of Aristotle, MacIntyre means that reconstructed Aristotelian points are vindicated *using Augustinian resources*: moral virtues made *entirely* dependent on charity (*TRV*, 140–41).

15. MacIntyre may think Thomas holds that people necessarily lack prudence absent orientation to beatitude (*WJ*, 191–92). And, while he rightly notes that without belief in God one cannot "be *perfectly* obedient to the natural law," for Thomas the impossibility of *perfect* obedience does not entail the impossibility of a great deal thereof, enough even to attain virtue (my emphasis, 188). McIntyre notes: "even if . . . parts of my interpretation . . . could not withstand criticism [related to its accuracy], . . . this would itself strengthen the tradition which I am attempting to sustain and extend" (*After Virtue*, 260). I intend my points as such a contribution, and *WJ*, 182, 192–93 and *TRV*, 137, themselves suggest a more capacious trajectory.

16. Thomas insists that the nature of faith itself must not be changed in the process, but it would misunderstand his metaphor and involve us in idolatry to think Augustine's teaching—or even one's prior *conception* of faith—could not undergo change for the better.

17. I here claim neither an *exclusively* Aristotelian provenance for such dialectic or *quaestio*-style distinction-drawing nor deny its earlier theological use. On my point, see, e.g., M. D. Chenu, *Nature, Man, and Society*, 270–309, esp. 280, 287–95, and *TRV*, 124–26.

18. We can thus better grasp Thomas's battle against those who claimed that, contrary to Aristotle, the world could be shown non-eternal by reason alone. While Thomas believes the world is not eternal, such knowledge, he argues, comes through revelation and thus Aristotle is not guilty of intellectual error.

19. While full treatment of these dimensions of Thomas's context is beyond our

scope, on the preceding points see, e.g.: Kent, *Virtues of the Will*; Frederick Bauer-schmidt, *Faith, Reason, and Following Christ*, Ch. 1; Stanley Cunningham, *Reclaiming Agency*, esp. Ch. 3; and Odon Lottin, "*Les vertus morales.*" "Since the early twelfth century," Cunningham notes, "the only kind of good intention was one rooted in charity . . . and directed by faith" (*Reclaiming Agency*, 48). When Lottin contends that, for the most part, from at least Stephen Langton (d. 1228) up to Thomas "the source (*facteur*) of moral goodness was [thought to be] charity," the implications for pagan virtue are obvious (*Psychologie et Morale*, vol. 3, 480). Of course, some of Thomas's contemporaries and predecessors such as Philip the Chancellor (d. 1236) had more positive views of pagan virtue.

20. In cases of injustice, e.g., sexual abuse, Thomas demands public reckoning and punishment (II.II 33.1). It is no "fraternal correction" to allow injustice or protect the guilty at the victim's expense. See too *RC* 14.3.1137.

21. Recall that most Dominicans were not university-trained nor would their learnedness necessarily mirror that of those whose work has endured to this day.

22. And assume, more doubtfully, continuity between Augustine's *consuetudo* and Artistotle's *hexis*—that Augustine and Thomas (and his Aristotle) are referring to the same thing.

23. While knowingly conveying false teaching is heresy (II.II 11.2), unnecessarily doing publicly what may spiritually damage someone constitutes scandal (II.II 43.1 ad 4).

24. Thanks, in part, to Christianity's precedence in Thomas's synthesis, we have already seen numerous case where, departing from Aristotle, Thomas vindicates Augustinian positions on Aristotelian grounds.

25. Robert Markus, *The End of Ancient Christianity* (New York: Cambridge University Press, 1991), 45–62.

26. Complexities obtain here, thanks to the relations between grace and free will, for even the turning toward God is a gift of grace even as it is, simultaneously, a movement of free will (109.6 and 7). In I.II 109.6, Thomas makes his case using *Aristotelian* points. Most precisely, Thomas insists that this is a matter of divine *help* (see, e.g., I.II 109.7 ad 3 and *De veritate* 24.15), and, as we will soon see *that* is the key. Whether Thomas ultimately succeeds in all this, the point is his relentless effort to do so.

27. For Aristotle, those who are not an act's immediate source can nonetheless count as its author. See, e.g., *Politics* I.4.

28. Shanley sketches an argument like this in *APV*.

29. Henri de Lubac, *Mystery of the Supernatural*, 76–77.

30. Timothy Jackson, *Priority of Charity*, 56, 15.

31. Ralph Waldo Emerson, "Experience," 491.

32. The political good is not had "without divine assistance" (*adiutorium divinum*) (I.II 62.1).

BIBLIOGRAPHY

PRIMARY SOURCES

Aristotle. *The Nicomachean Ethics*. Translated by W. D. Ross, edited by Lesley Brown. New York: Oxford University Press, 2009.

———. *Politics*. Translated by C. D. C. Reeve. Indianapolis: Hackett Publishing Company, 1998.

Augustine. *Concerning the City of God Against the Pagans*. Translated by Henry S. Bettenson. New York: Penguin Books, 2003.

Bacon, Roger. *The Opus Maius of Roger Bacon*. Translated and edited by Robert B. Burke. Sterling, VA: Thoemmes Press, 2000.

Bartholomew of San Concordio. *Summa de casibus conscientiae*. Augsburg, 1475.

Bonaventure. *Collationes in Hexaemeron et Bonaventuriana quaedam selecta*. Edited by F. Delorme. Ad Claras Aquas (Quaracchi): Collegium S. Bonaventurae, 1934.

Francisco de Vitoria. *Political Writings*. Edited by Anthony Pagden and Jeremy Lawrance. New York: Cambridge University Press, 1991.

John of Freiburg. *Summa confessorum*. Paris: Jehan Petit, 1519.

John of St. Thomas. *Cursus Theologicus in Iam–IIae. De Virtutibus*. Edited by Armand Mathieu. Québec: Presses Universitaires Laval, 1952.

Thomas Aquinas. "*Ad ducissam Brabantiae*." In Vol. 42, *Opera omnia iussu Leonis XIII p.m. edita*, Cura et studio Fratrum Praedicatorium, 357–78. Rome: Typographia Polyglotta, 1979.

———. *Commentaria in octo libros Physicorum Aristotelis. Opera omnia iussu Leonis XIII p.m. edita*, Vol. 2, Cura et studio Fratrum Praedicatorium. Rome: Typographia Polyglotta, 1884.

———. *Corpus Thomisticum: Opera Omnia*. Edited and maintained by Enrico Alarcón. http://www.corpusthomisticum.org/iopera.html

———. *Disputed Questions on Virtue*. Translated by Ralph McInerny. South Bend, IN: St. Augustine's Press, 1999.

———. *In duodecim libros Metaphysicorum Aristotelis expositio*. Edited by M. R. Cathala and R. M. Spiazzi. 2nd edition. Turin: Marietti, 1971.

———. *Opera omnia cum hypertextibus in CD-ROM*. Edited by Robert Busa. 2nd ed. Milan: Editoria Elettronica Editel, 1992.

———. *Quaestiones disputatae* [including *De virtutibus*]. Edited by E. Odetto. Vol. 2. 10th ed. Turin: Marietti, 1965.

———. *Quaestiones disputatae de malo. Opera omnia iussu Leonis XIII p.m. edita*, Vol. 23, Cura et studio Fratrum Praedicatorium. Rome: Typographia Polyglotta, 1982.

———. *Quaestiones disputatae de veritate. Opera omnia iussu Leonis XIII p.m. edita*, Vol. 22, Cura et studio Fratrum Praedicatorium. Rome: Typographia Polyglotta, 1970–1976.

———. *Sentencia libri De anima. Opera omnia iussu Leonis XIII p.m. edita*, Vol. 45.1, Cura et studio Fratrum Praedicatorium. Rome: Typographia Polyglotta, 1984.

———. *Sententia libri Ethicorum. Opera omnia iussu Leonis XIII p.m. edita*, Vol. 47, Cura et studio Fratrum Praedicatorium. Rome: Typographia Polyglotta, 1969.

———. *Sententia libri Politicorum; Tabula libri Ethicorum. Opera omnia iussu Leonis XIII p.m. edita*, Vol. 48, Cura et studio Fratrum Praedicatorium. Rome: Typographia Polyglotta, 1971.

———. *The Sermon-Conferences of St. Thomas Aquinas on the Apostles' Creed* [*Collationes Credo in Deum*]. Translated and edited by Nicholas Ayo. Notre Dame, Indiana: University of Notre Dame Press, 1988.

———. *Summa theologiae. Opera omnia iussu Leonis XIII p.m. edita*, Vol. 4–12, Cura et studio Fratrum Praedicatorium. Rome: Typographia Polyglotta, 1888–1906.

———. *Summa Theologica.* Translated by Fathers of the English Dominican Province. Vol. 1–5. New York: Benziger Bros., 1947.

———. *Super Boetium De Trinitate; Expositio libri Boetii De ebdomadibus. Opera omnia iussu Leonis XIII p.m. edita*, Vol. 50, Cura et studio Fratrum Praedicatorium. Rome: Typographia Polyglotta, 1992.

———. *Super epistolas S. Pauli lectura.* Edited by Raffaele Cai. Vol. 1–2. Turin: Marietti, 1953.

———. *Super evangelium S. Ioannis lectura.* Edited by Raffaele Cai. Turin: Marietti, 1972

———. *Summa contra Gentiles. Opera omnia iussu Leonis XIII p.m. edita*, Vol. 13–15, Cura et studio Fratrum Praedicatorium. Rome: Typographia Polyglotta, 1918–1930.

———. *Thomas d'Aquin: Commentaire de l'Épître aux Romains.* Translated and edited by Jean-Éric Stroobant de Saint-Éloy. Paris: Cerf, 1999.

———. *The Treatise on the Divine Nature: Summa Theologiae I, 1–13.* Translated by Brian J. Shanley. Indianapolis: Hackett Publishing Company, 2006.

William of Rubruck. "Itinerarium." In *The Principal Navigations, Voyages, Traffiques, and Discoveries of the English Nation*, edited by Richard Hakluyt. Glasgow: J. MacLehose, 1905.

SECONDARY SOURCES

Adams, Robert M. *Finite and Infinite Goods: A Framework for Ethics.* New York: Oxford University Press, 1999.

Bauerschmidt, Frederick C. *Thomas Aquinas: Faith, Reason, and Following Christ.* New York: Oxford University Press, 2013.

Boguslawski, Steven C. *Thomas Aquinas on the Jews: Insights into His Commentary on Romans 9–11.* Mahwah, NJ: Paulist Press, 2008.

Bowlin, John R. "Augustine on Justifying Coercion." *Annual of the Society of Christian Ethics* 17, (1997): 49–70.

———. *Contingency and Fortune in Aquinas's Ethics*. New York: Cambridge University Press, 1999.

Boyle, Leonard E. "The Setting of the *Summa Theologiae* of St. Thomas—Revisited." In *The Ethics of Aquinas*, edited by Stephen J. Pope, 1–16. Washington, D.C.: Georgetown University Press, 2002.

———. "The Setting of the *Summa Theologiae* of Saint Thomas." In *The Gilson Lectures on Thomas Aquinas*, 19–45. Toronto: Pontifical Institute of Mediaeval Studies, 2008.

———. "The *Summa Confessorum* of John of Freiburg and the Popularization of the Moral Teaching of St. Thomas and of Some of His Contemporaries." In *Facing History: A Different Thomas Aquinas*, 37–65. Louvain-la-Neuve: Fédération Internationale des Instituts d'Études Médiévales, 2000.

Bradley, Denis J. M. *Aquinas on the Twofold Human Good: Reason and Human Happiness in Aquinas's Moral Science*. Washington, D.C.: Catholic University of America Press, 1997.

Bretherton, Luke. *Hospitality as Holiness: Christian Witness Amid Moral Diversity*. Burlington, VT: Ashgate Publishing, 2006.

Brock, Stephen L. *Action and Conduct: Thomas Aquinas and the Theory of Action*. Edinburgh: T&T Clark, 1998.

———. "Harmonizing Plato and Aristotle on *Esse*: Thomas Aquinas and the *De Hebdomadibus*." *Nova et Vetera* (English edition) 5, no. 3 (2007): 465–93.

Budziszewski, J. *Written on the Heart: The Case for Natural Law*. Downers Grove, IL: InterVarsity Press, 1997.

Burrell, David B. "Thomas Aquinas and Islam." *Modern Theology* 20, no. 1 (2004): 71–89.

Chenu, Marie-Dominique. *Nature, Man, and Society in the Twelfth Century: Essays on New Theological Perspectives in the Latin West*. Translated by Jerome Taylor, edited by Lester K. Little. Toronto: University of Toronto Press, in association with the Medieval Academy of America, 1997.

Cohen, Jeremy. *Christ Killers: The Jews and the Passion from the Bible to the Big Screen*. New York: Oxford University Press, 2007.

———. *Essential Papers on Judaism and Christianity in Conflict: From Late Antiquity to the Reformation*. Essential Papers on Jewish Studies. New York: New York University Press, 1991.

———. *The Friars and the Jews: A Study in the Development of Medieval Anti-Judaism*. Ithaca: Cornell University Press, 1982.

———. *Living Letters of the Law: Ideas of the Jew in Medieval Christianity*. Berkeley: University of California Press, 1999.

———. "Towards a Functional Classification of Jewish Anti-Christian Polemic in the High Middle Ages." In *Religionsgespräche im Mittelalter*, edited by Bernard Lewis and Friedrich Niewöhner. Vol. Bd. 4, 93–114. Wiesbaden: Harrassowitz, 1992.

Congar, Yves. "Christ in the Economy of Salvation and in our Dogmatic Tracts." *Concilium* 1, no. 2 (1966): 4–15.

——. *The Meaning of Tradition*. San Francisco: Ignatius Press, 2004.

Coolman, Holly Taylor. "Romans 9–11: Rereading Aquinas on the Jews." In *Reading Romans with St. Thomas Aquinas*, edited by Matthew Levering and Michael Dauphinais, 101–112. Washington, D.C.: Catholic University of America Press, 2012.

Cooper, John M. *Pursuits of Wisdom: Six Ways of Life in Ancient Philosophy from Socrates to Plotinus*. Princeton: Princeton University Press, 2012.

Corbin, Michel. *Le chemin de la théologie chez Thomas d'Aquin*. Bibliothèque des Archives de Philosophie. Vol. nouv. sér., 16. Paris: Beauchesne, 1974.

Cunningham, Stanley B. *Reclaiming Moral Agency: The Moral Philosophy of Albert the Great*. Washington, D.C.: Catholic University of America Press, 2008.

Davis, G. Scott. "Conscience and Conquest: Francisco de Vitoria on Justice in the New World." *Modern Theology* 13, no. 4 (1997): 475–500.

de Lubac, Henri. *The Mystery of the Supernatural*. Translated by Rosemary Sheed. New York: Crossroad Publishing Company, 1998.

Dewan, Lawrence. *Form and Being: Studies in Thomistic Metaphysics*. Washington, D.C.: Catholic University of America Press, 2006.

Emerson, Ralph W. *Essays and Lectures*. Edited by Joel Porte. The Library of America. New York: Literary Classics of the United States, 1983.

Emery, Gilles. *The Trinitarian Theology of St. Thomas Aquinas*. Translated by Francesca Aran Murphy. New York: Oxford University Press, 2007.

Finnis, John. *Aquinas: Moral, Political, and Legal Theory*. New York: Oxford University Press, 1998.

Gallagher, David M. "Aquinas on Goodness and Moral Goodness." In *Thomas Aquinas and His Legacy*, edited by David M. Gallagher, 37–60. Washington, D.C.: Catholic University of America Press, 1994.

——. "The Will and its Acts." In *The Ethics of Aquinas*, edited by Stephen J. Pope, 69–89. Washington, D.C.: Georgetown University Press, 2001.

Gardet, Louis. "*La connaissance que Thomas d'Aquin put avoir du monde Islamique*." In *Aquinas and Problems of His Time*, edited by Gérard Verbeke and D. Vehelst, 139–49. Leuven, Belgium: Leuven University Press, 1976.

Garrigou-Lagrange, Reginald. *The Three Ages of the Interior Life: Prelude of Eternal Life*. Translated by M. T. Doyle. Vol. 1. Charlotte, NC: TAN Books, 2013.

George, Robert P. *Natural Law Theory: Contemporary Essays*. New York: Oxford University Press, 1992.

George, Robert P. and Christopher Wolfe. *Natural Law and Public Reason*. Washington, D.C.: Georgetown University Press, 2000.

Grayzel, Solomon. *The Church and the Jews in the XIIIth Century: A Study of their Relations During the Years 1198–1254, Based on the Papal Letters and Conciliar Decrees of the Period*. 2nd ed. New York: Hermon Press, 1966.

——. "The Papal Bull *Sicut Judeis*." In *Studies and Essays in Honor of Abraham A. Neuman*, edited by Meir Ben-Horin, Bernard D. Weinryb, and Solomon Zeitlin, 243–80. Leiden: E. J. Brill, 1962.

Grisez, Germain G. *The Way of the Lord Jesus*. Chicago: Franciscan Herald Press, 1983.

Grisez, Germain, Joseph Boyle, and John Finnis. "Practical Principles, Moral Truth, and Ultimate Ends." *American Journal of Jurisprudence* 32, (1987): 99–151.

Hauerwas, Stanley. *The Peaceable Kingdom: A Primer in Christian Ethics*. Notre Dame, IN: University of Notre Dame Press, 1983.

Hauerwas, Stanley and Romand Coles. *Christianity, Democracy, and the Radical Ordinary: Conversations between a Radical Democrat and a Christian*. Eugene, OR: Cascade Books, 2008.

Hauerwas, Stanley and Charles R. Pinches. *Christians Among the Virtues: Theological Conversations with Ancient and Modern Ethics*. Notre Dame, IN: University of Notre Dame Press, 1997.

Hector, Kevin. "Apophaticism in Thomas Aquinas: A Re-Reformulation and Recommendation." *Scottish Journal of Theology* 60, no. 4 (2007): 377–93.

Henn, William. *The Hierarchy of Truths According to Yves Congar*. Analecta Gregoriana. Vol. 246. Rome: Editrice Pontificia Università Gregoriana, 1987.

Herdt, Jennifer A. *Putting on Virtue: The Legacy of the Splendid Vices*. Chicago: University of Chicago Press, 2008.

Hillgarth, J. N. "Who Read Thomas Aquinas." In *The Gilson Lectures on Thomas Aquinas*, 46–72. Toronto: Pontifical Institute of Mediaeval Studies, 2008.

Hood, John Y. B. *Aquinas and the Jews*. Philadelphia: University of Pennsylvania Press, 1995.

Inglis, John. *Spheres of Philosophical Inquiry and the Historiography of Medieval Philosophy*. Boston: Brill, 1998.

Irwin, T. H. "Splendid Vices? Augustine for and against Pagan Virtues." *Medieval Philosophy and Theology* 8, no. 2 (Fall 1999): 105–27.

Jackson, Timothy P. *The Priority of Love: Christian Charity and Social Justice*. Princeton, NJ: Princeton University Press, 2003.

Johnson, Mark. "The Sapiential Character of the First Article of the *Summa Theologiae*." In *Philosophy and the God of Abraham: Essays in Memory of James A. Weisheipl, OP*, edited by R. J. Long, 85–98. Toronto: Pontifical Institute of Mediaeval Studies, 1991.

Jordan, Mark D. *Rewritten Theology: Aquinas After His Readers*. Malden, MA: Blackwell Publishing, 2006.

———. "Theology and Philosophy." In *The Cambridge Companion to Aquinas*, edited by Norman Kretzmann and Eleonore Stump, 232–51. New York: Cambridge University Press, 1993.

Keating, Daniel A. "Aquinas on 1 and 2 Corinthians: The Sacraments and Their Ministers." In *Aquinas on Scripture: An Introduction to His Biblical Commentaries*, edited by Thomas G. Weinandy, Daniel A. Keating, and John Yocum, 127–48. New York: T&T Clark, 2005.

Kent, Bonnie D. "Habits and Virtues." In *The Ethics of Aquinas*, edited by Stephen J. Pope, 116–30. Washington, D.C.: Georgetown University Press, 2001.

———. "Moral Provincialism." *Religious Studies* 30, no. 3 (1994): pp. 269–85.

———. *Virtues of the Will: The Transformation of Ethics in the Late Thirteenth Century*. Washington, D.C.: Catholic University of America Press, 1995.

Kerr, Fergus. *After Aquinas: Versions of Thomism*. Malden, MA: Blackwell Publishing, 2002.

Knobel, Angela McKay. "Aquinas and the Pagan Virtues." *International Philosophical Quarterly* 51:3, no. 203 (2011): 339–54.

Levering, Matthew. *Scripture and Metaphysics: Aquinas and the Renewal of Trinitarian Theology*. Malden, MA: Blackwell Publishing, 2004.

Lott, Micah. "Have Elephant Seals Refuted Aristotle? Nature, Function, and Moral Goodness." *Journal of Moral Philosophy* 9, no. 3 (2012): 353–75.

Lottin, Odon. *Psychologie et Morale aux XIIᵉ et XIIIᵉ siècles*. Vol. 4. Louvain: Abbaye du Mont Cesar, 1954.

———. "*Les vertus morales acquises sont-elles des vraies vertus? La réponse des théologiens de Pierre Abélard à S. Thomas d'Aquin*." *Recherches de théologie ancienne et médiévale* 20 (1953): 13–39.

MacIntyre, Alasdair C. *After Virtue: A Study in Moral Theory*. 2nd ed. Notre Dame, IN: University of Notre Dame Press, 1984.

———. *Three Rival Versions of Moral Enquiry: Encyclopedia, Genealogy, and Tradition*. Notre Dame, IN: University of Notre Dame Press, 1990.

———. *Whose Justice? Which Rationality?* Notre Dame, IN: University of Notre Dame Press, 1988.

Maritain, Jacques. *Science and Wisdom*. Translated by Bernard Wall. New York: Scribner, 1940.

Marshall, Bruce D. "*Quasi in Figura*: A Brief Reflection on Jewish Election, After Thomas Aquinas." *Nova et Vetera* (English edition) 7, no. 2 (2009): 477–84.

McCabe, Herbert. *God Matters*. London: Continuum, 2005.

McInerny, Ralph M. *Ethica Thomistica: The Moral Philosophy of Thomas Aquinas*. Rev. ed. Washington, D.C.: Catholic University of America Press, 1997.

McKay, Angela. "Prudence and Acquired Moral Virtue." *The Thomist* 69 (2005): 535–55.

Milbank, John. *Theology and Social Theory: Beyond Secular Reason*. 2nd ed. Malden, MA: Blackwell Publishing, 2006.

Milbank, John and Catherine Pickstock. *Truth in Aquinas*. New York: Routledge, 2001.

Nelson, Daniel M. *The Priority of Prudence: Virtue and Natural Law in Thomas Aquinas and the Implications for Modern Ethics*. University Park: Pennsylvania State University Press, 1992.

O'Brien, T. C. "A Commentary on 1a2ae 89,6." In *Summa Theologiae: Effects of Sin, Stain and Guilt (1a2ae. 86–89)*. Translated and edited by T. C. O'Brien. Vol. 27, 125–33. New York: McGraw-Hill, 1974.

O'Meara, Thomas F. *Thomas Aquinas: Theologian*. Notre Dame, IN: University of Notre Dame Press, 1997.

Osborne, Jr., Thomas M. "The Augustinianism of Thomas Aquinas's Moral Theory." *The Thomist* 67 (2003): 279–305.

———. "Perfect and Imperfect Virtues in Aquinas." *The Thomist* 71 (2007): 39–64.

Pesch, Otto H. *Theologie der Rechtfertigung bei Martin Luther und Thomas von Aquin:*

Versuch eines systematisch-theologischen Dialogs. Walberberger Studien der Albertus-Magnus-Akademie. 2 Aufl ed. Vol. Bd. 4. Mainz: Matthias-Grünewald, 1985.

Pilsner, Joseph. *The Specification of Human Actions in St. Thomas Aquinas*. New York: Oxford University Press, 2006.

Pinckaers, Servais. "*Le vertu est tout autre chose qu'une habitude.*" *Nouvelle Revue Théologique* 82 (April 1960): 387–403.

Porter, Jean. *The Recovery of Virtue: The Relevance of Aquinas for Christian Ethics*. Louisville, KY: Westminster/John Knox Press, 1990.

Preller, Victor. *Divine Science and the Science of God: A Reformulation of Thomas Aquinas*. Princeton, NJ: Princeton University Press, 1967.

Rahner, Karl. *Foundations of Christian Faith: An Introduction to the Idea of Christianity*. New York: Seabury Press, 1978.

Rogers, Eugene F. *Thomas Aquinas and Karl Barth: Sacred Doctrine and the Natural Knowledge of God*. Notre Dame, IN: University of Notre Dame Press, 1995.

Shanley, Brian J. "Aquinas on Pagan Virtue." *The Thomist* 63 (1999): 553–77.

Shatzmiller, Joseph. *La deuxième controverse de Paris: Un chapitre dans la polémique entre Chrétiens et Juifs au Moyen Age*. Paris: E. Peeters, 1994.

Smith, James K. A. *Introducing Radical Orthodoxy: Mapping a Post-Secular Theology*. Grand Rapids, MI: Baker Academic, 2004.

Southern, R. W. *Western Society and the Church in the Middle Ages*. The Pelican History of the Church. Vol. 2. New York: Penguin Books, 1970.

Staudt, Robert Jared. "Religion as a Virtue: Thomas Aquinas on Worship through Justice, Law, and Charity." PhD diss., Ave Maria University, 2008.

Stump, Eleonore. *Aquinas*. New York: Routledge, 2003.

Thompson, Michael. *Life and Action: Elementary Structures of Practice and Practical Thought*. Cambridge, MA: Harvard University Press, 2008.

Todeschini, Giacomo. "Franciscan Economics and Jews in the Middle Ages: From Theological to Economic Lexicon." In *Friars and Jews in the Middle Ages and Renaissance*, edited by Susan E. Myers and Steven J. McMichael. Vol. 2, 99–118. Boston: Brill, 2004.

Torrell, Jean-Pierre. *Aquinas's Summa: Background, Structure, and Reception*. Washington, D.C.: Catholic University of America Press, 2005.

———. *Saint Thomas Aquinas, Volume 1: The Person and His Work*. Washington, D.C.: Catholic University of America Press, 1996.

Turner, Nancy L. "Jews and Judaism in Peter Auriol's *Sentences* Commentary." In *Friars and Jews in the Middle Ages and Renaissance*, edited by Susan E. Myers and Steven J. McMichael. Vol. 2, 81–98. Boston: Brill, 2004.

Velde, Rudi A. te. *Aquinas on God: The 'Divine Science' of the Summa Theologiae*. Burlington, VT: Ashgate Publishing, 2006.

Wawrykow, Joseph P. "Grace." In *The Theology of Thomas Aquinas*, edited by Rik Van Nieuwenhove and Joseph Wawrykow, 192–221. Notre Dame, IN: University of Notre Dame Press, 2005.

Weisheipl, James A. *Friar Thomas D'Aquino: His Life, Thought, and Work*. Garden City, NY: Doubleday, 1974.

Wetzel, James. "Splendid Vices and Secular Virtues: Variations on Milbank's Augustine." *Journal of Religious Ethics* 32, no. 2 (June 2004): 271–300.

Williamson, Timothy. *Knowledge and Its Limits.* New York: Oxford University Press, 2000.

Wippel, John F. *The Metaphysical Thought of Thomas Aquinas: From Finite Being to Uncreated Being.* Washington, D.C.: Catholic University of America Press, 2000.

Wyschogrod, Michael. "A Jewish Perspective on Incarnation." *Modern Theology* 12, no. 2 (1996): 195–209.

INDEX

Abraham, 5, 316n36

act, pure, God as, 48–50

action: complexity of, and determination of end, 206; good, done well, 91, 124–27, 160, 168, 303; good, virtue as perfection of capacity for, 107–8, 126–27, 133, 264–67; as inevitably affecting others, 122; as morally significant by nature, 114–15, 122; as specifically or generically indifferent, 188; virtuous, vs. virtuously-done, 314–15n23. *See also* operations

acts, as generic or specific vs. individual, 199, 200–201, 312n1

acts ordered to *infidelitas*, 202–15; complexity of intention and, 207–16, 221, 223–24, 235, 316n33, 319–20n59, 319n56; as evil, 200, 203–6; meaning of, as issue, 202–3, 208; range and complexity of final ends and, 208–15, 316n33; religious-only (*sola religio*) acts as, 206–8

acts ordered to *infidelitas*, virtuous: as "accidental" divergence from sin, 203–5, 218, 314n21; good ends of human nature and, 205–6, 208–15; *sola religio* interpretation of, 206–8

acts ordered to strong *infidelitas*, as evil, 218, 234

acts ordered to weak *infidelitas*, goodness of, 218–24; good of human nature within pagans and, 205–6, 208–15, 219, 220–24, 234–35, 318–19nn51–52, 319n54; imperfect but good ends and, 233; resistance to good end and, 222–23, 226–27, 234, 322n87

acts without charity, ordered to that by which one lacks charity: distinguishing from those ordered to natural good, 215–16; as evil acts, 198–99, 200, 201, 202–3, 215; range of salient final end-constitutive beliefs and, 208–15, 316–17n38, 316n33, 316n36, 317n40, 317n44; religious-only (*sola religio*) acts as, 206–8

acts without charity ordered to true good short of beatitude, 198–99, 312n1; distinguishing from those ordered by that by which one lacks charity, 215–16; ends suitable for, 201–2; as good but not perfectly good, 198, 199, 201–2, 215; Thomas's welcoming of as unconsummated Christwardness, 202

actuality: *esse* as, 46, 50–51; perfection as, 46, 50–51

Ad ducissam Brabantiae (Thomas Aquinas), 23, 29–30

Albert the Great, 19, 22

al-Kāmil, 34

Ambrose, on unity of virtues, 156

animals: and habit, lack of, 85, 95–96, 291–92n47; lack of *usus* in, 95–96, 292n48

Summa contra Gentiles (Thomas
Aquinas), 18, 20, 25, 36, 277–78n25,
277n22
Summa theologiae (Thomas Aquinas):
as Christological, 62–63, 64, 70; as
climax of Thomas's work, 56, 285n43;
context of arguments in, 64–65; on
the good as what all desire, 40, 43–44;
influence of, 27; on Jews' crucifixion
of Jesus, 25, 26–27; pedagogy of, 20, 33,
64–65, 69–70, 172–73; as *sacra doctrina*,
20, 66; *sacra doctrina* as *scientia* in,
56–60, 63, 286n57; structure of, 285n2;
as synthesis of Aristotelian *scientia*
and Augustinian Trinitarianism, 63,
65–66, 70–71; treatment of virtue in,
72, 106; as Trinitarian, 62–63, 64, 70;
use of Aristotelian methods in, 257;
writing of, 20–21. *See also* ethics of
Thomas as transformative synthesis of
Aristotelian and Augustinian convictions; *sacra doctrina*
suppression of truth: as *infidelitas*,
228–33; and instinct toward religion, as
imperfect guide, 229–31; types of suppressors, 229–30, 234
S-virtue, 92, 93, 156, 157, 160, 290n34,
304n8. *See also* S-habit
synderesis, 295n23, 297n40

Talmud: medieval Christian perceptions
of, 22; 13th-century efforts to suppress,
17, 19, 22
Tatars, 37, 281–82n65
temperance: imperfect, 157; as individual-
ized virtue, 101; necessity of for other
virtues, 122–23, 128, 160; as operative
habit, 76; as pagan virtue, 259; as single
virtue, 162–63, 181; as virtue *simpliciter*,
295–96n25
Theology and Social Theory (Milbank), 6,
253–54, 273n3, 273n8, 325n27, 325n1–2
theology of Thomas: complexity of,

multiplication of distinctions and, 73,
259–60; Dominican orientation of,
20, 33, 64–65, 172; as enacted in his
writing and way of being, 3, 8, 64–65,
253, 256, 257–60; radically Christian
nature of, 55–56; *Summa theologiae*
as climax of, 56, 285n43; Trinitarian
character of, 61, 63, 70. *See also* ethics
of Thomas as transformative synthesis of Aristotelian and Augustinian
convictions
Todeschini, Giacomo, 23–24
Torrell, Jean-Pierre, 22, 277n22
Trinity: and Christology, 63; and doctrine
of the Word, 70, 103; and friendship,
266–67; and Godseeking, 68; and
infidelitas, 316n32, 318n47, 320n63;
Summa theologiae and, 63, 64; and
theological vision of Thomas, 20, 40,
55, 61, 68, 70; and Thomas's theology of
goodness, 66; wedding of Augustinian
doctrine of with Aristotelian *scientia*,
55, 63, 70; and welcoming of outsider,
40–41, 266–67
truth, hatred of, 293–94n10

University of Naples, Thomas's studies
at, 19
University of Paris, Thomas at, 19–20, 21
usus, 95, 96, 107, 108, 112, 127, 292n49

vegetative powers, 85–86
velleity, 316n36
venial sin, Thomas on, 314n21
vice, 100–101, 128, 165, 295n17, 299n58
vice, splendid, 181, 248, 258, 273n1. *See
also* virtue, false or counterfeit
virtue(s): adverbial character of, 123–25;
as attainment of relative mean, 101;
Augustine's definition of, 72; capacity
for, as gift of grace, 269–72; capacity for, as human characteristic, 12;
complexity of conception of, 117–18;

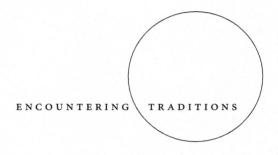

ENCOUNTERING TRADITIONS

Francis X. Clooney, SJ, *His Hiding Place Is Darkness:*
  A Hindu-Catholic Theopoetics of Divine Absence

Muhammad Iqbal, *Reconstruction of Religious Thought in Islam*

Lightning Source UK Ltd.
Milton Keynes UK
UKOW04f0442290917
310094UK00001B/91/P